D1340341

Hillfort and Hill-top Settlement in Somerset in the First to Eighth Centuries A.D.

Ian Burrow

BAR British Series 91
1981

B.A.R.

B.A.R., 122 Banbury Road, Oxford OX2 7BP, England

GENERAL EDITORS

A. R. Hands, B.Sc., M.A., D.Phil.
D. R. Walker, M.A.

B.A.R. 91, 1981: 'Hillfort and Hill-top Settlement in Somerset in the First to Eighth Centuries A.D.'

Price £12.00 post free throughout the world. Payments made in currency other than sterling must be calculated at the current rate of exchange and an extra 10% added to cover the cost of bank charges. Cheques should be made payable to 'British Archaeological Reports' and sent to the above address.

ISBN 0 86054 137 1

BAR publishes monographs and collections of papers on all aspects of archaeology and on related subjects such as anthropology, classical and medieval history and numismatics.

BAR publishes BAR International Series which is concerned with world archaeology and BAR British Series which covers the British Isles.

For details of all BAR publications in print please write to the above address. Information on new titles is sent regularly on request, with no obligation to purchase.

Volumes are distributed direct from the publishers. All BAR prices are inclusive of postage by surface mail anywhere in the world.

Printed in Great Britain

CONTENTS

PLATES

EARTHWORK PLANS

SUMMARY AND INTRODUCTION

Human communities of many kinds in many places have used hill top locations for a variety of purposes in the past. In Britain hill-top activity is documented in the Neolithic, it peaks in the Iron Age, and occurs sporadically elsewhere in the archaeological record. Like many other facets of that record, hill-top evidence has until recently been interpreted by archaeologists in purely utilitarian and 'obvious' terms. It was therefore 'obvious' that hill-top settlements were defensive, or, if not obviously defensive, then 'ritual'. This is an oversimplification, but it remains true that British archaeology has only recently become more aware of the importance of the purely cultural considerations which influence the choice of settlement sites. The use of a hill-top site by a particular cultural group is a reflection of choices made by that group, conditioned by its own perceptions of the 'obvious'. It is among the archaeologist's tasks to try to discern what those perceptions were.

This study examines this general problem within a specific chronological and geographical context. The chronological framework is the Roman and immediately post-Roman centuries. This period is one of massive cultural change, but following the obsession with continuity that distinguished Migration Period studies in the early 1970s this study discusses the problem throughout the period in an attempt to detect unifying factors. The geographical context is in fact a political one, being based on an administrative unit, the county of Somerset, which existed from the end of the study period until 1974 when it was partly dismembered. The area faces both west to the Atlantic Province and east towards Wessex and straddles and border between 'Highland' and 'Lowland' Britain. In the context of Migration Period Studies it is thus of considerable importance as a zone of cultural contact between the Celtic West and the Germanic East. It is also an area which has produced a relative abundance of archaeological evidence from the Roman and Post Roman centuries. The Roman background for the southern part of the area has been stimulatingly discussed by Leech (1977), and the AD 400-700 period has also received treatment in some detail (Rahtz and Fowler 1971).

Hilltops and particularly hillforts were used in a variety of ways in this period and location. In the Roman centuries the evidence is sufficiently diagnostic for there to be little doubt that religious belief was one major element in that use, although others can be detected. In the immediately post-Roman centuries we enter a minefield of more ambivalent data. In 1970 it almost seemed enough to show that an Iron Age hillfort had been 'reoccupied' in the Dark Ages, until it was appreciated that Iron Age scholars themselves were unable to decide on the functions of the original occupations. To say that a hillfort was re-used does not explain what it was re-used for, and tacit assumptions about the re-emergence of pre-Roman patterns of hillfort use are inadequate. The tenuous documentary record is not especially helpful either, and there is no discussion here of the role of specific historic figures such as Arthur.

This study has a number of purposes. The first four chapters are an attempt to evaluate various types of evidence for their relevance to the identification of hilltop sites. It is very unlikely that all sites that were used have been located by direct archaeological research and the relevance of topography, morphology, place-name studies and fieldwork are all therefore assessed for their potential contributions in this and other areas. Chapters 5 and 6 concentrate on interpretation of the archaeological evidence from known sites with especial reference to the excavations at Cadbury Congresbury. The final chapter discusses in detail the various models which can be applied to the data.

The work is a revised version of a Ph.D. thesis submitted to the University of Birmingham in 1979. Minor modifications and additions to the bibliography have been made but no basic changes to the main text written in 1975-1977 have been felt desirable even though some aspects now seem somewhat dated. This is especially true of the analysis of pottery from Cadbury Congresbury in Chapter 6, the statistical potential of which has not been realized and which is one of many future directions research on this problem must take.

I am indebted to the individuals and organizations below for a range of practical assistance and moral support. Many other individuals have also contributed directly or indirectly to this thesis, although it is not possible to list them all here. My especial thanks are offered to Cambridge University Committee for Aerial Photography; West Air Photography, Weston-Super-Mare; The National Monuments Record; Archaeology Division, Ordnance Survey; Mr. D. Bromwich, Local History Library, Taunton; Dr. and Mrs. R. Everton, Bristol; Dr. P. J. Fowler; Mr. K. S. Gardner; Mrs. S. Minnitt, Taunton Museum; The late Professor E. K. Tratman.

I would also especially like to thank my mother, Mrs. J. M. Burrow, who did all the preliminary typing, and my wife Cathe who has constantly given me support and encouragement.

Finally, I must thank my supervisor, Professor Philip Rahtz, whose enthusiasm, dedication and imaginative thinking have been a great inspiration to me, both in this work and in my general approach to archaeology.

CHAPTER 1

THE AIMS AND BACKGROUND OF THE STUDY

Introductory remarks

The profound changes which affected Britain and Western Europe between the third and seventh centuries AD are the ultimate concern of this study, although its subject matter is limited to a more restricted geographical area and to one specific aspect of settlement history. The area concerned lies on the western limits of 'Lowland' Britain,[1] and an examination of the evidence for the use of defended or defensible hilltop enclosures and other sites within that area is the primary aim of the study.

While it may not be wholly justifiable to isolate any one period as crucial in historical terms, it is difficult to disagree with the opinion, expressed in the major studies which have appeared in the last ten years, that our period was one in which the pace of fundamental and lasting cultural changes was very considerable, notwithstanding the recent stress on continuity in various forms.[2] There were very evident linguistic, political and social developments whose broad outlines are relatively well known, but which still demand wholly satisfactory explanation. A key factor, population size, defies quantification at present, and so the significance of the apparently very extensive abandonment of settlement sites of all types at the end of the Roman period can still not be adequately assessed. The degree to which the organization of the agricultural landscape, and the economic relationships arising from it, were affected by these other changes has also provoked considerable controversy, but here too any generally applicable conclusions seem far off.

The relative abundance of data of various types, the difficulty of interpreting and correlating the evidence from different disciplines, and the undeniable drama of the historical events may account for the increase in both academic and popular interest in the period in recent years. One aspect of the ' data explosion' was the confirmation that some of the larger Iron Age Hillforts of Britain had indeed been ' reoccupied' in the post-Roman centuries, and the initial intention of this study was to examine the phenomenon of ' hillfort reoccupation'. In the early 1970s this phrase, carrying with it various attractive though unstated implications for the nature of post-Roman Britain and its similarity to the Iron Age, was thought to require no further qualification. It will become apparent that this concept did not provide a solid basis from which to work, nor was it feasible or useful to attempt to cover the whole of the British Isles as had at first been envisaged.[3]

The broad aim of the study is to evaluate the data relevant to an assessment of the extent, chronology and function of activity within hillforts and on hilltops in the period. A secondary aim has been to explore the means by which the identification of sites can be achieved, without resorting to the impracticable solution of total excavation of the population of sites. To this end the settlement background, the evidence of place names and the relevance of surface fieldwork have all been explored with the intention of formulating hypotheses which can ultimately be tested by excavation. The experience gained in evaluating this material may prove methodologically valuable in any future studies of this kind, though it should be immediately stated that, in the one instance where a postulated re-use of a hillfort site was tested by excavation, the hypothesis was firmly refuted.[4] It has also been the intention to question whether past and present excavations provide data adequate to resolve the fundamental issue; the place of these sites in the social structure and settlement pattern of Somerset. It must be admitted that understanding of these aspects remains partial, but the final discussion suggests that these problems, though complex, are not insoluble.

Before the consideration of these points in detail in subsequent chapters it is necessary to set the study in its academic and geographical context. There therefore follows a discussion of the relevant developments in Romano-British and later studies, and of the physical and historical background of the study area.

Developments in Romano-British studies

It was suggested above that change in the size and distribution of population through time must be regarded as of fundamental importance to our understanding of the developments in Britain in the period under consideration. It has become apparent in recent years that the population of Roman, and probably also of Iron Age Britain, was very much larger than earlier evidence had suggested. The increase in systematic archaeological survey, both from the air and on the ground, stimulated in a large degree by the 'rescue' outlook of the last two decades, has produced a great mass of new material.

The implications of this are threefold. Firstly the large size of the late Roman population in particular makes the evidence for large-scale abandonment of settlements of all types in the fifth century even more difficult to explain than previously. Secondly, it is no longer possible to maintain the view that Anglo-Saxon settlers initiated the large-scale exploitation of forested areas carrying soils less tractable, though potentially more productive, than the valley gravels and chalk soils from which the bulk of settlement evidence had earlier been obtained. Romano-British rural settlement may now be regarded as perhaps as extensive as that of the thirteenth and fourteenth centuries, and as complex and dynamic. Unless we envisage the massive depopulation of most of the country, perhaps as a result of epidemics, and a subsequent collapse of social organization at all levels, it is probable that Germanic settlement was fundamentally influenced by the pre-existing pattern.[5]

The third implication has the most direct relevance to the present topic, and follows from the previous two. Settlements in upland areas and on lighter soils are probably now to be regarded as marginal, rapidly abandoned during periods of population decline or climatic deterioration.[6] One of the questions to be considered in more detail below is the extent to which the hilltop settlements with which we are concerned should be regarded in this way. Does the use of hilltop sites in the Roman period and later reflect merely an expansion of settlement, or are there more specific reasons for the selection of these sites?

4

'Continuity'

Since it now seems improbable that the Germanic settlement and domination of Lowland Britain was marked by a complete change in all aspects of life, much attention has been paid in recent years to evidence for direct links between Roman Britain and Anglo-Saxon England. It is relatively easy to demonstrate from archaeological evidence alone that a settlement site, for instance, has been successively occupied by individuals using Iron Age, Roman and Anglo-Saxon ceramics. This may demonstrate continuity in cultural attitudes towards desirable settlement sites, but does little to indicate whether the site was continually occupied, or if the inhabitants in the seventh century were direct descendants of those in the fourth. At least five aspects of continuity can be isolated: continuity of population, of settlement form and location, of material culture, of political and social structure, and of division of the landscape. These will now be briefly considered.

Continuity of population in a genetic sense can scarcely be doubted in many areas. The western areas of Britain, in which Somerset lies, were not affected by major Germanic infiltration until the seventh or later centuries, and even in the east the political and cultural dominance of the Anglo-Saxons was probably out of proportion to their numerical strength. Positive demonstration of survival of the British population chiefly comes from place-name and documentary studies, but the potential of skeletal evidence from cemeteries in use over a long period has scarcely been realized.[7]

It has been suggested that settlement sites are one of the least stable elements in the landscape at all periods.[8] Continuity of occupation of such sites over a long period may prove to be the exception rather than the rule. The reasons for such instability are more likely to be economic and local than linked to major political and social upheavals, and we cannot as yet rely on settlement evidence as an indicator of more general trends. Even so, the impression that a great many sites were abandoned within a relatively short time at the end of the Roman period remains, though as suggested above a proportion of this may represent desertion of sites on marginal land. The main areas of settlement may have remained in occupation, and this possibility will be considered in more detail in chapter 4.

The physical form and scale of settlements clearly underwent major change in the first millennium AD, though recent research has tended to emphasise that such changes were more gradual and evolutionary than previously envisaged.[9] This model is in direct contrast to the long-established, though never wholly unchallenged, view that the typical settlement pattern of Lowland England, with nucleated villages and open arable fields cultivated in common, was a Germanic importation owing virtually nothing to the Roman past.[10] This pattern was certainly established by the thirteenth century, but is increasingly seen as coming at the end of a long sequence of gradual changes. The antithesis between the 'Celtic' individual farmstead and the 'Germanic' nucleated village can no longer be maintained in the face of archaeological and documentary evidence.[11] It may therefore be possible to demonstrate a continuous development of settlement from the Roman period through the first millennium at some sites, and 'continuity' in this form may be envisaged.

The greatest discontinuity from the fourth century to the seventh was in political and social organization. Instead of a centrally organized, urban-based and highly complex society, Britain by the seventh century had one which was fragmented politically, economically and culturally, and in which only Christianity was capable of maintaining a broader outlook. The degree to which these massive changes are reflected in the archaeological record from AD 400-700 will be one of the topics considered in the final chapter.

Continuity of material culture is likewise difficult to demonstrate. Large-scale production of utility and luxury goods seems to have ceased relatively rapidly in the early fifth century. Pottery either ceased to be used on any scale, or was reduced to the scale of a domestic industry.[12] High quality metalwork, based on Roman or Germanic models, developed very rapidly. Subsistence equipment probably remained broadly the same, but this material rarely survives.[14] The ability to build in mortared stone or brick was lost, the Church again providing the only tenuous continuity with Roman practice.

Much attention has been paid in recent years to the land units described in early charter material. It has frequently been found possible to equate these both with modern parishes or townships, and with earlier land units definable by archaeological means alone.[15] While the full implications of this are far from clear, it may indicate that the basic divisions of the agricultural landscape remained stable even though settlement within them may have undergone continuous change.[16]

Data of this sort has lent support to the more controversial suggestions of Professor G. R. J. Jones.[17] He has attempted to demonstrate that the social structure of medieval Wales, as implied by Welsh legal texts, is part of a long-established system reflecting not only the settlement pattern of medieval Wales, but also underlying that of late Saxon England, which may have its origin in the Pre-Roman Iron Age.[18] This view has been heavily criticised from an archaeological standpoint by Alcock,[19] on the grounds that uncritically used archaeological data is at present inadequate to confirm the hypotheses put forward. For present purposes, however, the most important aspect of Jones' work is that it suggests that what has been regarded as the 'typical' English landscape was a relatively late development from a pre-English pattern, and that hillforts may have played an important role in that pattern. Although these views have not met with a wholly favourable academic response, they do suggest that the possibility of links between hillfort re-use and the basic economic organization of the surrounding land is worth consideration.

Developments in settlement archaeology, AD 400-700

The character of the settlement evidence recovered in the last two decades still reflects differences between the western and eastern parts of Britain. In eastern England settlement sites and buildings are now known in some quantity,[20] a number being in close association with late Roman sites.[21] A range of social status can be identified in this material, from the large royal halls at Yeavering, to humbler settlements such as Catholme (Staffs), West Stow (Norfolk) or Chalton (Hants).[22] The only fortified sites so far identified on the ground are the forts associated with the royal sites at Yeavering and Millfield (Northumberland), though other sites mentioned in documentary sources, such as Taunton and Bamburgh, remain unidentified on the ground.

6

In the west and north, and in Ireland, a number of factors have reversed this situation, and settlement evidence from these areas comes largely from sites which can be loosely described as fortified. The lack of prolific local pottery types, and a modern emphasis on non-arable farming which reduces the incidence of cropmarks and artifact scatters, hinders the identification of types of settlement not defined by upstanding earthworks or walling. The material poverty of most sites, and the difficulty of dating them on purely morphological grounds are added hindrances to identification. The archaeological sample in the west is therefore more heavily biased towards some classes of settlement than others, with consequent effects on our overall view of the period.

Between these two contrasting areas lies a third, within which our area of study is located, and where the identification of settlement sites of all types in the period AD 400-700 is still at a very early stage. It can be broadly defined as the zone lying between the Jurassic Ridge and the uplands of the South-West Wales and the southern Pennines. It thus comprises the West Midlands and Welsh Marches, parts of south-east Wales and most of Gloucestershire, Somerset, Dorset and Devon. This zone is one in which the level of Romanization was markedly higher than in the areas to the west and north, and which also remained outside Germanic cultural or political control for as much as 250 years after AD 400. In this lies its wider significance for the study of the period as a whole, since any developments in settlement form, agricultural and economic organization, or social structure cannot be directly attributed to intrusive Germanic influences. The area therefore probably contains the data from which the debate over various types of continuity can be resolved (Fig. 1). It is here termed 'Western Lowland Britain'.

At present, however, settlement archaeology has been confined largely to the identification of a number of hilltop sites, all but one of them fortified. Aerial survey has led to the identification of several hundred sites on tractable soils in various parts of the zone, and at least two are probably to be dated to the period AD 400-700, but the vast majority are of unknown date.

A basic weakness of this study is therefore that it perpetuates a pre-existing bias towards a certain type of site. It is unlikely, whatever the specific role of hilltops and hillforts both before and after AD 400, that they at any stage formed more than a small percentage of the total settlement pattern. It follows that factors affecting their use or disuse, or their interior arrangements, may have little or no relevance to general trends in settlement development. Nevertheless an attempt has been made to set these sites in a wider context, and to evaluate such evidence as is available for the location of the other types of settlement which must have existed contemporaneously.

The historiography of the study

By the 1920s it was becoming clear that the large complex hillforts of the British Isles were to be regarded as phenomena of the Pre-Roman Iron Age.[23] Wheeler, however, was still able to suggest at that time that archaeological evidence from a number of Welsh sites, when considered in conjunction with developing views of the character of the Roman occupation of Wales, justified the assertion that hillforts may actually have been constructed

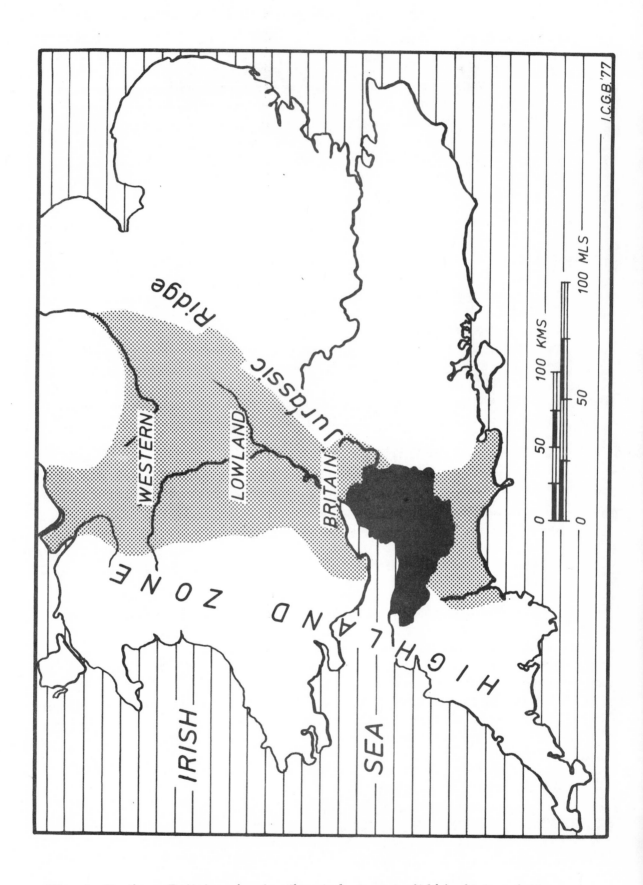

Fig. 1 Southern Britain, showing the study area (solid black) in relation
to major physiographical features

in the Roman period in the area, possibly as a reaction to Irish raiding.[24]
Simpson's paper swung academic opinion against such a view, but the evidence
Wheeler assembled for Wales was clearly indicative of intensive use of some
sites within the Roman period. This was itself something of a challenge to
the view that the Roman attitude to hillforts was one involving solely their
depopulation and destruction.

However, Wheeler's own excavations at Maiden Castle lent considerable
support to the latter view, with the dramatic evidence of sacking and massacre
at the east entrance,[25] and similar evidence was forthcoming on other sites.
This model predisposed excavators to see any indications of activity within
hillforts in the first to fourth centuries in terms of 'frequentation', 'squatting'
or 'picnicing', the implication being that any occupation was small-scale, illicit,
temporary, or squalid, and of no great inherent interest. Nevertheless in 1931
Curwen published evidence clearly indicating settlement and cultivation within
the defences of Cissbury in Sussex, and the existence of a major late or post-
Roman addition to those defences.[26, 27]

At both Lydney[28] and Maiden Castle Wheeler had revealed a major religious re-usage of Iron Age sites in the Roman period. Since that time excavation at both rural Romano-British temples and within hillforts[29] has indicated
that the sanctity of such sites in the later Roman period may well be a continuation of Iron Age practices, the direct superimposition of Roman temples
on Iron Age shrines at such sites as Frilford and Maiden Castle[30] lending
support to this view. This religious function for hilltop sites provides the
main alternative to the secular and aristocratic model which has received
so much attention.

At Lydney, Wheeler had also recovered evidence for a refortification
of the site, probably in the fifth century or later. His comments on the
occupation implied by that evidence indicate a striking lack of sympathy or
interest in the fortunes of the post-Roman Britons at that time:

> 'In its final phase, therefore, the character of the occupation of the
> Lydney promontory reverted substantially to its aboriginal type.
> The intermediate phases of Romanization had for a time given the
> native population much that otherwise lay beyond its grasp, but in
> giving this they had at the same time taken from that population such
> cultural initiative as it had possessed before the coming of Rome.
> The poverty of the post-Roman relics upon the site is eloquent of a
> population which, behind its refurbished second-hand earthworks,
> eked out a sort of second-hand existence entirely lacking in cultural
> initiative'.[31]

In view of such an attitude it is surprising that any advance was made in the
study before the war. In the late 1930s however, the recognition of imported
Mediterranean pottery at Tintagel and in Ireland (where it was initially regarded as Roman) provided a new stimulus to the identification of sites occupied
after c. 450 AD. A number of defended sites, two with historical references
indicating their royal connexions, had also been the subject of large-scale
excavations in Ireland at the same time.[32] These produced a wealth of information on material culture of the period, and indicated the type of data which
might be anticipated on sites in Britain if these could be identified.

The scanty documentation, and the wealth attested by high-quality metalwork and imported pottery, was, by about 1940, suggesting that defended and defensible sites of the period post AD 400, and possibly earlier, were the dwellings of 'kings' and petty local rulers who figured prominently in the contemporary written sources in western Britain. However, in his interim report on the eminently defensible site of Tintagel, Radford interpreted the structures excavated there as those of a monastery, separated from the mainland by a bank and ditch interpreted as the vallum monasterii mentioned in early hagiographical material.[33] This interpretation of the evidence can be criticized,[34] but it did set a third model, that of the Christian community, against that of the pagan site and the princely court. With the development of active field research into the archaeology of early Christianity in Britain it became clear that many ecclesiastical sites were located within enclosures indistinguishable from those of pre-Christian or contemporary settlements whose secular character was not in question.[35] The limitations of the archaeological evidence for establishing the exact status of sites in a partly documented period such as this were therefore already apparent.

By the late 1950s, however, a number of sites in Wales and the north and west of Britain had been examined which seemed to fit the picture of small, secular, prestigious fortifications.[36] The evidence from these was discussed in Alcock's report on the Glamorgan site of Dinas Powys. This major landmark in post-Roman studies appeared in 1963, and was the first full publication of a large and varied body of material from a western British site, and included a discussion of the social, economic and political background of the site by drawing on a wide range of archaeological and historical material. Alcock's conclusion was that

> 'The evidence of domestic and industrial activities at Dinas Powys can best be reconciled if we interpret it as the llys or court of a local ruler, with its neuadd or hall .... surrounded by subsidiary buildings of stone and timber, and forming the centre of a variety of agricultural, industrial and domestic pursuits.'[37]

In this and a series of papers in the 1960s Alcock proceeded to develop a model for the form and function of post-Roman defended sites in the west of Britain. These were seen as predominantly aristocratic centres, their weak defences reflecting the unimportant role of fortified sites in the warfare of the period implied by documentary sources. Within these sites lived the lord, his immediate followers, and his warband, the establishment being supported by various dues and services owed by the local population. Such sites comprise the 'heroic' environment to which the poetry surviving from the period relates and in which peripatetic bards and metalworkers were maintained. The small size of the defended unit was seen as in marked contrast to the Iron Age situation in which very large areas were enclosed by elaborate schemes of defence involving work by a much higher proportion of the population.[38]

It will be suggested that this model requires modification in the light of recent evidence. The small sites to which it applies are mostly located in relatively un-Romanized highland areas in which the average size of the known defensive snclosures, many of them Iron Age date, is itself much less than in western parts of lowland Britain. It is from these latter areas that evidence

for the late and post-Roman re-use of large hillforts has begun to emerge.
A more basic criticism, recently argued by Dumville[39] relates to the documentary material upon which Alcock's model depends. Dumville has re-emphasized that very few of the surviving sources which relate to the period from AD 400 to the seventh century were written in their original form during that time. Reliable contemporary witnesses are therefore confined to the works of Patrick and Gildas, and deductions concerning social change and organization in western Britain based on other source material are liable to impose concepts from later centuries onto the archaeological data. This minimal view is unlikely to go uncontested, but is a major challenge to the use made of the documentary material by Alcock and Morris.[40]

The archaeological evidence for the use of large hillforts in the period AD 400-700, which was largely obtained in the 1960s and early 1970s, fitted Alcock's model less well than did that from the smaller sites. Since relatively few of these larger sites have as yet been shown to have been intensively used after AD 400, Alcock has suggested that such usage is indicative of exceptional historical circumstances.[41] It will be argued that this view is untenable, if only because so few major hillforts have been sampled on a scale comparable with that of Cadbury Congresbury or South Cadbury, from which the most important data has been recovered.[42] One of the advantages of the regional approach to this topic is that it enables the evidence from these sites to be seen in relation to their local historical and geographical setting. Alcock has pointed out that the military affairs of the latter part of the AD 400-700 period, at least, were not carried out wholly on a minor local scale,[43] but in view of the cultural and political fragmentation observable in these centuries, explanations are here sought chiefly in terms of local responses to local factors. This is not to deny that our archaeological material may be directly related to specific recorded historical episodes of more than local significance in some cases, but it is suggested that such explanations should only be sought when the data cannot be fitted to any one of a range of models based on the local environment.

The study area

Somerset[44] has been selected as the area for detailed consideration for a variety of reasons, both academic and personal. The data already available, which was considerably more extensive than that from most other parts of Britain, was summarized in 1972,[45] and this, combined with the writer's prior involvement in excavations in the area, made it an obvious choice once the conept of studying hillfort reoccupation in the British Isles as a whole had been abandoned.

Somerset's geographical position renders it susceptible to external influences from both the Highland Zone and from areas to the east. The Bristol Channel coastline brings Somerset into contact with the Irish Sea Province,[46] which, had certain specific effects on the area in the sixth century. To the east, the Jurassic Way provided communication with the Cotswolds and the Upper Thames, though direct contact with the chalklands of Wessex must have been less easy, and this will be commented on further at a later stage.

Somerset contains geological and topographical features typical of both Highland and Lowland Zone areas as they are conventionally described, and this 'frontier' character of the area also influenced its selection (Fig. 2).[47] The area to the west of the River Parrett consists predominantly of sandstone moorland areas with thin soils and steep gradients. Intermediate low-lying areas consist of marly, water retentive soils. Settlement is characteristically more scattered here than in the eastern parts of the county, and large areas of upland remained uninhabited until the last century.

The southern and eastern parts of the area are of a Lowland character, consisting of calcareous Oolitic hills fronted by complex and varied Lias and alluvial deposits which provide a range of soil types. North Somerset is dominated by plateaux of Carboniferous Limestone and Triassic sandstone, rising to around 250-300 m O.D. These areas are fringed by areas of fertile outwash or 'head' deposits.[48]

Most of central, and part of north Somerset consist of the low-lying alluvial and peat deposits of the Somerset Levels. With shallow gradients, and lying at about 6 m O.D., these areas have been subject to both marine and fresh water flooding in the past. Their condition in our period is still a matter for debate, the controversy centring around evidence for late-Roman marine transgression.[49]

Despite its variety, the area possesses a certain unity imparted by physical boundaries, which are largely reflected in political ones. On the north-east the River Avon forms a considerable barrier, only easily crossed in the vicinity of Bath. Further to the south the band of Oxford clay which marks the former area of the Forest of Selwood separates the Oolite hills from the chalklands to the east. Much of the southern boundary is defined by the Blackdown Hills, and only the Devonshire boundary on Exmoor does not follow any obvious major line of demarcation. Discussion of the emergence of Somerset as a political entity is largely beyond the direct scope of this thesis, but as this took place within our period, the adoption of the county as the region of study is not entirely without historical justification. The archaeological and historical background of the area will now be considered.

Historical and archaeological resumé, AD 0-700

Whatever its later political or cultural unity, numismatic and other evidence suggests that the territory of at least three late Iron Age groupings included parts of Somerset. The northern parts fell within the tribal area of the Dobunni, the southern in that of the Durotriges, and the western in that of the Dumnonii. Precise tribal boundaries cannot be reconstructed, but the area of the Somerset Levels probably provided a common natural boundary.

Initial Roman control was established by c. 50 AD, Roman forts were established at various points, and at some time in this initial phase many of the inhabitants of at least two hillforts were massacred.[50] Civilian settlement at Bath was well developed by the end of the first century,[51] and exploitation of Mendip lead by its middle decades.

The later third century seems to have been a time of radical changes, especially in the rural landscape, and the character of fourth-century and later Somerset may have been greatly influenced by these. Large and opulent

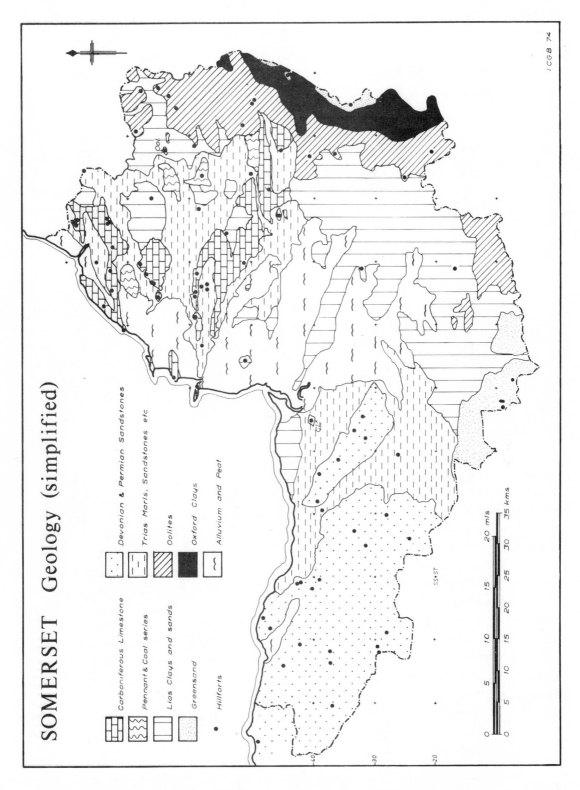

SOMERSET Geology (simplified)

Carboniferous Limestone	Devonian & Permian Sandstones
Pennant & Coal series	Trias Marls, Sandstones etc
Lias Clays and sands	Oolites
Greensand	Oxford Clays
Hillforts	Alluvium and Peat

SS ST

ICGB 74

Fig. 2 Somerset; Simplified geology and distribution of hillforts and related enclosures

13

villa estates, some of them perhaps founded with Gallic capital, [52] typify the fourth century, though numerous other settlements characterized by rectangular stone buildings are also known. [53] A number of rural temple sites attest to a flourishing paganism until at least the end of the fourth century. In contrast to this evidently flourishing rural society, urban development was notably slight in comparison with eastern England. [54] Slight evidence for military activity at Sea Mills (Abonae) in the later fourth century, and for the destruction of a number of villas, has suggested that barbarian raids were affecting the area at this time. [55]

Political and administrative arrangements in the fourth century are obscure. The area was probably within Britannia Prima, [56] but the geographical location of the civitates which formed the main areas of local administration are unclear. In the south, Ilchester was the focus of the Civitas Lendiniensium. [57] The remainder of the county east of the Parrett is normally ascribed to the artificial Roman creation of the Civitas Belgarum, [58] and western areas to the Dumnonii. [59] It is to such groupings that Honorius addressed his letter in 410, empowering the inhabitants to undertake their own defence, [60] and from which political arrangements of the fifth century and later may derive. There is, however, no direct evidence as to what these may have been.

Political developments may have had little effect on the bulk of the population, but the length of time for which they continued to make use of distinctively Romano-British artifacts and to occupy fourth-century sites is uncertain. Some sites remained in use until some time after the collapse of the commercial production of pottery and the virtual cessation of imports of coin, but at some stage most were abandoned. Among their successors are the hilltop sites we shall be considering, but it cannot be doubted that the majority of the sites of the fifth and later centuries were not located in such places and await detection.

English settlement of the area, on documentary evidence a phenomenon of the seventh century, must be considered under three main headings. English domination can too easily be equated directly with the first; the establishment of political control of the area by the West Saxon kingdom. The documentary references in the Anglo-Saxon Chronicle and from charter material suggest that this was complete by AD 700, and had been effected by victory in battle against British opposition. [61] This westward extension of Wessex into Somerset was part of a general wave of aggressive and expansionist activity by the English kingdom from the mid-sixth century onwards. By AD 700 the whole of the intermediate zone defined above was under English political control. It has been suggested by Morris[62] that this expansion was qualitatively different from that of the initial English land-taking in the fifth century, being subject to much greater royal control and direction. This is an important point, since there may have been a direct concern for the conservation of the existing resources of land and manpower as ready-made revenue for the royal house. Disruption at a local level may therefore have been relatively slight once pitched battles had been decisively won or lost.

It is often tacitly assumed that victory in battle and the extension of political domination over a new area are the concomitants of land-taking by English-speaking settlers. This process may have taken place quite independently of such events, and have preceded or succeeded them by a considerable interval. It is, however, extremely difficult to document in western areas of England because of the paucity of closely datable Germanic artifacts, their uncertain cultural and ethnographic implications, and the lack of adequate skeletal data which might indicate intrusive elements in the population.

Following from this it is possible that English political, cultural and linguistic dominance in the area was effected less by a major change of population than by the adoption by the local population of the cultural patterns of the dominant English. There is reason to suspect that this occurred in the case of place names, and many other aspects of life may have been effected similarly.

It is however probable that greater changes took place at the top of the social scale. Although it is clear from Ine's laws that British nobles had a recognised, though subordinate, place in West Saxon society,[63] a range of other evidence indicates expulsion and death in battle of the local rulers at the hands of the English. As the sites under consideration in this study have been regarded as the habitations of local lords, the English settlement could have had a major and immediate affect on the occupation of hilltop settlements.

English domination of the area was not, however, the only major intrusive element into the Somerset area at this time. There may have been limited Irish settlement in some areas,[64] but the most significant changes may have been brought about by the establishment of Christianity as the sole organized religion of the area. There is at present no conclusive evidence for Christianity in the region in the fourth century, and as will be discussed in chapter 3 the evidence of 'Celtic' church dedications suggests that active evangelization of the area from South Wales may have taken place in the sixth century.[65] Paganism in various forms may also have remained much more active than the limited documentary evidence would suggest. Religious activity, pagan or Christian, may therefore continue to be relevant to evidence for hilltop activity in the fifth to seventh centuries, as it had in the fourth or earlier.

Identification of settlement and other sites of this period remains closely linked to archaeologists' ability to recognize a very limited range of artifactual material, chiefly imported Mediterranean pottery and Teutonic and Celtic metalwork. Some types of site, in particular cemeteries with particular characteristics,[66] are also regarded as diagnostic of the period, but recognition of field monuments, with the exception of Early Christian inscribed stones and linear earthworks, is at present extremely hard.

In the next chapter the data from the Iron Age hillforts of Somerset are examined. This basic discussion aims to assess the general field evidence for hilltop settlement as reflected by these major monuments.

NOTES

1. Using 'Lowland' and 'Highland' as defined in Fox, 1943. This division has been criticised recently (e.g. Evans, 1975, 1-2), but is felt to be still useful in the Roman and post-Roman centuries under consideration here.

2. Alcock, 1971a; Morris, 1973; Thomas, 1971a, b; Laing, 1975a.

3. Explicit statement of the personal motivation for the study is felt to be desirable in order that any bias detected in the approach to the data or its interpretation may be more explicable, although it is hoped that no such biases are present. See Clarke, 1972a, 3-10.

4. Burrow, 1976a.

5. Much of this material has not yet been fully published, but recent trends are summarized in various papers in Rowley, 1974, and Rodwell and Rowley, 1975. For epidemics, see Wacher, 1975, chap. 10. For a valuable discussion of the problem locally see Leech 1977, esp. chapters 10-12.

6. Taylor, 1974b.

7. Rahtz, 1977, 56.

8. Taylor op.cit., 7.

9. Taylor, op.cit.

10. Maitland, 1897, especially 221-3 gave the classic exposition of this view. See Applebaum, 1972, 250-67.

11. Taylor op.cit., Jones, 1972.

12. Myres, 1969, 21; Alcock, 1971a, 198-201.

13. Laing, 1975a, chaps. 12 and 13. Alock, 1971a, chap. 10, refs.

14. Laing, op.cit. chap 11.

15. e.g. Bonney, 1972.

16. Taylor op.cit., note 6.

17. Summarized in Jones, 1972.

18. Jones, 1961a.

19. Alcock, 1962; 1963a, 195-99; 1964; 1965a.

20. Rahtz in Wilson, 1976, 49-96.

21. Shakenoak; Brodribb et al., 1972, but see Alcock, 1973. Rivenhall; Rodwell and Rodwell, 1973. Kent; Med. Arch. 17, (1973), 145.

22. Chalton; Addyman et al., 1973a, 1973b. Cunliffe, 1973a, 1973b. West Stow; West, 1974. Catholme; Current Archaeology 59 (1977), 358-64. Yeavering; Hope-Taylor 1979.

23. Cunliffe, 1974, chap 1, for a résumé of development of Iron Age and hillfort studies.

24. Wheeler, 1925, 261-2. The problem has been reviewed, and Wheelers theory discounted, in Simpson, 1964. Savory, 1976.

25. Wheeler, 1943, 61-8.

26. Wheeler, 1943, 72-3.

27. Curwen and Williamson, 1931.

28. Wheeler and Wheeler, 1932.

29. Lewis, 1966 for temples. See Frilford (Bradford and Goodchild, 1939) and South Cadbury (Alcock, 1970b, 18-20).

30. Wheeler, 1943, 143.

31. Wheeler and Wheeler, 1932, 64-5.

32. Ballinderry Crannog (Henken, 1942), Garranes (O'Riordain, 1942), Ballycateen (O'Riordain, 1943), Lagore Crannog (Henken, 1951).

33. Thomas, 1971a, 29-31.

34. Burrow, 1974.

35. Thomas, 1971a, 32-8; Rahtz, 1974a.

36. In Scotland Dunadd (Craw, 1930) and the Mote of Mark (Curle, 1914) had already been examined. The major sites in Wales and the West were Pant-y-Saer (Phillips, 1934), Castle Dore (Radford, 1951), Carreg-y-Llam (Hogg, 1957), Dinas Emrys (Savory, 1960), and Garn Boduan (Hogg, 1960, 3-10).

37. Alcock, 1963a, 55.

38. This model is most specifically outlined in Alcock, 1971a, 347-9, but see also 1962, 1963a, 1963b (especially 302, note 3), 1964, 1965a, 1965b.

39. Dumville, 1977.

40. Morris, 1973.

41. Alcock, 1971a, 347-9.

42. Fowler, 1971, 203.

43. Alcock, 1971a, 338-40.

44. The study area consists of the County of Somerset, and the City and County of Bristol as they existed before local government re-organisation of April 1974. The northern part of the area now lies within the county of Avon.

45. Rahtz and Fowler, 1972. Somerset sites will not normally be other-
     wise referenced in this chapter.

46. Alcock, 1970a considers this problem archaeologically.

47. Institute of Geological Sciences 1948, 1969.

48. Findlay, 1965; Avery, 1955.

49. Cunliffe, 1966; Hawkins, 1973; Coles, 1975; Leech, 1977, Chapter 5.

50. Alcock, 1971b, 3-4; Dymond and Tomkins, 1886.

51. Lead; Frere, 1967, 284. Bath; Cunliffe, 1969, 3.

52. Branigan, 1972 and 1974. For a contrary view see Leech 1977, 194-195.

53. Fowler, 1970, Lilly and Ussher, 1972, Leech, 1976.

54. Rahtz and Fowler, 1972, 190ff. Leech 1977. The latter regards
     South Somerset and North Dorset as a more logical study area within
     a Romano-British framework (Leech 1977, 1-6).

55. Branigan, 1972, 120-21.

56. Frere, 1967, 211.

57. Frere, 1967, 171.

58. Rivet, 1964, 140-41.

59. Thomas, 1966, 83-4.

60. Frere, 1967, 366-8.

61. Hoskins, 1960, Porter, 1967.

62. Morris, 1973, 296.

63. Stenton, 1947, 300.

64. Rahtz, 1976.

65. Radford, 1962. 'Celtic' is used here in the dual sense of persons
     speaking Celtic languages and originating from ecclesiastical centres
     in Celtic speaking areas. Other similar semantic problems, with
     which the post-Roman centuries are replete, will be discussed as they
     arise.

66. Rahtz, 1977.

CHAPTER 2

SOMERSET HILLFORTS AND HILL-TOP SITES—
A REVIEW OF THE EVIDENCE

Over much of Southern Britain hillforts figure prominantly in the archaeological record as striking and dominant features in the landscape. It is
probable that they have constantly been frequented for motives ranging from
mere curiosity to a need for security or seclusion. They have also been an
attraction to archaeologists of the recent past and the study of the motives
and function of hillfort utilisation must take into account the bias in the data
caused by archaeological concentration on sites, such as hillforts, which are
readily identified and defined. This study runs the risk of perpetuating this
bias by attaching greater significance to Roman and post-Roman material
from hillforts than that material would warrant in its overall context. Similarly the single-minded study of hillforts as a class of monuments standing
alone—except in areas where they form the only known settlement type—cannot
easily be justified if the aim of the study is to make deductions concerning
settlement patterns and relationships.

In both the Roman and post-Roman periods a small number of sites,
located on hilltops but lacking enclosing defences, is known. Their recognition has thus been more difficult than that of hilltops and re-emphasises
the problems of bias mentioned above. As will be discussed further in cha-
ter 7, assessment of the significance of the presence or absence of pre-existing
or refurbished earthworks around these sites is a matter of great complexity.
For the present, however, attention will be confined largely to the analysis of
the general evidence from hillforts themselves.

Definition and function

It is widely accepted that the term 'hillfort' is unsatisfactory, applied
as it is to a numerous and very varied body of sites located throughout the
British Isles. It has proved a convenient shorthand term, however, and is
here used in the broad sense followed by Hogg,[1] and Forde-Johnston[2] and
others. The expression thus encompasees all those sites referred to by the
Ordnance Survey[3] as 'Hillforts and similar defended enclosures', there being
a school of thought which would restrict the use of the term 'hillfort' to larger
more strongly defended sites,[4] although precisely where the division lies is
unclear.

It could be argued that the application of this term to Somerset sites as
diverse as the 85-hectare multivallate hillfort on Ham Hill and the weakly
defended enclosure only 1/800th of this size at Wraxall (No. 79) is a hindrance
rather than a help to understanding. The sites under consideration here do,
however, share two characteristics. In the first place they are all defined by
artificial banks and ditches of a more or less defensible character, and secondly

the vast majority do not fall readily into any other earthwork classification. It must nevertheless be stressed that the material is extremely diverse, and that observed variations must be related to social, functional and chronological differences. In particular, there is a danger in assuming that all earthworks were defensive in intention, however much they may now appear to be so. Banks and ditches may be built for a wide range of purposes, of which the following may readily be brought to mind: as defences; as an expression of social importance; as a legal barrier; as a religious barrier; to control game; to control livestock; to control drainage.

It is with the function of hillforts within the Iron Age that much recent research has been concerned. It is inappropriate here to discuss in detail the development of archaeological thinking on this problem, but four main hypotheses can be discerned in the literature. These may ge termed the military, refuge, agricultural/domestic and proto-urban models, and all of these may be applicable in the periods with which we are concerned.

The military model, little favoured in current Iron Age studies, would see the hillfort as an instrument of defence, conquest and subjection, a 'native' equivalent of the Roman forts with which hillforts were frequently identified by earlier antiquaries. This strand of thought is still evident in the 'invasion'-orientated discussions prior to the last war, but is rarely cited now.[5] It has, however, continued to find favour in post-Roman contexts.

The refuge model sees hillforts as defended enclosures located conveniently enough in relation to permanent settlement areas to be used in times of danger by surrounding communities. Arguments in favour of this view are the extremely inhospitable and inconvenient locations (from a present-day viewpoint at least) of many larger hillforts, and the lack of any clear indication of occupation at many sites. Both these points can now be seen in the light of work in Wales[6] and elsewhere, which has suggested that even the most exposed sites were permanently occupied or at the very least regularly frequented on a seaonsal basis.

For smaller sites in particular a function related either to the herding of stock or to the simple defensive enclosure of an essentially small domestic community is indicated. The type of site interpreted in this way is so unspecialised that its wide chronological and geographical distribution is not surprising, and to judge from the known date range it is likely that a considerable number will ultimately prove to date from the Roman and later periods.

It is a commonplace of Iron Age studies that the average size of hillfort enclosures decreases towards the west and north of Britain, probably reflecting different social and economic conditions away from the south-east. As will be argued later, this distribution pattern may have exerted an influence both on Roman and post-Roman developments and on recent interpretations of those developments. Larger hillforts are more characteristic of western and southern England, where their density and size is taken to imply larger, better organised populations. In recent years there has been a tendency to consider many of these sites as permanently occupied settlements possessing urban or proto-urban characteristics in the Iron Age.[7] Among these characteristics are evidence for elements of planning in the interior placing of structures, specialist activities and industries, social and religious functions, redistribution of regional products and more long distance trade. Although there is likely to be considerable regional variation, this model of hillfort function is now being widely adopted, and as a result attempts have been made to analyse the relationships of hillforts with each other and with other settlement types.[8] Attempts have been made to define 'territories' within which the hillfort would have been the dominant settlement.[9] There has also been an increased understanding of the possible economic and social relationships between the hillfort and other contemporary settlements.[10] While such approaches have severe limitations and have been much criticised, they have made it possible to explore further the implications of the data recovered from recent hillfort excavations, and have tended to stress the major role of the hillfort in Iron Age cultures in large areas of Britain.

The Somerset data (Fig. 3)

With these points in mind the basic data from Somerset may be considered. Up to April 1975 a total of 89 sites which fall under the broad definition of 'hillfort', adopted above, had been located. It is probable that more remain to be discovered or have been totally destroyed, this being especially true of the smaller sites. Recent work on Exmoor for example has indicated that small hillslope enclosures are more numerous than previously supposed.[11] Nevertheless, the general pattern of survival and discovery is by archaeological standards excellent.

Classification and distribution

The great range in scale of defences, siting and enclosed areas in the Somerset sites necessitates some attempt at ordering of the material, since these observed differences must represent different social, cultural or historical conditions. Any hillfort classification is, however, bound to depend very largely on above-ground indications, since so few sites have been adequately excavated or recorded. Lady Fox's analysis of the wide-spaced rampart forts of South-West England provides a model here in its use of criteria such as size, location and disposition of the defences to define a distinctive group of sites for which an approximate date could be suggested on the basis of a small amount of excavated material.[12]

Somerset has not been regarded as a unity by recent workers on Iron Age problems, the tendency being to see the western areas as part of the South Western peninsula, the north as an extension of the Cotswold region and the south as part of Wessex.[13] These divisions are based both on geographical and Iron Age cultural criteria, and so may have a greater validity in a purely Iron Age context than in a study concerned with later aspects of the sites. It was, however, argued in chapter 1 that the Somerset area should be treated as a whole for the purposes of this study, and in the light of this a classification for the Somerset sites has been devised. The aim of this classification is chiefly to analyze the topographical and other physical characteristics of the hillfort sites without any cultural or chronological implications attached. It has relevance only in the context of this study and makes no claims of universal applicability. For the Somerset sites, the basis for classification is restricted to the size of the enclosed area, the form and scale of the defences, and the situation of the sites. On this basis four broad groups (I-IV) were isolated, the distribution of which is shown in Figure 4, and the characteristics of which will now be considered.

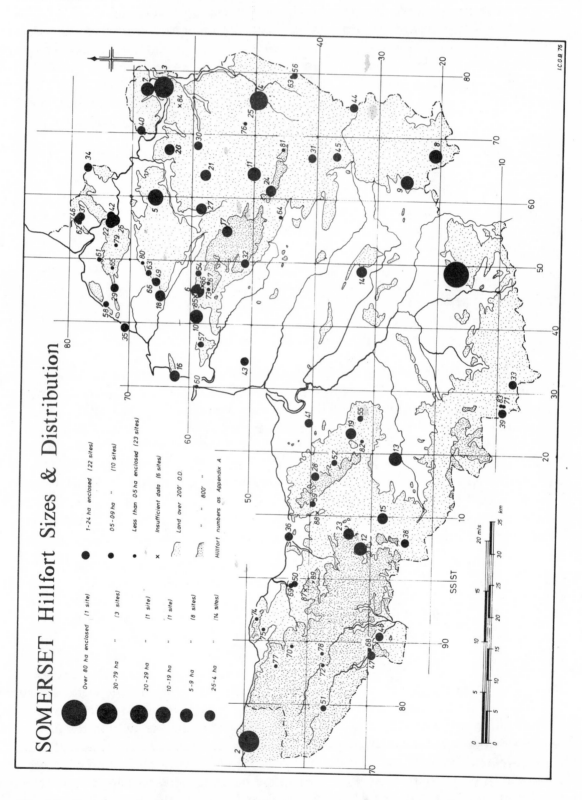

Fig. 3 Somerset; Hillfort sizes and distribution in relation to topography
and the National Grid

22

Sites of Group I are essentially 'classic' hillforts. The enclosed area varies from the enormous area of Ham Hill (site 1)[14] to the small, but strongly defended, site of Brewer's Castle (68) of only 0.3 hectares. Most of the 33 sites are, however, over one hectare in area, and all are in prominent defensive positions and possess defences of considerable size and complexity. It is these sites for which a proto-urban function may be envisaged in the latter part of the Iron Age, and are also those from which positive evidence of Roman and post-Roman activity is most plentiful.

The distribution of these hillforts shows an even scatter over the county; one site is exceptionally located in the upland of Exmoor (51), another in the Polden Hills in the middle of the Somerset Levels (14), and the distribution is such that it is nowhere possible to be more than 15 kilometres from one of these sites. Most sites are in much greater proximity than this last figure, which only applies to the area to the west of Ham Hill. The construction of unweighted Thiessen polygons[15] around sites of Group I and a number of larger sites of Groups II and III emphasises this distribution pattern (Fig. 5). This technique has severe drawbacks as an analytical device, other than as a simple way of indicating spatial relationships, since the construction of polygons as an indication of hillfort 'territories' depends on the assumption that all the points used as centres are in contemporary use. The technique clearly has a limited predictive value, as positive evidence for contemporaneity is normally lacking. Nevertheless, the pattern observable in Figure 5 is a stimulus to the consideration of aspects of the distribution of our sites.

In detail, it is noteworthy that many sites are located near the nodal points of geographically defined areas. Thus Ham Hill and Norton Fitzwarren (13) are located in the upper parts of the Parrett river catchments, polygons based on them roughly defining areas bounded by higher ground. A number of other sites also appear to be located with a regard to areas defined by river systems, for example Bat's Castle (50), Daw's Castle (36), Cannington (41) and Cadcong. Many of the Group I sites are also sited close to, or actually on, major geological and topographical changes. This may be partly explained by the defensive advantages that such junctions frequently possess in Somerset. The steep scarps at the edge of the Carboniferous Limestone of North Somerset, and the Upper Lias and Oolite in the south and east of the county, for instance provided locations for several of the largest hillforts. This characteristic choice of siting at the junctions of different topopgraphical zones is, however, shared by all groups, especially Group IV, in which defensive considerations seem to be a minor factor. It may therefore be suspected that this choice of location was influenced by economic considerations, and possibly by a desire to have ready access to a number of types of land.

Some Group I sites are, however, located in areas of relatively uniform geology and topography, and a number of factors may be involved in these cases. Do such sitings, for example, represent a deliberate choice of a uniform resource area and a rejection of the more varied agricultural opportunities of a location at the edge of different zones? Clearly such a question is only relevant if it is assumed that hillfort communities were self-sufficient for their food production, and that such production took place close to the hillfort itself.

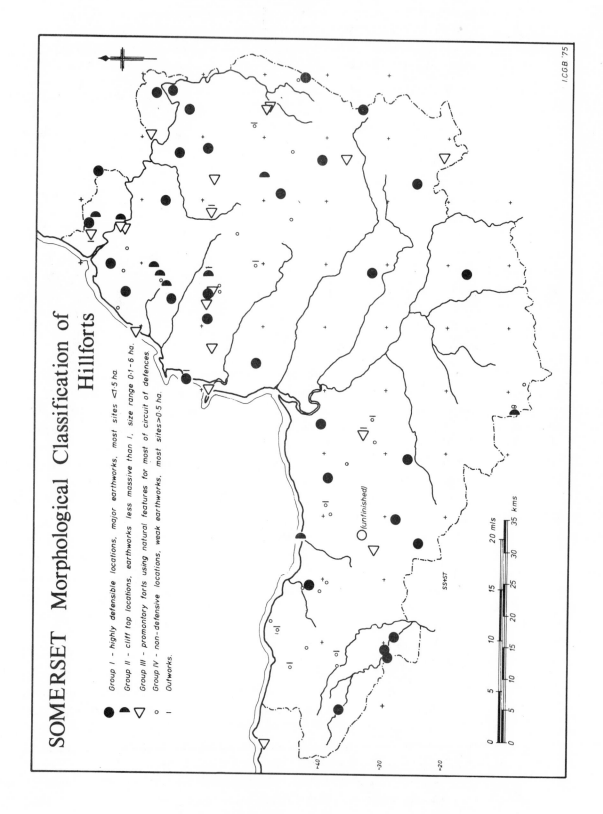

Fig. 4 Somerset; Morphological classification of hillforts

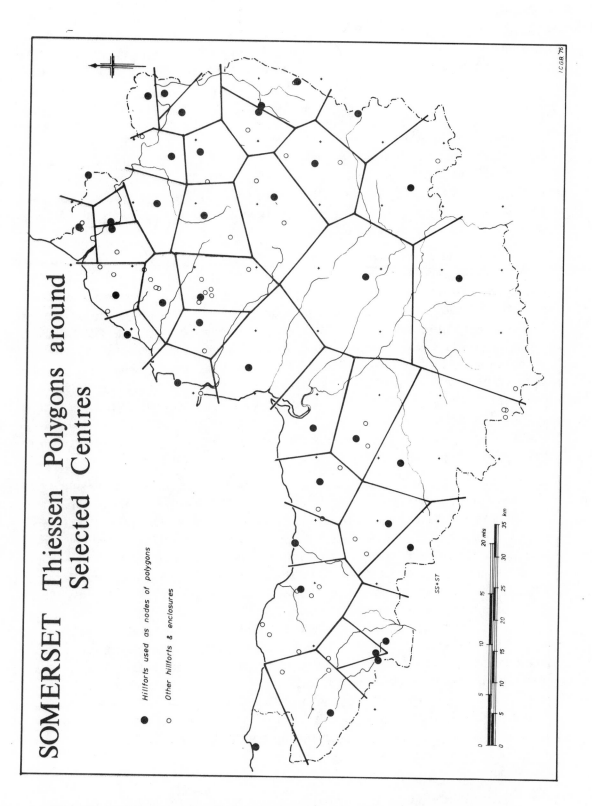

Fig. 5 Somerset; Spatial relationships between selected hillforts
expressed by Thiessen Polygons

25

The most marked examples of such sites are Maesbury (24) and Cow Castle (50). Both are in upland areas thinly populated even today, and apparently lacking any substantial settlements even by the end of the first millennium A.D. Maesbury (Plate 1) is representative of Group I sites, a bivallate enclosure of about 2.8 ha. with one entrance on its west side, apparently original, and a later breach on the east. Sited on a rise in the limestone plateau at 950 feet (289 m) O.D., the hillfort has wide views over the surrounding country, but is not well defended by natural slopes except on the south side. A Roman road passes close to the site on the north side, running along the Mendip plateau towards the lead mining areas to the west, and the hillfort is bisected by the parish boundary between Croscombe and Dinder. Clarke[16] has suggested that this hillfort was the Iron Age regional centre upon which the Glastonbury settlements depended for much of their exchange, but the impression gained from its present setting, especially when compared with most other sites of Group I, is one of isolation and remoteness from concentrations of settlement, and archaeological and place-name evidence will be adduced to reinforce this view in later chapters.

Cow Castle, Exmoor is to an even greater extent a 'marginal' site and here a specialised economic function may be guessed at. This small (0.9 ha.) univallate hillfort is located on a knoll at the confluence of two streams in the heart of Exmoor, and land within an eight kilometre radius is marked by steep inclines and thin peaty acid soils. Even allowing for climatic deterioration since the construction of the site, a specialised economy based on livestock rather than arable cultivation would be indicated here. Most of the interior is unusable for permanent habitation because of the steep slopes and rock outcrops. It is possible, therefore, that Cow Castle is just that, a strongly fortified enclosure designed for the coralling of large numbers of cattle. It might then be seen as complementary to the Group IV enclosures dotted around the edges of the upland moors.

The relatively isolated character of these sites has been stressed because it is in such marked contrast to the majority of the Group I sites. The location of the latter on dramatic hilltops should not be allowed to conceal their proximity to potentially productive and varied agricultural land. The sites of Group I may in general be regarded as, in origin, communal settlement sites in which various social pressures have made the need for hill-top siting and defensive structures outweigh the advantages to be gained from lowland living. This is now a commonplace on Iron Age studies, but needs to be emphasised in the Roman and post-Roman periods, when we may expect the same factors to obtain —firstly that there will have to be a local population of some size to make intensive use of a hill-top site feasible, and secondly that there must be a powerful stimulus or stimuli to cause any such use. This suggests that we should look for any re-use of sites of Group I in areas of especially dense occupation, and not at such relatively isolated sites as Cow Castle and Measbury. An important caveat to these assumptions must be the possibility that some sites had a wholly religious use not dependent on a large population.

This discussion of sites of Group I has anticipated to some extent the more general comments to be made on the overall data, but this is due to the smaller number of sites of both Groups II and III, to the special problems of the Group IV enclosures, and to the greater importance which the sites of Group I apparently possess.

Plate 1 Maesbury Hillfort (no. 24) from the east
(West Air Photography, Weston-Super-Mare; neg. AJ935/9)

Group II is defined more by the disposition of its defences than from the size of the area enclosed. The chief characteristic of the sites of this group is the use made of cliff top locations at the edge of plateaux. The sides without natural defences are protected by earthworks, but no defences are now present at the top of the severe or vertical slope, which forms less than 50% of the total enclosed circuit in most cases. This is a device which might naturally suggest itself where the topography is suitable, but it can be argued that the nine sites showing this form share other common features which merit their isolation as a group. The largest, Blacker's Hill (11) (Plate 2) encloses about six hectares, while the smallest, the now destroyed Backwell Camp (80) enclosed only 0.1 hectares. Only in two cases can the defences be described as at all formidable. At Clifton Camp (42) the surviving, much mutilated inner rampart still stands 4 m high above the outer ditch, and Blacker's Hill is a bivallate site with banks averaging $3\frac{1}{2}$ m in height. At the latter site the present disposition of the defences is very unusual in that, because of the downward slope towards the interior, the outer bank is noticeable higher than the inner at places where both survive.

The remaining sites, however, are distinguished by small-scale defences and it is improbable that they could ever have posed serious problems to an attacker. These are Daws Castle (36), Come Hill (37), Horsepool (39), Cleeve Toot (49), Tap's Combe (53), Burrington (54) and Backwell (80). This group of sites will be considered in more detail in chapter 4. At this point it may merely be noted that all the sites except Daw's Castle and Horsepool are in locations at the junction of different land types in the northern part of the county, and that three sites are in very close proximity, spaced regularly along the northern edge of the limestone plateau of Broadfield Down a short distance east of Cadcong.

The eighteen sites belonging to Group III are coastal or inland promontory forts, at which natural features account for more than 50% of the defensible circuit, and normally much more than this. Even more than with Group II, this type of location presents obvious advantages which have been utilised for many purposes and at many periods. Some of the larger sites in this category, such as Roborough (19) and Clatworthy (12) are of sufficient size and strength to be included among Group I sites, but Littledown (40 and Plate 3) is more typical of promontory sites, being artificially defended by a single bank only, and that of moderate size, the present vertical difference between the bottom of the ditch and the top of the bank being only about 3 metres. Clearly, the distribution of this group will be largely a reflection of suitable topography, and no conclusions can be drawn from it. It seems probable that the isolation of promontory sites as a class is only of limited value, but it does help to distinguish a number of sites from those belonging to the final Group IV.

The remaining sites fall into this category, and are defined as enclosures with small-scale enclosing ditches and banks, in locations not chosen for their defensive potential. The majority of the sites have an enclosed area of less than 0.5 hectares. The shape of the enclosed area is variable, some sites, such as Road Castle (72), being nearly square or rectangular, others circular or polygonal. Whether such variations reflect actual differences in date, function or cultural background cannot be assessed, but it must be regarded as unlikely. The provision of outworks—lengths of bank and ditch set across

28

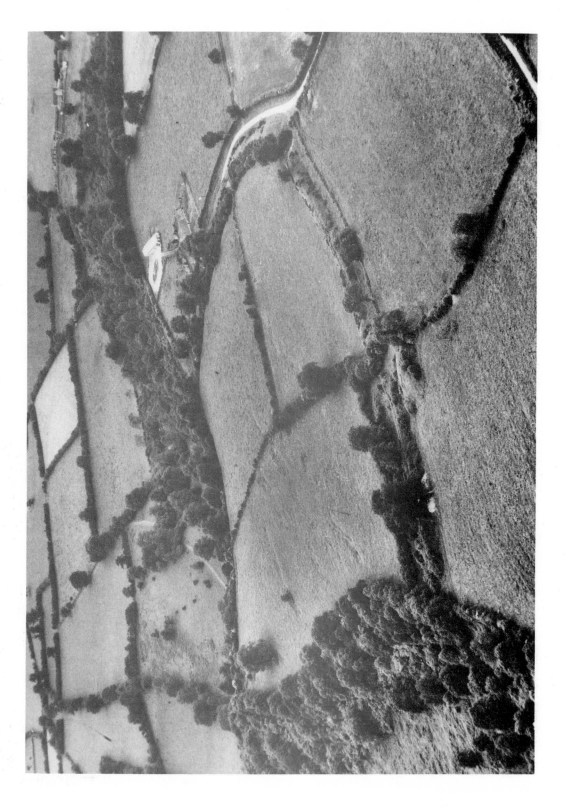

Plate 2 Blacker's Hill Hillfort (no. 11) from the east
(University of Cambridge Collection, neg. no. LX14)

Plate 3 Littledown Camp (no. 40) from the east
(UCCAP neg. no. CD71)

the easiest approach to the site and located some distance away—links a number of sites to Lady Fox's south-western hillslope enclosures, and the five sites which most clearly fall into this class (55, 59, 70, 75 and 77) all lie in the hill country of West Somerset.[17]

Clearly, these enclosures are of such a simple and non-specific character that a wider date range is to be expected in Group IV than in the other three groups, and analysis based on general form will probably be misleading.[18] In advance of more detailed discussion in chapter 4, we may, however, make some general observations on this group, in particular comparing it with the large defensive enclosures of Group I.

Somerset hillfort and enclosure distribution is a microcosm of that of Southern Britain as a whole. If the river Parrett is taken as a division between Western Somerset and the remainder of the county the following results are obtained:-

West of the Parrett	30 sites average 2.47 ha.
(omitting No. 2, 34 hectares)	29 sites average 1.38 ha.
East of the Parrett	53 sites average 4.86 ha.
(omitting No. 1, 85 hectares)	52 sites average 3.32 ha.
[Six sites have no size information available]	

It is clear from these figures that enclosures in the western, highland parts of the county are on average only half the size of those in the rest of the county —the large hillforts of Group I are both rarer and smaller, and small univallate enclosures predominate.

Many of these small enclosures, such as Trendle Ring (Plate 4) are constructed on considerable slopes, and the interior of the sites show no sign of the levelling which might be anticipated had permanent dwellings or structures been erected within them. These 'hillslope' enclosures are virtually confined to the area west of the Parrett, although there are four sites at the edge of Mendip and in the east of the county which also fall into this subdivision of Group IV. The association of this choice of siting with cross-dyke and outwork features may suggest a specialist economic function related to stock corralling. Similar sites on the Welsh Border have recently been interpreted in this way.[20]

In the east of the county, be contrast, many Group IV enclosures are located on the flat plateaux formed by the Carboniferous Limestone, although never very far from other types of land. Only one enclosure of this type, Kingsdown Camp, is to be found on the Oolitic soils of the eastern part of the county, and the remaining sites are located on poorly drained Greensand and clay soils in the east and south. This remarkable concentration on the limestone areas may be a product of selective survival of the evidence—these areas having been used predominantly for grazing for many centuries in contrast to the more productive soils around the margins—or it may indicate an actual situation in which small earthwork enclosures fulfilled a function in upland limestone areas which is not reflected elsewhere in the county. As with the hillslope enclosures in the west, an explanation linked to economic factors associated with livestock comes to mind. In support of this, a number or sites of a different character, but presumptively also falling somewhere in the period 1000 B.C. - 1000 A.D., are known from the Wrington area. These are ' open'

Plate 4 Trendle Ring Hillslope Enclosure (no. 59) from the south
         (UCCAP neg. no. ARJ4)

settlements with associated 'Celtic' field systems and are located off the plateaux and on lower terraces flanking the valley.[21] Only one of these sites has been excavated but it is at least a testable hypothesis that these differences in character and location are functional and not chronological. If this is so it would probably be incorrect to see at least the majority of the Somerset enclosures as strictly analogous to the raths of Ireland, where available evidence, both of distribution and economy, suggest an unspecialised character and a mixed economy for this type of site.[22]

A small number of sites of Group IV are considerably larger than the majority. The average size of sites of the group is 0.6 hectares, the but majority are of 0.4 hectares or less. Pitchers Enclosures, now destroyed, was however a ditchless embanked enclosure of 3.6 hecateres with a single entrance, possibly surrounded by a field system.[23] Westbury can be classed topographically with the hillslope enclosures of West Somerset, but encloses 2.4 hectares. The defences are now badly damaged by ploughing and quarrying, but seem never to have been of any strength. Two linear banks run north and eastwards from the main enclosure, but detailed examination does not suggest that they are functionally linked to it.

Wambrook Camp, now also almost destroyed by ploughing, lies at 200 m on the highest point of gently rising ground. The view is extensive on all sides and the location is thus that favoured for the majority of the Group I sites, and this site thus emphasises the problems of establishing a wholly consistent classification. Ascription to Group IV is predominantly on the apparently weak, univallate character of the defences so far as their form can be assessed.

In conclusion, therefore, it can be said that enclosures of Group IV show a distribution which is somewhat different from that of the larger sites of Group I, showing a marked preference for the western parts of the county and for plateau locations on the north Somerset limestone but close to its margins. The group shows considerable variety both in size and location, but the enclosures around the fringes of Exmoor and the Quantocks stand out as a clearly defined consistent sub-group which may be explained in terms of a specialised economic purpose.

General comments

The body of data presented by the 89 sites of the four groups discussed above is therefore considerable even before chronological problems are considered. Each site represents a considerable investment in time and manpower by the community which constructed it, and it is therefore certain that the choice of location was not made lightly. If it is accepted that the vast majority of the sites served as essentially domestic and economic function, rather than being constructed for ritual or short-term military purposes, it follows that a range of deductions may be made about the probable land use and distribution of population in the county.

Changes in geological formations are strongly reflected in the topography of much of Somerset. The concentration of hillforts on some formations and their avoidance of others is not therefore at first sight surprising. The Carboniferous Limestone, as has been discussed, presents a number of topographical advantages exploited by sites of Groups I-III, and was also favoured by enclosures of Group IV, perhaps for more specific economic reasons. The hill country of the west of the county also shows a large number of sites but, as has been seen, many of these are also small enclosures of Group IV positioned on hillslopes and not making defensive use of the local topography. As with the enclosures of north Somerset, their avoidance of the high central areas of Exmoor and the Brendons, and the summit plateau of the Quantocks suggests a concern as much with adjacent lowlands as with the hill areas themselves.

The Oolite scarpland of south-east and east Somerset shows a preponderance of large sites of Group I and two especially large sites of Group III, nos. 4 and 8. The small sites are noticeably absent from this area.

The complex Lias areas of the south of the county contain only two sites. Ham Hill is located on upper Lias limestone formations overlooking the Levels and Lias hills around Ilchester and with extensive areas of Oolitic uplands within 5 km to the south. The nearest hillfort, Dundon Hill (14) is over 15 km to the north, South Cadbury on the Oolite is 17 km to the east, and no major hillforts lie within 25 km to the south. The size of Ham Hill and the distance which separates it from other sites must indicate that it was of outstanding importance for a long period and supports the idea that it was the centre of a hillfort 'territory'.

Dundon Hill itself is a smaller site, but is still considerable by county standards. Once again, this site appears to naturally dominate a discrete area—the Lias Polden Hills which run westwards from it above the surrounding Somerset Levels.

North Somerset, with a very varied topography and geography is, consistently, the area with the greatest range of enclosure types, small sites of Group IV being interspersed with larger hillforts along the limestone ridge of King's Weston, the Failand Ridge and the northern and southern fringes of Mendip. Without detailed chronological information on all the sites no firm conclusions can be reached, but it does appear that dispersed single homesteads and communal nucleated settlements can only be readily intermingled where opportunities are sufficiently varied for both to function.

No real attempt can be made to assess the population represented by the construction of these enclosures, as the imponderables are too great. What can, however, be considered is the relation of hillfort distribution to the later distribution of population. While the hillforts of Somerset are most numerous in the north and west of the county, their enclosed areas are on average much smaller than those in the south and east. A comparison of the overall distribution of hillforts with that of, for example, Domesday vills reveals very little except that there is a broad correspondence between the two—the uplands of the Mendips and Exmoor and the Somerset Levels being alike avoided by both.

What has, however, been attempted in Fig. 6 is to adopt the regions defined by workers on the Domesday material, and within those regions to work out the proportion of the area enclosed by hillfort earthworks to the total area of the region. In this way some idea of the actual quantity of land occupied by

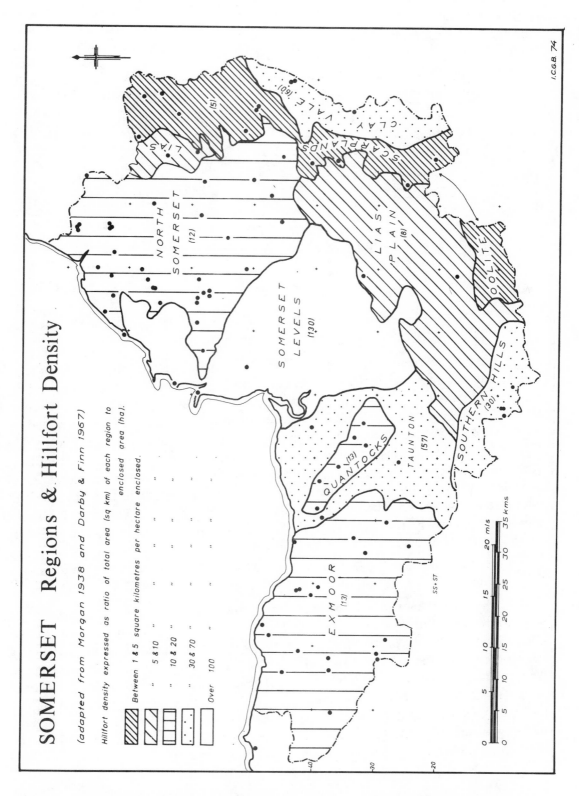

Fig. 6 Somerset; Economic regions related to hillfort density, expressed
in terms of the total areas enclosed

hillforts can be obtained. This can then be directly compared with types of data extracted from the Domesday survey.

It can be immediately seen that the Oolitic areas have the greatest density of hillforts, followed by this Lias area which essentially forms the 'territory' of Ham Hill. These two areas, as we have seen, are distinguished by the presence of a few very large and strongly defended hillforts. Out of the seven regions into which the county has been divided by Morgan,[24] the Olitic region consistently shows the highest figures of all the economic indicators evaluated. The Lias area lies third in population density, but second in most other analyses.

This comparison of Domesday data with hillfort density may be summarised as follows:-

	Hillfort Density	Population 1086	Value 1086
Oolites	1	1	1
Lias	2	3	2
North Somerset	3	5	5
Western Hills	4	7	7
Taunton	5	2	3
Clay Vale	6	4	4
Somerset Levels	7	6	6

The correspondences in the upper and lower parts of the list are thus close, but the lack of similarity between the Domesday data and hillfort density in the cases of north and west Somerset and Taunton Vale are noteworthy. It must be recognised that the two bodies of material are only to a limited extent comparable. In particular the order of difference between categories is very much larger in the hillfort data. Hillforts are in effect twenty-six times as dense in the Oolite region than in the Somerset Levels, whereas the Domesday population on the Oolites is less than twice that in the Levels, and value per 1000 acres (405 hectares) only just over twice. The striking fact remains, however, that the large multivallate hillforts of Group I are concentrated in the Lias and Oolite areas that later emerge as the most prosperous in the county, and which apparently, on the evidence of villas and other settlements supported a dense Romano-British population as well.

It seems reasonable to deduce from this that the largest and most highly organised Iron Age communities were to be found in the south and east of the county, and that this population was a reflection of an agricultural prosperity which continued throughout the main period with which we are concerned. The re-use and recommissioning of a hillfort would not be an enterprise easily undertaken, and we may suggest therefore that such re-use would be most likely to occur in well-populated and prosperous areas where the necessary manpower and organisation would be available. This point will be returned to in more detail in chapter 7.

Chronology within the Iron Age

So far in this chapter hillforts and enclosures have been treated as far as possible without reference to their absolute dating. The date of most sites is unknown, although most are placed within the pre-Roman Iron Age on typological grounds. In addition, it was felt desirable to consider hillforts merely in terms of their form, size and choice of location in an attempt to analyse these more basic factors, since these form the essential background to hillfort use or re-use in the period with which we are chiefly concerned.

The body of evidence built up, locally and nationally, over the last fifty years confirms that the majority of sites are of Iron Age origin. As will be discussed in chapter 5, however, excavation techniques and policies have in the past been geared towards the recovery of Iron Age evidence to the detriment of later phases of activity on hillfort sites. The evidence for the development of hillforts in the Iron Age remains inadequate, but will now be reviewed since it provides the background for later developments, and may give insights into the factors affecting the use of these enclosures.

Figure 7 shows the current extent of major archaeological research on all the Somerset enclosures, which has supplied the larger part of the data on which chronological schemes can be cased, although casual finds and topographical evidence also play some part in this. Twenty-six sites, of 29% of the total of all groups have been excavated to a greater or lesser extent, and recent detailed descriptions of the earthworks are available for a number of others. Excavation has been heavily biased towards the larger sites however:

Group I	15 sites sampled	(45%)
Group II	1 site sampled	(11%)
Group III	4 sites sampled	(22%)
Group IV	6 sites sampled	(21%)

The available data is therefore not only limited but uneven in its distribution. With this in mind certain aspects of the Iron Age development of Somerset hillforts will be considered, treating each group in turn.

Group I

The Iron Age development of the large, frequently multivallate hillforts of southern England has become much more clearly understood in recent years. The excavations at Maiden Castle[25] first positively demonstrated the chronological and structural complexity of the larger hillforts, and the major operations at South Cadbury and Danebury[26] have supported and enlarged on this picture. Many Group I sites may have their origin as late Bronze Age settlements, although few can as yet be shown to have possessed defences at this time.[27] Such enclosures frequently consist, in their initial phase, of a single timber-framed or dry stone wall defence fronted by a single ditch. The elaboration of this scheme into the typical close-set multivallate schemes of southern England was interpreted by Wheeler as a reaction to sling warfare, but must be seen at least partly as a natural result of the necessity for periodically clearing the silt from the ditches.[28] This second explanation of multivallation implies that hillforts with this charateristic will prove to have a long structural history, and the 19 Somerset sites of Group I which possess two or more ramparts should probably be seen in this light.

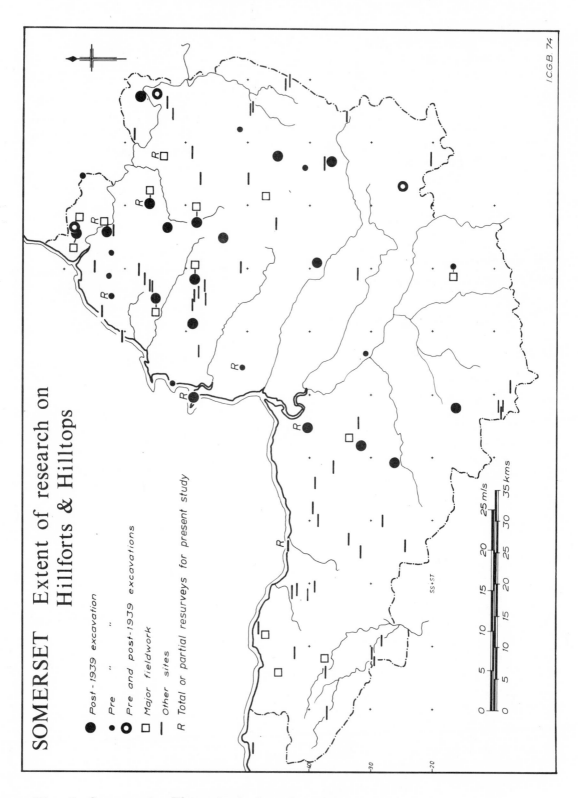

Fig. 7 Somerset; The extent of archaeological research on hillforts and
hill-top sites (to 1977)

Multivallation is frequently accompanied by the elaboration of defensive works around the entrances and by the adoption of 'glacis' style ramparts of dump construction. In general, it would appear a valid generalisation that large hillforts with these characteristics were in occupation in the last few centuries of the Iron Age. Using these criteria and the available absolute dating evidence, Cunliffe has proposed a model for hillfort development on the Wessex chalkland.[29] He suggests that there is a tendency towards the occupation of fewer, larger hillforts towards the end of the Iron Age, indicating the consolidation of political power and growth of social cohesion at this time. He has not hesitated to describe such sites as urban settlements.[30] Whether such a model is applicable over the whole of Somerset is debatable, but the Oolite scarpland and the adjacent Lias with their few large multivallate hillforts, two of them, Ham Hill and South Cadbury, with demonstrated long structural histories and both occupied up to the Roman Conquest, seem to fit the model well.

The other parts of the county, we as have seen, show a more complex pattern of hillfort distribution. This complexity is compounded by the relative scarcity of datable material. Fifteen Group I sites have produced no datable material of any kind.[31] The majority of excavated Group I sites have, however, produced evidence consistent with Iron Age construction and use.

Refinement within this period remains difficult, dependent as it is upon sealed finds of datable material. The Iron Age chronology of the area is a fragile construction based largely on pottery or metalwork typology.

Apart from various groups of more distinctive finer wares, the bulk of the Iron Age pottery recovered from Somerset sites, especially in North Somerset, consists of various soft, poorly-fired black and brown wares of undistinctive form. This material is so lacking in distinctive features that it may have remained in use for a considerable period. It appears to have continued to do so, at least in North Somerset, until the end of the Iron Age, being therefore contemporary with the finer wares of Glastonbury, Belgic and Durotrigian types.[32] The virtual absence of the finer types from some sites evidently occupied at a time when they were current elsewhere raises a number of social, political, and economic issues.[33]

The ceramic and other dating evidence from the sites of Group I does, however, show a late Iron Age emphasis of occupation within the defences. The dating of a defences themselves is, however, less certain. Termini post or ante quem falling within the Iron Age have been obtained for the defences of five sites.[34] At Solsbury the rampart was found to have collapsed onto an occupation level containing Glastonbury-type pottery, with a further level developed above the collapse.[35] It is difficult now to assess whether the apparently simple one-phase dump or dry-stone constructions reported by earlier excavators are merely a reflection of inadequate excavation techniques or whether the great structural complexity at South Cadbury and Ham Hill are indeed exceptional. The possible failure to identify replacement or alteration of ramparts during excavation is of great significance in the present context and will be discussed further in chapter 5.

It seems probable, however, that many sites of Group I were in use at the time of the Roman conquest. Direct evidence for this in the form of Roman finds or structures has been obtained at Ham Hill, South Cadbury, Norton Fitzwarren, Cadbury Tickenham, Bury Hill, Brent Knoll and Blaise Castle. To this list it might be permissible to add a number of sites with late Iron Age evidence, such as Worlebury, Dolebury and Cannington. Even this somewhat inadequate evidence is sufficient to indicate that almost one-third of the Group I sites were in use in the immediately pre-Roman decades and it must be suspected that many more would prove to be so if excavated.

Group II

Sites in this group pose a more difficult problem, since only one site, Burrington (54) has been excavated. A rampart section and 15 sondages in the interior failed to produce any datable artifacts and only one object, a possible pot lid of red sandstone, was recovered.[36] Clifton Camp, which, as has been noted above, possesses rather more massive defences than most sites in this group, has produced Roman material but no prehistoric finds. No other datable material is known from this group of sites and it may be doubted if they are all of Iron Age date.

Group III

The promontory forts of Group III similarly lack many positive indications as to their chronology within the Iron Age or otherwise. If the evidence from Stokeleigh may be taken as representative of the larger, more strongly defended sites of this group, the defences were probably constructed during the currency of Glastonbury pottery, but apparently before the arrival of 'Belgic' material in the final part of the Iron Age. Occupation here probably continued into the Roman period.[37] The other large, strongly defended promontory forts, Tedbury, Wodbury, Littledown and Milbourne Wick on the Oolite, and Ruborough, Clatworthy and perhaps Countisbury may have their origin at this time. At the smaller end of the range, the defences of Brean Down have a terminus post quem of 310 ± 510 B.C. and a terminus ante quem of 100 ± 100 B.C., again pointing to an origin for the defences in the Iron Age though probably some time before its end. Here also, occupation probably continued into the Roman period although by that time the defences were in decay and may even have been deliberately slighted.[38] At the rather similar enclosure at Kings Weston a similar sequence is implied by the available data.[39]

Group IV

An Iron Age date can be demonstrated for five sites of the 29 sites of this group, and a sixth produced no dating evidence on excavation.[40] With the exception of the 'banjo' enclosure on Walton Down, which is of a type distinctive enough to be classed as an Iron Age site on form alone, although even here a later data cannot be ruled out,[41] most sites are undated. Only at Berry Castle are finds recorded, 'swords and other instruments of war' being reputedly found within it.[42] This site is one of a number already noted which, by their position and possession of networks, appear to be linked to the multiple enclosure sites of Dumnonia, but reliable dates are lacking for the majority.

For the majority of the Group IV enclosures no direct dating evidence is therefore available and, by analogy with similar sites in other parts of Britain, a date-range from the earlier part of the first millennium B.C. into the later Middle Ages might be encountered. In default of a large-scale excavation programme on these sites our understanding of them can only be refined by detailed analysis of their form and location. As was discussed above, the two major geographical groups, that of West Somerset and the North Somerset limestone, possess within their regions shared characteristics of siting in particular, which suggest a common economic function. Although it cannot be certain that this similarity also implies contemporaneity it may be valuable to consider those sites which do not fall into these groups as of potentially different date to them. The larger size of three sites has already been noted, and additionally three sites which stand out on account of their location should be considered.

The better preserved of two sites at Wortheal Farm (71) is a well-constructed oval stone-walled enclosure about 60 metres across on a hillslope in broken, poorly drained country near Chard. It is located on Greensand which here supports a water retentive soil, in contrast to the location of the majority of Group IV sites. In addition, clear signs of a 'Celtic' field system are present in the field immediately to the west of the site. Of the sites to the west and north, only Wraxall is in such close proximity to field systems of this type. It seems, therefore, that at Wortheal we may be seeing an arable site in contrast to the more pastoral emphasis suggested for most of the Group IV sites.

The same comments may be applied to the siting of the now destroyed Curdon Camp, on Trias Marl to the west of the Quantocks, and Hales Castle on the Oxford Clay. Hales Castle has been regarded as a Medieval site,[43] and this could also be true of the other two. Certainly their choice of siting sets them apart from the majority of sites of Group IV, although the form of their enclosing earthworks does not.

To sum up the evidence for Iron Age chronology on the Group IV sites it is clear that some at least have their origin in this period and continue into the Roman period. A small number of sites seem to possess features which set them apart functionally and perhaps chronologically from the majority. Even so we must acknowledge that information on all these sites is scanty and among them may be numbered sites of the first millennium A.D., either continuing in use from the late Iron Age or newly constructed and used.

Finally, the possible chronological relationships between groups of sites in close proximity must be considered. There are two situations. The more common is that in which enclosures face each other across steep ravines or rivers; there are five instances of this.[44] In two cases a smaller enclosure is located on falling ground below a larger site of Group I. Forde-Johnston[45] has argued that in the latter circumstances the two sites are interdependent and contemporary, although this view has been much criticised,[46] and the topography of one pair of sites, that of Black Ball Camp and Bats Castle, whereby one is virtually invisible from the other, renders any military co-operation between the two of the type envisaged by Forde-Johnston extremely unlikely. It must be thought probable that in both Somerset cases the two sites are of different dates although direct evidence is lacking.[47]

The remarkable clustering of relatively large and strongly defended sites on the Bristol Avon and on Mells Stream may represent a different situation. Here the forts are separated by major natural obstacles which may have been used as political boundaries. O'Rian has pointed out that a number of major sites in pre-Roman Gaul and in Ireland were located on or close to political boundaries and were thus used as places where contact could take place between different groups on relatively neutral ground.[48] Such an explanation seems appropriate to the examples mentioned above, but other reasons, such as one of a pair of sites being abandoned and replaced by another for religious or political reasons, may be as important here.

To what extent were hillforts of importance at the time of the Roman conquest of the area? Later developments may perhaps have been strongly influenced by the events of this time. A hillfort which had already stood deserted for some generations before Roman control was established might have much less significance in the eyes of the indigenous population than one from which the population had, for instance, been forcibly removed by the Roman army but remained in the vicinity. The assumption here is that in the relatively stable conditions of the Roman period traditions relating to hillfort sites may have survived to influence their later usage, and for this reason it is important to attempt some assessment of hillfort occupation in the first decades of the first century A.D.

Positive evidence of the use of Group I sites at this time is available at Ham Hill, South Cadbury and Bury Hill where there are signs of Roman military activity. Evidence of a massacre possibly of this period at Worlebury, and early Roman material from Cadbury Tickenham, Blaise Castle and Cannington (in the latter case from the settlement outside the fort) may also indicate occupation in c. 50 A.D. Positive evidence of desertion prior to the Roman conquest has not been so forthcoming. Five sites of Group I were clearly in use during the currency of late Iron Age pottery.[49] The four sites which have produced only undiagnostic coarse wares,[50] may also prove to be occupied at this time but data is lacking except at Cadcong where the presence of a La Tène III brooch at the top if Iron Age levels suggests a late date. The large univallate sites of Maes Knoll and Bathampton both appear on present evidence to date from early in the Iron Age and have not produced any later material, but this evidence again is from small scale investigations.[51] Although recent work has tended to call in question Cunliffe's hypothesis that the trend in the later Iron Age was towards fewer and larger hillforts,[52] it seems probable that many of the large Somerset hillforts of Group I sites were occupied immediately prior to the Roman Conquest. The difficulties of establishing a chronology for the other groups has already been discussed.

To sum up, therefore, the data available from Somerset hillforts points to regional and functional variations among them which may be largely social and economic rather than military. The degree of correspondence between the intensity of hillfort construction and later evidence indicates that the distribution of population implied by Domesday evidence had been established over 1000 years previously and that some areas of the county supported much higher populations than others. Where information is available an Iron Age origin for most sites is indicated, but sites of Group II in particular have unique features and may not be of Iron Age date. Many sites of the other groups, perhaps a third of the total, were probably in use at the time of the Roman Conquest, including all those from which post-Roman evidence has been recovered.

Hill-top settlements

What are the implications of the presence or absence of enclosing earthworks for the interpretation of a hill-top settlement? The answer to this question may be of great significance for our understanding, not only of the nature of late and post-Roman settlement use, but of Iron Age developments as well. Evidence is now accumulating from a number of hillforts in Britain that the construction of Iron Age defences was preceded by an undefended phase when the settlements were of an open character.

What is as yet lacking is evidence to confirm or refute the suggestion that the construction of defences denotes a change in the character of the settlement within them. Permanent or frequent use of a hill-top site may be a response to a number of factors, but two, religious and defensive motives, may be regarded as of central importance. Iron Age evidence for the pre-defensive use of a hillfort site for 'ritual' purposes is at present confined to Danebury,[53] but the discovery of undoubted Iron Age temple sites both within hillforts and beneath later Roman hill-top temples[54] demonstrates that the 'ritual' use of hilltops was well developed in the Iron Age and continued into the Roman and, it will be argued, the post-Roman period. Clearly, on present evidence, the use of a hilltop for religious purposes will not necessarily result in the construction of enclosing earthworks and it must be anticipated that many Iron Age and Roman religious sites were located on hilltops which have no surface indications of such activity.

The presence of temples within hillforts emphases that we should not expect 'religious' and 'secular' functions necessarily to be separated, but we must consider whether the choice of a hill-top location from motives predominantly of security necessarily resulted in the construction or artificial; works. In an Iron Age context research has stressed the increasing emphasis and elaboration of defensive systems with the passage of time, and evidence is lacking for hill-top settlements of any size without defences of some kind by the later Iron Age.

The possibility must therefore be considered that settlement and other permanent or semi-permanent occupation did take place on undefended hilltops in the Iron Age although by the nature of the evidence their discovery will be largely a matter of chance. How far are the Roman and post-Roman situations likely to be analogous? The ritual use of hill-tops clearly remains important throughout the Roman period and a number of permanent settlements in Roman Somerset are also located on hilltops. In the subsequent centuries the direct archaeological evidence already demonstrates that both defended and undefended hilltops were in use, but on the general analogy with the Iron Age presence or absence of earthworks should not by itself be allowed to coloured our interpretation of the activity on the site.

Topographically, Somerset contains a large number of potential hill-top settlement sites. The broken country on the east side of the Brendons, and the numerous Lias erosional remnants to the south of the Levels and flanking the south-west side of the Mendips all provide possible locations. Surface indications have, however, only been detected at one site, Nyland Hill, a prominent hill rising 225 feet above the Levels at ST 458505. Just below the summit, and chiefly on the north side are about twenty platforms in the hillside. These are sub-rectangular and average 7 metres along the slope and 5 metres wide with slightly sloping bases. The regularity of these features and their shallowness calls in question their interpretation by the Ordnance Survey as quarry hollows. There remains the possibility that they are house platforms of unknown date.[55]

At Pagans Hill a multi-period use of the site has been demonstrated, with early Iron Age features preceding the construction of a Roman temple complex in the late third century one element of which at least, the well, was still open in the seventh century and later.[56] Another possible hill-top site is the prominent hillock of Burrow Camp (ST 359305). Excavations here produced samian ware, fourth century material and a Roman flue tile. None of these was stratified or associated with structures and they were regarded by the excavator as 'fortuitous'.[57]

Crucial to the understanding of hill-top sites without enclosing earth-works is, however, Glastonbury Tor.[58] The specific historical motives for the excavation of this site have been outlined by the excavator, and there were no surface indications, prior to excavation, of the complex of post-Roman and late Saxon features present on the hilltop. Disturbance of the stratification rendered the interpretation of the small amount of Roman material difficult, and there may have been a Roman phase of occupation of which all structural evidence has been destroyed. The absence of Iron Age pottery, in an area where it is relatively prolific, may be more significant. At Glastonbury the difficulties of interpretation of excavated data and of the identification of hill-top settlements without enclosing earthworks are both highlighted. The first is that the stratigraphic problems encountered on exposed summits prevent the elucidation of satisfactory sequences. The second is that there was no archaeological evidence, prior to excavation, upon which to base a hypothesis that the site might have been in use in the Roman or post-Roman period.

In this chapter the archaeological material which is our chief concern, has been defined and a number of points relating to the form, distribution and function of hillfort and hill-top settlements have been discussed. The following chapter considers data which is more specifically related to the historical circumstances of post-Iron Age hillfort use by an examination firstly of place-name evidence relating to the sites and their surroundings, and secondly in a discussion of the evidence relating to the establishment of Christianity in the area as evinced by church dedications.

NOTES

1. Hogg, 1972b, 293 n.1.

2. Forde-Johnston, 1976, passim.

3. Ordnance Survey, 1962.

4. Cunliffe, 1974, 153.

5. Forde-Johnston, 1964 stresses the military aspect of hillforts. For the development of thinking on hillforts see Avery, 1976, especially 28-34.

6. Hogg, 1960, 23-4. Alcock, 1965b.

7. Cunliffe, 1974, 254-63.

8. Haggett, 1965.

9. Cunliffe, 1971a, 60. Hogg, 1971, 118-122.

10. Clarke, 1972b.

11. McDonnell 1980.

12. Fox, 1952a, 1961. Forde-Johnston 1976, 249 & 258-261.

13. Cunliffe, 1974 and Forde-Johnston, 1976.

14. The numbers cited refer to the hillfort gazetteer (Appendix A) in which the sites are ordered by size, No. 1 being the largest.

15. Haggett, 1965, 247-8.

16. Clarke, 1972b.

17. Whybrow, 1967.

18. Alcock, 1972b, 104-5.

19. West of the Parrett: sites 52, 55 (outworks), 59 (outwork), 69, 70, 75 (outworks), 77 (outworks), 78 (outworks), 82, 86, 88, 89.
    East of the Parrett: 32 (outworks), 63, 73, 81.

20. Guilbert, 1975b, with refs.

21. Fowler, 1970.

22. Proudfoot, 1961.

23. Site 17, 1968.

24. Morgan, 1938, 142.

25. Wheeler, 1943.

26. Cunliffe, 1971b.

27.   e.g. Ivinghoe Beacon, Bucks - Records of Bucks vol. 18 (1968), 187-260.

28.   Wheeler, 1943, 48-51, Frode-Johnston, 1976.

29.   Cunliffe, 1971a, 59-61.

30.   Cunliffe, 1974, 166.

31.   Sites 14, 15, 23, 24, 28, 30, 44, 47, 48, 50, 51, 56, 61.

32.   Hand-made pottery: ApSimon in Rahtz and Greenfield, 1977, 7-14, 193-201, Burrow, 1976a, 151. Glastonbury Ware: Cunliffe, 1974, 43, 102, 104, 276. Durotrigian Ware: Alcock, 1972a, 164-5.

33.   Burrow, 1976a, 147-8.

34.   Nos. 3, 9, 18, 29, 31.

35.   Dowden, 1957.

36.   Tratman, 1963b.

37.   Haldane, 1975.

38.   Burrow, 1976.

39.   Rahtz, 1957.

40.   17, 65, 74, 79, 82. No. 81 produced no dating evidence.

41.   No. 58, see Perry, 1966.

42.   Savage, 1830, 92.

43.   King and Alcock 1966, 121.

44.   Sites 37, 46 and 62; 22, 26, 42; 4, 25; 47, 68; 6, 85.

45.   Forde-Johnston, 1964, esp. 86-7, 89-90.

46.   Alcock, 1965a, Hogg, 1973.

47.   Sites 50, 69; 56, 63.

48.   O Rian, 1972.

49.   Dolebury, Solsbury, Cannington, Brent Knoll, Blaise Castle.

50.   Banwell, Cadcong, Stantonbury, Smalldown.

51.   Bathampton, 1967. Maes Knoll 1963.

52.   Cunliffe, 1971a, 59-67. Cunliffe, 1974, 305. Much recent work, emphasising the chronological complexity of hillforts remains unpublished (Hillfort Study Group).

53.   Cunliffe, 1971b, 241-45.

54.   Lewis, 1966, passim.

55.   Arch. Rev. 7 (1972), 24.

56.   Rahtz et al., 1958. Rahtz and Harris, 1957. Rahtz, 1951.

57.   Gray, 1940.

58.   Rahtz, 1971.

CHAPTER 3

PLACE-NAME EVIDENCE AND CELTIC CHURCH DEDICATIONS

The discipline of place-name study is, as Wainwright stressed,[1] one independent of, though linked to, history and archaeology. This chapter attempts a synthesis of place-name research in Somerset in so far as it may throw light on two main aspects of relevance: the names applied to Somerset hillforts, with especial concentration on the place-name element -bury, and the general problem of Celtic Survival and the bearing of such names on the location of pre-English settlement sites in the area. Finally, Celtic church dedications are discussed.

This selectivity is imposed both by the scope of the study as a whole, but more fundamentally by the absence of any comprehensive work on the place names of the county. Hill's work, published in 1914,[2] is now of little use, but Turner's[3] papers and thesis on North Somerset place names contain much useful information when considered in conjunction with the standard work of Ekwall.[4]

Turner's material is now twenty-five years old, and Ekwall's is similarly becoming outdated in many respects. Place-name identifications based on these works are therefore subject to revision in the light of more recent research. The study of place names has developed very rapidly, and major hypotheses are reassessed as frequently as those in archaeology. The material under consideration here fortunately avoids one of the most contentious areas, that of the chronology of the earliest English place-name elements, but Celtic linguistic problems are almost equally severe.[5] These have been treated at length by Jackson,[6] but more work remains to be done on the western counties of England before Turner's work on Somerset can be seen in perspective.

In a study of aspects of settlement development, place-name evidence must be used with caution. Recorded place names, even from such a relatively comprehensive contemporary survey as Domesday, do not represent the total number of settlements, nor is it safe to project the existence of a recorded settlement backwards or forwards from the date at which it is mentioned, because of the demonstrable fluidity of settlements already commented on in chapter 1.[7] Such problems become especially acute when the spatial distribution of place-name types is considered.

Wainwright pointed out that, strictly speaking, place names provide 'direct evidence only of language and speech habits',[8] and that further inferences made from place-name evidence rely on a variety of assumptions about the material. He went on to argue, however, that because of their largely 'unconscious' formation, place names provide a source for a different range of historical information than archaeological and documentary material.

Because place names are created in this way 'the assumptions behind non-linguistic inferences from place names are less prominent and less strained than the assumptions behind non-archaeological inferences from archaeological material'.

It is to be anticipated that place names will provide some indication of the form and siting of settlements and landscape features. If pursued in depth, analysis of topographical elements in Somerset place names would clearly assist the study of landscape history, but for present purposes we shall concentrate on the implications of one element; the suffix -bury and related forms, as applied to hillfort and other names.

In the virtually total absence of direct archaeological evidence, place names provide some indication of the general distribution of population. Despite the chronological difficulties involved, place names containing, or wholly composed from, Celtic elements are considered as possible pointers to the location of pre-English settlement. These places may have formed one element in a settlement pattern which included hillfort and hill-top sites which, in contrast to other settlements, did not retain their Celtic names, except possibly in a few instances.

Hillfort names and place names implying fortification (Fig. 8)

Of the 89 hillfort and enclosure sites under consideration, 21, or nearly 25% have, or had, names apparently incorporating the element -bury or similar forms. There are in addition at least 28 other places in the area containing this element named on Ordnance Survey maps. The significance of -bury will first be considered, and other elements and hillfort names then discussed.

In the absence of detailed documentary work on these names, the presumption is that the suffix -bury and similar words such as berry, are predominantly derived from the O.E. burh or burg, having the general meaning of a fortified place. A note of caution is necessary, however, as the large and impressive Class III hillfort of Ruborough (19) is recorded in 854 as Rugan beorh and in 904 as Ruwanbeorge, the second elemnnt in both cases being beorg 'hill'.[9] It is therefore possible that other hillfort names at present ending in -bury are also derived from beorh, which can also mean 'burial mound', and which it clearly does in a number of instances. An additional element is bearu 'grove, wood', which appears in Elenberwe, Elborough,[10] and from which may also derive modern names such as Rowberrow.

There are a small number of hillforts, referred to in pre-Conquest sources, at which we can be certain that the final element is burh. Of these the best known is South Cadbury, clearly known as Cadanbyrig in the early eleventh century.[11] The others are Tedbury (4)—Todanbrigge or Todanberghe,[12] Stantonbury (20—Merces burh or Byrig aet Stantune[13] and Maesbury (24)—Merkesburi.[14] Additionally there is a fourteenth-century reference to Kings Castle (15) as Castrum de Hethenberi.[15] This last is also a reminder that place names are subject to change and substitution.

For the remainder of the hillforts now ending in the element -bury it can be suggested that this does derive from burh in the majority of cases. It may be reasonable to infer that the other two Cadburys contain the same elements as South Cadbury. It would be surprising if Wadbury (25), on the

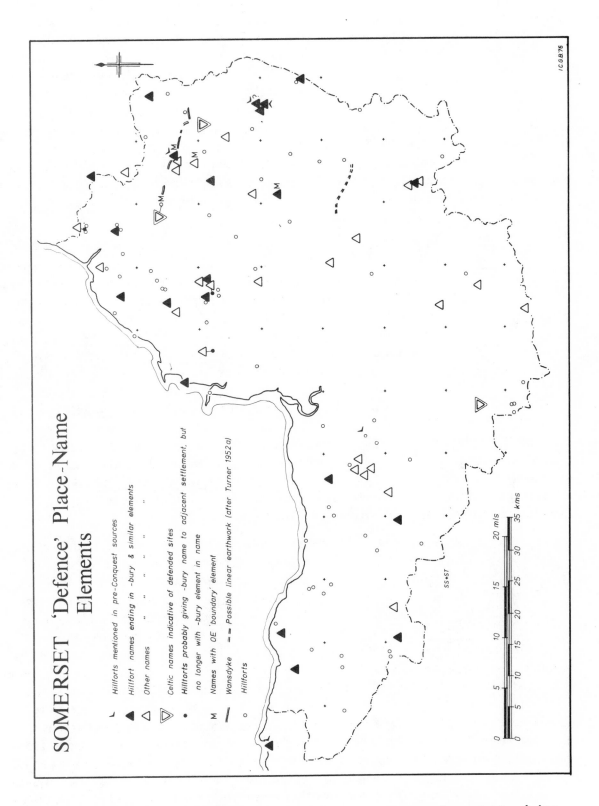

Fig. 8 Somerset; Distribution of selected place-name elements implying
the existence of fortifications

opposite side of a ravine from Tedbury and, like the latter, not on a prominent hilltop, was not also thought of as a burh. This topographical argument may be used with reference to Bury Castle (75), Bury Hill (76) (not on an outstanding summit), Berry Camp (77), Burwalls (26) and Oldberry (48). At Burrington (54) the modern name of the camp is borrowed from the village, the meaning of which, 'tun by the burg', [16] is almost certainly a reference to the hillfort. There may be other instances of this type of transfer of names; for in tance at Blaise Castle (46), the original name of the site may have been Henbury, but this is now borne by the adjacent settlement. This leaves seven sites where such topographical arguments are not valid, as they are situated on large commanding hills, and one (28) contains a barrow, increasing the uncertainty of identification. The sites are Countisbury (2), Dolebury (6), Solsbury (7), Worlebury (16), Highbury (21) Dowsborough (28) and Roddenbury (56). As has been seen, the large defences possessed by these sites does not automatically allow the assumption to be made that the places were called burh.

What characteristics did a place therefore have to possess to be referred to as burh in the Anglo-Saxon period? The complexity of this problem renders impossible its adequate discussion here, but must be considered in some detail. We may start with a brief examination of the use of this suffix at places other than hillforts, although the lack of adequate place-name research is a major hindrance, especially in the matter of confusion between burh, beorg and bearu. Among the earliest recorded names containing burh are two ecclesiastical centres, Glastonbury and Congresbury.[17] Use of burh in this context is not uncommon, the best known example being Peterborough.[18] If we follow Phillips; 'Anglo-Saxon place names containing the element burh will normally indicate features which appeared at the time to have been strongholds of various kinds.'[19] In the specifically religious context of these sites a military fortification seems out of place, and reference is probably being made to an enclosing feature, perhaps identifiable with the vallum monasterii. Such a feature has perhaps been located at Glastonbury,[20] but nothing similar has been identified in the present village of Congresbury.

Two points, however, arise from this. The island location of Glastonbury and the marshy surroundings of Congresbury raise the alternative possibility that strong natural defences could lead to the description of a place as a burh, and that artificial works were not a prerequisite. This may account for the apparent use of the term at Winsbury, Wineces burug[21] and at Montacute, Lodegaresburgh,[22] although in the latter case a separate reference to Logderesdone[23] (last element dun, 'hill') may indicate that in the first case beorg or bearu was intended rather than burh. Both of these places are steep-sided prominent hills. Montacute has had any earlier earthworks on it obscured by its adaptation into a Norman motte, but Winsbury has no visible defensive works and here the difficulty is compounded by the presence of a small barrow on the summit. From the survey of the general evidence from hillforts (chapter 2) it appears unlikely that major earthwork defences can be destroyed without trace, and it therefore must be accepted, if the place-name evidence is reliable, that Winsbury was regarded as a burh either because of its natural strength or because of slight, perhaps wooden, defences which it possessed but which have since vanished. It is in either case clear that there is no simple equation of burh with massive defences.

Secondly, the application of <u>burh</u> to known monastic sites raises the question whether other <u>burh</u> names may be accounted for in this way, among them perhaps hillfort sites. None of the other early known monasteries in Somerset appear to have ever included the element in their names, but there may have been small pre-English foundations, for which no documentation survives, at some <u>bury</u> places, and this is clearly important in relation to the archaeological evidence from both South Cadbury and Cadbury Congresbury.

Superficial examination of the siting of the remaining <u>burh</u> names in the study area confirms the impression that neither a naturally strong position or large artificial defensive works are the sole criteria for the use of the term. Portbury,[24] with a small hillfort (61) above it, and possibly another instance of the transfer of names from a hillfort to the settlement at its foot, is situated at the base of a scarp and at the edge of coastal marshes. If the name here originally did apply to the fort then the first element, perhaps implying trading, is of considerable interest. Neither Westbury-on-Trym nor Westury-sub-Mendip are in advantageous positions defensively, and although place name Old Ditch[25] at the latter may indicate former defence works, this is far from the present centre of the settlement, apparently unrelated to it.

From this brief survey it is therefore apparent that in pre-eleventh century Somerset <u>burh</u> could be used to describe monastic sites, places without prominent natural defences, but also perhaps places having such features, and hillforts. It is probable that artificial defences or enclosing features which have now disappeared existed on several sites termed <u>burh</u>, but clearly the earthworks of some hillforts were immediately recognised as also deserving this appellation. The nature of the documentation for the other <u>burh</u> place names makes it probable or certain that these were functioning settlements and not abandoned sites, and it is therefore worth enquiring whether the calling of a hillfort <u>burh</u> might not imply that it too was an occupied stronghold at the time the name was coined, or simply perhaps that any place <u>suitable</u> to be a <u>burh</u> might be so termed.

Direct evidence for the first of these is lacking, and the weight of opinion is against such a view, e.g.

> 'The Anglo-Saxons could not ignore the many ancient hillforts...
> which were apparent everywhere. In any case they were convenient
> landmarks and were used as such, but most of these gave rise only
> to minor names and had themselves become no more than a recorded
> point on a land boundary by the time the middle ages were well
> begun.'[26]

The hillfort names recorded in pre-Conquest sources, with the exception of South Cadbury, are merely points on charter boundaries. The position of the sites at the periphery of land units of the later first millennium may reflect a major change of land organisation from the Iron Age, when hillforts may have possessed their own discrete territories. For our present purposes it seems probable that the application of <u>bury</u> to a hillfort cannot of itself assist in the identification of sites in use in the period under consideration.

The first element in <u>bury</u> hillfort names may, however, be of some relevance in this context, and these will now be discussed. The name Cadbury, held by at least five hillforts and earthworks in Southern England, [27] probably links a personal name <u>Cada</u> with <u>burh</u> in the manner frequently met with in English place names as a whole. The alternative suggested by Hill, [28] that the British *<u>Catu</u>, meaning battle or fortification, is involved also deserves attention, although the first recorded spelling indicates that at least by the eleventh century, the first element was regarded as a personal name. [29]

The name <u>Cada</u> itself, however, may incorporate a British element, perhaps deriving from *<u>Catu</u>, in the same way as do the names of two early Wessex kings recorded in the <u>Anglo-Saxon Chronicle</u>, Cerdic and Caedwalla. [30] As it is generally accepted that some British and English intermarriage at a high social level is indicated by such names, it is of considerable interest to find three Somerset hillforts described as 'cada's <u>burh</u>' when two have produced archaeological evidence for use in the centuries preceding English domination of Somerset. There is clearly little hope of ascertaining whether 'Cada' was a real individual or individuals, and whether the application of the name to widely-scattered hillforts reflects ownership of their sites by such as individual or individuals at some time prior to their first documentation. An alternative view would be that 'Cada' was a heroic figure in some way associated with hillfort earthworks and perhaps with other locations also, [31] and whose name therefore became attached to a number of sites. A parallel to this may be seen in the attachment of the name of Caratacus to several Welsh and Border hillforts, as in 'Caer Caradoc'.

The possibility may also remain that the original name of the Cadbury forts did in fact incorporate the element *<u>Catu</u>, and that this was later distorted into a personal name. That distortion of this type did take place is demonstrated by the derivation of the name Rochester, discussed by Alcock. [32] Such a situation would imply a bilingual stage in which appropriate British and English elements could be combined together. As will be discussed below, there is evidence to indicate such a bilingual phase in Somerset in the seventh and eighth centuries. In this instance the meaning intended may be something like 'battle-fort', although if *<u>Catu</u> also implies a fortification we may be seeing an instance of a tautological compound in which the second, English, element has essentially the same meaning as the first, British, one and had been added because the first was not understood. [33] Whichever of the possibilities is the correct one, it remains true that Cadbury is a name of great interest, either because it is the only one containing a Celtic element which is certainly known to have been applied to a Somerset hillfort, or because it incorporates an English personal name derived from a Celtic one.

Why so many forts should receive this name is unclear. South Cadbury is an impressive and outstanding site, but neither Cadbury Tickenham nor Cadbury Congresbury are especially large, and the latter has weak, unimpressive defences, as also does Cadbury Tiverton in Devon. In this case neither the sites association with a hillfort-building hero, nor their naming as 'battle-forts' seems entirely justified if the names were merely attached as convenient descriptions to deserted sites. This is admittedly a subjective assessment, but taken with the archaeological evidence from the Cadbury hillforts, which clearly demonstrates use of five of them in Roman or post-Roman times, it does suggest that Cadbury is an important name. The date at which Cadbury Tickenham and Cadbury Congresbury obtained their names in unknown, but there is no evidence to suggest that the latter was ever called Congresbury, as implied by Alcock, [34] and it seems more probable that, like South Cadbury, they had acquired their names by the tenth century if not earlier.

The attachment of personal name elements to hillforts and other locations is demonstrated by the earliest recorded form of Tedbury, Todanberghe, incorporating a personal name, Toda. Such names can clearly refer to real owners of places, as shown by the case of Tickenham, probably named after Abbot Tica or Ticca, Abbot of Glastonbury in the eighth century. [35] In a post-Conquest context the small hillfort of Mounsey Castle (47) may take its name from possession by the Monceaux family. [36] Other instances of the use of personal names may be seen at Wadbury, [37] Lodgaresburgh, and possibly at Elworthy. [38] Solsbury, first recorded by Camden, may contain the word Sul, a reference to Sulis Minerva, Goddess of nearby Bath. [29] As with the majority of hillfort names, however, the earliest record is so late that it is impossible to be certain if this is a genuine early name. In this specific instance an antiquarian influence on the name may be suspected.

Of the remaining -bury hillfort names, three appear to have a descriptive and topographical element which, if one could be certain of the antiquity of the names, indicate abandonment and reversion to waste land. Of this group are Worlebury, [40] Dowsborough, [41] and Roddenbury. [42]

Two hillforts, both recorded in pre-Conquest charters, incorporate the Old English Mearc 'boundary'. Maesbury, traversed by the parish boundary between Croscombe and Dinder, is recorded as Merkesburi in 705, [14] and Stantonbury, a boundary point between Corston and Stanton Prior was Merces burh in 941, though simply Byrig in 963. [13] Maesbury may be an example of the use of a hillfort simply as a landmark in boundary definition, and otherwise an irrelevance in the landscape at the time of the compilation of the charter, and it may be noted at this point that both Croscombe and Dinder are names incorporating Celtic elements, [43] and therefore perhaps land units of early origin.

The position of Stantonbury is, however, less clear. Although in the Stanton charter it is used as a boundary mark, which may be sufficient to account for its name, its position on the Wansdyke, the earthwork evidence for which is discussed in chapter 4, may cast doubt on this explanation of the name. It may be that the site was called the 'Boundary Fort' because of its prominent position near the mid point of the Wansdyke, mentioned in the charter of 963 as Ealdan Dic. This raises the possibility, supported to some extent by the earthwork evidence, that the name was applied to the hillfort because it was thought to have some role related to its position on the dyke.

Of the remaining hillfort names a great number are of recent origin and many do not specifically refer to the hillforts themselves. These names are briefly discussed in Appendix A. At this point, however, the lack of direct reference to the fortification of some hilltops may be noted. Particularly noteworthy in this respect are Ham Hill and Dundon, neither of those names appears to imply the existence of a fortification. Ham Hill is one of the largest hillforts in the country, and Dundon is a well-preserved example of a class 1 site. It is therefore strange that neither site has a recorded name including the element burh. The time-span involved, and the probable instability of hillfort names, makes it unsafe to draw any firm conclusions from this, but it does at least reinforce the suggestion that the use of burh may be influenced by more complex factors than might at first be assumed.

Finally, consideration must be given to a small group of names which imply the existence of fortified sites and which are probably of purely Celtic origin. They should be considered in the light of the general comments on Celtic place names below. Dundry, a name now applied to a dominant flat-topped hill south of Bristol, upon which lie the hillfort of Maes Knoll and the probable end of Wansdyke, may mean 'fort of refuge', [44] presumably a reference to an actual or assumed function of the hillfort. It might be suggested that this name was assumed by English speakers to contain the element Dun and was therefore applied to the whole hill. The hillfort then acquired a name probably related to its situation on the Wansdyke, including the element maeres, 'boundary'.

Dommett, a hill mentioned in a charter of 762, [45] may be a similar instance of a transfer of names. According to Turner the first element in this name is also the Celtic Din 'fort', [46] and may in this instance refer to the site of Castle Neroche immediately to the north. Although excavation demonstrated that the main features of the site are those of a complex motte and bailey castle, a univallate enclosure without associated datable material may predate the other earthworks by a considerable period and be those of the fortification referred to in 762. [47] This would suggest an Iron Age or early post-Roman date for the first phase at Castle Neroche, rather than the late-Saxon one favoured by Davison.

The third instance is perhaps the most interesting. This is Dunkerton, a small river-side village south-west of Bath close to the Fosse Way. This is not the type of location one would expect to find the 'fort on a rock' implied by the first two elements in the name. [48] One mile to the north is Duncorn Hill, a knoll at the end of a NE-SW spur. Although fieldwork failed to identify defensive earthworks on this site it is possible that this is the location of the 'dun-Caer' from which the village took its name. This place name suggests the existence of an otherwise unknown defended site in the study area, one of the three for which a pre-English name can therefore be suggested.

Celtic place names (Fig. 9)

Place names consisting entirely of Celtic elements or containing such elements are relatively numerous in Somerset. Despite the lack of recent research on the county, 66 such names may be identified in Domesday and pre-Domesday sources, or over 10% of the Domesday total. Additionally, Turner cites 22 places recorded in post-Domesday material. The majority of the river names of Somerset are of Celtic derivation, as are those of many major topographical features. On the basis of the work of Ekwall and Turner, Appendix C lists 106 probable Celtic place names, and this must be regarded as a minimum figure. This is a greater proportion than that of Gloucester-shire, but less than that of Dorset, [49] but the contrast between the high survival of Celtic names in Somerset and their relative scarcity in Devon has probably been overstressed. [50] Devon possesses 33 'pure' Celtic names (i.e. uncombined with English elements) [51] compared to 30 in Somerset, and it is

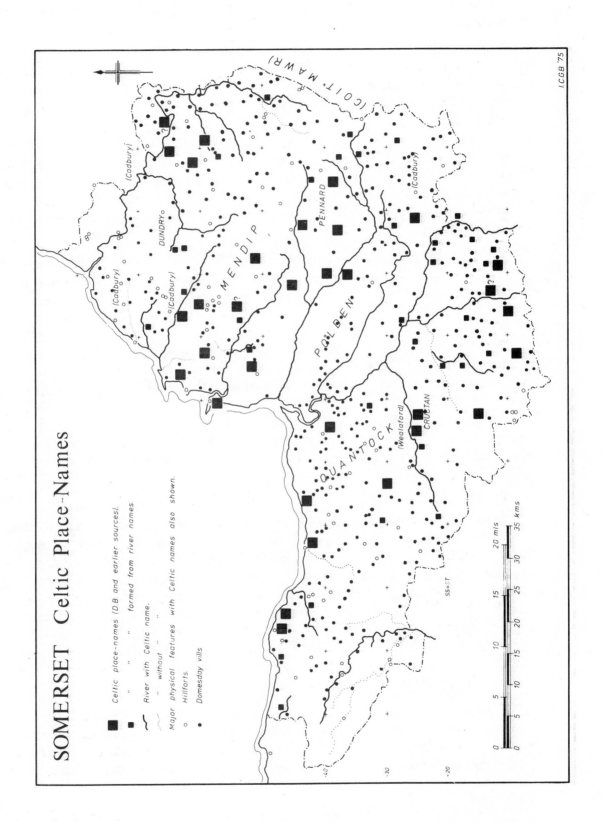

SOMERSET Celtic Place-Names

■ ● Celtic place-names (DB and earlier sources).
■ ● " " " formed from river names.
        ⌐ River with Celtic name.
        ⌐ " " without " " .
        Major physical features with Celtic names also shown.
   ○ Hillforts.
   ● Domesday vills

Fig. 9 Somerset; Celtic place-names in relation to Domesday vills

only the higher incidence of 'hybrid' names in the latter that increases the Somerset total to the relatively large figure of 106. An additional complicating factor must be competence and quality of the place-name research done in the two counties, and it may be that some of Turner's identifications for Somerset would not now be accepted.

There appears to be little agreement on the significance of the survival of Celtic place-name elements. The relatively frequent survival of the names of major features such as hills and rivers, seen in Somerset as elsewhere need not, according to one view, imply a close contact between English and British speakers or the extensive survival of the latter.[52] By contrast, however, Jackson has argued that the survival and mutation of British place names to suit English pronunciation is a reflection of the presence of a British population adopting the 'superior' English language and adapting local place names accordingly.[53] This view is in accord with the general trend against the 'extermination' view of the Anglo-Saxon settlement, especially in the western parts of England:

> '... the proponents of this view ... must presumably have imagined the Saxons as capturing a Briton, demanding of him the name of a neighbouring river or hill, and then slaughtering him on the spot, while being careful to remember the form he told them.'[54]

If Jackson's view is accepted, it must imply that those places which retained Celtic names were in fact occupied by British speakers at the time when those names become generally accepted. Finberg[55] has taken this a stage further and asserted, on the basis of Devon evidence, that the survival of Celtic names is also indicative of the survival of pre-English tenurial arrangements and land units. Celtic place names may therefore give some indication of the location of population in the early stages of the English domination of Somerset.

There are, however, complicating factors. Many places which now have purely English names may originally have had Celtic ones later altered, survival or alteration depending on local factors now undiscoverable. Such alteration could materially alter any distribution pattern, and render any deductions about overall settlement location invalid. It is possible to see this process in action in the West Monkton charter,[56] which may belong to the late seventh century. The document mentions a hill 'qui dicitur britannia lingua Cructan, apud nos Crycbeorh'. This is Creechbarrow hill, Taunton, and the charter shows an English place name adapting the first element of a British one, clearly in current use by local British speakers whose presence is further attested by the name Wealaford in the same charter.

The second factor is that many settlements with Celtic names may have been abandoned. Clearly, those Celtic settlement names which are recorded are only those which were in use at the time, and it is difficult to assess the extent to which English domination may have disrupted the general pattern of settlment from place-name evidence alone.

With these factors in mind some consideration may be given to the distribution of known Celtic place names, plotted on Figure 9 against the background of Domesday vills and hillforts. While the latter does not give a wholly reliable indication either of population density or of the total number of settlements in 1086, it is probably a good general guide to the general distribution of population in the latter part of the first millennium.

The general model which sees the Anglo-Saxon Settlement in terms of expulsion, if not extermination, of Britons, would imply that places with Celtic names should be found in unfavourable locations, their British inhabitants having either been left alone on undesirable land or forced to move to such locations when better land was seized by English settlers. Ravenhill's work in Devon suggests that this view is not tenable there, and that places with Celtic names are generally located on good quality land.[57] In the case of Somerset a simpler analysis than that undertaken by Ravenhill has been attempted. The proportion of Celtic to non-Celtic place names has been worked out as a percentage for each of the regions defined in Figure 6. The results are as follows:

Percentage for whole county	10.8%
Oolites (Highest Population)	13.7%
Taunton	7.1%
Lias	11.3%
Oxford Clay	9.5%
North Somerset	10.8%
Levels	15.6%
Western Hills (Lowest Population)[58]	7.6%

The numbers involved are too small for firm deductions to be made from these figures, but the relatively high proportion of Celtic names both in the Oolitic areas, which appear to have supported a high population at Domesday, and in the relatively thinly-populated levels are noteworthy. The former does not suggest that a major displacement from good quality land had occurred, and the places with Celtic names in the Levels region are located on outwash and Head deposits rather than in unfavourable positions on marginal land. The low figure for the Taunton region cannot be readily explained. It could be suggested either that English settlement in this area was numerically strong compared to the Oolitic areas and the Levels, resulting in greater replacement of place names, or that pre-English settlement was sparse in this area because of difficult soil conditions. Recent trends in archaeological thinking would treat the latter view with considerable caution, and it may be that the early charter evidence, and the enigmatic reference to Taunton in 722, do reflect considerable English settlement here towards the end of the seventh century.[59]

Broadly, the place-name evidence suggests that pre-English settlement sites exploited all the types of land later favoured for occupation. From this it may be inferred that there was no fundamental expansion or change in settlement pattern from the seventh century onwards. This in turn implies a high probability of survival of early land units, estates and general tenurial arrangements among which may be territories linked to hillforts and hill-top settlements.

Although the distribution of these place names provides useful general information it does not directly assist in the identification of hill-top and hillfort sites in use in the period of study. Names with Celtic elements show no tendency to cluster around hillfort sites, nor does Turner's opinion that Celtic church dedications, a number of which are very close to hillfort sites, are to be found in areas with a high concentration of Celtic place names, stand up to close analysis.[60]

Historical deductions from place-name evidence can only be tentative, but the forms of the Somerset names led Turner to conclude that:

> 'the British language in Somerset had developed into a stage corresponding to Primitive Welsh before it finally gave place to English'.[61]

Such a conclusion reinforces the impression gained from the documentary sources that English control of Somerset was not secured until the second half of the seventh century and that settlement by English speakers may only have been on a small scale for some time after that. Turner felt that the lack of Celtic place names to the north of Wansdyke was evidence of its use as political, cultural and linguistic boundary over a considerable period.[62] In general, therefore, the evidence from the Celtic place names supports the historically-derived view of the English settlement of Somerset and suggests that the area remained linguistically British for three hundred years after the separation of Britain from the Empire.

In detail, however, the place names only provide a limited range of historical information. In contrast to English names, the use of personal names appears to be virtually absent in those of Celtic derivation. The only use of possible Celtic names is at Congresbury, Cadbury and at Kewstoke where the final elements are English, and at Lantocai (Leigh by Street)—a purely Celtic name combining the personal name Cai with Lan, meaning church.[63] Names such as these, implying connexions with Celtic saints' touch on other aspects, discussed shortly.

The majority of the names are, however, purely topographical in character. A few, as we have seen, refer to fortified locations, but most either take their forms from descriptive adjectives applied to rivers or hills. One interesting exception is Ridgehill, apparently incorporating the element iâl 'upland cultivated land'.[64]

The contribution made by the study of Celtic place names is thus threefold. Firstly, it may identify two defended sites previously unknown, those at Dommett and Dunkerton, and also gives the pre-English name of one hillfort, Maes Knoll. Secondly it may tentatively be deduced from the overall distribution that the British-speaking population were not forced into marginal areas by English settlement, and were probably occupying areas of high quality land before the English conqusst. Finally, the form of the names indicates that the language continued to develop to the Primitive Welsh stage before it was wholly replaced by English. Such replacement was presumably a result of English conquest and settlement, and it seems probable from all available data that this process took place in the later seventh century.

'Celtic' church dedications   (Fig. 34).

The initial expansion of Christianity in both Eastern and Western Europe was achieved by close alliance between the church and secular powers, and there are documented instances of Christian centres being established within pre-existing fortified sites or close to major political centres.[65] The location of churches dedicated to saints from Celtic-speaking areas can thus potentially provide a clue to either or both of these situations, and in this lies their relevance to the present study.

The traditional view of the historical value of Celtic church dedications was summed up by Bowen:

> '... ancient churches and chapels now bearing the names of Celtic Saints owe their foundation in the first instance to the fact that the saint in question or one of his immediate followers, actually visited the church and established thereon a small religious community, which became the forerunner of the modern church.'[66]

This view has, however, been challenged in recent years, stress being laid on the lack of genuinely early evidence for the dedications, and on the complex social and historical factors which could account for the later adoption of the names of Celtic Saints for churches which may have had no original association with the saint in question.[67] Additionally, early church dedications to Celtic saints may be replaced by later ones to better-known saints. This process may be seen in Somerset at Congresbury, where the church is now dedicated to St. Andrew.[68]

In Somerset, due allowance must be made for the interests of the abbey of Glastonbury and the bishopric of Bath and Wells, both of whom may have influenced church dedications by their possession of relics of saints with no direct association with the area. Thus the dedications to the Irish Saint Brigit at Brean and Chelvey are probably due to the strong cult of Brigit at Glasbonbury the origins of which are obscure but which are unlikely to be earlier than the late Saxon period, although there is a strong tradition of Irish links with Glastonbury.[69] Similarly, the relics of St. Petrock, commemorated at Timberscombe, were probably the gift of Athelstan in the tenth century.[70]

Despite this, however, there does appear to be a genuine early group of church dedications which may be of pre-English origin. These are those to Dubricius (Porlock), Carantoc (Carhampton), Decuman (Watchet), Congar (Congresbury and Badgworth), Paternus (Nailsea - possibly with Glastonbury connexions),[71] and probable dedications to Kew at Kewstoke and Cai at Lantocai near Glastonbury.[72] The distribution of these dedications is markedly coastal, with the single exception of the St. Cai dedication. (Fig. 34).

This coastal distribution may be most readily explained as indicating missionary activity based on the sea-routes of the Irish Sea area, and has more specifically been regarded as evidence that Somerset was evangelised from South Wales.[73] In this context the dedication of Dubricius is of most relevance.

The hagiographical material relating to Carantoc and Congar give the dedications to these saints added importance, since both these locations are associated with fortified sites. The Life of St. Carantoc[74] is of twelfth-century date and does localise the saint to the Carhampton area where he encounters Arthur and a certain Cato in a fort called Dindrarthou.[75] Where a twelfth century hagiographer would have obtained such material is unknown, but it is tempting to think that Dindrarthou may have been the earlier name of the hillfort above Carhampton, now known as Bat's Castle (50).

59

With Congar the problems are much more complex, the difficulties being compounded by the archaeological data from the hillfort. It is clear that Congresbury was associated with Congar by the late ninth century, as the donation of the monastery there to Asser by Alfred demonstrates.[76] By the early eleventh century Congresbury was regarded as Congar's place of burial.[77] The Life of Congar survives in two manuscripts but is, like that of Carantoc, an eleventh or twelfth-century compilation probably written at Wells because of the interest of the bishopric in Congresbury at that time. The Life shares many incidents with contemporary Welsh hagiography but topographical detail suggests that the compiler of the work was familiar with the supposed location of Congar's monastery, the Habitaculum and cemetery being laid out by the saint in a place 'shut in by water and reed beds'. If this detail is more than a literary device it does indicate that the present site of the church, on the edge of the Levels, was intended rather than the hillfort, to which no tradition of sanctity appears to be attached. No mention is made in the Life of any fortified sites, but the chapter describing the alleged donation of the site for the monastery by Ine of Wessex relates that the king

'freely gave ..... all the territory lying around Cuggrisberia (sic), and promised that its sanctuary (refugium)...... should never be disturbed by the noisy presence of the royal soldiers'.[78]

The textual and genealogical problems associated with Congar will not be further discussed here,[79] except to note the equation of the saint's name with that of 'Docco' twice in one of the two extant texts.[80] Docco is independently attested in Irish sources,[81] and in the life of St. Samson, where a monastery with this name is mentioned, also later associated with St. Kew. The probable dedication of a church to St. Kew at Kewstoke less than 10 km from Congresbury similarly located on the edge of coastal marshes at the foot of a hill surmounted by a major hillfort (Worlebury, 16), may indicate a positive link between the two dedications in Somerset also, although it must be stressed that the equation of Congar with Docco may be of very late origin.

The main points to be noted from the brief survey above are the coastal emphasis of the distribution of those dedications which may be regarded as of early date, and the broad correspondence of this with certain classes of archaeological evidence, especially that of cemeteries. The relatively close proximity of the dedications to Congar, Kew, Decuman and Carantoc to hillfort sites may be noted in view of the documentary evidence from other areas of Britain for the association of early Christian foundations with local power centres and fortified sites, but the density of hillforts and the restricted availability of land for settlement are such that no deductions can be made from this evidence on its own.

Several of the points raised here will be returned to in the final discussion. The importance of this material will be more clearly seen when considered in conjunction with the more specifically archaeological data to be discussed in the following chapters. The first of these is an examination of the surface evidence from hillfort and hill-top sites, and is based to a large degree on fieldwork carried out as a central part of this study.

NOTES

1. Wainwright, 1962.

2. Hill, 1914.

3. Turner, 1950, 1951, 1952a, b, c, 1954.

4. Ekwall, 1960.

5. Cameron, 1969, 33-46.

6. Jackson, 1953.

7. See above, chapter 1.

8. Wainwright, 1962, 43.

9. Sawyer, Nos. 311, 380. Ekwall, 1960.

10. Finberg, 1964c, No. 465 (AD 946X955).

11. Alcock, 1972a, 27.

12. Sawyer, 481 (AD 941).

13. Sawyer, 476 (AD 941) and 711 (AD 963).

14. Sawyer, 247 (AD 705).

15. Grinsell, 1970, 93.

16. Ekwall, 1960.

17. Cungresbyri c. 894 (Stevenson, 1904, chap. 81). Also possibly Conbusburie 688X726 Finberg, 1964c, No. 372.

18. Anglo Saxon Chronicle 'E' S.A. 656 (Whitelock, 1961).

19. Phillips, 1974, 10.

20. Radford, 1957.

21. Sawyer, 711 (AD 963).

22. Turner, 1950, an alternative early form is Lutgaresberi (info. M. Gelling).

23. Finberg, 1964c, No. 414 (AD 871X874).

24. Portbrig Finberg, 1964c, 425 (AD 899X925).

25. At ST 503 494.

26. Phillips, 1974, 10.

27. Fowler, Gardner and Rahtz, 1970, 45, to which should be added Cadbury, Overton, Wilts, a possible univallate hillfort of 16 ha. SU 544 494.

28. Hill, 1914, 36-7.

29. Ekwall, 1960.

30. Stenton, 1947, 38-9.

31. No earthworks have been identified at Cadbury Heath, Bristol.

32. Alcock, 1971a, 194-5.

33. Cameron, 1969, 33-4.

34. Alcock, 1971a, 219. Since it is clear that <u>burh</u> may be applied to monastic sites not located in hillforts, there is no need to assume that Congres<u>bury</u> refers to the hillfort.

35. Barker, 1961, 106.

36. Page, 1890, 85.6.

37. Ekwall suggests a personal name Wada, but citing the possibilities <u>wad</u> 'woad' and <u>gewaed</u> 'ford'. In view of the topography the latter may be most probable.

38. Ekwall, 1960.

39. Hill, 1914, 26.

40. 'Grouse-Wood', Ekwall, 1960.

41. ' Jack Daw' s Hill', 1914, 312-3.

42. 'Valley of Roe Deer', Ekwall, 1960.

43. See Appendix C.

44. Turner, 1952a, 12.

45. Finberg, 1964c, No. 392.

46. Turner, 1952c.

47. Davison, 1973.

48. Ekwall, 1960.

49. Taylor, 1970, 47. Leggatt, 1935, 116.

50. Stenton, 1947, 63-4.

51. <u>Place Names of Devon</u>. English Place Name Society, Vol. I.,1931.

52. Cameron, 1969, 33-4. Wainwright, 1962, 59.

53. Jackson, 1953, 241-6.

54. Idem, 229.

55. Finberg, 1964a, 116-130.

56. Sawyer, No. 237.

57. Ravenhill, 1970.

58. Morgan, 1938.

59. Anglo Saxon Chronicle (Whitelock, 1961). Leech 1977, 169 and *passim* suggests that Taunton Deane may have had a considerable population in the Roman period.

60. Turner, 1952a, v.

61. Turner, 1952b, 150.

62. Turner, 1952a, vi.

63. Turner, 1952b, 149.

64. Turner, 1952c.

65. Thomas, 1971b, 33-5.

66. Chadwick, 1954, 176 n.2.

67. Chadwick, 1954, 173-88. Pearce, 1973.

68. Bates, 1905, 120-1.

69. Finberg, 1967. Rahtz and Hirst, 1974, 9-13.

70. Doble, 1946.

71. Rahtz and Hirst, 1974, 11.

72. See above and note 64.

73. Radford, 1962.

74. Doble, 1965, 31-52.

75. cf. Caer Draithou, one of the 'cities' of Britain named in Harl. 3859.

76. Stevenson, 1904, 68 (chap. 81).

77. Doble, 1945.

78. Doble, 1945. The mention of Ine in the life may be due to the existence of a Charter (now lost) giving land at Conbusbirie to Sherborne by King Ine (Finberg, 1964c, No. 372).

79. Chadwick, 1954, 51-2. Morris, 1973, 350.

80. Doble, 1970, 20-23 (chapters 6 and 16 of the later text, 11).

81. Chadwick, 1961, 71ff.

CHAPTER 4

THE EARTHWORK EVIDENCE

'I have been greatly deceived at times by the external
appearance of earthworks'   (Pitt-Rivers 1892, xi)

Can criteria be established by which sites may be ascribed to 0-700 AD
predominantly on the evidence of their own earthworks? There are very strict
limitations to such an approach, but a number of sites were found to possess
earthwork features which may date from the period with which we are concerned. New surveys were made of these sites and these are described and
discussed below. In conjunction with other evidence in chapters 5 and 6, this
material provides the basis for predictive hypotheses which may be tested by
excavation in the future.

The examination of sites for evidence of this nature depends in the first
instance on two assumptions, firstly that activity on hilltops involved the
construction or modification of earthworks at least in some cases, and secondly,
that such earthworks have survived in recognisable form to the present time.
As the examples of the Roman hill-top temple sites and of Glastonbury Tor
make clear, however, the construction of earthworks is not an essential feature of Roman or post-Roman hill-top activity in Somerset. Disregarding the
limitations of the earthwork evidence itself, it is clear that by concentrating
on this class of data some sites will by their nature not be detected at all.

In approaching the data two main situations were envisaged in our period
which would result in the construction of earthworks. In the first case totally
new sites may have been built in new locations in the Roman and post-Roman
centuries. It might be anticipated that such sites would show morphological
differences, and perhaps different choices of location, from the main Iron Age
sites of hillforts.   In the second instance pre-existing earthwork sites may
have been re-used, and their defences and other features modified or renovated,
showing distinctive features again setting them apart from the majority of
earthworks. A purely subjective view would be that the second situation was
more common, merely because a large number of the available hill-top sites
already possessed hillforts by the first century AD.

Methodology and limitations

Much of field archaeology depends on the assumption that approximate
dates can be ascribed to distinctive types of earthwork on the basis of their
similarity to dated examples. The number of examples of any given earthwork
type (e.g. motte and bailey castle, long barrow) adequately dated by independent means is normally very small in relation to the whole, but the attributes
of the type are such that unexcavated and undated examples are seen to belong
to the same type and, by extension, are normally presumed to be of similar

date. This process is a commonplace of archaeological techniques as a whole, but it needs stressing here since in principle it may be applied to the problems of earthwork sites of the first millennium AD.

However, several factors combine to render the isolation of specific earthwork types relevant to this study particularly difficult. The first is the small number of well-dated sites which can be used as analogues to the data from the mass of unexcavated sites. The example of Cadbury Congresbury, where earthworks possessing distinctive features have been satisfactorily dated by excavation, remains, regrettably, isolated. Secondly, earthworks built with similar functions in similar locations and with similar material may have a very similar appearance, even if their dates of construction are separated by as much as a millennium. This is especially true of the sites of our Group IV. One simple bank and ditched enclosure of less than 0.5 ha. looks much like another, although their dates and even the techniques used in their original construction may differ considerably. The present surface appearance of earthworks is the result of a protracted process of settlement and decay. Although no earthwork experiments of the nature of those on the chalk of Overton Down and on sand at Wareham[1] have been undertaken on the major subsoil types of Somerset, it is clear from excavations of earthworks of single phase construction at least, that after an initial period of fairly rapid decay and collapse banks and ditches reach a state of equilibrium in which the material is at its angle of rest. It is improbable, therefore, that observed differences in earthwork profiles are simply the result of chronological differences. All other factors being equal, an earthwork of the twelfth century AD will today probably have a profile very similar to that of one constructed in the fifth century BC. Marked variations in profile are more likely to be due to differences of structure, for example to surviving dry-stone walling, than to chronological divergence.

Since the basic classification of earthworks by the Ancient Earthworks Committee in the early part of this century[2] the isolation of distinctive groups or classes of hillforts and other sites with the aim of identifying the chronological and cultural realities which lie behind such classifications has proceeded. With some exceptions,[3] however, hillfort studies have continued to make use of the simplified scheme used by the Ordnance Survey,[4] since in most areas systematic fieldwork has not been undertaken with these problems in mind.

Distinctive classes of small enclosure have, however, been isolated in the Highland Zone areas of North Wales[5] and Northumberland[6] and in both cases the evidence suggests that their occupation was predominantly in the Roman period, although in both areas the settlements probably have roots in the local Iron Age, and continued to be frequented into the fifth century or later.[7] Their importance here lies in the fact that they form distinctive groups which can be isolated and ascribed to the period under review, and suggests the possibility that distinctive characteristics may be identified on Somerset sites, although it is immediately apparent that no earthwork in Somerset possesses any of the distinctive specific features of northern or Welsh enclosures.[8]

Much attention has been paid to the possibility of identifying sites of the fifth-seventh centuries by their surface form, both in Wales and Scotland, but Alcock has cast doubt on the valdiity of such an approach in Wales at least.

> '... a survey of the known or supposed sites of Arthurian date in Wales has revealed that they display no features to distinguish them from sites characteristic of the pre-Roman Iron Age....'[9]

In Scotland, a number of forts have been tentatively ascribed to the early post-Roman centuries because of consistent similarities of form and documentary references to some sites.[10] Some of them are small, simple defensive sites, the Duns, which àre the predominant form of enclosure in Western Scotland, ranging in date, like small enclosures elsewhere, from 1000 BC to 1000 AD or even beyond, and lacking really distinctive surface features.[11] The sites to which historical references can be ascribed, the 'nuclear forts', have defences which, utilising rock outcrops, characteristically define a strong central 'citadel' with surrounding enclosures at lower levels. This arrangement is not entirely dictated by the topography and it has been argued that such sites lie at the end of a typological development starting with small simple enclosures, which become elaborated by the addition of outer works. Some sites can be shown to overlie earlier, larger enclosures,[12] suggesting that this typology may also have a chronological validity, but this should not be pushed too far.[13]

It is clear that such valid typological schemes have only emerged from intensive, highly organised fieldwork in areas where the preservation of sites is particularly good. In Somerset, although, as has been argued above, preservation of sites is good, more extensive use of wooden construction is probable on sites, at least east of the Parrett, and much detail observable on stone sites will have been lost in this way, explaining, for example, the scarcity of visible hut sites within enclosures throughout the area. In addition, agricultural activity, while tending to avoid the major earthworks, has frequently damaged the interiors of sites, even at quite high altitudes in West Somerset. The preservation of distinctive earthworks at Cadcong is due to the fact that the site has never been ploughed, and similar evidence may well have been lost on other sites. On these grounds it is not therefore to be anticipated that Somerset will produce such clear-cut results as areas in the Highland Zone, but the evidence from the latter areas can be usefully compared with that from Somerset itself.

Enclosures of Group IV

As has been emphasised, the chronological range of these small enclosures is likely to be very wide. Three Somerset examples have produced evidence of Roman date, but on analogy with evidence from Cornwall[14] and Wales,[15] there is no fundamental reason why occupation whould not also have occurred in the fifth-seventh centuries at some sites. It is perhaps among this class of sites that distinctive earthwork types might therefore be hoped for. This was not, however, found to be the case and the limitations of earthwork study alone are most clearly shown in relation to these sites.

Groups II and III

It has been argued above (chapter 2) that the form of the sites of Group II represents a deliberate choice not wholly dictated by the topography. This need not, however, have chronological implications, and the non-isolation of this type in other areas renders it difficult to locate comparable dated examples. Many promontory forts of our Group III have produced material of both Roman and post-Roman date, particularly coastal examples in the South West of England and Wales, but again there is no evidence of distinctive earthwork types in association with the material.

Group I

Earthworks of Roman date are frequently found within sites of this group and some may yet prove to be entirely of Roman or post-Roman construction. Outside the areas of direct Roman control fourth-century dates have been demonstrated for the final phase of the defences of Traprain Law[16] and for the initial construction of those of Freestone Hill, Co. Kilkenney in Eire.[17] Occupation of major hillforts continued in Wales[18] and in numerous hillforts in lowland England. During the fourth and into the fifth century, refurbishing and reconstruction of hillfort defences certainly occurred, the best documented examples being the widely separated sites of Cissbury (Sussex)[19] and Lydney (Glos.);[20] in each of these cases considerable additions were made to existing earthworks. In none of these instances, however, was such activity suspected from the surface indications.

The gradually accumulating evidence for major activity on Group I sites in the period AD 400-700 presents the same picture—the absence of earthwork features recognised as unusual or distinctive before exacavation. However, despite the failure to identify distinctive earthworks of our period on Group I sites in the past, these large and structurally complex sites are perhaps more likely to produce relevant data than the simple small enclosures of Group IV. Very many large hillforts can be seen from their surface remains alone to incorporate successive phases of enlargement or other alternations to the defences and enclosed area, and detailed field examination of such sites can convincingly demonstrate relative sequences.[21]

Somerset field survey

The Somerset data was therefore approached with these points in mind. In the first place it was realised that ultimately only earthwork types dated by excavation could prove the validity of any ascription of a site, or part of it, to one period. This led to the comparison of the Somerset sites with other excavated earthworks of Roman and post-Roman date in order that any similarities, arguably indicating similar date and function to other unexcavated sites, could be detected.

Other questions were considered jointly with this. In particular, sites which appeared to be structurally complex, even though they might not have specific similarities to known sites of our period, were examined with the hope of establishing sequences of construction. This approach proved especially fruitful in relation to the two hillforts which have a direct structural relation to the Wansdyke, where the conclusions of earlier workers were modified.

Methods

The method adopted in the field study of the earthwork evidence was to visit every known site at the time of lowest vegetation growth in the early months of the year in 1973 and 1974. On the basis of field notes and photographs a number of sites were then selected for detailed or total re-survey (indicated on Figure 7), which was carried out in August 1974 and March 1975. The total time spent on work in the field amounted to 78 days.

A number of difficulties were encountered which limit the validity of the data. In the first place 25 sites are severely overgrown in whole or part throughout the year, making detailed investigation extremely difficult. Even in February and March the dense undergrowth of brambles and hazel coppices which cover sites on the Carboniferous Limestone especially, effectively masks large areas of the defences and the interiors of such sites.

It was in all cases assumed that the 25 in. O.S. plan was broadly accurate and that detailed correction rather than total resurvey was the most practical approach, given the time and circumstances.[22] There is no doubt that the majority of Somerset sites need detailed attention and would repay large-scale resurveying of their interiors and defences, but the O.S. plans, mostly revised in the 1960s, will probably remain the basis of work for the foreseeable future.

The earthwork data is considered under the following headings:

1. Cadcong and Brent Knoll.
2. Hillforts with features structurally later than the major defences.
3. The forts on the Wansdyke.
4. 'Anomalous' sites.

1. Cadcong and Brent Knoll (Fig. 10, Plan A, and Plate 5)

Here it is necessary to anticipate somewhat the discussion of the evidence from Cadcong in chapter 5, by stating that the excavated material indicates that the bank which bisects the summit plateau (Bank A on Fig. 10) of the hill, and that which runs around the perimeter (Bank B on Fig. 10), were constructed in the fifth or sixth century AD, although their precise relationship to each other is not yet clear.[23]

These banks both show several distinctive features which should enable comparable examples to be identified. The perimeter bank, which was clearly visible before excavation, will be concentrated on here, and can be traced around the entire circuit with the exception of the western end of the hill, where it has been damaged by quarrying. It is clearly visible as a bank with a flattened top, 3 metres in average width and about 0.5 m high, set some 2-3 m back from the edge of the steep wooded slopes that delimit the plateau on all sides except the east. At the east end of the hill is an entrance gap through the bank, which at this point is elaborated by two irregular flanking, looped enclosures. The northern enclosure (C) consists of a curving length of bank, apparently added to the front of the perimeter bank, at this point turning to the SW to flank the entrance gap, the whole forming a 'D' shaped structure about 10 m x 5 m internally. The southern enclosure (D) is more complex. From surface indications it appears that here the main perimeter

Fig. 10 Cadcong; General plan (based on Rahtz and Fowler, 1972, 195, with additions). For lettering see text

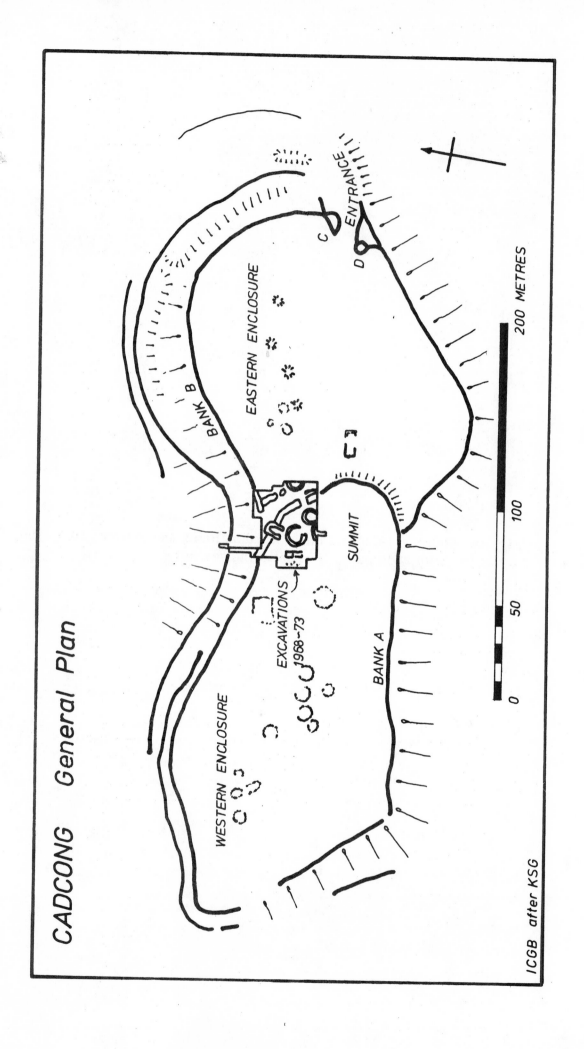

CADCONG   General Plan

WESTERN ENCLOSURE

EXCAVATIONS
1968-73

BANK A

SUMMIT

BANK B

EASTERN ENCLOSURE

C

D

ENTRANCE

0   50   100   200 METRES

ICGB after KSG

Plate 5   Brent Knoll Hillfort (no. 43) from the north-east, showing the
eastern entrance (UCCAP neg. no. BMC71)

bank is not inturned, but ends abruptly at the outer end of the entrance passage. From its end a slighter bank returns westwards for about 20 m and then runs southwards to rejoin the main perimeter, thus defining a roughly triangular area 20 m long and a maximum of 10 m wide. At the western apex of this area is an ambanked circle about 5 m in diameter. If these enclosures are additions to the main bank, as seems possible, its original form would have been that of an 'inturn - out-turn' entrance, with the northern side forming the inturn and the southern the out-turn. The addition of the enclosures may therefore be a device to further increase the length of the entrance passage and to emphasize it. The circular enclosure on the south could, on this inter-pretation, be a 'guard hut' or similar structure. A small cutting across the northern enclosure in 1959[24] gave only an Iron Age terminus post quem for the collapse of the bank, but its structure, form, and obvious continuation of the line of the post-Roman bank in the excavated area strongly suggests that it belongs to the same scheme. If this deduction is correct it indicates a late or post-Roman interest in elaborate entrance works for which Maiden Castle provides a parallel,[25] and which may also be seen at Brent Knoll, discussed shortly.

The extremely slight character of these banks immediately sets them apart from the general run of earthworks on Group I sites and even on most of those of Group IV, and this raised hopes of locating other examples of hill-forts with similar features. The earthworks of some of the 'anomalous' sites discussed below show definite similarities, but enclose a much smaller area, and no other medium or large sites in the study area were definitely found to possess these low banks. In the densely overgrown sites of Cannington (41) and Dundon (14) occasional glimpses were obtained of slight earthworks pos-sibly of the same form but sufficient lengths of them were not clear of under-growth for positive identification.

As will be seen, the evidence from Cadcong does not point conclusively to these slight banks having a primarily defensive purpose, and it is even possible that pre-existing defences were destroyed for their erection, and on the basis it might be predicted that such structures would not be constructed on top of large-scale pre-existing earthworks, even if they could be detected in such positions.

At Brent Knoll, however, the earthwork evidence suggests that, although the main earthworks here are of considerable size, the entrance at least may have been altered to create a similar arrangement to that at the eastern en-trance of Cadcong.

Brent Knoll camp (43) is a contour fort of Group I, set on the highest point of a prominent Lias 'island' rising to 139 m O.D. above the surrounding levels, the defences of which enclose 1.6 ha. Most of the interior of the fort has been lowered some 2-3 m by quarrying for the sandstone which caps the hill, and this had occurred before 1812.[26] Roman and Iron Age material has been, and continues to be, found here and will be discussed further later.

The defences consist basically of an inner bank with two outer terraces which may represent banks fronting on totally silted-up ditches, or be simple terracing of the hillside. Across the easiest approach up the spine of the hill from East Brent village to the north east is a third major terrace. The inner bank has been largely removed for 40 metres on the western side and the outer terrace has been much damaged by Home Guard trenches, but the middle terrace and most of the inner bank are relatively undamaged, the latter standing about 3 m above the terrace.

The only visible entrance is on the east side, and Plan A indicates its form. As at Cadcong, the entrance passage is flanked by two enclosures of unequal size. In both cases the front of the inner bank and the first terrace appear to have been quarried subsequent to their construction and the material pushed outwards to form hollow 'bastion' type structures. While it is possible that these features are the fortuitous result of stone quarrying on each side of the entrance passage, the lack of spoil heaps or stone in the vicinity, and the apparently deliberate creation of slight, curving banks argues against this.

The southern, smaller, structure is the more regular of the two, the rampart and outer bank enclosing an area 12 m north-south and 6 m from east to west, most of which is on a steep slope which renders it unsuitable for a hut site or other structure, the outer bank being 4.25 m below the crest of the main rampart.

The northern side is an irregular kidney shape, a maximum of 23 m north-south and 11 m east-west, the interior of which slopes very steeply down to the east, the surface of the ground being broken into a series of terracettes probably caused predominantly by cows walking on the unstable clay soil. Roman pottery and fragments of Pennant sandstone, not native to the area, were found near the top of this slope and their positions marked on the plan. The vertical distance between the crest of the inner bank and the top of the outer is again just over 4 metres. The central portion of the outer bank appears to have been partially removed.

The interior of the hillfort in the immediate vicinity of the entrance has been disturbed by quarrying, but on the south side are the slight remains of an inturning length of rampart running westwards for about 10 m from the crest of the inner bank. Disturbance behind the northern side is too great to assess whether the same situation obtained there.

This entrance arrangement shows both similarities to and divergences from that at Cadcong. The major variation is the much greater difference in vertical height between the front and back of the looped enclosures at Brent Knoll compared with those at Cadcong, where the entrance was built on very gently sloping ground. The vertical difference there is only about 1 m from west to east. However, if, as is suggested here, the Brent Knoll entrance represents alteration to a pre-existing major scheme of defences, while the builders of the Cadcong structures were not faced with problems of the same magnitude, the differences become explicable. To construct the enclosures on relatively flat ground at Brent Knoll would have involved either placing them behind the inner rampart (where it may be suspected the major banks of an inturned entrance existed in any case) or demolishing lengths of the rampart on each side of the entrance to utilise the flatter ground on which it is placed. The observable scheme would be the most economical of these three alternatives.

If the differences of siting are therefore regarded as being totally dictated by the pre-existing topographical features the similarities between the two sites can be more clearly seen. In the first place the sizes of the enclosures are very similar in both cases (11 x 23 m compared with 20 x 10 m; 12 x 6 m compared with 10 x 5 m) although this could be more coincidence and several examples would be needed to confirm that this is a significant correlation. Secondly, the slight nature of the banks is similar, and unless the earthworks formed the basis for major timber structures, they cannot be held to have had a defensive purpose.

In both cases, however, the intention seems to have been to emphasise the entrance by elongating the entrance passage and flanking it with curving structures. Without excavation nothing further can profitably be said until the other evidence from the two sites is considered. No other examples of this type of structure were identified in the study area, but we may note in passing their possible affinities to sites in North Britain.[27]

2. Sites with other features structurally later than the defences.

In very few cases are the interiors of hillforts entirely featureless. A great many show evidence of surface quarrying of unknown date, and others contain slight earthworks which would require detailed contour surveys to show them adequately. In six instances, the earthwork evidence is of a scale to imply activity on the sites subsequent to the main construction of the defences. In four cases, Ham Hill (1), Dolebury (6), Bury Hill (34) and Clifton (42) these take the form of internal enclosures and banks; at Cadbury Tickenham (29) the evidence suggests the construction of a subsidiary entrance after the ramparts were completed. Finally, at Cannington (41) the earthworks of a settlement and fields secondary to the outer bank of the hillfort were surveyed. All of these sites have produced Roman material, which is discussed in chapter 6.

Dolebury is an extremely impressive site of 9.15 ha. situated on a limestone spur overlooking the Churchill gap, one of the main routes through the Mendips (plate 6), the defences consisting of bank, ditch and counterscarp with entrances at the east and western ends, the latter with indications of outworks, the former a simple gap in the defences. To the east are two cross-ridge dykes and a field system.[28] At the highest point of the interior are the remains of a warrener's hut inside a circular enclosure, but the major features are the north-south banks, about 1 m high and 10 m wide, visible on the air photograph. The area was certainly a warren in the nineteenth century and the best explanation for these features is that they are pillow mounds constructed to provide tractable material for rabbits to burrow into.[29] They may be medieval, since they were not used as such at the time of Dymond's survey,[30] and the air photograph suggests that the area between them has been cultivated subsequent to their construction.

The rectangular depression 47 x 36 m in the south-west corner of the hillfort could be related in some way to warrening activities, perhaps as a sheltered breeding place for does,[31] but similar features appear in corners of both Ham Hill and Clifton.

Plate 6   Dolebury Camp (no. 6) from the south
(West Air Photography neg. no. H343/10)

At Ham Hill a depression known locally as the 'Frying Pan' and which was interpreted by Collinson and later workers[32] as a Roman amphitheatre, is located in the north-eastern corner of the northern part of the fort. This is a sub-circular hollow about 2 m deep and 30 m across, located in an area where large amounts of Roman material have been found. This area was also a warren in the thirteenth-fourteenth centuries.

Clifton Camp (plan Be; plate 7) is situated on the eastern side of the Avon Gorge, in an area that was largely waste until the eighteenth century, and which might have contained rabbit warrens, although there is no direct evidence.[33] The bivallate defences and entrances have been damaged by quarrying and landscaping, and the present enclosed area of 1.7 ha. may originally have been considerably larger before quarrying of the sides of the gorge in the last century.

Towards the north-western corner of the fort is a rectangular enclosure 45 x 40 m defined by a bank about 30 cm high with a very shallow ditch on the outside. The bank is only well defined in its southern part. On the eastern side it comes to an end some 10 m to the south of the inner rampart of the camp, behind which is a large quarry hollow. On the western side the bank is less regular and has been cut through by a path. About half-way along this side two short lengths of bank about 5 m apart run eastwards from it for a short distance. This enclosure is clearly earlier than two other features in the interior of the fort. The north-south hedge bank clearly overlies it and also cuts through the inner rampart, but at its southern end appears to have been itself destroyed by the buildings associated with the windmill. Secondly, a linear depression, running SE-NW and visible both on the air photograph and on the ground cuts through the enclosure near its south-east corner. This depression runs from the pronounced oval parch-mark just north of the windmill and which is the site of a nineteenth-century reservoir.[34] A cutting through the enclosure bank in 1900 produced no datable material.[35]

The enclosures at these three sites are clearly too small to be fields but too large to be the remains of buildings, and as all are of the same order of size a common function might be suspected for them. Their appearance on sites producing Roman material may be significant, but the majority of such sites do not contain these enclosures. On balance a medieval or later date might seem more probable, but they potentially belong to the period of study.

At Bury Hill the interior of the hillfort contains a number of complex earthworks, which were described in two separate papers in 1926.[36] The original enclosed area, defined by two banks and ditches, was probably of the order of 2.2 ha. Davies' and Phillips' excavations demonstrated that some at least of the earthworks are of Roman date, but the site well demonstrates the problems of distinguishing earthworks of different periods from surface indications alone. Quarrying for iron ore deposits is sufficient to explain most of the hollows and mounds in the interior.

The major visible feature is a bank 10 metres wide and 30 cm high running almost due east-west across the interior, dividing it into two unequal portions. Sixty metres west of the inner rampart a second bank runs northwards from this but is difficult to trace for more than 10 m, although it may

Plate 7   Clifton Camp (no. 42) from the north
(West Air Photography neg. no. AL1000/10)

have originally extended as far as the inner rampart on the north, thus defining a sub-rectangular area of about 60 x 90 m in the north-eastern corner of the fort in a similar manner to the features at Clifton, Dolebury and Ham Hill.

Aligned on the east-west bank are two embanked rectangles. That on the west, excavated by Phillips and now covered by quarry spoil, appeared to him to be of early Roman date, and the similar alignment of the smaller one, 16 x 4.6 m overall, suggests that it may also be of this date. The only deduction that can be made from the surface evidence, however, is that all these features are likely to post-date the hillfort defences and although their rectilinear character suggested to Willmore and Tratman that they were of Roman date there is nothing in their superficial appearance to distinguish them from medieval features.

At <u>Cadbury Tickenham</u> (29, plan Ba, plate 8) the breach through the ramparts on the north-west side is distinguished from other gaps on the west and south of the enclosure. These are narrow and were produced by partially pushing the ramparts into the ditches to form rough causeways for agricultural access.[37] Its greater width, the inturning of the ends of the inner rampart on each side of the gap, and a slightly sunken approach about 5 m wide which runs slightly north of west for 40 m from the lip of the outer ditch distinguish the north-west gap from these. Like the other gaps this is clearly later than the defences, and its construction involved their demolition and the filling up of the ditches. The ramparts at this point were, however, much more thoroughly levelled. It is therefore possible that this gap is an ancient subsidiary entrance to the hillfort, supplementing the complex original entrance on the north side, partially excavated by Gray.[38]

<u>Cannington</u> (41) (plan C) appears to be unique among Somerset hillforts in having the earthworks of an extra-mural settlement immediately adjacent to, and probably post-dating, its defences. Combined with the material from the cemetery and hillfort itself, this evidence makes Cannington one of the most important areas for the study of settlement in the South-West.

The hillfort itself, one of the most overgrown in the county, was re-surveyed by Quinnell[39] in 1963, and consists of two lines of defences enclosing 1.8 ha. on a low but prominent carboniferous limestone hill rising above rolling country of Keuper marl and Lower Lias clay. It is the only hillfort in the roughly triangular area bounded on the north by the sea, on the east by the Parrett and to the south-west by the dip slope of the Quantocks, which support less fertile soils.

The inner defence originally comprised a drystone wall, at least on the north.[40] There are indications of an entrance on the north, but the main access was at the south-east corner, where the second bank reaches its greatest height. A third bank (A) has been added, extending 100 m east and west of the entrance passage but then fading out. There is a possibility that this bank is of late Roman date.[41]

The field immediately to the south of the fort slopes fairly steeply down towards the south, the average gradient being about 1 in 10 in a line due south from the hillfort entrance but much less in the western part. The area has been subjected to surface quarrying which has produced irregular hollows and

Plate 8   Cadbury Tickenham (no. 29) from the north-north-east
(West Air Photography neg. no. AN1038/10)

mounds, and towards the western end are the remains of buildings associated with a rifle range. Flat rectangular platforms (T) cut into the outer banks of the entrance works are probably golf tees.[42]

Distinct from these, and clearly visible on air photographs are earthworks forming a series of sub-rectangular enclosures and embanked trackways. It is probable that the area was emparked in the later Middle Ages,[43] and these features predate the emparkment. Towards the south-east corner of the field they have been destroyed and disturbed by surface quarrying. The limits of the earthworks are unclear, as the fields to the south and west are under plough, although vague crop marks are visible on the air photograph. The field to the east (Little Park) is some 15 m lower than Great Park, and the eastward limit of the earthworks, with the exception of one enclosure (B) which may not be related, is defined by a steep drop.

On the east the earthworks consist of at least three terraced enclosures (C, D, E), possibly containing house platforms defined by low ditches and banks, terraced on the downhill side, the banks averaging 1 m in height. The northern enclosure utilises the ditch of the outer bank of the hillfort and appears to have been laid out in relation to it. Against the eastern side of the enclosure are slight traces of a sub-rectangular area, perhaps a building (F). In the two enclosures to the south Romano-British and Iron Age pottery and animal bone were found in areas very superficially disturbed by cattle.

Westward from these enclosures run two hollow-ways flanked by wide low banks and which bifurcate towards their western ends, where they appear to be blocked by a continuous bank (G) which runs for 200 m up the slope from the modern road. On the north this bank fades into the steep hillside. A major scarp, changing into a bank (H), runs from that point eastwards, turning towards the outer bank of the hillfort and butting onto it 25 m west of the entrance. Other enclosures are present on the western side of the field but are not physically connected. In the north-west corner a series of slight terraces runs along the contours of the steep slope, delimited by a bank on the north and a 'hollow way' on the east.

These earthworks are best interpreted as those of a settlement with associated fields, through which 'droveways' provide access to the small (? homestead) enclosures at the eastern side. The relationship of the earthworks to the hillfort, combined with the surface finds suggests a Roman or later, rather than a pre-Roman, date.

3. The hillforts on Wansdyke

The problems of the Somerset Wansdyke, its date, extent, function and relationship to the Wiltshire section will be discussed below (chapter 7). The dyke is unique among the linear earthworks assumed or known to be post-Roman in incorporating two major hillforts in its line. Wat's Dyke in Shropshire runs up to the hillfort of Old Oswestry,[44] utilising its western side as the frontier line, but Offa's Dyke either ignores or deliberately avoids the hillfort of Pen-y-Gardden.[45] The Bedwyn Dyke in Wiltshire, argued to be a separate work from Wansdyke, may have used the hillfort of Chisbury as a terminal point,[46] but in general linear earthworks do not show a great interest in hillforts.

Maes Knoll (5) (plan D) is now generally held to mark the western end of Wansdyke. Attempts to trace it beyond this point have failed, despite documentary indications of its continuation.[47] The hillfort has been adequately described only once,[48] and field study produced evidence which alters the hypotheses there proposed.

The site, of 12.1 ha. is virtually a promontory fort, the only easy access being eastwards along the plateau from Dundry, and of which the fort occupies the eastern extremity. This access is blocked by the very large earthwork, The Tump, which Tratman regarded as the terminal work of Wansdyke on the basis of comparison with the degraded nature of much of the rest of the probably Iron Age defensive system. The north-south ditch on the north-east was also interpreted as part of Wansdyke, cutting through an earlier defence line now represented by an isolated length of bank and ditch immediately to the east. Tratman suggests that Wansdyke then ran along the top of the steep unstable scarp on the north side of the hillfort, but has since collapsed.[49] This hypothesis agrees better with the field evidence than the description by Fox and Fox, who claim that the Wansdyke bank and ditch, running north-westwards up the hill, stopped some 75 m to the east of the north-south bank and ditch, the intervening gap being occupied by a ditch running on the same line but described as a 'typical hollow way'.[50]

Tratman's explanation is not totally satisfactory, primarily because it fails to explain why the builders of Wansdyke changed the alignment of the dyke so markedly in the vicinity of the hillfort. If it was intended to utilise the northern scarp of the fort it would seem more logical to run the line of the dyke directly towards it. Moreover, it is clear from the plan that the line of N-S bank and ditch interpreted by Tratman as Wansdyke is a northward continuation of the much ploughed-down scarp which runs as far as the south end of the fort. On this basis it appears more probable that Wansdyke here made use of a pre-existing work which may have been refurbished.

The point of junction between the Wansdyke ditch and the north-south ditch was therefore resurveyed in 1974 (Plan D). On the southern side of the Wansdyke ditch only a very slight ridge indicates the former presence of a bank, and its relationship to the 4-metre north-south scarp cannot be assessed. The ditch itself swings round northwards on reaching the foot of the scarp, and the large north-south ditch runs from this point as far as the northern slope of the plateau. It appears, however, that what is here interpreted as the Wansdyke terminates just beyond this change of direction, as the ditch becomes markedly shallower at this point, suggesting termination of work in an existing feature. The pronounced terrace which separates the Wansdyke ditch from the foot of the scarp to the west might, on this interpretation, be merely the silting deposits in the pre-existing ditch, cut into by the constructors of the dyke, or could be the remains of the Wansdyke bank. It seems probable, in any case, that the pre-existing defences to the south were already degraded by the time of the construction of the dyke.

The large earthwork of the Tump is not without parallels in probable Iron Age contexts, and though it might be a deliberately impressive final flourish to the Wansdyke it should be noted that at Countisbury (2) and Milbourne Wick (8) a similar combination of large size, weaker earthworks on all but the most exposed side, itself defended by a very large scale bank and ditch, is present.

The tentative conclusions with regard to Maes Knoll and the Wansdyke are therefore that the Wansdyke builders made use of a pre-existing, probably Iron Age, defence on the east side of the hillfort, but did not undertake major alterations to this and probably stopped work once they had reached the well-preserved portion of the Iron Age ditch. The Tump may be part of the Wansdyke scheme, but there are probable Iron Age parallels for its huge scale.

Stantonbury (20) (Plan E) is on a prominent oolite hill rising about 60 m above the surrounding land, and is situated half-way along Wansdyke. The view obtainable over most of the course of the dyke from this position led Fox and Fox to suggest that the hilltop had been used as a vantage point from which to plan its line.[51]

Previous descriptions of the hillfort and its relationship to the Wansdyke have been inaccurate and misleading due to inadequate field observation, which until recently was hampered by dense vegetation cover and unco-operative landowners. Extensive clearance of the interior and northern defences in 1973-4 and easier access to the site enables a fuller examination of the earthworks to be undertaken, and on this basis a structural sequence can be suggested.[52]

The hill on which the hillfort is located is steep sided, its long axis running east-west. The easiest and most visually advantageous approaches are from the north-west and east, where less steep ridges forming the spine of the hill are utilised by the Wansdyke, which joins the hillfort at its north-western angle and runs downhill to the east. It has been levelled by cultivation on the lower slopes of the hill.

The hillfort itself consists of two enclosures, only the western one of which, enclosing about 2 ha., has previously been considered in descriptions of the site, although perhaps Phelps had noted the earthworks to the east, which partly define a smaller enclosure of about 1 hectare.[53] The relationship of these two enclosures to each other and to the Wansdyke was tentatively resolved by close examination of the earthworks and detailed re-planning of crucial junctions.

It is suggested that the western enclosure is primary. This is defined on the west and south by a bank very much obscured from the interior by ploughing. Numbers of large oolite blocks lying on the surface and tumbled down the slope on the south suggest originally stone walled defences. The western slope has been much disturbed by quarrying, but on the south side a ditch and counterscarp are present, and the main bank is here 3.3 m high, increasing to 5 m towards the east. Iron Age pottery was found in rabbit disturbances here by K. S. Gardner in 1974.

The eastern side of the enclosure is delimited by a broad shallow ditch with a low much spread bank visible to the east. There is no sign of one on the west except towards the north end. Collinson describes the ditch as 7 feet (2.2.m) deep, which is much in excess of its present dimensions except at the north end, and it seems probable that the rampart here has been ploughed into the ditch.

The defences on the northern side are still prominent from the interior. The bank stands about 1 m high from the inside, and there are prominent quarry hollows behind it. On the exterior the bank drops about 5 m to a terrace about 5 m wide. This has a counterscarp bank on its outer edge immediately to the north of the point at which the ditch on the east side of the enclosure reaches the northern slope of the hill.

At this point the bank bulges outwards markedly and drops some 50 cm, strongly suggesting that here it runs across the pre-existing ditch. This therefore originally ran to the top of the slope to complete the circuit of the western enclosure. From this point the bank runs eastwards with the terrace still present but damaged by quarrying, the dimensions being similar to those to the west. A pronounced terrace about 10 metres wide with a 1.5 metre scarp on its southern side runs behind the bank for most of the distance along the plateau. Towards the eastern end of the plateau the bank curves southwards, the terrace ends and is replaced by a ditch and counterscarp which are the distinctive feature of Wansdyke on both sides of the hill.

The line of this curve is continued by that of the middle of three banks or terraces which run around the end of the plateau immediately to the south and define the eastern enclosure but fade out after running along the steep slope on the south side of the hill for a short distance. The outer terrace (bank 3) is very low, and its junction with the Wansdyke at its northern end is obscured by the modern track which runs over it. The inner terrace (1) curves round to run parallel to the northern defences for a short distance, forming what appears to be an inturned entrance which was approached along the top of the terrace (2). The line of this entrance is continued westwards by the terrace running behind the northern rampart. Shortly before the ditch of the western enclosure is reached a slighter ditch joins the terrace, running across the plateau to the south-west and becoming a terraced way as it runs down the southern slopes of the hill. This was probably a trackway across the hill.

As there are no indications of any defences along the southern side of the eastern enclosure it is possible that it is unfinished. This, combined with the evidence at the north-eastern corner of the western enclosure, and the general form of the two enclosures, strongly suggests that the eastern one is an addition to the original scheme.

The configuration of the bank at the north eastern corner indicates that at this point Wansdyke was added to the earthworks of the eastern enclosure probably covering the slight earthworks of bank 3, and butting against those of bank 2, which has since been much degraded by the present track immediately to the south. The superficial impression which is gained from the plan that banks 1, 2 and 3 are flanking works to an entrance utilising Wansdyke and therefore secondary to it, is therefore probably incorrect.

At the north-western corner of the hillfort the Wansdyke also runs up to the western enclosure in a manner which indicates that the dyke is secondary. Fox and Fox inexplicably described the dyke here as 'ending in an open patch of ground below the former Iron Age defences',[54] but this is incorrect. The dyke runs up the slope from the north-west and is here at its most impressive, being 5 m high and fronted by a ditch and counterscarp. At the point of junction with the north-western corner of the hillfort the main bank of the dyke is some 50 cm lower than the hillfort defences, resulting in a marked break in slope.

Immediately below this, as at the eastern end of the hillfort, the ditch and counterscarp of Wansdyke fade into the 5 m wide terrace which runs along the north side of the hillfort. Fox and Fox suggest that this terrace might post-date the construction of the hillfort.[55] Its presence below both the western and eastern enclosures, combined with the larger dimensions of the defences as a whole along the northern side of the hillfort compared to those on the rest of the circuit might support this idea, but it is possible that the pre-existing defences were refurbished to some extent at the time of the construction of the dyke.

In summary, therefore, the sequence deduced from the earthwork evidence is as follows:-

I The construction of the western enclosure. Possibly defended by dry-stone walling, ditch and counterscarp. The position of the entrance of this phase is unclear, but was possibly on the east side. With this phase may be associated the early Iron Age pottery mentioned above.

II The addition of the eastern earthworks, which were carried over the ditch of the western enclosure at its north-eastern corner. An inturned entrance was constructed at the eastern end, but the evidence suggests that the scheme was not completed on the south edge of the plateau.

III Wansdyke was brought up to the north-west and north-eastern corners of the plateau, and at this point was built on a large and impressive scale with the addition of a counterscarp bank on the outer edge of the ditch. Possibly some renovation of the existing defences on the north side, but no indication of any concern with the defences of the rest of the hillfort.

IV Track across eastern defences and enclosures, ploughing of interior etc.

Without precise information on the physical, social and political restraints which operated on the constructors on the dyke and conditional to its line, it is very difficult to assess the significance of the incorporation of the hillforts into it. If it is accepted that the blocking of the Jurassic Way south of Bath was the primary object of the dyke,[56] and that the length from Englishcombe westwards is an addition, even if not separated from the original construction by any great interval, there was probably time for the choice of line to be carefully considered. While it certainly possesses a good field of view to the north from Maes Knoll and Stantonbury, the rest of the dyke is not well positioned visually, and has control neither over river traffic on the Avon nor over the Roman road running north-west from Bath along the south side of the river.[57] The more logical line from a military point of view would be along the edge of the flood plain of the river, but clearly other factors influenced the choice. The possibility that the existence of two hillforts to the south was one of those factors may be put forward, but cannot be proved with the data available. Further implications arising from the construction of Wansdyke will be considered in chapter 7.

4.   'Anomalous' sites

A small number of enclosures possess characteristics of form and siting which set them apart from the majority of Somerset sites. Although many sites have features which do not immediately agree with the picture of a 'typical' Iron Age enclosure, it is obvious that the variation in hillfort plans is very great and for a site to be described as 'anomalous' it must possess a number of attributes which differ markedly from those possessed by other sites, and which appear consistently together.

On this basis there are three enclosures in North Somerset which can be so described, and two more which share some of their features. None of these sites has any direct evidence of date.

The three sites of Cleeve Toot (49), Taps Combe (53) and Backwell (80) are spaced along the northern edge of the Carboniferous Limestone outcrop of Broadfield Down (Plans Bc and d). Cleeve Toot is 2.2 km from Cadcong and 2 km south-west of Taps Combe, which in turn is 2 km south-west of Backwell. This even spacking, combined with similarity of location may indicate that the three sites are contemporary.

All three sites are located at the top of low limestone cliffs at the sides of the combes which form a distinctive feature of the Somerset limestone. In common with many enclosures on the limestone, their position is such that access to the fertile soils at the base of the limestone scarp and to the plateau to the south is equally easy (see above, chap. 2).

The characteristic feature of the plans of the group is the use of the limestone cliff to reduce the length of artificial defences required to form the enclosures, the enclosure banks terminating at the cliff top. This logical idea is not used frequently in Somerset, despite a large number of suitable locations, and the close proximity of the Cleeve Hill enclosure (66) to Cleeve Toot emphasises the deliberate nature of the choice of these particular locations. Cleeve Hill is a univallate enclosure 200 m NNE of Cleeve Toot on the opposite side of the combe. The siting and character of the two sites is largely identical except that Cleeve Hill, instead of making use of the cliff top, is set back some 20 m from it, and the enclosure had thus to be defined by a bank around its full circuit. While this difference could represent a mere whim on the part of the builders of Cleeve Hill it does emphasise that Cleeve Toot, Taps Combe and Backwell were constructed to a plan which did not immediately suggest itself to other people in the area wishing to construct small, weakly defended enclosures at the edge of the limestone.

The three sites are defined by low wide banks, those at Cleeve Toot being 1.2 m high and 9 m wide. Those of Backwell were of similar dimensions,[58] but Taps Combe's defences are 1.5 m high and the site has a ditch and slight counterscarp bank on the north side. The latter site also has an embanked track which runs downhill NNW for about 50 m from the north-western corner of the enclosure. In this direction the ground falls away gently onto the intensively cultivated soils along the north side of the limestone, and on which are remains of 'Celtic' field systems.[59]

The interiors of the sites are level and featureless and there is no evidence of hut sites or other activity.

It is therefore argued that these three sites form a distinct morphological group, the validity of which is reinforced by their close proximity. There are, in addition, two other sites which share some of the distinctive features of these enclosures and which may belong to this group also.

Burrington Camp (54)[60] is located on the east side of Burrington Combe and is overlooked by higher ground to the south, a feature shared by the three sites discussed above. Direct access to the lower ground in the area of Burrington Village is hindered by the steep slope to the north of the site, but the slope is more gradual to the north-east.

The main enclosure of the camp, of 0.8 ha., the same as the enclosed area of Taps Combe, utilises the cliff top on its western side, but in contrast to Cleeve Toot and Backwell (but not perhaps to Taps Combe),[61] a low bank was constructed here with material from the inner quarry ditch which forms a distinctive feature of the site. On the north and south sides lengths of bank and ditch continue westwards to enclose small additional areas. The earth-works on the south definitely run to the head of the combe and it seems probable that those on the north did also, although they have been disturbed by later quarrying.[62] The defences are larger in scale than those of sites 49, 53 and 80, the inner bank being up to 2.5 m high in places along the eastern side and fronted by a ditch and counterscarp, but the site otherwise shows the same features as the group to the north.

Daw's Castle (36, plan Bb) may also belong to this group of cliff-top sites, but possesses some unique features. It is located on unstable Lias cliffs about 70 m above O.D. on the coast west of Watchet. In its present form the enclosure bank ends at the cliff top on the west, but on the east it was probably destroyed by the construction of lime kilns in the late nineteenth century.[63] The original size of the enclosed area is impossible to assess, since the cliff in the vicinity is eroding continuously. The cliff below the site is fairly stable at present.

The defences on the south-west and south consist of a bank, which for most of its length is merely a scarp up to 2 m high with a steep profile, fronted in places by a terrace about 4 m wide. The bank becomes much less distinct towards the east, but the course of the road from Watchet strongly suggests it originally ran around pre-existing works at this point, and there are slight traces of the bank at the edge of the field immediately to the west of the road, which is about 2 m lower than the interior of the site here. Burrow recorded a length of bank 300 yards to the east of the fort which has since been destroyed by a landslip.[64] The interior of the site slopes down-wards from the cliff top towards the south.

Hillforts not on highly defensible promontories are very uncommon in coastal locations. The nearest examples to Daw's Castle are on the South Devon coast at High Peak[65] and Berry Cliff.[66] High Peak, which proved on excavation to be of post-Roman date (although no suggestion that this might be so had been made) consists of a scarp fronted by a ditch, not visible before excavation, enclosing a semi-circular area at the top of the coastal cliff. There was also a second bank on the east side perhaps providing an additional defence for the entrance. The scale of the inner scarp is similar to that at Daw's Castle. Cliff erosion here also makes assessment of the original size and form of the enclosure impossible, though Pollard suggested that as originally constructed the site was some distance from the edge of the cliff, and this may also be true of Daw's Castle.

Berry Cliff is in a similar location on a cliff top, the earthworks enclosing an area about 3.5 ha., but on a larger scale.

Daw's Castle, therefore from its position and form resembles a known post-Roman site in the South-West, and the sites share a type of location which is not common in the British Isles. The presence of a cemetery within it, and a 'Celtic' dedication and holy well 1 km distant at St. Decuman's, gives the site a particular interest in this context. There are additionally indications of an Anglo-Saxon Minster complex immediately to the east.[67]

Summary and conclusions

Although by its very nature field survey alone cannot precisely date earthwork forms, the approach adopted has produced results which can be used in conjunction with other evidence. Using various criteria fifteen sites, of 16% of the total, were found to possess features worth consideration. Eight are Group I sites and the remainder are of Group II, and none of the promontory forts of Group II or smaller enclosures of Group IV showed distinctive or unusual features, although it is clear from other evidence that sites of both types were in use in our period. It is also clear, however, that this does not wholly invalidate the concept of earthwork study for signs of activity in the first to seventh centuries.

Fieldwork can contribute positively towards the study of earthwork sites in the period of study, although it is unlikely to produce conclusive dating evidence of itself. The methods adopted could probably be profitably applied in similar surveys of adjacent counties, although the much less productive Welsh sites may suggest that highland areas in general require a different approach. Clearly in Somerset and other lowland areas we are dealing with a much more complex archaeological pattern at all periods, reflecting a much higher population density, and the observed alterations and additions to hill-forts are one aspect of this. It is still true that the bulk of fieldwork on the post-Roman centuries especially has taken place in Highland Zone areas, and that conclusions about the sizes and types of site in use in this period continue to be influenced by this evidence, whereas the study of the Somerset evidence may well indicate an entirely different picture, of which the weight of emphasis on Group I sites from fieldwork is one indication.

It has been stressed that excavation, to the highest standards and on the largest possible scale, is essential for the elucidation of the questions posed at the beginning of this study. Having therefore explored the limitations of the surface evidence we may proceed to an examination of excavation, considering the particular problems involved in the identification and interpretation of Roman and post-Roman occupations on our sites.

NOTES

1. Summarised in Coles, 1973, 69-82.

2. VCH I 1911, 467-9.

3. Especially Hogg, 1972a and 1972b, Fox, 1952a, 1961.

4. Ordnance Survey 1962, 13-14.

5. Hogg, 1966 especially 31-36 with refs.

6. Jobey, 1966, with refs.

7. The implications of these sites in relation to Somerset will be further discussed in chapter 7.

8. See Appendix A for earthwork descriptions.

9. Alcock, 1971a, 148.

10. Feachem, 1955, 1966; Maxwell, 1969; Laing, 1975a. Alcock 1980a.

11. Maxwell, 1969, 45.

12. Feachem, 1955, 71-5.

13. Hogg, 1973, 83.

14. Miles and Miles, 1974; Saunders, 1973.

15. Alcock, 1956b etc.

16. Feachem, 1956.

17. Raftery, 1969.

18. Simpson, 1964a.

19. Curwen and Williamson, 1931. The date of this refurbishment remains unclear, however.

20. Wheeler, 1932, 63-5.

21. For good examples of this approach see Feachem, 1971 and Curwen and Williamson, 1931.

22. Taylor, 1974a.

23. Descriptions of the visible earthwork in 1970a, 7-9 and 1970b, 339.

24. Fowler et al., 1970, 9.

25. Wheeler, 1943, 120-22.

26. Skinner, B. M. Add. MS. 33646 f.10 (see Appendix B).

27. Hope-Taylor, 1979, 205-209.

28. Tratman, 1927a.

29. Sheail, 1972, chap. 3.

30. Dymond, 1882.

31. Sheail, 1973, 41. Note also Dymond, 1883, 106 suggests a pond. The ploughing avoids it.

32. Collingson, 1791, 310; Colt-Hoare, 1829; VCH 3 9174, 242.

33. Information from Mrs. F. Neale.

34. No. 42, 1893.

35. Lloyd Morgan, 1900.

36. Willmore and Tratman, 1926; Davies and Phillips, 1926. The former plan is inaccurate in outline.

37. They are still used as such, and are shown on Grover's plan of 1868, Grover, 1875.

38. Gray, 1922.

39. Rahtz, 1969, 59.

40. Rahtz, 1969, 60.

41. Rahtz, 1969, 64-66.

42. Rahtz, 1969, plates and R.A.F. FS/CPE/UK/1944 2107.

43. Greswell, 1905, 254. Tithe Award field names.

44. Fox, 1955, 249.

45. Fox, 1955, 81-3.

46. Fox and Fox, 1960, 18-20, especially note 2, p. 18.

47. Collinson, 1791 III, 140. Field work by K. S. Gardner and others continues, however.

48. Tratman, 1963a,11-15.

49. Tratman, 1963a,14.

50. Fox and Fox, 1960, 26.

51. Fox and Fox, 1960, 32.

52. The main points of the following description were agreed on site with K. S. Gardner, P. J. Fowler and myself.

53. Phelps, 1839, 95.

54. Fox and Fox, 1960, 30.

55. Fox and Fox, 1960, 32.

56. Fox and Fox, 1960, 36.

57. Tratman, 1963a, 14.

58. The site has been destroyed by quarrying since Tratman's description (1935).

59. Fowler, 1978, Fig. 5.4 no. 84 and p. 42.

60. Tratman, 1963b.

61. Thorburn, 1925, 280.

62. No. 53, 1963, 19.

63. Page, 1890, 241.

64. Burrow, 1924, 140.

65. Pollard, 1966. SY 104 860.

66. VCH 1906, 575. SY 188 881.

67. Ex inf R. W. Dunning, Victoria County History of Somerset.

CHAPTER 5

THE EVIDENCE OF EXCAVATION

Excavation strategies on hillfort and hill-top sites have been, until recent years, primarily concerned with the examination of limited areas of the defences and, less frequently, with small portions of the interiors. The aims of such excavations have normally been limited to establishing the chronological range of occupation and chronological or cultural links with other sites. The greater financial resources of recent years have enabled large continuous areas of the defences and interiors of a number of hillforts to be examined, with major implications for Iron Age studies.[1] Among these relatively large-scale excavations were those at two of the Somerset Cadburys, where in both cases the post-Iron Age aspects of the sites were, exceptionally, the primary targets of the research programme.

Assessment of the value of the excavated data for our present purposes must therefore take two factors into account. The first is the stated or implicit research aims of the excavators themselves, the majority of whom will, since the 1920s at least, have investigated hillfort sites on the presumption that they contain data relevant to Iron Age studies; the second, the limitations of the excavation techniques employed. Consideration of these points is preliminary to the discussions which follow in chapters 6 and 7.

Hillforts have been natural targets for excavation programmes since the early nineteenth century. Early investigators, locally typified by Skinner and Warre, undertook excavations to confirm preconceived notions, an endeavour in which they were normally successful.[2] Excavations of this nature tended to be of small size and, at this stage, in the interior of sites rather than on the defences, with a minimum of recording other than the mere listing of the objects found.

The first excavation to approach modern standards of recording and objectivity was that of Worlebury by Dymond and Tomkins.[3] Previously, Warre had opened a number of the interior pits, and had argued that the site was prehistoric, employing anthropological parallels to support his interpretation.[4] He linked observed archaeological data uncritically to known historical circumstances, associating Roman material and skeletons with a presumed massacre subsequent to the Battle of Dyrham in c. 577. Dymond and Tomkins were sceptical of these claims on both stratigraphical and artifactual grounds, finding no support for them in their own work. Their approach to the data was far more rigorous, involving surveying and elevation drawing, and the selective examination of the defences and pits. They did not, however, open up large areas of the interior. Their approach reflects a much greater appreciation of the limitations of archaeological data.

91

A further advance in the excavation methods applied to hillforts came with H. St. George Gray's attempted application of Pitt-Rivers' axioms to various Somerset sites on behalf of the Somerset Archaeological and Natural History Society. Gray published accounts of a number of hillfort excavations between 1904 and 1930.[5] There was, however, no coherent excavation policy. The reasons for the choices of Smalldown, Norton and Cadbury Tickenham were not wholly academic, being related to the itinerary of the Somerset Society's Archaeological summer excursions.

The general emphasis of Gray's work was to cut sections through the defences in all cases except Kingsdown (where the site was sufficiently small for most of the interior to be excavated). This indicates Gray's intention of obtaining a dateable structural sequence, although the reliance he placed upon ditch deposits for dating evidence would not now be accepted. The examination of the interiors was evidently not regarded as sufficiently rewarding, the narrow trenches favoured by Gray being incapable of producing coherent plans of features, and where he attempted area excavation at Kingsdown his techniques were clearly inadequate. This traditional concentration on the defences of hillforts is a greatly distorting factor in the evaluation of the extent of hillfort utilisation in our period—Roman and post-Roman activity which did not alter or make use of the defences may have gone undetected on the sites examined in this way. Only large-scale internal examination of sites can conclusively demonstrate that they were not so utilised.

Any 'rescue' element was absent from these excavations, since although it is clear from Gray's accounts that parts of both Norton and South Cadbury were under plough, he did not examine the areas affected. The first excavation for which the immediate stimulus was the destruction of the evidence was that of Bury Hill. In this case quarrying was encroaching on the interior of the camp, a threat whose extent and character would now probably result in the stripping of the area immediately affected. It is indicative of the emphasis placed on sections and on small-scale sampling of sites at that time that this was not done. An unthreatened portion of the defences was sectioned, and the sites of two of the three other cuttings were so far from the quarry edge that they still survive.

With the exception of Norton Fitzwarren, all excavations until the mid 1960s were small in scale, and not designed to elucidate the character of the interior occupation. The decision to undertake programmes of excavation involving the opening up of large areas of the interiors of the two hillforts of South Cadbury and Cadcong in the late 1960s was influenced by a number of factors which had previously affected hillfort study in the area or in Britain as a whole. The first and most important of these was the desire to explore the post-Roman aspects of the two sites, by the presence of imported Mediterranean pottery in surface collections from South Cadbury and from small-scale trial excavations at Cadcong. An academic and popular interest in the Western British sites of the period AD 400-700 was combined with the recognition that the slight structures and shallow stratification to be expected on such sites could only be dealt with by large-scale open-area excavation, the adoption of which in British archaeology has been traced by Barker but which had not, in 1966 when South Cadbury began, been applied to hillforts to any great extent.[6] Previously Alcock had intended to examine the whole interior of the much smaller site of Dinas Powys by this method, but had been prevented by logistical problems for achieving this.[7] Despite the unsatisfactory preservation of post-Roman features and stratification within the defences of Dinas Powys, the excavation demonstrated clearly that anything less than the 50% examined would probably have failed to locate and elucidate the slight traces of buildings which provide part of the supporting evidence for Alcock's interpretation of the site.

The implications of this are clear. The methods adopted for the excavation of Somerset hillforts until the two Cadbury projects would not necessarily have detected slight timber buildings or the comparatively small quantities of post-Roman material generally encountered on sites in Western Britain, or subtleties of rampart construction and alteration. Roman or post-Roman additions to pre-existing defences are naturally the most vulnerable to later disturbance in any case, and may leave traces so slight as to be virtually undetectable except in large cuttings. At South Cadbury instability of the front of the inner bank in site J (1969) resulted in the major part of the late or post-Roman bank falling down the slope in antiquity, leaving a 'tail' of bank material only 2 m in length and 20 cm deep in the south side of the cutting, and not detectable at all on the north.[8] Such slight features may either have disappeared on sites with similar topography to South Cadbury,[9] or have not been detected where excavation took place. The former existence of vanished Iron Age ramparts could be inferred at South Cadbury from the accumulation of deposits behind and below the surviving phases, and data of this kind may enable late or post-Roman enclosure banks to be postulated on sites where direct structural evidence is lacking.

Of the twenty-seven Somerset hillforts (30% of the total) and the five known Roman and post-Roman hill-top sites which have been excavated, only the extensive stripping of the temples at Brean Down, Pagans Hill, Henley Wood and Lamyatt, of the summit of Glastonbury Tor, the examination of 6% of the area of South Cadbury and 5% of Cadbury Congresbury and the near total excavation of Kingsdown can in any way be regarded as samples of the sites useful for our present purpose. In addition, none of the seven excavated sites which failed to produce Roman or post-Roman material on excavation can be wholly dismissed as candidates for occupation in the period under consideration on this basis alone.

The range of available information from past excavations on our Somerset sites is thus very restricted, as indeed it is in most areas of the British Isles. The dating of defensive schemes, and the recovery of groups of usefully associated groups of artifacts, have been the most explicitly defined aims of past work. Other aspects of hillfort studies have been barely examined, and interest in post-Iron Age problems was minimal until the 1960s. In order to put this material into perspective, aspects of both the South Cadbury and Cadcong excavations will be discussed. The Cadcong material is being prepared for publication, and only selected aspects will be covered here. The aim here is to outline methods developed for the recovery and academic presentation of the Cadcong data, comparing these where appropriate with those at South Cadbury. The technical difficulty of expressing the complex and shallow stratification and its relationship to artifactual and environmental evidence in the two-dimensional medium of drawings or through tabulated lists has been considerable. The ways in which this has been attempted are discussed here because they are felt to have a methodological importance for future work, though as models they are unlikely to remain wholly satisfactory for any length of time.

Excavation strategy at Cadcong and South Cadbury

The 1959 excavations at Cadcong were designed to locate a Roman site thought to exist on the hill, and the discovery of Bi and Bii amphorae in one of the test holes just to the north of the highest point of the hill influenced the choice of location of the 1968 area.[10] The success of this cutting in locating two structures of post-Roman date in turn resulted in the decision to extend this area outward to the north, south, east and west, so that a continuous area of 1375 square metres had by 1973 been completed. By virtue of its location this excavation programme has examined many structural aspects of the site, investigating both the interior occupation, the stone perimeter banks and an entrance way.

Apart from the 1959 excavations, there is, however, no way at present of assessing the extent to which the density of occupation in the excavated area relates to that in the remainder of the site. In this context we must consider the rather different approach adopted at South Cadbury, where larger financial resources available enabled both a larger total area (7,700 square metres), and a number of different areas to be sampled.[11] The percentage of the total area examined is not much different in each case, but the disposition of the South Cadbury cuttings was not solely dictated by post-Roman considerations. Despite the greatly increased research effort, direct comparison between even these two sites is considerably circumscribed. This difficulty can best be appreciated if the types of evidence from the two sites are considered together under various headings. Detailed discussion of Cadcong will chiefly relate to the SE part of the excavated area (Green Cutting), mostly excavated under the writer's supervision in 1973. Technical description of the Cadcong excavation method is also included here, as its understanding is an essential preliminary to the consideration of the Roman material in chapter 6.

Cadcong and South Cadbury—Types of evidence from excavation

a) Stratification and soils

At South Cadbury a long history of ploughing and the topography of the hilltop had combined to remove virtually all vertical stratification from the summit plateau. The summit area, upon which the evidence for fifth-sixth century buildings was found, thus lacked any floor levels or other occupation surfaces, while the complex structural and erosional history of the area of the defences combined to limit the exploration of these areas.[12] At Cadcong apparently undisturbed stratification was present, but was generally shallow, averaging only 20 cm deep in areas without major rock-cut features. The natural soil is an alkaline reddish clay loam whose clay content and red colour increase with depth.

Stratigraphic units at Cadcong were distinguished by variations in soil colour and texture, and by the quantity, size and degree of weathering of stone in the soil matrix. For the most part such variations were extremely slight and could only be seen when large areas were exposed. Vertical sections were only of use for stratigraphical analysis where deep deposits were present (Fig. 12). Nor was the significance of the defined units in relation to human activity at all evident, since it may be suspected that worm action and other natural processes account for many observed colour and texture variations.

Because of this difficulty it was found necessary to adopt an arbitrary terminology for these areas of the excavation where clear stratigraphic units could not be readily defined. The procedure was to isolate four or five layers —in effect stages of definition—in successive trowellings of the whole cutting extending vertically from immediately below the turf to the bedrock.

A crucial stratigraphic problem was that of identifying utilised or artificially laid surfaces related to the 5th-7th century occupation, in order to understand the interior layout of the site, the purpose of the many rock-cut features and the significance of various artifact distributions discussed below. In some cases, such as with the rectangular Structure I (Fig. 11)[14] it is possible to suggest that the natural bedrock may have been used as an interior surface or floor, but the majority of the structures defined contained no direct evidence of this kind. The difficulty was especially acute within the 'entrance' through the N-S enclosure bank in Green Cutting (Fig. 13). There was no doubt that a gap existed in the banks at this point, since the southern bank terminated at the top of a vertical drop of about 50 cm, and the terminal of the northern bank was defined by rows of large limestone blocks. It was therefore anticipated that evidence for a worn or laid surface for some type of traffic, and perhaps for gate structures, would be encountered, especially since such features had recently been identified at South Cadbury.[15]

Three successive layers were defined in the area, but only the middle, GF133b, had characteristics which suggested that it had been consolidated for traffic. On trowelling it was marginally more compact than the overlying material, and on its surface were found two iron objects possibly from a gate hinge or from a vehicle. This evidence was however far from satisfactory, and understanding of both the natural and human-derived processes which have affected the Cadcong stratification is still at an early stage.

b) Rock-cut and other excavated features

At Both South Cadbury and Cadcong a significant part of the evidence for occupation in the period AD 300-700 took the form of excavations into underlying deposits or into the parent bedrock. At South Cadbury the features on the summit, interpreted as the postholes and wall trench for a post-Roman hall structure, were cut into the bedrock and into the fill of earlier rock-cut features. The absence of vertical stratification in this area forced the structural interpretation of these features to rely on formal similarities between them and on the use of datable finds in the fill of other features in the area to eliminate them as portions of the structure.[16]

The greater and more consistent depth of the stratification at Cadcong did not however greatly assist in the interpretation and dating of rock-cut features here. In the area excavated in 1968 the stratification was thinner than elsewhere and the two major structures, I and II (Fig. 11), could be so interpreted because of their coherent plans, and were dated to the post-Roman period by the finds in the deposits with which they were filled.

95

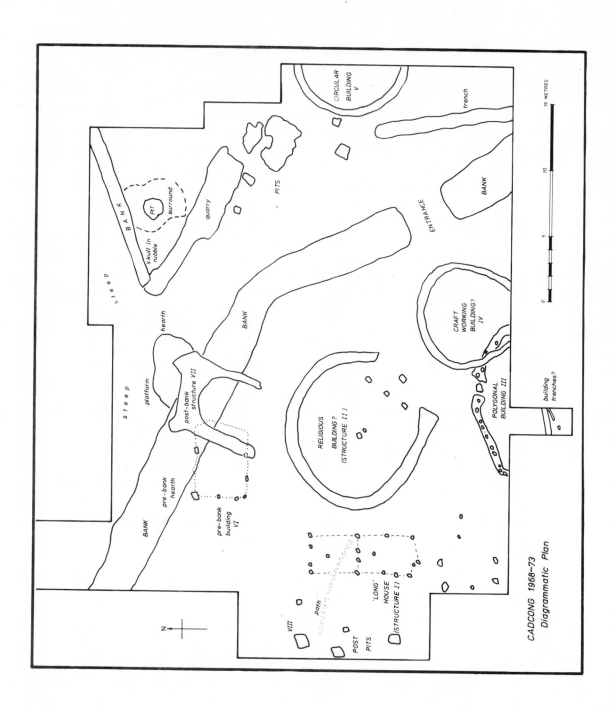

Fig. 11 Cadcong; Preliminary diagrammatic interpretation plan of
excavated area, 1976 (by P. A. Rahtz)

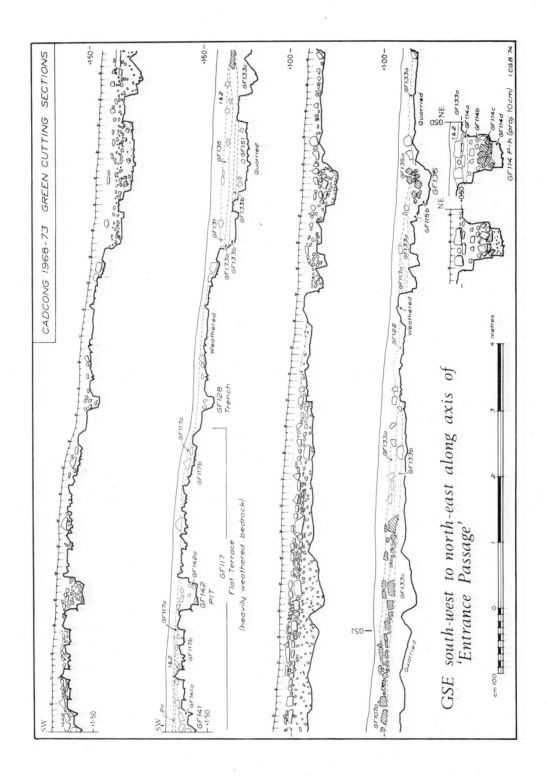

CADCONG 1968-73 GREEN CUTTING SECTIONS

GSE south-west to north-east along axis of 'Entrance Passage'

Fig. 12 Cadcong; Section GS E

Fig. 13 Cadcong; Section GS B

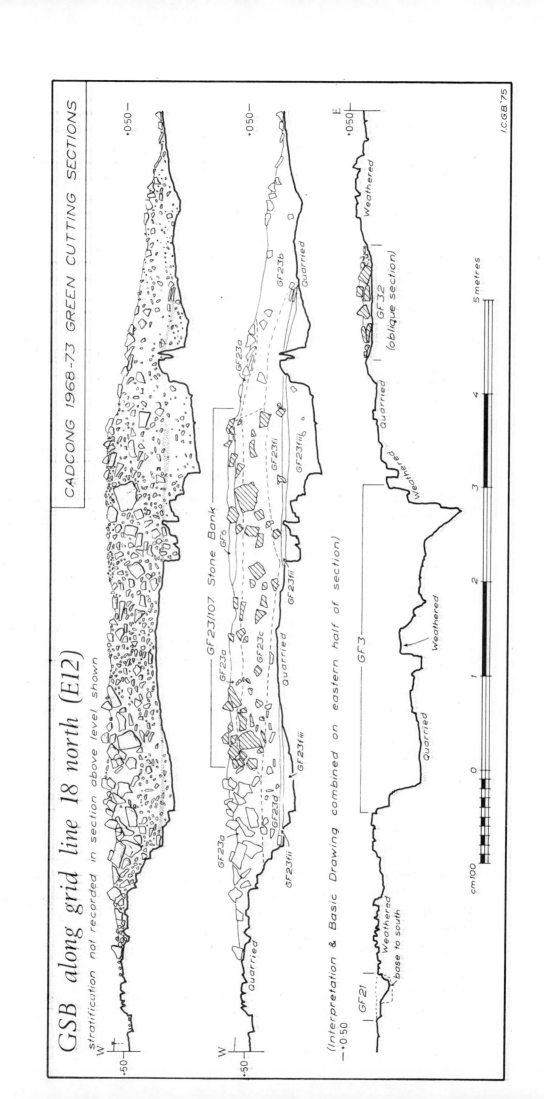

GSB along grid line 18 north (E12)

stratification not recorded in section above level shown

CADCONG 1968-73 GREEN CUTTING SECTIONS

I.C.G.B. '75

In the deeper parts of Green Cutting the situation was more complex. In only one area, beneath the bank north of the entrance, was a feature identified which could be regarded as separating the pre- and post-Roman stratification and features—a fine stone-free humic soil interpreted as a decayed turf line (Fig. 14, GF107h). Finds from the deposit below this (GF133c) were almost entirely prehistoric and lay directly on the bedrock, suggesting that GF 133c was a developed Iron Age or earlier soil.

When finally uncovered, great variations in the character of the bedrock were observed. In the deeper areas of the cutting the rock was unweathered and sharp and appeared to have been quarried to create smooth surfaces in some areas. In the shallower areas it was rounded and easily dislodged along different planes. This contrast might simply be accounted for by differential percolation of humic acids from the topsoil leaving the deeper areas unaffected, were it not for the fact that some of the deeper areas had been modified by human agency and a number of features apparently cut from bedrock level. In the areas so far opened it is difficult to establish the date of this quarrying: the stratigraphic evidence in general favours an Iron Age date. Establishing the date of rock-cut features has proved difficult because of the lack of readily observable stratification, and a number remain unassigned. The value of datable finds within such features is particularly limited unless seen against the general distribution of finds on the site as a whole. It is impossible in the majority of cases to distinguish between, for instance, the packing of a posthole and its natural or deliberate silting subsequent to its structural use. The three-dimensional recording of the majority of the finds thus formed an essential element in the analysis of the stratigraphic sequence.

c) Structures

The interior buildings at the two sites were all apparently of wood or other perishable materials, and the major upstanding features in both cases were sets of linear banks. At South Cadbury a single bank constructed after AD 393[17] was shown to have encircled the hilltop; at Cadcong the plateau was similarly enclosed but also in this case bisected by a second bank of which almost 50 m had been examined by 1973 (Fig. 10).

The South Cadbury bank had been first identified in section both from its stratigraphic position and from the presence of dressed stone in its make-up, indicating a Roman or later date. The short lengths of the rampart examined suggested that drystone walling and rubble had formed the basis for a timber framework comprising both vertical and horizontal members.[18]

Definition of the banks at Cadcong was less easy and their nature and function are extremely enigmatic. Where most clearly observed, the cross bank took the form of a low flat-topped spread of rubble up to 5 m wide but normally less than 1 m high. It was differentiated from the surrounding stratification chiefly by the closer-packed nature of the stone. In places the surface was fused by burning into a concreted shattered mass, and the body of the bank was in places delimited by a single or double line of large boulders up to 40 cm across.

Occasional shallow post settings, pieces of charcoal, and the small vertical height of the bank combine to suggest that it supported a superstructure of perishable materials, especially since there is no evidence that the stone element of the whole was substantially higher originally.

Assessment of structural evidence from Cadcong, as much as that from the general stratigraphy and from the rock-cut features, is clearly hampered by the very incomplete survival of organic materials. It is evident that the majority of the physical elements of the site were originally of wood or other perishable materials, but the soil conditions and the nature of the bedrock and rubble derived from it render the identification of traces of these elements oxtremely difficult, despite the undisturbed nature of the site and the considerable depth of deposits in some areas. Sites at which this material is preserved, such as crannogs and some forts, [19] will clearly supply a range of data almost wholly lacking at Cadcong and South Cadbury.

d) Finds

Soil conditions at Cadcong, however, did favour the preservation of animal bone, ceramics, metal, glass and slag or various kinds. The importance of the datable finds for the understanding of the site sequence and the significance of horizontal links across the site have already been stressed. Finds can potentially answer questions related to the social status and interior organisation of a site, and both these aspects will be discussed in the following chapters, but at this point the way in which the material was recorded and presented for publication will be discussed, followed by the treatment of the other types of data.

The finds were recorded three-dimensionally, with the exception of the most common, animal bone, which was merely recorded by weight, by stratigraphic unit and, in the case of the extensive layers, by one-metre squares. Some potential information has therefore been lost in relation to the faunal evidence, but the large quantity of fragmentary bone made its three-dimensional plotting an impossible task with available resources. Plotting of finds was done at the same scale as the basic planning in order that the two could be directly compared. From this data overall distributions of different classes of data were produced at 1:100 scale, and these will be considered in the next chapter. The quantity of this material is such that any multivariate analysis or comparison of distributions and their relationship to features and layers now is largely beyond manual retrieval.

Cadcong—presentation of excavated data

The finds are relatdd to the stratification most directly through the Feature Tables (Fig. 14). These are the fundamental record of the defined stratigraphy of the site, possibly for storage in archive rather than for publication, and are essentially a digest of the information on the pro forma record sheets, drawn plans and sections, and finds registers.

Visual presentation of the spatial relationships between the various elements of the site has proved more difficult to achieve. The solution adopted has been to produce a series of Definition Plans (Figs. 15-18) which show the site at stratigraphically significant stages, these being decided upon after the basic sequence had been worked out. The definition plans are therefore interpretative to some extent and are edited versions of the field drawings. Plan A, showing the features encountered immediately below the topsoil, is in

GREEN FEATURES

TABLE -

DIMENSIONS	DEPTH	PLAN	SECTION	NEG NO	FINDS SUMMARY	INTERPRETATION	FEATURE NUMBER	IDENTIFICATION	GRID REFERENCE	CONTEXT	DESCRIPTION
1.80 NS 1m EW	c5 cms	GPA	-	-	S/stone(1)Flint(4)ABCH(1) BC(1)Bii(1)RB(1)PRIA(1)	Soil accumulation. Post abandonment.	GF1	Soil patch	E12 14/15-19/15	Redder soil within layer 2.	Red stone-free soil. Sub. Div. into a & b.
40x40 cms	c10 cms	GPA	-	-	Stone sample		GF2	Discrete patch of oolitic limestone.	E12 08/16	Base of layer 2, above layer 3.	3 small pieces of oolitic limestone.
2.2m NS 4.6m EW	1m	GPA. BC	GSA see also YSC	D18, 80	See individual layers	Pit or quarry.	GF3	Large excavation in bedrock	E12 14/19 (centre)	First defined at base of layer 2 as patch of stone-free soil within weathered bedrock edges – YF100/128.	Sub-rectangular hole in bedrock with irregular quarried sides and bottom. Bedrock at lip weathered, remainder unweathered.
as above	40cms max	GPA	GSA	D12	Pennant(8)st(4)Flint(1) Slag(2)BC(1)IR(2)Med(3) Glass(1)RB(2)?D(1)A(1)	Accumulation in top of pit.	a	Soil patch	ditto	Base of layer 2 delimited by bedrock edges, above GF36 = YF100a,b.	Red-brown stone-free soil.
as above	40-10 cms	GPB	GSA	D10, 12	Pennant(5)Flint(1)BC(1) Glass(1)Bii(2)	Deliberate backfilling?	b	Stone layer	ditto	Below GF3a, above GF3c&d – YF128b.	Large weathered CL blocks in brown soil with lrg.bone frge
2m NS 80 cms EW	20 cms	-	GSA	D12	Glass(1)	Weathering.	c	Stone and soil patch	E12 15/19	Wedge on east side of feature only, below GF3b and above GF3d.	Small angular CL in reddish soil.
2m NS	25cms max	-	GSA	D12	Pennant(1)Slag(1) PRIA(1)Animal bone.	Interruption in silting or deliberate backfilling with humic material	d	Soil wedge	E12 14/19 (centre)	Below GF3b and GF3c wedge commencing from east side of feature and becoming thinner to west, not filling feature. Above GF3f = YF128c YF100c.	Dark brown worm-sorted humic soil with a few isolated large stones and much bone, esp in SE corner of GF3.
	20cms	-	GSA	D12	Glass(1)BB(2)MT(1)		e	Stone and soil wedge	E12 15/19	Wedge of material at east and W sites of GF3 belo. GF3d above GF3g.	Brown clayey soil with angular CL.
1m NS 2m EW	40cms	-	GSA	D12	PRIA(1)		f	Stone and soil layer	E12 14/19 (centre)	Below GF3d on bedrock in lowest part of GF3, YF100d but partly overlying 3g.	Large unweathered CL blocks with some brown soil.
1m NS 1.30 EW	30cms	-	GSA	D12	PRIA(5)RB(10)	Primary silting? Assoc with 40 :B sherds from 10 find-spots.	g	Bottom layer within GF3		Wedge only in E part of GF3 below GF3d,e,f, and on bedrock – YF125d.	Sticky red clayey soil with close packed small angular CL no bone.

Fig. 14 Cadcong; Part of feature table, Green Cutting

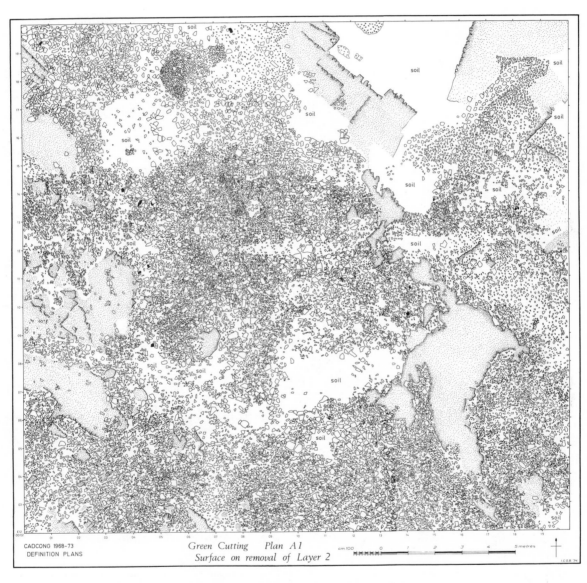

soil soil soil soil soil soil soil soil soil soil soil soil soil soil soil soil soil soil

CADCONG 1968-73
DEFINITION PLANS

Green Cutting   Plan A1
Surface on removal of Layer 2

cm 100   0   1   2   3   4   5 metres

Fig. 15   Cadcong;   Green Cutting Definition Plan A1

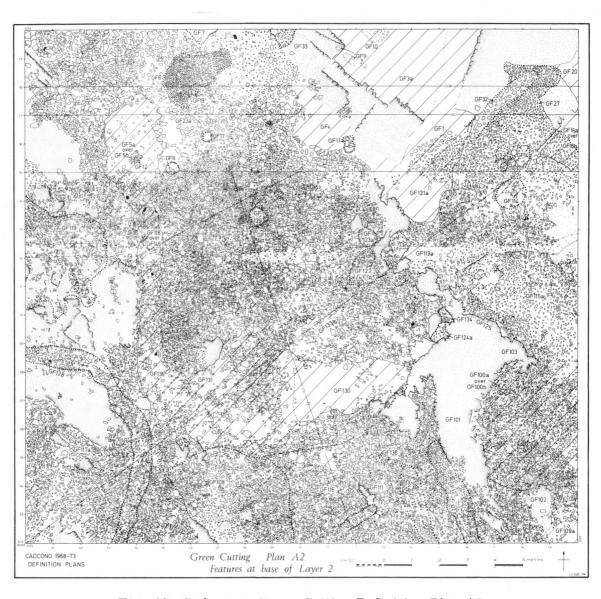

Fig. 16 Cadcong; Green Cutting Definition Plan A2

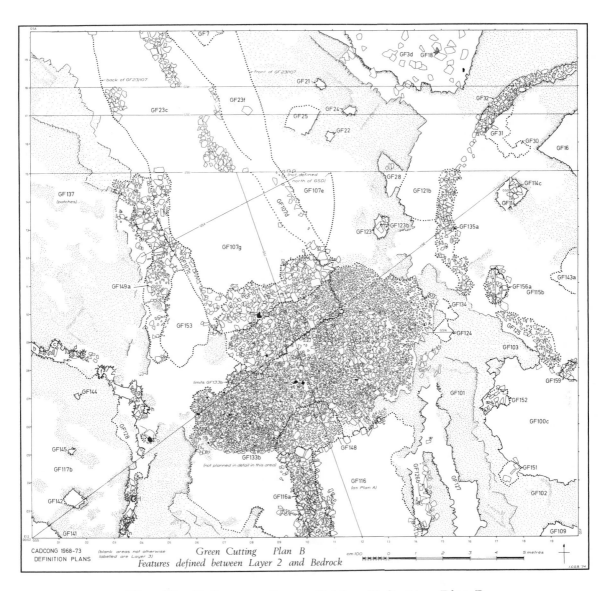

Fig. 17   Cadcong;   Green Cutting Definition Plan B

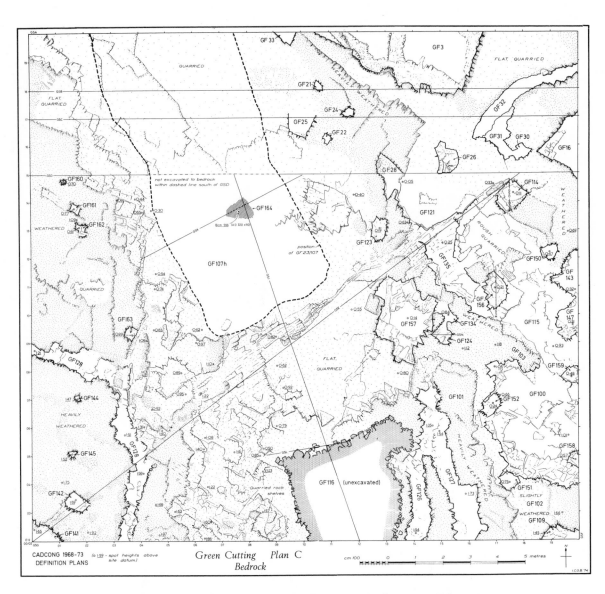

Fig. 18   Cadcong;   Green Cutting Definition Plan C

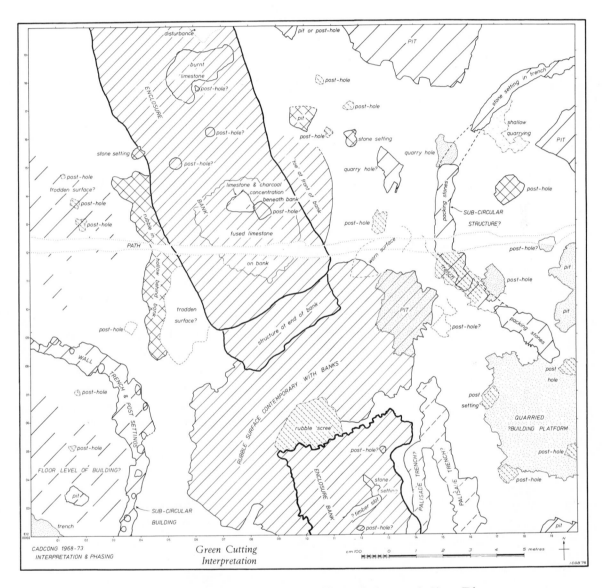

Fig. 19 Cadcong; Green Cutting Interpretation Plan

this sense the most objective of the plans, the bedrock plan, C, being somewhat less so, and the intermediate plan, B, which attempts to show the major features associated with the main occupation phase, is much more selective.

Vertical relationships are expressed in sections (Figs. 12 and 13), laid across areas felt to contain particularly significant stratification. This procedure is clearly highly selective and subjective and is based on predictions about the site made at an early stage in the excavation. An ideal alternative to this procedure would be the three-dimensional recording of each stratigraphic unit, enabling sections to be constructed in any desired direction. Because of the shallowness and ambiguity of much of the stratification the sections are probably the least useful of the various recording methods used since the basic understanding of the site could only be effected by examining features in plan.[20]

On the basis of tables, plans, and sections a phased Interpretation Plan (Fig. 19) and a stratigraphic account of each cutting was produced. The integration of the accounts from the separate cuttings is the next major process in the site analysis, the aim being to produce an overall picture of the history of the excavated area.

Discussion

The post-Roman evidence from Cadbury Congresbury is a great deal more complex than that from any other Somerset site, both in its basic stratigraphic data and in the amount of structural evidence it contains. Whereas at South Cadbury only three major structures, the timber aisled building and perhaps other structures on the summit plateau, the enclosure bank and the gate tower are assignable to the AD 400-700 period, the continuous area at Cadcong contains at least eight buildings and other structures. Direct comparison between these two sites, and between them and Glastonbury Tor, where later disturbance drastically reduced the survival of structural evidence, is possible only to a limited extent, even had the data from these three sites been published in comparable ways.

Even such a basic issue as the precise extent of the area occupied by buildings is as yet uncertain, though the existence of the delimiting banks at South Cadbury and Cadcong, and the steep gradients around all three sites, do at least define the potential area. The arrangement of the interior space of the sites is unknown: at Cadcong the past excavation strategy in effect sacrificed an assessment of the overall distribution of features within the site to a better understanding of one continuous area, and the value of this strategy will be discussed further in the final chapter. The larger available resources at South Cadbury enabled a number of cuttings to be opened on a reasonable scale, but the selection of these areas was made not on the basis of a sampling procedure for assessing the extent of the post-Roman phase, but in order to examine areas in which important structural and chronological sequences relating the whole history of the site might be anticipated. One cannot therefore suggest that the apparent contrast between the density and complexity of structures at Cadcong and South Cadbury is a significant difference which affects the ultimate interpretation of the sites in functional terms. Comparison of the material culture, as represented in portable artifacts, is however felt to be potentially more valid, and in the next chapter attention is focussed on one particular aspect of the material culture of the Somerset sites, the functional and chronological implications of the presence of Romano-British pottery on hillforts and hilltops.   In contrast to the several studies of the nature, chronology and distribution of imported post-Roman ceramics on sites of the 5th-7th centuries,[21] Romano-British material, commonly also found in these contexts, has been somewhat neglected.   Its interpretation is, however, of considerable importance for the study of settlement in western Britain in this period.

NOTES

1. Guilbert, 1975.

2. B.M. Add. Ms. 33726 f106, 110 (June 1st, 1832).

3. Dymond and Tomkins, 1886.

4. Warre, 1851, 66-7.

5. Gray, 1904, 1908, 1913, 1922, 1924, 1926, 1930.

6. Barker, 1970 and 1977.

7. Alcock, 1963a, 12-13.

8. South Cadbury site J typescript page 5. Typescript and drawings of these two cuttings made available to me in advance of publication by Professor Leslie Alcock, University of Glasgow.

9. Sites where instability and steep slopes have probably resulted in the collapse of large portions of the ramparts are:-

Ham Hill	(1)	Maes Knoll	(5)	Dolebury	(6)
Solsbury	(7)	South Cadbury	(9)	Dundon	(14)
Kings Castle	(64)	Stantonbury	(20)	Wains Hill	(35)
Cannington	(41)	Brent Knoll	(43)		

and at these sites in particular earlier investigators might well have failed to detect traces of later additions to the banks.

10. Fowler, et al., 1970, 9-10. They were also found in other cuttings.

11. Three major areas in the interior, five rampart excavations and the south-western gate area (Alcock, 1971b, fig. 1).

12. Alcock, 1972a, 25, 102-103. Alcock 1980b.

13. The soils have not been fully studied. Cornwall, 1969.

14. Fowler et al., 1970.

15. Alcock, 1972a, plates 77-79.

16. Ibid., p. 79.

17. Cutting J typescript report, p. 2. Coin of Honorius in body of rampart.

18. Alcock, 1968b, 15; 1970b, 17.

19. e.g. Dundurn Med. Arch. 21 (1977), 218 and Alcock pers. comm.

20. Compare South Cadbury, where the post-Roman defences were identified in section in the first instance (Alcock, 1972a, 66-67; 1968b, 14-15).

21. Summarised in Thomas, 1976a with refs.

CHAPTER 6

ROMAN MATERIAL FROM HILLFORTS AND HILL-TOP SITES

Background

Roman material has been widely encountered in British hillfort excavations and in quarrying and cultivation. Given the abundance of Roman material culture, with mass-produced pottery, glass and metalwork, it is not surprising that some Roman artifacts found their way onto hillforts even if these had been abandoned for all but infrequent use. The density of Roman finds within a hillfort may be no greater than that of any equivalent surrounding area, where it would have little significance as a pointer to settlement or any continuous activity; it is only the context of the find which appears to give greater weight to it. Criteria for deciding on the 'significance' of Roman finds from hillforts have remained highly subjective, and the analysis in this chapter may go some way to deciding between the various interpretations which can be put forward.

Although a certain amount of 'random' Roman material is thus to be anticipated in hillforts, there is sufficient evidence from a number of sites to demonstrate that more intensive activity did take place. The structural remains of temples and a range of other building types of Roman date provide the clearest instances of this.[1] It is evident, however, that the interpretation of much Roman material from hillforts has been heavily influenced by assumptions concerning the attitude of the Roman government towards hillforts. The historical and archaeological evidence for the capture and slighting of hillforts, in particular Maiden Castle, by Roman troops, and for the diminution of activity at the hillfort in the early Roman period[2] have provided a model for what is anticipated at most Iron Age hillforts. It is assumed that the threat posed by these defended enclosures prompted a Roman reaction involving the capture of the hillforts and the forcible dispersal of their populations,[3] the sites then being for the most part abandoned. While it is clear that the defences of many hillforts ceased to be maintained and the archaeological evidence from the interiors, where it is available, suggests a decline in activity, it may be unjustifiable to assume that this was a direct result of Roman military policy. Similarly, there is a persistent tendency to view evidence for use within the Roman period in terms of exceptional historic situations and a low level of social attainment. The latest example of this view may be cited as typical:

> 'In the recent excavations Period III (the mid third century A.D.) seems to be characterised by no structures of great importance. This may suggest.... that this site was re-used by squatters in response to the same conditions that resulted in the building of Gatcombe's defensive wall at around this time'.[4]

The assumptions here are that a return to hillforts in the Roman period can only be a response to external military threat or other disturbance, and that occupation at this time is by 'squatters'. This frequently used term has clear overtones of squalor, illegality and impermanence.

111

In Wales the quantity of Roman finds from a number of hillforts led Wheeler to suggest a military occupation of the sites and possibly construction of the defences themselves in the second century AD.[5] Reconsideration of the evidence has resulted in the abandonment of this hypothesis, on the twin grounds that construction of the defences can be shown in almost all cases to be a pre-Roman phenomenon, and that the Roman finds from within the forts are neither sufficiently numerous nor sufficiently homogenous chronologically to support it.[6] While, as has been seen above, the available evidence from Somerset hillforts indicates an Iron Age origin for their defensive schemes, the concept of a military occupation of some sites during the later Roman period is a possibility to be kept in mind, even though it may be considered inherently less likely than other models.

Some Roman material has been taken to indicate that the choice of hill-fort sites was influenced by their remoteness from official control. The counterfeiting of coinage which took place at Coygan Camp in the late third century is the major example of this, though the other evidence from the site at this time suggests a permanent settlement rather than a short-lived and presumably illegal establishment for forgery.[7] In this instance the small hill-fort is assumed to be 'isolated' in the contemporary Roman landscape and therefore regarded as appropriate for this type of activity—the 'controlling model' here being that of the general enforced abandonment of hillforts in the Roman period. If this interpretation is valid, then many Iron Age forts may have been used in this way, perhaps functioning as refuges for those outside the law.[8]

Other explanations for the presence of Roman material in hillforts are those linked to casual or agricultural use. Manuring of a hillfort interior converted to arable use in the Roman period, as may have occurred at Maiden Castle and South Cadbury,[9] could result in quantities of sherds being deposited on the hilltop, and this might well seem a plausible origin for much of the known material. Similarly, casual frequentation by herdsmen or even by 'picnickers' provide other contexts in which sherds or other artifacts might have been deposited during the Roman era.

Major re-use of the interiors of hillforts can in several instances be shown to have a religious purpose. Religious use, frequently held to indicate in some sense a continuity of function from the Iron Age, can only be confirmed when structural or artifactual remains indicative of masonry temples and associated buildings in an essentially Roman style can be located. Positive evidence for temples of this type has been discovered at at least seven hill-forts,[10] though they may be suspected at many more where Roman material has been found in quantity without direct evidence of structures. The slight nature of some rural religious buildings, especially those in the circular tradition, adds support to this possibility which, as will be discussed in chapter 7, supplies a radically alternative group of hypotheses to those normally advanced to explain hillfort use after c. AD 450.

The classic example of Lydney[11] shows how complex some of these certainly religious hillfort sites may be, and a strong 'secular' element must also be anticipated even in cases such as this. The small number of extensively excavated hillfort interiors has, however, prevented the adequate definition of any Roman agricultural settlement within them. Roman sites of villa status have even so been located inside hillforts, in addition to structures suggestive of a lower social level, such as the enclosures at Cissbury.[12] A range of settlement usage is probably involved here.

Some classes of material, in particular coin hoards, may be indicative of a neglect of the hillforts which contain them, an abandoned hillfort being seen as an appropriate place for the concealment of valuables. This interpretation would minimise the importance of the hillfort in the Roman landscape other than as a landmark.

This brief review of the explanations which may be put forward to account for the presence of Roman material in hillforts normally assumes that the material is representative of activity within the Roman period. This assumption restricts to a very large extent the types of explanation which are put forward; if it is not made a different range of possibilities is opened up.

It has long been noted that Roman material frequently occurs on sites or in phases on sites which, on other grounds, can be regarded as post-Roman. This material is in these cases in some sense 'residual' in that it is not in its original cultural and chronological context, but this term may be interpreted in various ways. The vast quantities of Roman sherds and coins lost during the Roman period will find their way into later contexts merely by disturbance of Roman levels or by casual collection from Roman sites. Other than potentially demonstrating continuity in the use of land, or an antiquarian curiosity on the part of some individual, this view does not give the Roman material any real significane as part of the material culture of the later period.

Even if the Roman material is residual in this sense, however, the specific circumstances of its appearance on a later site are of importance. Was it, for example, incorporated in soil or other material being deliberately brought to the site, or merely already present on the site and disturbed by later activity? If the former is the case, then the context is essentially a secondary one and the Roman material provides merely a terminus post quem for the activity which brought it to the site. Such a situation would immediately raise questions about the degree of deliberate selection of the Roman material by those who transported it.

The collection of Roman artifacts for use as raw material, curiosities, souvenirs or talismans in the post-Roman period may have been very widespread. Metalwork, coins and glass in particular are all thought to have been utilised in this way,[13] and various uses may have been found for pottery sherds, even if complete vessels were not obtainable. This body of material would clearly have been readily available in the fifth, sixth and later centuries in Somerset. Even if it is considered that occupation of the villas and larger settlements ceased in the fifth century, their sites would probably remain evident for a considerable time. Roman material in hill-top locations may therefore be associated with the collapse of Roman material culture and disruption of the settlement pattern in the fifth and later centuries—Roman sites being used as 'quarries' for artifacts destined for other uses.

An alternative to these hypotheses would be that Roman material in post-Roman contexts is indicative of a real continuity of usage of these artifacts.

This is, of the various alternatives outlined above, probably the most difficult to demonstrate, but is at the same time the one with the most far-reaching implications for Migration Period archaeology in Britain, since it may call in question the conventional dating of a number of 'late Roman' sites, as well as current views on cultural change at this time.

The length of time for which Roman material continued to be a) produced and b) used for its original purposes after the ending of readily datable contexts on Roman sites in the early fifth century (because of the cessation of coin circulation) is a perennial archaeological problem, although attempts to resolve it have been concentrated on sites which have a long and continuous Roman history. Frere's essentially stratigraphic argument for the longevity of civic activity at Verulamium demonstrates the very great difficulties of establishing an absolute chronology on these sites after the ending of the coin series.[14]

On sites newly occupied in the fifth or later centuries, however, we may, theoretically at least be in a better position to assess this problem. An association of Roman with later material provides the necessary contexts for studying the possibility that the material culture of the people utilising the site included artifacts more appropriate to late fourth-century sites. The situation envisaged is that these artifacts were being used for their original purpose, implying the presence of pottery as complete vessels rather than as sherds, and metal ornaments or tools still serving the purpose for which they were designed. Despite the addition of some later elements, such as typologically more developed metalwork types or imported pottery, such a material culture would deserve the term 'sub-Roman' if its existence could be positively demonstrated.

It may be expecting too much of the evidence to attempt an extrapolation from sites where post-Roman evidence supplies some form of independent dating for Roman artifacts, to those where Roman material only has been found. Possibly, however, close study and comparison of assemblages will eventually demonstrate that 'sub-Roman' collections of ostensibly purely 'Roman' artifacts show features which distinguish them from late fourth or early fifth-century groups, and link them to Roman material from sites otherwise securely dated to later centuries. As yet groups of comparable material are not widely available, but as the problem is such a potentially crucial one it is desirable to explore the possibilities and to outline ways in which data might be collected to solve it.

If we can at some future date demonstrate that Roman material, and particularly perhaps pottery, was in common utilitarian use (at least in some areas) in the fifth, sixth or seventh centuries by people who otherwise possessed no distinctive surviving artifacts, this would put the problem of 'British survival' in particular in a new light. It must also cause some reassessment of the situation in the fifth and later centuries, especially in Western Lowland Britain. The excavated material from Cadbury Congresbury is in such a form as to make preliminary examination of this problem possible.

There are therefore various possible explanations for the presence of artifacts of Romano-British origin in hillforts, and these can be summarised:-

Fig. 20   Cadcong;   Models of Roman Pottery Use and Deposition

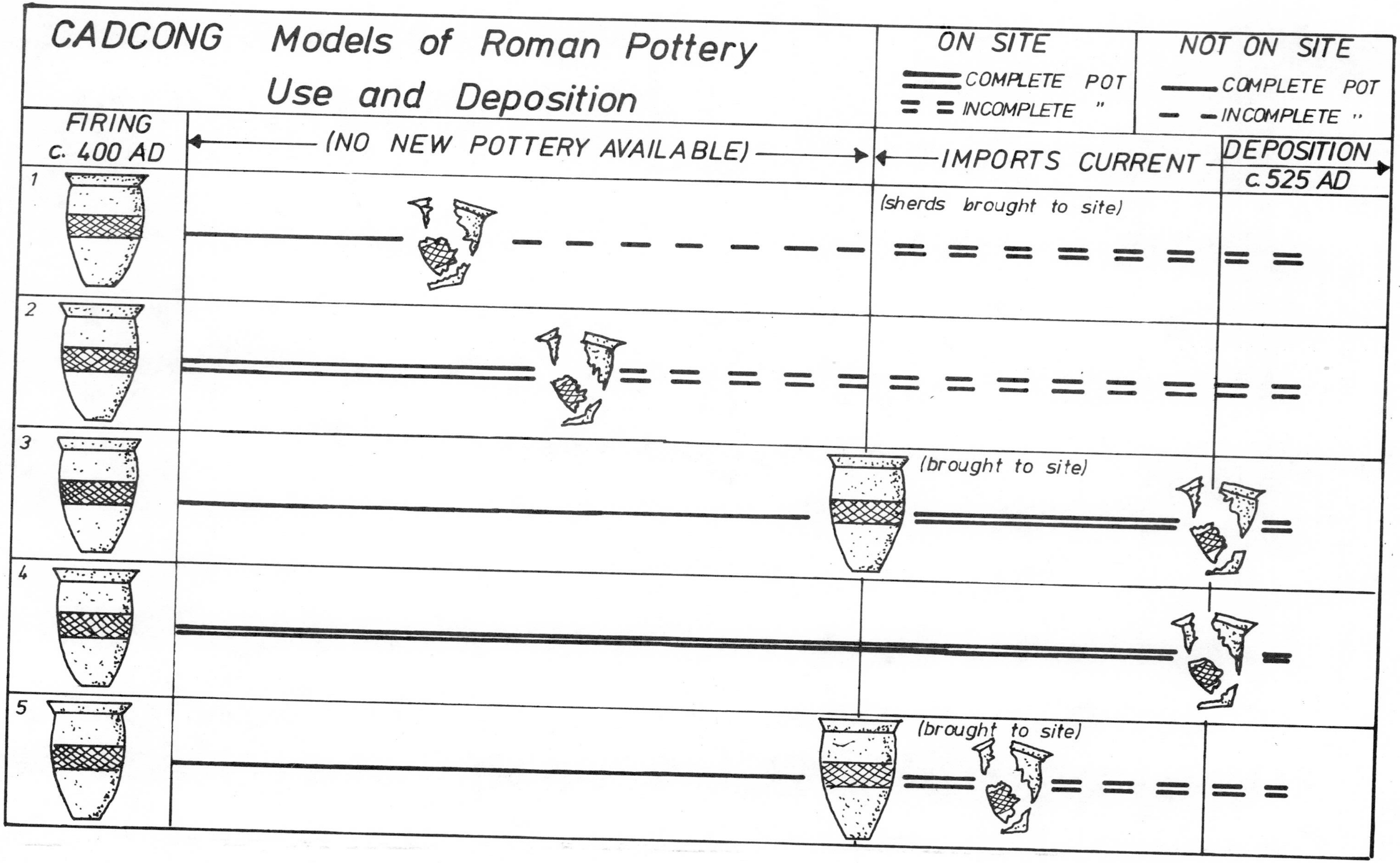

CADCONG Models of Roman Pottery Use and Deposition

	ON SITE		NOT ON SITE	
	COMPLETE POT ————	INCOMPLETE " ≡≡≡	COMPLETE POT ————	INCOMPLETE " – – –

FIRING c. 400 AD

IMPORTS CURRENT

DEPOSITION c. 525 AD

1 (NO NEW POTTERY AVAILABLE)

2

3 (brought to site)

4

5 (brought to site)

(sherds brought to site)

a) Within the Roman period

Military occupation	– by Roman troops
	– by native militia
'Illegal' use	– 'squatters'
	– coin forging, etc.
Casual/agricultural use	– 'picnickers'
	– manuring, etc.
Religious use	– temple complexes
	– infrequent visits to sacred area?
Major secular use	– villa settlements
	– others
	– continuing use from Iron Age
Concealment	– coin hoards

b) In the post-Roman period

Continued manufacture in area
Disturbance of pre-existing Roman deposits
Accidental importation in dumped soil etc.
Use as raw material, curiosities, souvenirs, talismans

| In use in original form | – continuous use from time of manufacture |
| | – recovered from Roman sites—cemeteries, villas etc. |

In Figure 20 the various ways in which a Romano-British vessel might eventually become deposited in a post-Roman context are expressed in diagrammatic form, and here related specifically to circumstances at Cadcong. Five models are presented, all of which share the common elements of an initial production of the pot before the end of commercial pottery production in c. AD 400, and a final and independently dated context of c. AD 525 from which the sherds were recovered in excavation. Between these two fixed points a number of circumstances can be readily envisaged, and the following discussion of the Cadcong data is intended to decide between them.

Model 1 suggests that the vessel had a relatively short life as a complete vessel, and that the sherds from the pot were at a later stage brought to Cadcong, incorporated in rubble or soil, for example.

Model 2 envisages that occupation on the site was continuous from the late-Roman period, the vessel being in use for some time, but being broken prior to the arrival of imported pottery on the site, and its component sherds ending up in their excavated context some time later.

Model 3 portrays the situation in which the vessel in some way remained intact, either by being carefully treated by its users throughout the period, or perhaps by being looted intact from an abandoned Roman site in which it had become concealed. The pot was then brought to Cadcong as part of the cultural equipment of its owners, who by the time they moved onto the hilltop also possessed exotic imported pottery. The Roman vessel then remained in use until broken and deposited in the context in which it was found in excavation.

Model 4   varies from 3 in postulating a continuous use of the Roman pottery on the site itself from the fourth and into the sixth century.

Model 5   differs from 3 only in suggesting that the broken pot was not immediately deposited in its final context, but that the sherds lay elsewhere for a time.

Various permutations of these models can additionally be suggested, and the stratigraphic evidence of other sites might produce further ones, but the proposed situations provide a basis from which to consider the Cadcong data itself.

Cadcong

Clearly only a detailed stratigraphic dissection of hillfort/hill-top deposits will decide between these alternative possibilities. At Cadbury Congresbury the three-dimensional recording of most classes of artifacts, combined with the absence of any major later disturbance of the stratification, enables complex analysis of the data to be made. It should be stated at the outset that the potential for the statistical evaluation of the vertical and horizontal distribution of artifacts, and their relationship to the defined stratigraphic units, is very much greater than has been attempted here. Computer storage of the three-dimensional data would enable simple randomness tests to be made on different classes of material to compare the degree of agglomeration or regular spacing.[15] This would lead on to further analysis to explain any observed differences in distribution patterns. Computer analysis of contexts might also produce results which are not readily obtainable by manual means—the frequency of association of some artifact types with others, or of groups of material with other groups, for example, might demonstrate stratigraphic links which were not clear during excavation, or test the validity of those which were postulated at the time.

Considerations of time and an innate innumeracy precluded the use of extensive statistical analysis of the Roman material for the purposes of this study, and the main concern has been to assess the character and distribution of the Roman pottery on the site, and its relationship to the stratigraphical evidence from the excavation; and specifically to the distribution and character of the post-Roman ceramics. This assessment is made in the light of the hypotheses concerning the occurrence of Roman material in hillforts discussed above.

The Roman pottery at Cadcong forms only one element in the Roman assemblage from the site. Also recovered were small quantities of metalwork and coins, glass (still undergoing analysis at the time of writing but believed to include both vessel and window glass), and building material, chiefly floor and roof tiles of Pennant sandstone but also including ceramic tiles and small quantities of Oolitic limestone. Some other material such as slag may also be of Roman date but this is not demonstrable.

Much of this material is clearly not in its original context or function. Fused and melted vessel glass strongly suggests its use as raw material, perhaps for enamelling or inlay work. In general the glass is extremely fragmentary and appears on preliminary investigation to come from very many different vessels, some probably fifth or sixth century in date. The

Pennant sandstone, small pieces of which were extremely numerous on the site, were also clearly out of their original context, in two instances being used to construct hearths. The remainder of this material is so widely distributed across the site and is in such small fragments that it is difficult to postulate that it was used on the site for its original purpose of roofing or flooring buildings, unless it is supposed that deliberate breakage took place after the tiles had ceased to be used. As has been discussed in chapter 5, later disturbance of the site appears to have been minimal and it is unlikely that this is the cause of this fragmentation. The suggestion is therefore that the Pennant tile was brought to the site, or at least to the excavated area, already in a somewhat fragmentary state.

The small number of Roman metal objects, in particular two toilet instruments, published in the 1968 report,[16] are by contrast complete and in a condition as good as that of the post-Roman metalwork. Everyday objects such as these may have continued in use for a considerable time and although any certainty is impossible it may be that here we are seeing an instance of the longevity of usage of 'Roman' articles rather than their re-use as raw material for recasting. The similarly perfect example of a La Tene III brooch in a possibly post-Roman context on the site[17] may, however, cast doubt on this interpretation since it seems improbable (although not totally excludable) that such a piece would still be in use in the fifth or sixth century. The coins, too, may support the 'scrap metal' hypothesis for a post-Roman context for metalwork finds, since it is generally accepted that a monetary economy had ceased to operate in Britain by c. 430-450[18] and thereafter Roman coinage would would presumably have been put to other uses. The coins, one of Tetricus (c. 270), one of Allectus (296) and two of Constantine (313/5 and 335/7) might, however, indicate activity centring on 300, and is not inconsistent with a date for much of the pottery.

The Roman pottery itself was, for a number of reasons, concentrated upon in this study. Firstly it was the most numerous body of Roman material on the site after the Pennant sandstone. Secondly it was much more readily classifiable into its probable original components than the latter, and thus one of the key problems—whether the Roman material is present on the site in its original form and usage during the post-Roman phase, might be resolved. The presence of post-Roman ceramics, of both imported and local origin, also provides a body of comparative material against which to consider the Roman pottery. Finally, as pottery is one of the most common and readily identifiable materials encountered in excavation or fieldwork, an assessment of the significance of the Cadcong material has the potential wider implications outlined above.

The main questions for which answers are sought in this discussion are as follows:-

1. What is the general character of the Roman pottery assemblage in terms of number of sherds and vessels, fabric types and chronology?

2. Does the pottery belong to the post-Roman phases of activity on the site or to a separate episode in the Roman period?

3. Were there complete vessels on site, or was the material brought to the excavated area, and therefore perhaps to the hilltop as a whole, as sherds?

4. What function did the pottery have, and how does this compare with that of the post-Roman ceramics?

5. Can any general conclusions be drawn about the presence of Roman pottery in hillfort sites in Somerset?

The general character of the material   (see Appendix B)

A total of 466 sherds identified as of Roman types were recovered in the excavations of 1959, 1968 and 1970-73. A basic macroscopic classification into fabrics was made with a further subdivision into vessels where possible. The small size of some of the sherds and the lack of distinctive rims means that identification is not always reliable and some fabric groups, especially 64-67, may in fact be medieval or of post-Roman imported origin. There is an especial difficulty over the red wares of the 'A/RB' category, consisting of fabrics which have a strong similarity to the imported Mediterranean red wares of Thomas Class A, but which are not universally accepted as such.[19] This material is not considered in detail here, and only sherds which seem more likely to be Roman than otherwise are examined. The definition of fabrics was essentially subjective and based only on macroscopic criteria, combined with comparison with the Butcombe and Chew Valley pottery series.[20] The chief aim of the classification was, however, to define individual vessels, which the relatively small number of items made feasible. It is worth emphasising the contrast here between Cadcong and Roman settlements—at Butcombe, a small rural non-villa settlement site, about 8000 sherds were recovered from two seasons' excavation. This difference immediately suggests that the Cadcong assemblage is a result of circumstances other than those encountered on at least lower order settlements of Roman date in the area.

Most of the sherds are small, a rough average would be a 6 cm^2 exterior surface area. Forty-four of the sherds are rims ($9\frac{1}{2}$%), whereas only twenty are from bases. In no case does more than half of the circumference of a pot survive, and only a few sherds or joining groups or sherds have any linear dimension in excess of 10 cm. This means that reconstructions of rim angles and diameters illustrated here are subject to error in many cases, although they are approximately accurate. The overall general impression is therefore one of great fragmentation and small sherd size.

Apart from the very soft wares, especially 81 and 82, the sherds are not severely abraded. Most breakages are fairly sharp, although this varies from fabric to fabric. The degree of abrasion is certainly no more marked than that of the A and B wares which show a comparable range of hardness. Joining groups of sherds, however, in particular 41 and 40i, comprise larger sherds, the edges of which are generally speaking equally weathered all around their perimeter. This weathering is considered to be slightly greater than on the joining edges of the sherds. This is a very difficult and subjective matter as so many variables are involved, but it may indicate that a minimum of two 'breakage episodes' is involved, the earlier breaking the material into a few large sherds, and the later reducing them to much smaller elements.

The broad divisions into fabric groups based largely on colour give the following breakdown of material:

Groups 1-9 (Grey Wares)	213 sherds from a minimum of 65 vessels - average 3.3 sherds/pot
Groups 40-44 (Black-Burnished Wares)	115 sherds from a minimum of 33 vessels - average 3.5 sherds/pot
Groups 61-67 (Buff/Red Wares)	43 sherds from a minimum of 30 vessels - average 1.4 sherds/pot
Groups 81-84 (Colour-Coated Wares)	9 sherds from a minimum of 8 vessels; - average 1 sherd/pot
Groups 91-95 (Mortaria etc.)	30 sherds from a minimum of 14 vessels - average 2 sherds/pot
Samian	56 sherds (at least 6 vessels)

The data from the first two is biased by the relatively large numbers of sherds from vessel 4(i) and 40(i). If these are removed the results are:

Groups 1-9	165 sherds from 64 vessels - average 2.5 sherds/pot
Groups 40-44	77 sherds from 32 vessels - average 2.4 sherds/pot
The overall figures are:	466 sherds from a minimum of 150 vessels - average 3.1 sherds/pot

These figures may be immediately contrasted with the imported pottery where a much higher sherd/vessel ratio is seen—an average of 13 sherds/pot being found among the B wares and of 4.75 sherds(pot among the A wares. In this respect the A/RB material with 1.3 sherds/pot shows a greater affinity with the Roman pottery than with imports.[21] In any event, the sherd/vessel ratio of the Roman pottery is strikingly low and although comparative data from Roman occupation sites is not obtainable the ratio would normally be much greater than this.

Where dates can be allocated to the forms or fabrics they fall generally in the later part of the Roman period. The lattice on vessel 40(i) provides a typological date of the mid third century. Exceptions are the Samian, where the identifiable forms are all first or second century, with no third century material, and group 41 which on the basis of the Chew Valley dating belongs also to the first or second centuries. Three sherds (81(iii), 83(i) and 84(i)) may be from late fourth century vessels. The chronological isolation of the Samian is thus noteworthy.

The finer colour-coated wares and the mortaria together make up only 8% of the sherds and 14% of the vessels. The bulk of the material is therefore of coarse wares, chiefly in the forms of dishes, bowls or jars where these can be identified. This contrasts with the post-Roman imported ceramics which consist predominantly of much larger containers or the fine table ware of Class A; the Roman material being thus much more utilitarian and 'domestic' in character. The majority of the grey wares (apart from Group 8, which appears to be of South Welsh origin), are probably local products of the Congresbury kilns. The black wares, similarly, were probably produced by the 'Black Burnished' ware industry of the Brue Valley and elsewhere in Somerset. In sum, therefore, the assemblage is representative of the late Roman ceramics of the area so far as they are known.

The problem of the chronological context of this material was approached in various ways, by analysis of the vertical and horizontal distribution in relation to the stratification and other classes of material, and these are now considered.

The two crucial contexts in this discussion are the rock-cut pit GF3 discussed above (chapter 4) and a complex succession of structures at the northern end of Yellow Cutting. The chief features of interest here are layer GF3g, a sticky red clay soil in and upon the surface of which were 40 Roman sherds from ten finds spots, and the deep soil wedge GF3d in which finds other than animal bone were rare. In the stone layer above this (GF3b) were two Bii sherds and one glass fragment, and in the humic fill in the top of the pit one sherd each of D and A ware and two Roman sherds.

Ostensibly, these contexts demonstrate the stratigraphical separation of Roman material from post-Roman (apart from a few 'residual' sherds). The Roman pottery in GF3g is chiefly from two grey-ware vessels, 3 and 4vi, were found in YF133c—one of the lowest layers defined in the linear quarried feature fronting the banks, and also one containing only Roman material. Much clearly depends on the function of GF3 and the circumstances of its filling. If GF3d is a natural accumulation of soil over a bedrock weathering to produce red clay, then the case for a separate 'Roman' phase in which no imported pottery was present, is strengthened. It can be argued, however, that the disposition of the layers in GF3 indicates that the pit has been deliberately back-filled with varying types of material and the apparent chronological separation of the pottery types may be no more than fortuitous. This argument does seem to strain credibility, however, and does not explain, in particular, the origin of GF3g. The very high sherd/pot ratio in this layer is also exceptional on the site and suggests the dumping of near-complete broken vessels rather than the scattering of already dispersed sherds.

The deep stratification at the northern end of Yellow Cutting is shown in plan in Figure 21 and a tentative stratigraphic analysis is given in Figure 22.[22] Interpretation of the excavated data from this area is difficult, and the loose character of the rubble makes the position of finds unreliable, but the general sequence appears to involve, a) the initial digging of an irregular quarried area, the earliest accumulation in which contained Iron Age material; b) a mass of large stones and rubble (chiefly YF133b—the 'Skull Tumble') was thrown in at the northern end. This contained human skull fragments (weathered) and 43 of the 48 sherds from vessel 4i, an indented grey-ware jar which may possibly be a waster, and one sherd from vessel 40i. Other sherds from this latter vessel came from the lowest layer on the level platform YF122. c) The stone bank YF105 was constructed. d) A carefully laid area of stones (YF132) was placed adjacent to the bank and a void (YF129) left within it, perhaps intended as an emplacement for a large timber. This then silted up with

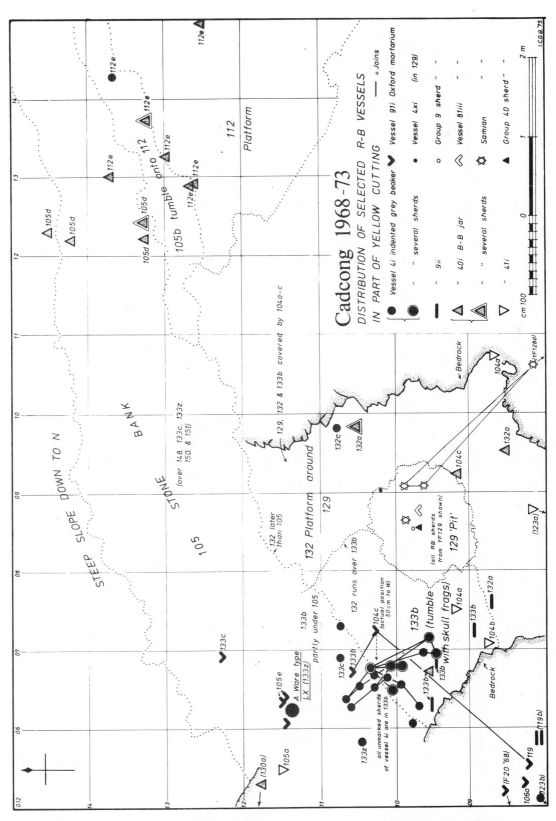

Fig. 21 Cadcong; Plan showing the distribution of selected Romano-
British vessels in relation to major excavated features in the
northern part of Yellow Cutting

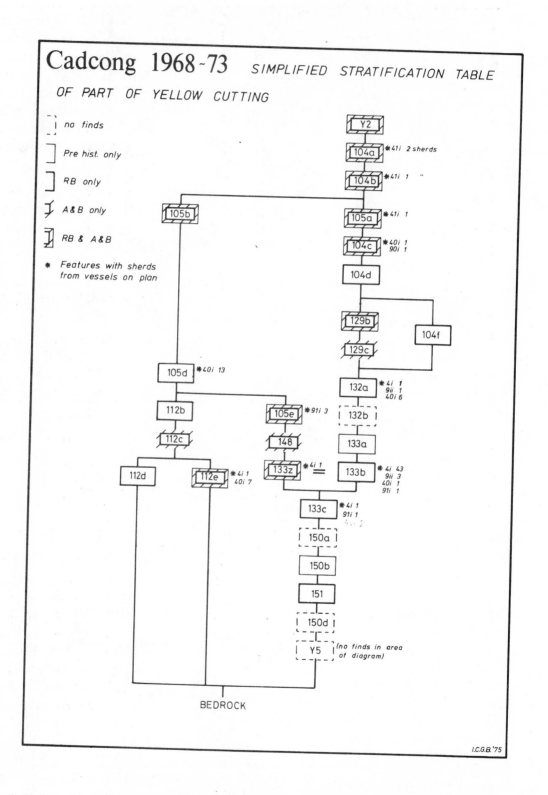

Fig. 22 Cadcong; Simplified stratification diagram of area of Yellow
Cutting shown on Figure 21

black humic soil containing a wide range of artifacts, among them seven Roman sherds including three of samian.

The proportion of the total surface area of these pots recovered in the excavation is similar to that of some of the vessels of Bi and Bii and vessel BMv and may suggest that the circumstances of deposition are similar. It may be that the post-Roman pottery was itself brought to the site in a fragmentary state (the apparently deliberate deposition of two amphora handles in the entrance post-holes of structure II supporting this suggestion[23]) but the presumption is that this was not so, and we may therefore envisage that vessels 40i and 4i also arrived on the site as complete or near complete vessels.

As in the case of the pottery from context GF3, these two vessels are virtually isolated from post-Roman material, although a North African Red Slip ware sherd (A LX) was in a context contemporary with the main concentration of sherds from vessel 4i. A small quantity of post-Roman pottery was also present in YF112e, the lowest defined layer on the platform, but none in the area of the lowest layer of the bank, YF105d. It is also notable that one sherd from each of the vessels 4i and 40i is present near the main concentration of sherds from the other.

Both vessels have clearly been incorporated into material which has been deliberately dumped, although 40i may have been lying on YF112 before being incorporated in the rampart YF105. The deposition of the 'skull tumble', and the distribution pattern of sherds from the Oxford Colour-coated mortarium, 91i, suggest that this material was pushed down from the west into the quarry hollow.

Whatever the significance of this activity, it seems clear that the earliest post-Iron Age contexts at Cadcong, in those parts of the site where the stratification is most to be relied on, contain predominantly Roman material from a few vessels which have a much higher sherd/vessel ratio than average. These vessels are not necessarily, as might be expected, of the latest Roman types, since 40i should, on typological grounds, be dated to the mid 3rd century.

At this stage we may therefore suggest an early phase of occupation, perhaps with only a little imported pottery, when complete Roman vessels were available. The evidence from other types of analysis goes some way to support this hypothesis. In Green Cutting, where stratigraphic analysis was most complete at the time of writing, 28 contexts contained Roman pottery, but only one of these (GF3g) contained this material alone, and in 25 cases it was associated with post-Roman pottery or artifacts. In 21 of these, however, Iron Age material was also present and it therefore seemed possible merely that disturbance of earlier occupations containing Iron Age and Roman pottery was producing this homogeneity. However, analysis of the contexts of the Iron Age pottery showed that in almost half of the cases (31 out of 70) Iron Age pottery occurred either alone or with other prehistoric material only. With the (possibly major) exception of the pit GF3 it can therefore be suggested that the Roman pottery is more frequently associated with the post-Roman occupation than Iron Age material.

It was possible to divide the late/post-Roman occupation (phase 3) in Green Cutting into a, b and c sub-phases, although many features could only be generally assigned to period 3. In Figure 23 selected types of finds from Green Cutting are presented, firstly as percentages of the total finds in each period, and then as absolute totals. In the first instance it can be observed that the Iron Age and Roman pottery show 'peaks' in period 2 and period 3a respectively. There was a general scarcity of finds from 3a contexts, though the absence of glass is perhaps noteworthy. In 3b there is an increase of most types of material, including Iron Age pottery, but the total quantity of Roman pottery and its 'share' of the total of artifacts recovered both drop. It would be unwise to make too much of these figures, since the quantities are relatively small. Similar analysis of the evidence from the whole site may confirm the indications here that the Roman pottery is most common in the earlier stages of the 'post-Roman' occupation and is not part of a general 'residual' background including Iron Age and other prehistoric material.

Is this postulated episode chronologically distinct from the main post-Roman phase? The small number of contexts where Roman pottery alone occurs, and the presence of post-Roman pottery in most contexts immediately subsequent to them does not suggest this. The general lack of coins of the third and fourth centuries would seem to preclude any activity on the site before the earlier fifth century, and none of the excavated features or buildings is demonstrably Roman in date. The overall horizontal distribution of Roman pottery (Fig. 24) does not show a marked association with any buildings other than the 'Long House' (Structure I) and in this case there is also a major concentration of post-Roman ceramics. Although it might be expected, for example, that Structure VI, under the bank in Blue Cutting, would be associated with more Roman pottery than later features this is not the case. The greatest concentration of Roman pottery is clearly in the deep deposits in the north-eastern part of the excavation, on the edge of the northern slope of the hill, and towards the 'summit' on the south.

This general distribution pattern is reflected in other classes of material also and seems to be a factor of the general movement of material on the site. The evidence from the prehistoric material is biased by the incomplete excavations of Blue Cutting. A purely visual comparison of the overall horizontal distribution of Roman pottery and A and B wares could, however, be made by showing the densities of finds in 4 m squares as percentages of the total finds of each class of material (Figs. 25 and 26). The general similarity of the two distributions can be readily seen, and the detailed correlation between the two types of material in the area of the 'Long House' and on the southern side of the cutting, and the lack of material from the area of the 'Religious Building' (Structure II), are also apparent. The A and B wares are slightly more widely dispersed over the site, occurring on just over half on the 4 m squares while the incidence of Romano-British is rather less than this, and the material is more agglomerated in the early contexts in Green and Yellow. Otherwise the overall distribution is similar.

There are, however, detailed differences in the distributions which may support the hypothesis that the two groups of material are chronologically separate. There is a notable concentration of A and B wares in the vicinity of the Post-Bank Structure, which is not reflected in the Romano-British

126

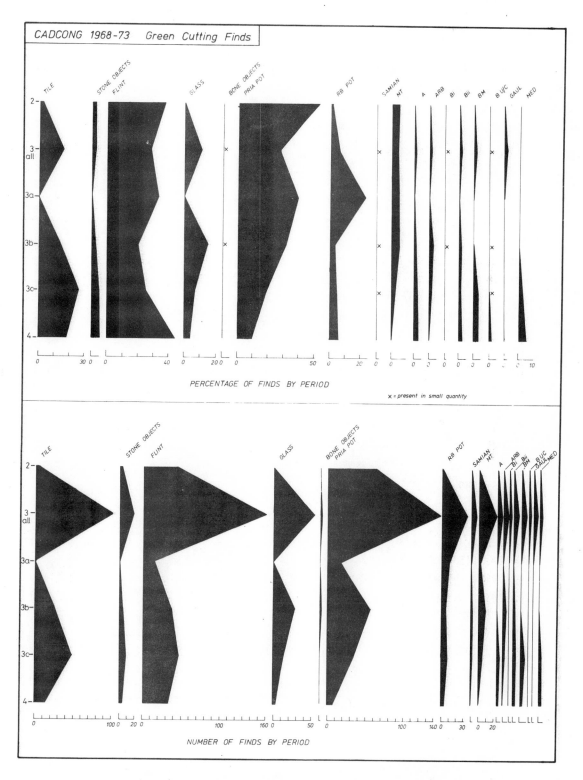

Fig. 23   Cadcong;   Finds from Green Cutting tabulated by period and
expressed as percentages (top) and numerical totals (bottom)

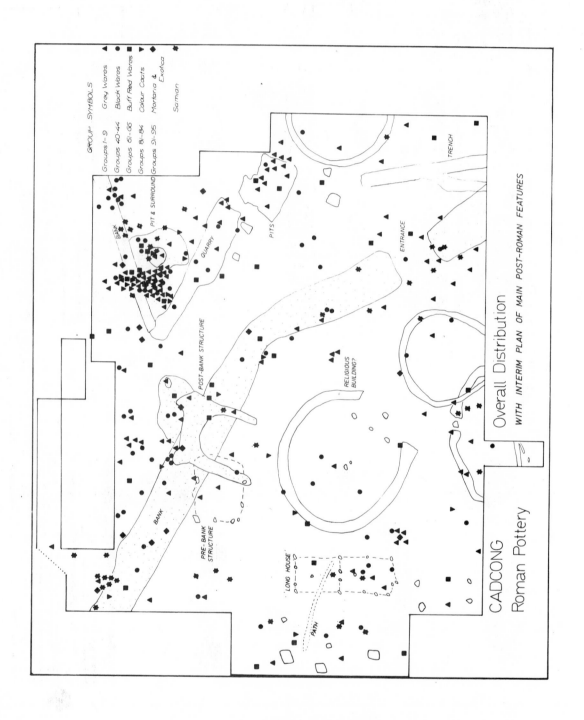

Fig. 24 Cadcong; Overall distribution of Roman pottery sherds

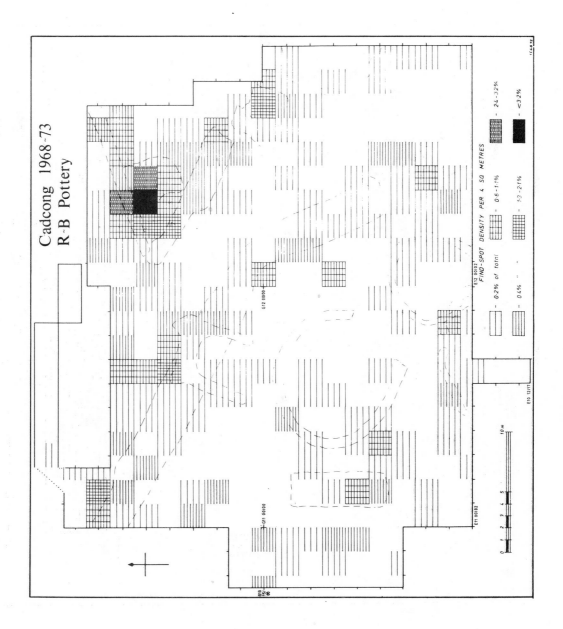

Fig. 25 Cadcong; Density of Roman pottery sherds by 4-square metre
units

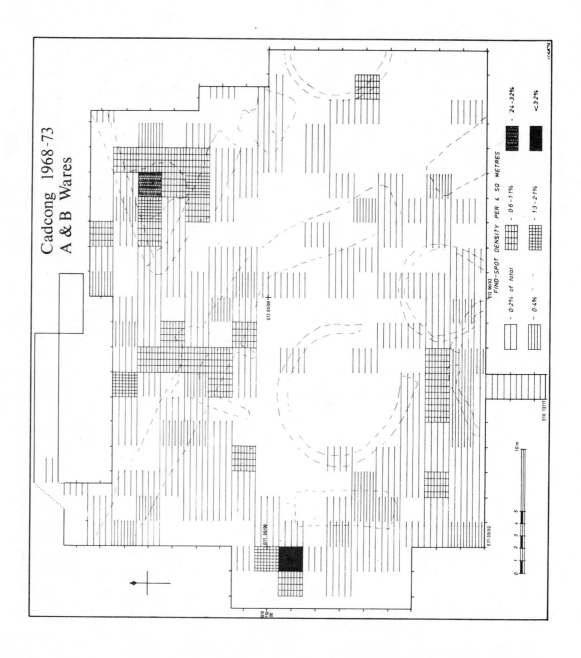

Fig. 26 Cadcong; Density of imported 'A' and 'B' ware sherds by
4-square metre units

pottery distribution. Similarly the 'pit' and its surround in Yellow Cutting, again late in the stratigraphic sequence, show a marked concentration of A and B wares and a relative scarcity of Roman pottery. Both these areas therefore confirm that Roman pottery is less common in the later phases of period 3. The major concentration of B wares south of grid point G11 is likewise not reflected in the Roman distribution.

In Figure 27 selected Romano-British and imported vessels have been shown on the same diagram, pots represented by the largest number of sherds being chosen. Sherds from the same Romano-British vessel are linked with lines to provide an impression of the scatter of each vessel. While it can be seen that the general pattern of distribution of the two classes of material is similar—with concentrations in the south-western and north-eastern areas of the excavation, the imported sherds from the vessels shown are much more clustered than those of the majority of the Romano-British pots, except for 4i and 40i. With these two exceptions the impression is thus reinforced that the Roman pottery has been subjected to greater disturbance and dispersal on the site than has the imported pottery, and this would be consistent with the emerging hypothesis that the Roman pottery is chronologically primary. Veseel 40ii, five large sherds (3 joins) of which were found, shows a distribution which illustrates the point. Four sherds of the pot are close together in the area of the 'Long House' and inside Structure II; the outlying sherd was incorporated in the rubble of the perimeter bank. This distribution suggests that a substantial part of the pot was broken in the concentration of Roman and post-Roman material in the 'Long House' area, but that one sherd was lying close enough to the edge of the hill to be quarried with the stone rubble of the bank.

The disposition of finds of both Roman and imported pottery around Structure II strongly suggests that if formed an enclosed area into which stray items of rubbish did not normally reach. The B-ware handles within the entrance post-holes would seem to imply that it was not built until this material was present on the site. Why, therefore, should the Roman pottery distribution also largely avoid it? It would appear that the major dispersal of the Roman pottery took place after the construction of Structure II, but as has been shown it is probable that complete or near-complete pots were present on the site before the advent of imported material, and features of the general distribution of Roman pottery suggest also that it may predate that of the imports. 40ii may be of some importance here, in that two of the sherds are from inside Structure II although the pot seems to have been broken in this area. It is suggested that this breakage occurred before the construction of Structure II, since it seems unlikely that the sherds would have got 'inside' this building had it been a standing, roofed structure.

So far the Roman pottery has been treated as a whole, but it was considered possible that different groups might be of different dates or functions. Distribution plots of sherds of the different groups were therefore prepared, but no major contrast in vertical or horizontal distributions was detected except in the case of the Samian. This is in any case chronologically isolated, and none of the identifiable vessels is represented by more than two sherds, though ascription is difficult with this material. Horizontally the distribution is

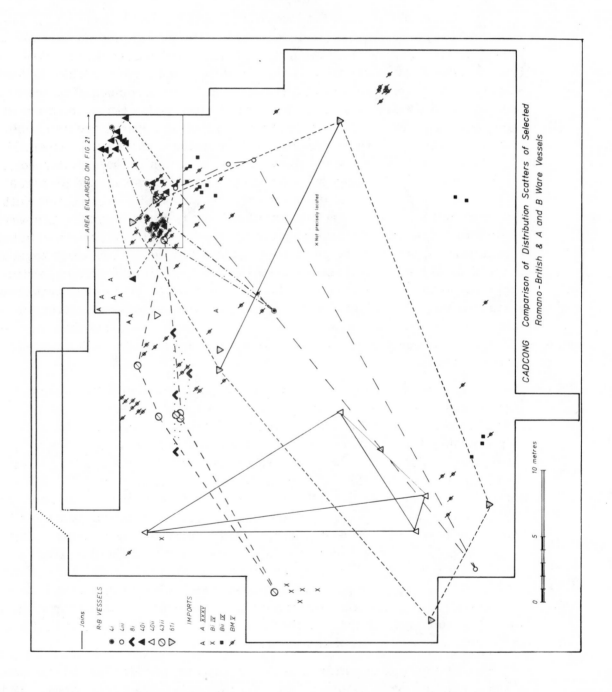

Fig. 27   Cadcong;   Comparison of distribution of selected Romano-
British and A & B ware vessels

notably clustered in three areas—at the top of the slope north of the stone bank at the NW corner of the excavation, and in the bank and stone setting around the 'pit' in Yellow. None of these contexts is stratigraphically primary, and Samian is absent from the 'skull tumble' in Yellow and GF3. Of the ten Samian sherds in Green Cutting, five were from the general layer G2, two from the rubble layers in the entrance, and one from the upper layers of the bank GF107. As far as the stratigraphic data can be relied on, it indicates the absence of Samian from early contexts on the site, and its general distribution seems to resemble that of the imported ware more than that of the other Roman pottery.

The function of the pottery on the site can now be considered. As has been demonstrated, some vessels were almost certainly present on the site in a complete state. It has also been argued that these vessels are from contexts which ante-date the occurrence of imported material, though probably by no long interval. It is, however, harder to accept that the bulk of the Roman sherds are from vessels in use and broken on the site. In two cases (vessels 4x and 40xix) re-use of sherds for other purposes seems probable. If the stratigraphic argument that the Roman pottery is slightly earlier than the imported wares is sound, more disturbance and breakage of the former would be anticipated. The material is, however, so fragmented that it must be considered probable that some Roman pottery at least was only brought to the site as sherds. Pennant sandstone roofing tile was re-used on the site, and pottery sherds may also have served some alternative use. It has been suggested, in a medieval context, that sherds may have had a lavatory function[24] or some types, notably perhaps Samian, were used in medicines.[25] The distribution of the Samian certainly suggests that it did not form part of the original body of Roman pottery on the site.

We are now in a position to attempt to answer the questions posed and to decide which of the models in Figure 20 is the most valid:

1. The Roman pottery assemblage is essentially a late Roman one, typical of the area in which the site lies, and is formed predominantly of coarse ware. The Samian sherds are the exception to this.

2. The balance of evidence suggests that some at least of the pottery was on the site prior to the appearance of the imported material. On a number of counts it appears that this pre-import 'phase' is not a separate episode in the history of the site, and that the 'post-Roman' occupation followed on directly from it. The current dating for the imported Mediterranean pottery makes it unlikely that the pre-import 'phase' is earlier than the fifth century, and probably falls in its second half.

3 & 4. In this earliest 'phase' a number of pots were present in a complete or near complete form, the implication being that they were in use as utilitarian vessels. The bulk of the material may, however, have been brought to the site as sherds for other purposes on merely as 'rubbish' from a Roman site. Models 1 and 3 therefore seem to represent the situation on the site most exactly.

Comparison with other sites

At Dinas Powys, the only fully published site with a comparable range of material, the Roman artifacts, although smaller in number, showed a contrasting emphasis on luxury items and exotic pottery such as Samian. The material was chronologically isolated, falling into the first two centuries AD, and not associated with a definable stratigraphic horizon. Alcock therefore concluded that in this case the Roman objects were wholly to be associated with the post-Roman phase.[26] Generalisations about the use of Roman material in later centuries are therefore clearly premature, but the material from other Somerset sites can now be discussed. In particular, similarities between the Cadcong assemblage and that from other hilltops have been sought. Twenty-five enclosures in the study area have produced Roman evidence of some kind, 28% of the total (Appendix B and Fig. 28) Roman material was recovered in excavations from 13 hillforts of Group I, with casual finds from a further three; only one site of Group II, Clifton, has Roman evidence; in four of the five sites excavated of Group III and both of those of Group IV Roman material was also found. This emphasises that any adequate hillfort excavation is likely to produce some Roman material, and it may be suggested that absence of Roman material will prove to be exceptional.

The quality and quantity of this evidence is, however, very variable. Structural evidence of Roman date has been recovered at seven sites, and may be suspected from casual surface finds at four others. In other instances Roman artifacts are not associated with structures or other features. Finally, coin hoards have been found at five sites.

Direct comparison with the evidence from Cadcong is difficult, but we may commence consideration of the conclusions reached there by discussion of South Cadbury, where Roman and post-Roman material have similarly been recovered. The wider aspects of the refurbishment of the defences at this site and the activity in the interior in the 5th-7th centuries will be considered in the next chapter, and at this point discussion is confined to the Roman evidence, based on the published accounts and information kindly made available by Professor Alcock in advance of publication.

Data from the excavations carried out at South Cadbury prior to 1966-70 is not susceptible to close analysis. It is hard to assess the various accounts of apparently Roman structures discovered in ploughing and which may have been, at least in part, natural features,[27] but clearly large numbers of Roman coins were frequently found in the interior, including late second-century issues. Gray's excavated material is not closely related to the stratification, and chiefly demonstrated the occurrence of Roman material at the south-west gate and on the summit plateau.

The early Roman material from the recent excavations can clearly be linked to two related circumstances, both of which are of some significance in demonstrating the varied fate of individual hillforts at the time of the establishment of Roman control, and underline the points made at the beginning of this chapter. The dating evidence from Samian finds and brooches from the 'massacre' level at the south-west gate indicate that the hillfort continued to be occupied for several decades after the Roman conquest of the area in the mid-40s AD, and that the defences were refurbished prior to Roman attack.[28]

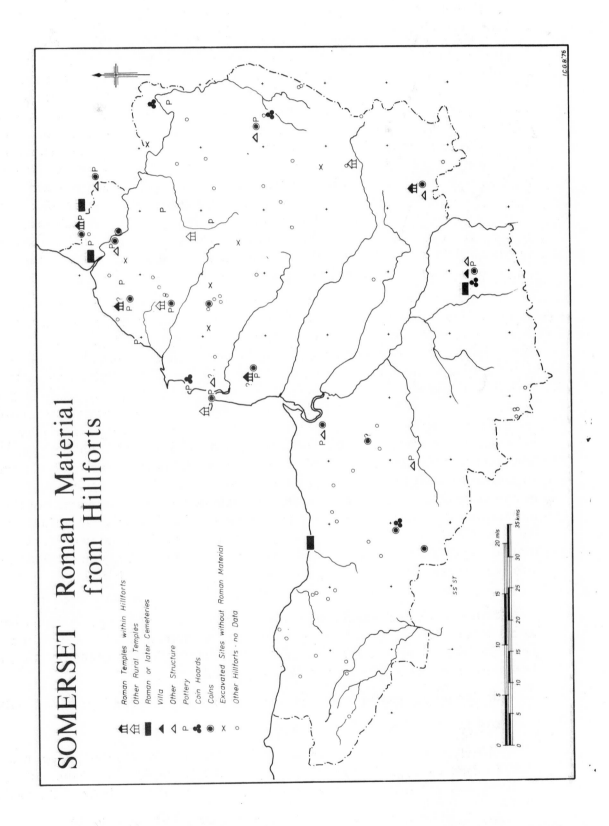

Fig. 28 Somerset; Romano-British material from hillforts and hilltops

In addition, a building interpreted as a temple was probably erected on the summit plateau at this time.[29] Roman military structures in the interior are, additionally, dated as late as the '60s by Samian finds.

After this the excavated evidence, both from relative absence of finds and the accumulation of humus against the rear of the final Iron Age rampart, suggest the use of the site for arable cultivation. This is useful regative evidence for a non-continuation of use of a major hillfort as a settlement site. The prominence of the late Iron Age/early Roman temple in the settlement and the probable re-use of the hillfort in the later period as a focus for religious activity might lead one to look here for 'continuity' at least of ritual usage of the hillfort throughout the period. Intensification of activity does not appear to have commenced until the latter part of the third century on coin evidence, but this is in some contrast to Stukeley's record of 'vast numbers' of coins of Antoninus Pius (138-161) and Faustina (before 175). An unknown number of these may of course have been from dispersed hoards, but the emphasis on finds of coins in earlier accounts does suggest similarity to the large coin deposition common at some Roman temple sites.[30]

Evidence for the later Roman temple itself is indirect. Roof tile and tufa were found within the body of the late/post-Roman rampart and the gilt bronze letter 'A' may be a further indication of such a building. In the context of the comparison between this site and Cadcong, the crucial question is the possibility of some sort of continuity between the temple activity, traceable down to the early fifth century on coin evidence, and the later occupation of the hillfort, probably in the late fifth century or later. Alcock has discussed the difficulty of resolving this problem, but considers the weight of evidence in favour of the abandonment of the temple at the end of the fourth century.[31] The general presumption that activity at rural temples was drastically declining with the spread of Christianity in the later fourth century can be challenged in a number of instances, and we shall be considering the implications of this in the following chapter, but final resolution of the problem at South Cadbury can only come from detailed stratigraphic analysis of the area around the temple site if it is still intact. However, the use of building stone within the late/post-Roman bank does suggest destruction of a nearby building by this time.

Against this background the evidence from the two cuttings on site J can be reviewed. These were designed to test the existence of the late/post-Roman and Aethelredan banks on the west side. J67 was dug by hand, J69 by machine. The general sequence in both was similar, consisting of

a) Humus accumulation on the last Iron Age bank (layer J115 in J67 only).

b) Late/post-Roman bank (J11, J112, J114, J012).

c) Lower levels of Aethelredan bank: consisting of reddish gravel and dirty earth (J109 and J107) and clay and gravel layers (J010a, J010, J009 and J008). These were distinct from the main body of the bank.

d) The main portion of the Aethelredan bank (J103 and J002-6).

e) Trench for the wall facing of the latter (J104).

f) Later field wall/revetment (J102, J002a?).

Of the contexts discussed only the topsoil, soil accumulation on the rear of the Aethelredan bank, the later field wall/revetment and the mortar spread within the Aethelredan bank produced no Roman material. Apart from an iron knife of probable 5th-7th century date in a pit, probably to the rear of the late/post-Roman bank, no later material was recovered in these cuttings.

The pottery assemblage, like that at Cadcong, is predominantly late Roman in date and is mainly utilitarian coarse wares, chiefly sandy grey/black 'black-burnished' ware vessels akin to Cadcong group 40 in fabric. There is also a small number of late Roman fine wares of Castor and Oxford ware types. The late/post-Roman bank is given a terminus post quem of 393 by a coin of Honorius of 393-402.

Otherwise, however, the differences are marked. Examination of the material showed that in general the sherds were much larger than those at Cadcong, and were also much more numerous in proportion to the area examined. The ratio of sherds/vessel was also much higher at South Cadbury, the implication being that some at least of the material was in a complete state or the sherds were in close proximity in the context immediately anterior to the one from which they were recovered.

The site lies at the foot of the steep slope leading up to the summit plateau, but despite this hillwash did not apparently build up to any great depth on the rear of the banks, although erosion of the late Iron Age defences complicates the issue. This, combined with the evidence of large numbers of sherds from individual pits, prompts consideration of the circumstances by which the pottery reached the position from which it was recovered in excavation.

The two contexts which might be considered to some extent discrete are the pit J125 and the quarried area J175, the latter possibly underlying the tail of the late/post-Roman bank. The filling of these features is late Roman or later, but includes pre-Roman material. The association of Roman and pre-Roman material occurs in the body of the late/post-Roman bank and in the humic layer on top of the latest Iron Age defence, but in stratigraphically later contexts Roman material preponderates.

Why should this be so? The context with the largest quantity of Roman material is the humus accumulation on the rear of the late/post-Roman bank. If this soil was derived simply from material washing down the slope we might expect to find a continued admixture of pottery types accumulating behind the banks. That this is not so may confirm the indications of early Roman ploughing, since this would destroy or bury much pre-Roman material. Only late Roman material post-dating this ploughing episode would thus be present in quantity in the topsoil at the time of the construction of the later banks and the development of soil upon them.

The presence of large numbers of sherds from individual late Roman vessels does suggest that the material was being deposited perhaps as rubbish, close to the ramparts in the late Roman period or later. It is possible, on stratigraphic grounds, that this was continuing to occur after the construction of the late/post-Roman bank, as the number of sherds in J110 and J010b indicates. However, among these are sherds from a substantial part of an early Roman dish, some more of which was found in the late/post-Roman bank itself. This is therefore in contradiction to the hypothesis related to ploughing outlined above. If a near-complete early Roman vessel could become incorporated in a deposit probably dating to between the sixth and eleventh centuries we must conclude that the similar incorporation of later vessels is no guide to their use as complete vessels in a post-Roman context. For it must be considered highly improbable that early Roman coarse ware would survive into the fifth century as complete vessels even if, as we have seen at Cadcong, this is probable for late Roman pots. Therefore some other explanation for the character of the Roman material in cutting J must be sought. The stratigraphic evidence from further into the area behind the bank, which might indicate the original contexts of the Roman pottery, is not, however, available.

The South Cadbury evidence is thus an immediate qualification to the tentative conclusions from Cadcong. Here the body of evidence suggests a considerable late Roman phase involving the use of relatively large quantities of pottery. While the stratigraphic evidence from cutting J raises the possibility that some of this pottery was complete after the Roman period, it must be suspected that conditions of deposition are more important here.

The undefended (though highly defensible) site of Glastonbury Tor presents different problems. Here the quantity of Roman material, and of post-Roman imported pottery, was small; the Roman pottery consisted of four sherds of Samian and seven of coarser wares, including two of Oxford ware. Despite the small quantity there are similarities with the Cadcong assemblage —the Samian being isolated chronologically and more closely linked to the main post-Roman occupation than the other Roman pottery, but sharing the distribution with Roman clay tile. Both these classes of material may therefore have served purposes in post-Roman contexts which were not shared by Roman coarse ware.

At Cannington, where fifth-seventh century occupation centring on the hillfort seems probable though it cannot yet be firmly demonstrated, 42 late Roman sherds were found in an occupation deposit behind the outer bank of the hillfort on the south side. Roman sherds and one Samian fragment were found on the surface in the earthworks to the south (see above, chap. 4). The apparent relationship of these earthworks to the hillfort and this evidence of Roman occupation close to the Roman and later cemetery must single out Cannington as a site where comparable evidence to that from Cadcong might be anticipated.

Apart from these post-Roman sites, there are a number of instances in which buildings and structures associated with Roman material alone have been located (Fig. 29). While it would normally be assumed that these structures do not date later than the earlier fifth century, the Cadcong evidence has raised the possibility that Roman material was in use later than this. The indications of continuing use of Roman temple sites in the county well beyond 400 should also draw our attention to the possibility of isolating sub-Roman groups of material. [32]

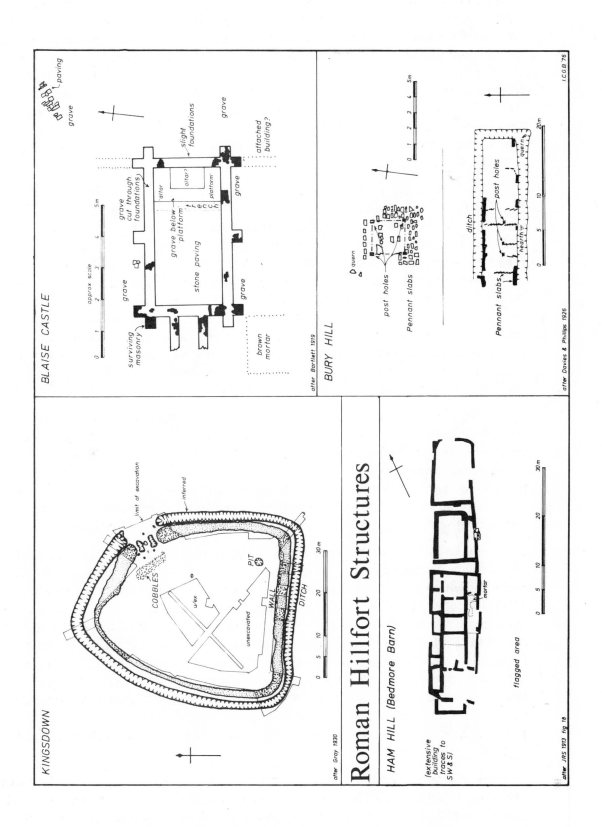

Fig. 29 Somerset; Structures of Roman date from hillforts

At Ham Hill and Bury Hill 'late Roman' structures have been excavated which indicate the use of hillfort interiors for non-religious purposes. At Ham Hill a structurally complex villa-like building was associated with coins ranging from the late third century to the end of the fourth. Branigan[33] has emphasised the apparent increase in villa and other building in the south-west in the late third century, and the establishment of the site at Ham Hill may well be part of this episode, although the evidence from the northern spur of the hillfort strongly suggests continuous activity throughout the Roman period. The evidence of surface finds south and west of the villa building indicates that it formed only a part of a much more extensive complex of buildings, perhaps similar to the site at Catsgore and elsewhere.[34]

Such evidence is as yet unparalleled in the study area, but less distinctive buildings have been located. At Bury Hill two rectangular structures were examined, one visible as an earthwork before excavation. Quarrying and iron working in the hillfort in more recent times, and the absence of clear dating evidence from stratified levels from within the structures make their dates somewhat uncertain, but early Roman pottery in the area of the first and Castor Ware and other types around the second suggest considerable Roman activity. The plan of the first structure, a long rectangle with internal unequal subdivisions, is clearly reminiscent of Roman barrack blocks, but as it apparently stood alone in the hillfort this may render this explanation less plausible. The second excavated building is a much slighter construction —a levelled square stone area with surrounding post-holes.

Excavated evidence from other hillforts too suggests that relatively insubstantial buildings of Roman date were erected. At Stokeleigh slight traces of structures were found in two of the cuttings—a hearth and a post-hole in one, associated with late Roman coarse wares and an undated, possibly two phase, rectangular structure which consisted of drystone walling and post-holes with an associated compacted layer on its eastern side. Similarly ephemeral structures may be implied by the evidence from Cannington.

Inadequate scale of excavation has clearly hindered the definition of these slight structures, and at a number of other sites the presence of Roman material without any indication of major structures may be more likely to be indicative of occupation than 'picnicking'. Late Roman sherds on the tail of the bank at Wains Hill and the Roman occupation deposit in the same position at Brean Down are both probably related to settlement within these coastal enclosures, and at King's Weston the quantity of Roman sherds in the ditch also suggests activity on a comparable scale to that of the Iron Age phase. Gray's interior cutting at Cadbury Tickenham located 'Roman' pottery also, although no features were encountered in his trench which was, however, only 2 feet wide. More recent evidence from here indicates more substantial activity (see below).

At Norton Fitzwarren more extensive areas were stripped in the interior and many features were encountered, associated with material chiefly of first century date. Roman material was found in all the cuttings, both on the summit of the hill and behind the earlier defences on the west and south sides and in the levels in the ditch silt. The excavator argued that absence of both Samian and coins implied that the occupation was early in the Roman period and soon ended.[35] It is difficult to accept this argument, since many local factors may have affected the availability of the former, and coins and indeed any Roman finds are scarce throughout the period in the Taunton region. Additionally, there is one unstratified red colour-coated ring-base which may imply later activity. Gullies, ditches and areas of cobbling were located, but again the areas examined seem to have been too small for the isolation of complete structures. Local iron ore, also in use in the earliest Iron Age phase, was apparently being worked on some scale in the Roman occupation of the hillfort. This raises the possibility that the settlement had a specialised economic function, inherited from the Iron Age phase. If Roman policy universally favoured the depopulation of hillforts it must seem improbable that such a settlement would have been allowed to continue in a defensible site. Roman control of the area is indicated by the presence of a fort at Wiveliscombe and it must be assumed that continuing use of the hillfort as a settlement was locally acceptable.

Economic specialisation may provide an explanation for the Roman material from the northern spur at Ham Hill, but the range of material is extremely wide. Again the scale and strategy of excavations militated against the identification of structures, but most cuttings made by Walter in the interior and around the ramparts by Gray produced relatively small quantities of Roman material, mostly of early date. It is almost certain that some of this relates to a Claudian military presence, although the various earthworks, the 'amphitheatre' and 'equestrian camp' discussed by Colt-Hoare[36] are probably unrelated to this.

The use of Ham stone in local Roman villas implies organised quarrying on the hill during this period, but it is not possible to be certain if there was also permanent occupation. Some evidence suggests that this was not so. Coins of all dates are known from the spur, but the majority date to after 250 when the demand for Ham stone may have been greater and this may thus indicate increased activity on the hill at this time. Of the five well-documented hoards from the spur four are also of the third and fourth centuries. The motives and choice of location for the concealment of hoards are undiscoverable but it is perhaps improbable that so many should be placed in the hillfort unless there was a considerable population reasonably close at hand. The lack of later Roman pottery in any quantity does not, however, suggest that domestic activities were being carried on on any scale on the spur.

Additionally, the site was clearly used as a cemetery in the later Roman period. Burials with late Roman material have been found at two locations, and some of the other inhumations found in the interior may also be Roman rather than earlier, especially those within the N.W. corner of the fort.[37] Adult burials are not normally found very close to Roman Settlement sites, though at the nearby site of Bradley Hill adult burials were closely associated with standing structures,[38] and there is also adequate room for both a settlement and cemeteries on the spur. Nevertheless, the evidence does seem to point to use of the hillfort's northern part as a source of raw material and a depository for valuables and the dead. The Saxon shield boss (Appendix B) may be an indication that this latter function continued beyond 400 AD.

The use of hillforts for burial may imply a specifically religious importance, and at Blaise Castle, although the evidence is slightly ambiguous, a late Roman inhumation cemetery of unknown extent was apparently related to a building which is best interpreted as a Roman temple. The alternative, that it was the medieval chapel of St. Blasius, may be doubted both on the artifactual and structural evidence outlined by Rahtz[39] and on the presence of burials, which would not normally be expected at a dependent chapel. One at least of the burials was fourth century or later, and the cemetery was clearly in use both prior and subsequent to the construction and abandonment of the building, since one burial was located beneath the tiled platform at the east end of the interior, and at least one other was cut through the foundations of the north wall.

Burials have been found at three of the four certainly identified rural hill-top temples in Somerset, and this is a feature known in other areas also.[40] At Henley Wood and Crrech Hill small E-W (head to west) cemeteries occur which are later than the partial demolition of the buildings, and the single burial at Brean Down was also subsequent to the collapse of the roof in the north annex of the temple there.[41] This phenomenon is known in other late Roman contexts, the Wint Hill villa being the closest local example.[42]

A further possible instance of Roman burials within defended sites is the poorly recorded cemetery at Daw's Castle, Watchet. The earthworks of this Group II site have been discussed in chapter 4, and the limekilns mentioned by Page[43] are located close to the line of the bank on the east side. The present access to these kilns apparently follows the course of the ditch, and it seems probable that the bones found during their construction were within the ditch silt. As there is no recorded dating devidence the problem must rest there, but this is certainly a site which would repay adequate excavation.

At two other hillforts there are indications of more substantial buildings than those considered above, and such evidence as there is indicates that Roman temples may have been constructed within them. The Roman altar or votive relief portraying Mars from Cadbury Tickenham (see Appendix B) was a casual surface find, and could clearly have been brought to the site from elsewhere.

The altar or relief itself cannot be even approximately dated within the Roman period. Other examples in the Cotswold area are likewise not closely dated, but it can be argued on general grounds that the inception of a Mars cult may be linked to the postulated arrival of Gallic finance and immigrants in the later third century.[44] None of the altars which form this Cotswold group have been found in situ in a Roman temple and the majority seem to have been hidden or deliberately damaged and thrown away, and it is by no means certain that these objects were always used in temples on the architectural scale of Brean Down, Pagans Hill, West Hill, Uley or the other well-known Romano-Celtic sites. Perhaps much slighter structures such as the shrine to Silvanus at Bowes (Northumberland) or Maiden Castle I, which contained a statuette of Diana, are involved here.[45]

A building of greater pretension is implied by the evidence at Brent Knoll, the earthworks of which have been discussed earlier. The structural evidence found by Skinner indicates the presence of a stone building with painted wall plaster and a tiled roof. Once again coins of the second half of the third century are known from the hill, though only one certainly from the hillfort itself. There is no clear evidence that this structure was a temple and it could have been a villa or some other building. The topographical setting of the site must, however, favour the temple theory. The hillfort is on the summit of a very steep hill to which access is inconvenient on foot and difficult tor wheeled vehicles, and such a location for a villa would set it very much apart from the general run of sites. Additionally, Brent Knoll is a striking landmark in much the same way as Brean Down, visible for many miles in all directions and thus perhaps a suitable temple site—although the precise circumstances and conditions which caused temples to be built are of course unknown.

Considerable quantities of Roman pottery have been picked up within the defences. The majority has come from a number of limited areas of disturbance and cow scrapes near the entrance and behind the inner bank below the topsoil. The relative proximity of this site to Cadcong and the similar quantity of material suggested that comparison with the Cadcong pottery might be worthwhile (Appendix B).

There is a general similarity between the two groups. At Brent Knoll there is a small quantity of Samian and other possibly early Roman pottery, but the bulk of the material consists of local coarse wares of third and fourth century date. In both cases the local grey wares form about half of the total, but at Brent Knoll black burnished wares form the bulk of the remainder, whereas at Cadcong a number of mortaria and colour coated wares were also present. As was noted at South Cadbury, the average size of the sherds from Brent Knoll was much larger than at Cadcong, and a large number of complete pots were clearly in use on the hilltop. Although circumstances of collection are widely different, and the precise character of the structure on Brent Knoll can only be elucidated by excavation, the evidence we have so far been considering suggests that a late Roman temple was built within the fort, and that a later occupation is not to be anticipated here (but see above, chapter 4).

It has already been suggested in the case of Ham Hill that the presence of Roman coin hoards in hillforts may indicate that the sites were not in use for permanent occupation at the time of deposition. The coin hoards from Tedbury (early fourth century) Solsbury, Kings Castle (late fourth century) and Castles Camp, Bathealton (late Roman) and possible finds from Ruborough, all stand alone, no other Roman finds being known from these sites. Casual coin finds from Dolebury and Clifton are also unaccompanied by other material. At Worlebury also, Warre's discovery of a varied collection of late Roman material in the hillfort interior suggests something more than the concealment of a hoard, since pottery, bronze and glass beads were found in addition to the coins. It has been argued that the deposition date of the coins may be as late as c. 500,[46] going some way towards agreement with Warre's hypothesis that this collection represented the worldly wealth of a sub-Roman Briton sheltering within the ramparts and killed in the Saxon attack after the battle of Dyrham. If this date is correct then the pottery may also date to the first part of the fifth century, but the small quantity of material which survives shows no distinctive features—grey, black-burnished and some colour-coated wares apparentely of typical late-Roman types. If this chronological assessment is correct and coins were still held in some value in the middle of the fifth century, then the virtual absence of coins from Cadcong may strengthen the hypothesis that the initial post-Iron Age activity there is in the later fifth century or later.

Only in one case can enclosing banks of Roman date be certainly demonstrated to have been constructed, at the Group IV site of Kingsdown (Fig. 29). It is much to be regretted that this enclosure was so thoroughly examined by Gray as he failed to record the stratification in an adequate fashion and his 'layers' are in fact only spits at set depths. Clearly, though, the initial ditched enclosure, with which no bank or wall was associated, began to silt up at a time when no Roman material was present on the site. This would suggest that this scheme was of pre-Roman inception, though it could date to the early decades after the conquest. The upper parts of the ditch fill, however, contained mid-first century material probably associated with hearths and ash deposits and a terminus post quem for the final silting of the ditch is provided by the two dupondii of Hadrian.

The succeeding enclosure scheme followed the earlier closely in plan and the area enclosed was much the same. This would suggest that there was little or no break in the occupation. No dating evidence is available from the 2.5 m thick stone wall as it was nowhere dismantled. The bottom of the V-shaped ditch produced sherds of Oxford ware-type imitation Samian material which should also indicate occupation in the earlier second century, [47] and there is no diagnostically late material in the pottery at Taunton museum.

Apparently therefore Kingsdown shows a characteristically Iron Age pattern of enclosure continuing into the Roman period unhindered. The earlier, presumably Iron Age, ditch was permitted to silt up until it had almost vanished, and was then replaced by a more ambitious scheme. The original height of the wall is unknown, but a figure equivalent to its width of 2.5 m would not seem unreasonable. The whole enclosing scheme thus presented a barrier 4.5 m wide and with a difference in height of over 4 m from the base of the ditch to the top of the wall. Clearly the size of the enclosure is such that it would not pose a major military 'threat' to the Roman administration, but for some reason these quite massive works were felt by the occupants to be necessary and were either tolerated by the local administration or unknown to them. The quantity of pottery and the remarkable collection of nineteen first-century brooches does not suggest that this was an improverished community, and the site lies only 5 km from the Fosse Way not far from Bath and so cannot be regarded as 'remote' in more than a very local sense. Nor does the evidence allow a specialised function for the site to be postulated. Iron slag, some of which may relate to on-site metal working, was found in small quantity, but there is no indication that this was the chief activity. The surrounding earthworks, though undated, are probably related to the main enclosure and are best interpreted as enclosures connected with farming activities. It can be suggested therefore that the site had an essentially agricultural base, though the occupants were clearly in a position to acquire articles of some value.

At present only one possible parallel to Kingsdown can be cited in Somerset. At Moat House, Wraxall a slight stone bank fronted by a ditch of similar profile to that at Kingsdown overlay a slighter ditch. Roman pottery was found in the upper fill of the outer ditch and 'black pottery' in the base, so here perhaps two Iron Age phases, rather than an Iron Age and Roman are involved. It can be postulated, however, that enclosing banks and ditches in drystone walling or making use of timber-lacing continued to be constructed well into the Roman period in Somerset, even in areas which would normally be considered heavily 'Romanised'. Excavation has failed so far to demonstrate that the defences of major sites were built or rebuilt during this time, although it can be shown that at some hillforts Roman-period occupation was prior to the major collapse and decay of the Iron Age defences.[48] Slight though this evidence is it must raise the possibility that many larger hillforts retained defences in a reasonably intact state well into the Roman period. Perhaps more importantly, however, the evidence from Kingsdown shows that new schemes of enclosure (hardly defensive in a military sense) were constructed, and thus that techniques of ditch digging and rampart construction would have been familiar, at least at some levels of society, through the Roman period.

The range of data considered above indicates that it would be simplistic to adopt any one model of hillfort usage in the Roman period in Somerset. At a number of sites timber structures and other features of Roman date appear to continue the pattern of pre-Roman activity, and we may suggest that this was much more common, at least in the earlier Roman centuries, than has been appreciated. The general assumption that hillfort abandonment quickly followed the Roman Conquest, and thus that only 'squatters' made use of the sites subsequently, needs careful reassessment in many areas. If a substantial population was permitted to remain in hillforts this has important implications for the developing settlement pattern in the Roman period, particularly perhaps on progress towards urbanisation. Such evidence as we have, however, indicates a gradual reduction in scale of activity at the larger hillforts, but a continuing occupation of the smaller enclosures, many of which may have been actually constructed in Roman times. While this may be viewed as evidence of differing official attitudes towards major communal sites and smaller enclosed settlements, local circumstances would have been a crucial factor in the continuing use of a major hillfort. The gradual, rather than sudden abandonment of such sites may be explained rather in economic terms —the growth of new settlements related to the road system for example—than in an official 'resettlement' policy.

In the later Roman centuries there seems to be a change of emphasis, with some larger hillforts being used for purposes related to 'ritual' activity. This has been seen as a concentration on one aspect of the Iron Age function of these sites, and thus in some sense indicating a continuity of use. There is, however, a chronological gap to be bridged, since this activity seems to be chiefly a third and fourth-century phenomenon, and four of the major hilltop temples in Somerest are not in hillforts and only one, Pagans Hill, shows any signs of activity prior to the construction of the Roman building. The current emphasis on 'continuity'—of settlement, population, land arrangements and ideas—may conceal major changes, and the use of hillforts for temple sites may have very little indeed to do with any earlier sanctity they possessed. The late villa and its associated features at Ham Hill seems also to be an entirely new element in the hillfort there, though considerable activity on the northern spur may be the only instance where some sort of usage may have been continuous from the Iron Age until the fifth or sixth centuries.

A religious use may also be implied by the presence of coin hoards and other collections of material. The majority of the coin hoards are late Roman, and while pure concealment within an obvious landmark may have been the only motive, the presence of small 'shrines' such as that at Cadbury, Devon[49] and possibly at Cadbury Tickenham, may have been an important factor in the deposition of such material.

There is no evidence to suggest military activity within hillforts or enclosures subsequent to the earlier phases of the conquest, and no late Roman military equipment or weapons have been recovered which might support the 'militia' theory or the use of late Roman Germanic troops at any of these sites. Late Roman military activity seems more probably to be related to coastal sites, in particular Sea Mills, and even hillforts in close proximity to estuaries or the sea—Cannington, Brean Down and Worlebury—have produced no positive evidence for military activity at this time, although as discussed in chapter 3, earthworks at Brent Knoll and Cannington could be of late Roman or later date.

It is not possible to demonstrate that any of these various uses to which hillforts were put in the Roman period continued into the fifth century or later. The analysis of the Cadcong material, which is crucial here, strongly indicates that a 'sub-Roman' occupation was not preceded by a late Roman one. It should probably be dated to the later fifth century or later, and linked directly to the subsequent phase with imported material. In contrast, an undoubted late Roman phase at South Cadbury cannot be satisfactorily linked to the later phase there, although the frequency of Roman pottery in post-Roman contexts behind the bank must leave the question open to some extent.

Consideration of the Roman evidence completes the discussion of the various types of data in chapter 2 to 6. This material will now be considered together and against a broader background in order to assess the wider historical implications and interpretations of hillfort and hill-top use in our period.

NOTES

1. For further discussion on Romano-British material from hillforts see Burrow 1979.

2. Wheeler, 1943, 61-8.

3. See, for example, Hogg, 1960, 21 (on Garn Boduan) 'it seems exceedingly unlikely that such a structure (the small fort) would have been permitted during effective Roman occupation'.

4. Haldane, 1975, 63.

5. Wheeler, 1922.

6. Simpson, 1964a. For a recent discussion see Savory, 1976, especially 282-91.

7. Wainwright, 1967b esp. p. 70. For coin hoards in the SW and in hillforts see Isaac, 1976.

8. Information from Mrs. M. Gelling, English Place Name Society.

9. Alcock, 1972a, 172.

10. Maiden Castle, Cold Kitchen Hill, Lydney Park, Chanctonbury Ring, Blaise Castle, South Cadbury, Borough Hill, Daventry.

11. Wheeler and Wheeler, 1932.

12. Curwen and Williamson, 1931.

13. Alcock, 1963a, passim. The assumption in Alcock, and that followed here, is that the production of recognizably, 'Romano-British' artifacts ceased more or less abruptly in the early fifth century. This view received considerable support from papers delivered to the Durham Conference on 'The End of Roman Britain' in 1978, British Archaeological Reports British Series 71 (1979).

14. Frere, 1967, 376.

15. Haggett, 1965, 231-2 with refs.

16. Illustrated 1968, 25. Fig. 10, nos. 1 and 2.

17. The context of this object is uncertain at present.

18. Alcock, 1971a, 197-8.

19. Fowler et al., 1970, 31 and 37; Thomas, 1976a, 246-7.

20. Fowler, 1970, 219-227; Rahtz and Greenfield, forthcoming, 217-72.

21. These figures (correct at 16.3.76) do not include sherds unascribed to vessels, if these are included then the figures are: A ware 10.2 sherds/ pot, B ware still at 13 sherds/pot, A/RB 4.5 sherds/pot. The Roman pottery figures are little altered by the inclusion of the few unascribed sherds.

22.   Analysis of Yellow Cutting is not yet complete and detailed relationships may be altered, but the overall sequence is correct. For the possible re-dating of African Red-Slip Ware see Hayes, 1977.

23.   Fowler et al. 1970, 16.

24.   Wilts, Arch. Mag., 1964, 141. (J. Musty).

25.   Rahtz, 1974b, 97.

26.   Alcock, 1963a, 22-5.

27.   Alcock, 1972a, 22-5. For discussion of ' residual' material here see Alcock 1980b.

28.   Alcock, 1972a, 168-9. Campbell, Baxter and Alcock, 1979.

29.   Alcock, 1970b, 18-20, 1972a, 163-4.

30.   Greenfield, 1963.

31.   Alcock, 1967b, 51-3 and personal communication.

32.   Brean Down (ApSimon and Boon, 1965), Pagans Hill (Rahtz, 1951, and Rahtz & Harris, 1957), Henley Wood (J.R.S. 1965, 216) and Creech Hill (info. Mr. R. Leech) all show sequences extending beyond 400. See below and chap. 7.

33.   Branigan, 1972.

34.   Leech, 1976.

35.   Langmaid, 1971, 119.

36.   Colt-Hoare, 1827.

37.   Walter, 1853, 87.

38.   Archaeological Review 7 (1972) 39-41.

39.   Rahtz and Brown, 1958.

40.   e.g. Frilford, Berks. Bradford and Goodchild, 1939.

41.   ApSimon and Boon, 1965, 211, 220.

42.   Search (Banwell Arch. Soc.) 1961-9 passim.

43.   Page, 1890, 241.

44.   Branigan, 1974; Burrow & Bennett 1979 for full discussion of the altar.

45.   Yorks. Arch. Journ., 1948, 107ff. Wheeler, 1943, 135.

46.   Hill, 1951, 25.

47.   Young, 1973, 107.

48.   Stokeleigh, Kings Weston, Brean Down.

49.   Fox, 1952b.

CHAPTER 7

DISCUSSION, INTERPRETATION AND CONCLUSIONS

Introduction

The use of hill-top locations by the inhabitants of Somerset in our period
was a cultural response to a number of pressures. The purpose of this final
chapter is to discuss, as far as is at present possible, all aspects of the cultural background to see if any particular stimulus was of paramount importance
in the establishment of functioning of these sites. The pressures involved
may have been very varied in character. Threat of attack from other groups
in the region or from outside it; a religious belief which attached importance
to hilltops; a social structure which expected certain of its members to re-
side in such places for reasons of status or prestige; or a desire to avoid
environmental hazards on lower ground such as flooding or disease; such
motives can be readily identified as potentially relevant to Somerset in our
period. The weight of the argument here is that hillfort and hill-top usage
cannot be seen as an isolated phenomenon solely produced by specific 'historical' circumstances, but as an expression of cultural attitudes in response
to certain stimuli. This difference in emphasis is important, in that it represents an attempt to evaluate aspects of the societies with which we are
dealing not illuminated by the sparse documentary data, although this has
provided the conceptual framework for many of the discussions of this period.[1]
The historical material is clearly of basic importance, but in a partially
documented period it can unnecessarily circumscribe the interpretation of
archaeological and other types of data, even though these take precedence in
the consideration of most aspects of the subject.

This discussion will be presented in five main sections. Firstly the
methodology employed in the previous six chapters will be reconsidered in
an attempt to establish the extent of hillfort and hill-top usage, since this
must be basic to subsequent discussion of the known sites. Basic to this also
is an evaluation of the significance of the cultural changes which took place
during the AD 0-700 period, it being especially important to decide whether
changes during the fifth century were so profound as to justify consideration
of the period in two parts.

The major discussion then attempts to define motives for hillfort and
hill-top usage in relation to the culture of Somerset, as far as this can be
perceived at present. A series of models is therefore put forward here and
related to the data from the sites themselves and to the general archaeological
and historical background.

Cadcong is then considered in more detail as a case study, as the data
from this site, although less than wholly adequate to resolve many of the
questions posed here, is of a quality which permits the potential of some lines

149

of approach to be more fully explored. In these discussions a number of models will initially be considered separately, and their integration then attempted.

The final section concentrates on future research strategies. Possible approaches to the continued excavation of Cadcong are outlined, together with proposals for small-scale work on other sites. In conclusion, the value of extending the thesis methodology to other areas is discussed.

The extent of hillfort and hill-top usage AD 0-700

While it must again be stressed that excavation is the only means by which hill-top and hillfort occupations can be firmly demonstrated, the non-excavational material discussed in chapters 3-6 does provide a basis from which some assessment of this question can be made.

The direct archaeological evidence, most of it in the form of the Roman material discussed in chapter 6, suggests that at least 25% of the Somerset sites were utilised in some way during the AD 0-700 period. Usage clearly ranged from permanent buildings and occupation, demonstrable in at least twelve cases, through the use of sites for burial or the concealment of coin hoards, down to the slight evidence of frequentation represented by stray finds. Reasons have however been put forward in chapter 6 for suggesting that the use of these sites for occupation was relatively frequent. Analysis of the material from Cadcong indicates that we must not be too ready to assume that the bulk of this material dates from the pre-AD 400 period, and each instance must be carefully examined on its own merits.

The majority of future excavations, particularly of hillforts, will probably therefore produce evidence for frequentation on our period in the form of Romano-British artifacts. It might be tentatively predicted that sites close to areas of known Roman activity such as Dundon (No. 14), Littledown (No. 40) and Creech Hill (No. 45) would produce evidence of occupation if excavated.

The artifactual evidence ostensibly indicates that the frequency of use of these sites declined during the fifth to seventh centuries. It has been suggested above that occupied sites with material dating to this period do not, on the at present limited evidence, develop directly from activity within the Roman period on the same sites. It is however a working hypothesis that Romano-British artifacts did form part of the material equipment of the occupants of Cadcong in the fifth-seventh century, and it must be questioned whether the apparent reduction in hillfort and hill-top frequentation after c. AD 400 is not simply a reflection of the decline in quantity of readily datable non-perishable materials available to the local population. A dwindling supply of Romano-British pottery and metalwork, such as postulated at Cadcong, would leave little archaeological trace, and once exhausted might be replaced by perishable materials only exceptionally supplemented by exotic and durable goods such as imported pottery. Such a model suggests that hill-top occupations entirely lacking in distinctive artifacts may occur and these may only be definable by stratigraphic means, by radiocarbon determination, or other dating techniques. The definition, in archaeological terms, of this sub-Roman, non-Germanic population of Western Lowland Britain must be a research priority, or the biases inherent in the present identification of sites of this period will remain.

The discussion of surface evidence and of the potential contribution of place-name studies in chapters 3 and 4 supplements to a limited degree the more tangible evidence provided by surface finds and excavation. It is clear that earthworks will repay further study in relation to this problem, and that alterations to existing structures during the AD 0-700 period can be anticipated, and have been tentatively identified in a number of cases. Place-name material, whose potential has certainly not been exhausted in this study, does appear to hold some promise, with a small number of significant hillfort names coinciding with other types of evidence suggestive of activity in our period.

While it is therefore possible to suggest, from the negative evidence of large-scale hillfort excavations such as Danebury, Moel-y-Gaer and elsewhere, that there was not a universal return to hillfort occupation in our period, it remains difficult to quantify its precise extent. Indications from the examination of the various types of evidence considered here do not however indicate that the sites so far identified are in any way exceptional, and a number of additional examples may therefore be anticipated.

The various analyses to which the Somerset sites have been subjected in the preceding chapters put forward various predictive criteria which may be applied to hillforts. It can be proposed that the pattern of re-use of these enclosures in the AD 0-700 period will eventually prove to reflect in general the pre-existing Iron Age size-distribution pattern. As discussed in chapters 1 and 2, the Iron Age pattern of smaller, more numerous enclosures predominating in the western parts of Britain does seem to be mirrored in the later evidence we at present possess. The suggestion therefore is that hillforts towards the large end of the size range will prove to have been re-used in eastern Somerset (and probably in adjacent areas of Wessex and the Cotswolds also), while to the west smaller sites will be more frequent.

It has also been noted that the sites with most positive evidence for use in the AD 0-700 period are those in close proximity to regions of high population density and high agricultural potential, rather than in areas which can be defined as more thinly populated. Cadcong and South Cadbury illustrate this point particularly well, and it will be further discussed below.

It is clearly not possible to predict in any specific way which sites will or will not prove to have been used in our period. The value of much of the analysis in the central chapters lies in the fact that the potential of the various types of evidence there discussed had not before been systematically examined in relation to this problem. Future workers in this field may be able to disregard some aspects explored here, but even the broad predictive statements put forward could not be made with any confidence had these data not been considered in some detail.

Cultural change, AD 0-700

Since it is not possible as yet to demonstrate that any of our sites was in continuous use throughout the study period, and in particular as positive demonstration of continuity from the fourth century into the fifth and sixth has not been forthcoming, it seems desirable to examine afresh the chronological treatment of the topic. Is there, in fact, a cultural break during the fifth century so profound as to render attempts to see common patterns through the

0-700 AD period invald?   If this is so then discussion of the re-use of hilltops will have to be undertaken in two parts using somewhat different frames of reference.

The consideration of 'continuity' in chapter 1 stressed that continuity of population and of basic economic and tenurial arrangements might be anticipated in Somerset in this period.   Other aspects of life do however seem to have been subject to accelerated change, especially during the fifth century, although it was suggested that current perceptions of apparently greater settlement instability at this time might be prejudiced by the difficulties of establishing the terminal dates of the occupations of sites after AD 400. Radical changes in other aspects of life can, however, be postulated.   By the end of the seventh century Christianity, the adoption of the English language, and West Saxon political control of the area in combination formed a major new cultural environment.   The economic and political structures of the fourth century both failed to survive, though the collapse of the former, suggested by the changes in material culture, is more positively demonstrable than the latter.

It is therefore difficult to avoid the conclusion that cultural changes, apparently at their most intense in the fifth century, were so profound as to render artificial any attempt to treat the first seven centuries AD as a continuum in this context.   We may perhaps assume that the Somerset population remained genetically the same throughout the period, and that broad patterns of land exploitation and land holding continued.   These aspects of continuity are clearly important, but the discussion below illustrates that complex phenomena such as hillfort and hill-top usage reflect cultural changes rather than any underlying regularity.

Models of hillfort and hill-top use AD 0-700

As we have seen, one model—the political/social one developed by Alcock—has dominated current attitudes to hillfort and hill-top sites in the AD 400-700 period.   For the earlier four centuries there has been little systematic consideration of the problem.[2]   An attempt is made here to present in a systematic way the various factors which influenced the establishment and functioning of these sites.   For this purpose it is necessary to treat these factors individually in the first instance in order that their individual significance can be assessed.   However, it must be assumed that the interaction of a number of circumstances would normally have been involved in any use of these sites, and the subsequent discussion of Cadcong is intended to examine the ways in which this interaction can be assessed.

The range of models to be examined can be summarised as follows:

I   Models Relating to Political/Social Function

    a) The llys model
    b) The burh model
    c) The 'tribal-centre' model
    d) Urban model

II Models Relating to Religious Function

       a) Sacred area - occasionally frequented
       b) Pagan shrine (and settlement)
       c) Christian shrine (and settlement)

III Economic Models

       a) Subsistence economy
       b) Local trade/market centre
       c) Long-distance exchange
       d) Specialised craft/industrial centre

Under each of the main headings we shall review the general relevant background data from the area, and then consider each model in relation to the Somerset sites themselves.

It is perhaps typical of studies concerned with this period that these models have diverse conceptual origins. Group I models are partly specific to the period considered here and a, b and d are ultimately derived from social concepts described in contemporary or near contemporary documentation. Other models, especially those in Group III have more affinity with approaches to the data being increasingly adopted by prehistorians.

I Models relating to political/social function

Historical archaeology has tended to stress this aspect of the cultural system it studies, and this is particularly noticeable in the archaeology of the AD 400-700 period, where archaeology can hope to resolve some of the basic questions relating to political and social developments hinted at by documentary sources. Thus Alcock has stressed the links between the Welsh sites and the literary milieu of the tyranni of Gildas, and the relationship of the refurbishment of South Cadbury to known or inferred political and military developments at the time. Laing similarly considers the evidence from Mote of Mark chiefly in relation to the Anglian occupation of S.W. Scotland.[3]

In order to assess the political and social status of hill-top sites in use in the AD 0-700 period, data is required both on the general political structure of Somerset in the period, and on the range of settlement forms and their modification through time. In this way possible motives for the use or re-use of hill-top sites in relation to these developments may be suggested.

The probable political development of the area was discussed in outline in chapter 1. There it was suggested that a complex Iron Age tribal pattern was perpetuated in Roman arrangements, the fate of which after c. AD 400 is unclear. External pressure from Irish or Germanic groups from c. 300-700 may have been significant in some areas,[4] but seems unlikely to have affected the whole of Somerset to the same degree simultaneously. We may envisage a relatively stable political environment up to at least AD 400, but after that a conventional view would expect political fragmentation to set in.

It is however possible to argue against this view. Morris suggested that Somerset was for some time part of the Kingdom of Dumnonia,[5] and by the end of the seventh century it was recognised as a distinct area within the West Saxon kingdom, administered by a patricius with considerable freedom

of action.[6]   This documentary evidence perhaps finds an archaeological
reflection in the linear earthwork of the Wansdyke, discussed, in relation
to the hillforts on its line, in chapter 4.   The date and function of this feature
must have a considerable bearing on the political background of the area.
It has been suggested that the delineation of territory by this means marks a
political development from earlier conditions in which 'tribal' groups were
separated simply by physical barriers of forest and marsh.[7]   The organisation
of resources needed for the construction of such a work must have been considerable, and, while a confederation of small political units could have undertaken the task, later historical analogies suggest that the conception of the
Wansdyke frontier may have been the product of a single mind rather than
many.[8]

The identity of the political organisation responsible for the dyke is
likely to remain obscure.   Both Fox and Fox, and Myres, favour a West
Saxon context, seeing the Wiltshire and Somerset sections either as a unitary
scheme built under Ceawlin in the late sixth century, or as two separate constructions, the Somerset section dating to 628-635.[9]   However, a British
origin for the dyke seems on balance just as likely, whether it is seen as one
scheme or two.   Ascription of the dyke to the West Saxons depends entirely
on its naming after the Germanic god Woden, although Myres has pointed out
that the linking of the deity's name to the work may indicate Pagan Saxon
ignorance of its true origin.   If a West Saxon construction is to be accepted
one must additionally envisage that the kingdom had a powerful interest in
the Somerset area before the middle of the seventh century, and this is difficult
to maintain on either archaeological or historical grounds, especially if the
conventional location and result of the battle aet Peonnum in 658 are accepted.[10]

The Somerset portion of the dyke accords well with the assumed situation
after the battle of Dyrham.   Its builders had clearly lost control of the Avon
valley, but were able to make use of the heights to the south to effectively
block the most ready access to the larger part of Somerset east of the Parrett
from the east—the eastern border being, as we have seen   protected by the
Selwood barrier.   It may be significant that the battle at Bradford-on-Avon
(661) took place in the only area where the dyke could be readily 'outflanked'
if such a concept is applicable to warfare in this period.

It can therefore be suggested that, rather than Somerset being fragmented politically, there may have been a tendency towards the creation of
political units larger than Roman civitates in the AD 400-700 period. Shadowy
(and possibly fictitious) figures such as Melwas of Glastonbury[11] or a ruler
of the Lichfield area who may have moved to Glastonbury in the seventh century[12] were perhaps local figures who acknowledged the overlordship of kings
claiming a wider authority.

While a model of this nature can be put forward in relation to the historical evidence it remains difficult to assess the archaeological evidence
from hill-top sites against the general settlement background, as this is still
so imperfectly known.   In the 400-700 period the character of types of settlement other than those on hilltops is almost wholly unknown.   The evidence of
Celtic place names (Fig. 9) and perhaps of Celtic Church Dedications and
cemeteries of this period, to be discussed further below (Fig. 30) probably

indicate in a general way the distribution of the population, but this does not assist in assessment of possible differences in status between sites. In the first four centuries AD the range of settlement types is better known. The evidence from the hillforts and hill-top sites in this period does not indicate any one particular type of usage. Building types, as discussed in chapter 6, range from villa-type structures, presumably used by the wealthier and more socially influential groups, to very slight and ephemeral constructions similar to those in other rural settlements.

With these points in mind we may consider the three suggested models under this main heading.

a) The Llys model

This envisages that the main function of some at least of the sites was to act as the defensible dwelling place of local rulers and their immediate following. It can also be suggested that the rudimentary political administration of the surrounding area would centre on the site. Alcock argued that the archaeological and historical evidence supported the interpretation of Dinas Powys in this way, the main criteria being the small size of the site, its apparent wealth, and the known historical background.

Such a function is unlikely for any of the sites dating to before AD 400, the key element being that of semi-independent political power. A site such as Kingsdown, apparently occupied in the first two centuries AD, is not dissimilar in size to Dinas Powys (though its location is much less imposing), and the large number of brooches found there indicates a community of some wealth. It is however inconceivable that this site had any role in the administration of the area during the Roman period, or that semi-independent rulers were tolerated while the Imperial government was functioning, and even in more remote west Somerset the model cannot be supported on any grounds. The only possible partial exception to this may be the intensive occupation at Ham Hill discussed in chapter 6. Here a villa-type building lies, exceptionally, within the ramparts of the Iron Age hillfort, and is probably contemporary with large-scale stone quarrying on the northern spur and an extensive occupation area to the south. The possibility may perhaps be considered that the Ham Hill complex aas an economically viable unit which had a degree of administrative autonomy, a leased-out Imperial estate for example, though this is hardly susceptible to proof. It might however form a basis from which later developments of the llys developed, and the possible B ware sherds from here may be relevant in this context.

In the post-AD 400 period the model has a potentially greater validity. We have seen that although all the sites of this date have Roman material, present evidence suggests that there is no continuity from pre-400 usage, and it must be envisaged that these sites were new creations. The one possible exception to this is Cannington, where the cemetery, which contains material perhaps from a nearby settlement, appears to have a chronological range from 'early or mid-Roman times to the 7th or 8th century'.[14] The fieldwork evidence combined with that from excavation[15] suggests that this settlement may have been located immediately outside the hillfort. Its character is uncertain, but the population, of hundreds rather than scores, indicated by the cemetery, fails to support the idea of a small-scale aristocratic defended unit implied by the llys model, as does the undefensible nature of the earthworks. The hillfort itself encloses 1.8 ha.—larger than the postulated llys sites in the West, although admittedly only a proportion of this is sufficiently level for building.

Glastonbury Tor is the only site which fits the llys model reasonably well. It is small, highly defensible, and produced evidence for craft metal-working. The faunal evidence does not however suggest that the community was in a position to obtain meat from animals in prime condition, as might be anticipated on a wealthy site of high social standing, although joints were clearly brought to the site from outside.[16] This secular interpretation was felt to be supported by the predominance of meat bones which were initially considered to preclude a Christian religious use, but this cannot now be regarded as conclusive, and the latter interpretation is now favoured by the excavator.[17] The historical evidence relating to the Glastonbury area emphasises the tradition of the great antiquity of Christian practices there, although these are not localised to the Tor itself. The later Christian use of the Tor summit cannot be projected back to the fifth-seventh century occupation with any confidence, but identification of the site as a llys finds little support in any aspect of the evidence other than its topographical location and small size. The interpretation of this site is considered further below under the Christian church model.

The size of the two Cadburys precludes them from the llys model as developed by Alcock, since the amount of space defended or enclosed at both sites seems far in excess of the requirement of the social unit envisaged. The fact that a defensible settlement of similar size to Dinas Powys could have been constructed on the highest part of the interior of South Cadbury emphasizes the contrast between these Somerset sites and those to the west,[19] and we must envisage a difference of function related to this contrast in size.

b) The Burh model

The second Political/Social model is based on the function of later first millennium defended enclosures, the burhs, and perhaps on late Roman constructions such as the fleiburgen of the Rhine and Danube frontiers.[20] It envisages defensive sites being available primarily as places of refuge for 'all the folk'[21]—the inhabitants of the surrounding area—in times of insecurity. This does not preclude their permanent occupation at other times, but the interior space would have to be adequate for the accommodation of a large transitory population and its possessions. Relatively centralised societies such as the late Roman Empire, and Wessex in the late ninth and tenth centuries, were capable of mobilising the forces needed for such schemes, and unsettled conditions within the third or fourth centuries might be seen as a likely context for such sites in the Somerset area,[22] although we have already suggested that the necessary political structure might have been present later also.

Archaeological evidence to confirm this model must demonstrate the defensive capability of a relatively large site of which the interior space is so organised as to accommodate sudden influxes of people and probably livestock.

Allowing for the limitations of the available excavated data, none of the sites in use up to c. AD 400 appear to possess features of the type implied by, for example, the Sisteron inscription of the early fifth century.[23] This records the provision, by a local magnate, of walls and gates to a site described as a vicus and castellum to be used by the local populace. Refortification of Cannington during the Roman period by the addition of an outer rampart on the south may have been carried out, but at no other site can a pre-AD 400 fortification or refortification of a substantial hillfort be demonstrated, and the known defensive systems belong to the AD 400-700 period, when the nature of political control had changed. It is of course true that the pre-existing Iron-Age defences may have been regarded as of sufficient strength to render refortification unnecessary, but this would not follow the pattern observed on the continental sites or in the West Saxon burhs, where elaborate new defences were constructed.

Considerable resources must have been required for both the timber-framed bank at South Cadbury and even for the lesser stone banks (perhaps with turf of peat superstructure) at Cadbury Congresbury. Both these schemes have termini post quos (and other evidence) which suggest that they are post-AD 400.[24] In this context it should be recalled that major hillforts were being refurbished on an elaborate scale before AD 400 in areas outside direct Imperial control.[25] All these schemes imply the availability of labour on a scale comparable with that envisaged by the Burghal Hidage for the actual defence and maintenance of these sites; four men to every $5\frac{1}{2}$ yards of rampart. On this basis South Cadbury could have been effectively manned (to tenth century standards) by a force of about 870, and Cadcong by 400 (for the western enclosure only) or 650 for the whole circuit of the hilltop. Since these would presumably be adult males for the most part, we must envisage a transitory population several times this size, and consequently a large 'catchment area' which relied on the sites as defensive centres.

The crucial evidence for the arrangement of the interior space to accommodate this periodic inflow is lacking. The Cadcong evidence might suggest that buildings occupied most of the interior, but the excavated sample is too small for this to be certain. There is, however, no clear evidence of planning such as might be anticipated on a site created for this specific purpose. At South Cadbury the dominant visual position of the possible aisled hall on the summit plateau might suggest a major 'social and administrative focus'[26] appropriate to a burh-type settlement, but at this site it is impossible to assess the internal disposition of buildings in the AD 400-700 period because of the stratigraphic difficulties, outlined in chapter 5.

If the defensive purpose of these sites was uppermost in the minds of those who built and used them it is relevant to consider whether they were not in fact intended as 'forts' in a purely military sense, rather than acting as refuges as the burh model suggests. The two sixth-century battles at or near hillforts in the Anglo-Saxon Chronicle,[27] only a short distance east of the Somerset sites, at least raises the possibility that hillforts did at times play a significant military role in this period. It is, however, difficult to envisage their use as permanent garrisons of a standing army. A comparison with earlier Roman forts indicates that such a garrison would need to be supported by a highly efficient commissariat, and that a site the size of South Cadbury would, in an early Roman context, be capable of containing a garrison of about 2000 mean.[28] This scale of operations seems out of keeping with what is at present known of the military capabilities of societies in the AD 400-700 period, and there is no hint in the archaeological evidence of a specialised military function for the excavated sites. Morris, however, suggested that hillforts might have been put to infrequent use by mobile mounted forces otherwise vulnerable to night attack.[29] Refurbishment of defences on any large or elaborate scale or the construction of permanent buildings would seem unlikely in this case, and its positive demonstration archaeologically would, in any case, be extremely difficult.

Of the overt military functions which can therefore be envisaged for these sites, the burh model merits serious consideration, both because of the documented near-contemporary use of similar sites for this purpose, and from archaeological evidence indicating the refurbishment of defences on sites large enough to have functioned in this way. The chief lack is evidence for the internal arrangements of the sites, and this indeed hinders the evaluation of the majority of the models we shall be considering here.

c) Sites as 'tribal' centres

Recent trends in Iron Age hillfort studies (see above, chapter 2) have stressed the communal nature of hillfort settlements and the probability that they formed a social focus for populations living in their vicinity. The model therefore envisages the hillfort being permanently occupied by a relatively small number of people, periodically supplemented by a larger number making use of the site for a variety of social, economic and religious purposes at certain times. The social relationship between the hillfort and non-hillfort populations has only been considered in the broadest terms in Iron Age studies, and then chiefly ith reference to geographical concepts such as settlement hierarchies more relevant to economic activity than to social and political links between settlements.[30] Such connections might be reflected in the Welsh Laws, where a complex social system linked settlements of unfree bondmen to local political and economic centres, though the system cannot firmly be demonstrated to have existed prior to the tenth century.[31]

It must be envisaged that political functions of this nature were largely taken over by the urban centres during the Roman period, though the scarcity of towns in Roman Somerset has already been remarked upon in chapter 1. The general background again renders a function of this type improbable for the period in which Roman government was functioning, but the apparent collapse of towns as administrative centres after 400 may provide a context for the development of this function for hillforts at this time.[32]

Identification of this use of hillfort and hill-top sites is, however, virtually impossible at present. Once again the interior arrangement of the sites may be the key factor, since provision would need to be made for the periodic arrival of non-residents as in the case of the burh model. Location of nearby sites, and the demonstration of links between them and the hillfort, would go some way to confirming the model, but would not be conclusive.

d) Urban model

Can any of these sites be regarded as having urban characteristics? These we can define in this context as the possession of a degree of political autonomy, expressing itself archaeologically perhaps in the provision of large public buildings, water supply, drains etc., in the manner familiar both in Roman and later medieval contexts. The economic function of urban centres will be considered further below, but in a social and political sense the only site which might fit the model is South Cadbury.

At South Cadbury we may postulate a settlement shift to the hillfort from a local urban centre, Ilchester (Lindinis), as a possible context for the refortification and re-use of the site. Once again the archaeological evidence is at present inadequate to confirm the suggestion, but both the refurbishment defences and the aisled hall building would be appropriate to a site with urban pretensions. South Cadbury merits attention under this heading both because, uniquely, there is a nearby Roman town of some importance, and also because later historical circumstances provide an analogy. Recent excavations at Ilchester have suggested that the peripheral areas of the town were abandoned during the late Roman period, and that flooding of the surrounding area may have occurred after the fourth century. A small number of unstratified finds does, however, suggest use of the site into the sixth and seventh centuries.[33] A combination of factors—the vulnerable position of the town on the Fosse Way, loss of surrounding agricultural land and perhaps pandemics—may have pre-cipitated the transfer of what remained of the civic functions of Ilchester to the hillfort. The hall structure on the summit plateau would, on this inter-pretation, have a function closer to that of a forum basilica than of an aristo-cratic feasting hall.

Such a shift certainly seems to have occurred in the early eleventh century. The minting of coins, at that time permitted only in urban centres, was transferred from Ilchester to the new burh at Cadanbyrig which was itself refortified and clearly intended as a permanent settlement. A similar se-quence of events may well have taken place in the earlier period, but this interpretation of the evidence has not been discussed by Alcock or other writers on the British evidence, despite indications of similar shifts in location on the continent.[34]

The four models outlined above cover a range of possible functions of our hillfort and hill-top sites in the political/social sphere. Although this is perhaps the aspect of the sites which seems most immediately important in historical terms, it is one which cannot easily be resolved with the evidence available. It can be shown, however, that Alcock's llys model cannot be made to fit the Somerset data even at this stage of research, and the presumption behind the present discussion, namely that the regional background of these sites is crucial for their interpretation, is confirmed. The local evidence indicates that the burh and urban models can be better supported than the llys model, and future research must be designed to investigate the evidence relevant to these.

II Models relating to religious function

Throughout the study period there is abundant evidence for religious activity centred on hillforts and hill-top sites both in Somerset and more generally in Britain.[35] There are two major questions to be resolved in relation to this data once a religious usage has been confirmed. Firstly, how intensive was the use of the site? A range of possibilities, from very infrequent visits to a sacred area to permanently occupied religious settlements such as Lydney or Christian monasteries, can be immediately envisaged. Secondly, what is the character of the religious use itself? In the following discussion major attention will be focused on the recognition of pagan or Christian elements on these sites, but it must be kept in mind that certain aspects of the function of Christian and non-Christian sites may have been similar, and the contrast between Christianity and other organised religions not as marked, at least in material terms, as it is sometimes presented.

The fundamental matter, however, is the recognition of religious activity from archaeological and other evidence. The possible relevance of the -bury place-name element in the identification of Christian monastic sites has been discussed in chapter 3, and the limitations of the archaeological evidence from the majority of sites examined in some detail in chapter 6. Neither class of evidence gives a clear indication of the extent to which hilltops were used in this way, although on some sites the religious function is clearly dominant and readily identifiable. It is possible, however, to envisage a religious focus existing within a settlement which had a variety of other functions, the analogy here being with the presence of temples in Iron Age hillforts which contain a number of other structures and features.

The use of hilltops for religious purposes in Somerset certainly continued throughout the period, as the seventh century finds from Pagan's Hill,[36] and perhaps the evidence from Glastonbury Tor, indicate, The nature of the religious and social background which produced this activity is, however, much less clear. The area has one outstanding cult centre, Bath, and the Cotswold area to the north has produced considerable evidence for the worship of classical deities,[37] but rural Somerset itself has produced little evidence for the cults practised in temples or elsewhere. All the known or suspected temple sites share the common feature of hill-top location, and two sites, Brean Down and Creech Hill, possess common plan elements which may suggest similar cult practices.[38] The motivation, economics and organisation of the construction and use of these elaborate buildings, however, remain unknown, though like later Christian foundations, we may guess that dominant local figures would be largely responsible for making resources of finance, land and labour available for the construction and maintenance of these establishments. Not all 'ritual' usage need have been as elaborate as this, and small shrines, sacred wells and natural features may also have formed important cult centres within some hillforts. We can, therefore, briefly examine the three models suggested above, although much of the discussion will be centred on Cadbury Congresbury, and some aspects have already been examined in Chapter 6.

a) Occasionally frequented sacred area

Direct evidence for this type of usage would probably take the form of very slight structural remains and quantities of finds in contexts which would suggest that they had been deposited as votives. However, extensive coin scatters such as found at Woodeaton may indicate periodic frequentation of these sites for functions akin to those of medieval fairs,[39] though evidence of this type will be confined to the period of coin circulation before c. 450, and after that date the detection of such sites will prove difficult. On the; limited evidence available none of the Somerset sites appears to fit this model. Even at Cadbury Tickenham, where the casual find of a Roman altar to Mars, or possibly Silvanus, might indicate a small rural shrine of the type exemplified at Bowes (Northumberland), some evidence for a stone tiled Roman building is present.[40] None of the excavated sites has produced evidence readily to be interpreted in this way—permanent occupation or massively built ritual structures intended for more than occasional use seem indicated at all sites. A possible exception is Worlebury, where the late Roman deposit of coins, pottery, glass and bronze ornaments was apparently unassociated with any structures and may be a votive offering similar to those in the well at Cadbury, Devon.[41] Although such sites may be suspected, the evidence available at present cannot confirm their existence in either a Christian or pagan context in our period.

b) Pagan temple (and associated settlement)

The evidence for major hill-top temple sites, at least one of which (Pagan's Hill) comprised a complex of buildings in addition to the main polygonal temple itself, is relatively abundant in Somerset. Ritual structures of this type are normally sufficiently distinctive to be readily interpreted archaeologically although in one case, Blaise Castle, the nature of the excavated building remains to be confirmed. The close association of burials with this structure, some of them at least of Roman date, is not conclusive evidence for a predominantly religious purpose for it, although major cemeteries are elsewhere associated with Roman temples[42] and this interpretation of the Blaise evidence may be accepted as a working hypothesis. The ambiguous evidence from this site apart, it is clear that the construction of sophisticated religious complexes on hilltops was especially esteemed by the inhabitants of Somerset in the period centring on the third and fourth centuries (when a small immigrant group may have been responsible for a growth of local interest in this particular form of religious expression[43]). Understanding of the precise functioning of these establishments is important, both because of the light it can potentially shed on the way Romano-British rural society functioned, and more particularly because of its possible relevance to the establishment and functioning of Christian centres in the area in the latter part of the study period.

Temples of this quality can perhaps be assumed to have been served by one or more priests whose maintenance must either have relied on gifts from visitors to the shrine, or from a more regular source such as payments in cash or kind or the donation of land from local individuals. It is difficult to imagine a large establishment such as Pagan's Hill maintaining itself solely by unpredictable donations,[44] though some of the smaller sites may have done so. It seems more probable that the initial establishment and donation of land for the temple itself would be accompanied by an endowment of some kind to enable the complex to function. More attention clearly needs to be paid to this problem. It is perhaps simplistic to imagine that this initiative came exclusively from the villa-owning class: sites could have been established on marginal land and maintained by a 'grass roots' local sentiment which valued the presence of a temple. Support of this type clearly continued in Gaul and elsewhere until at least the sixth century.[59]

Some hint of this local element may be seen in the association of cemeteries with temples, and also with hillfort sites, possibly retaining a religious function from the Iron Age. The identity of these sites could remain understood for many centuries, as the Anglo-Saxon description of the Chanctonbury Ring temple (Sussex) as Stan Erigan indicates.[45] This may account for the usage of some sites for pagan burials of the fifth to seventh century, some seventeen examples of which are listed by Meaney,[46] and the practice also seems to have found favour in Christian contexts.[47] Direct association of burials with the construction and main period of use of the Somerset sites cannot however be demonstrated except at Cannington, where an annular rock-cut ditch c. 7 m in diameter on the highest surviving part of the cemetery was coincident with only two graves, the main concentration of which was to the south. The one grave within this feature could not be stratigraphically related to it, but the excavated graves in the cemetery as a whole are not coincident with the slight evidence for buildings and this may suggest contemporaneity.[48]

In other cases, however, the use of the sites as burial places seems subsequent to the disuse of the buildings, graves cutting into walls and post-demolition deposits being located at Creech Hill, Brean Down, Henley Wood and Blaise Castle[49] and the context of the cemeteries at Daw's Castle and Kings Weston[50] seems likewise to post-date the silting of the defensive ditches on these sites, perhaps in these cases analogous to temple temené. Of the sites in use from the fifth century onwards only Glastonbury Tor has evidence for graves in situ,[51] though the data from Cadcong will be considered further below. Two cemeteries lie close to South Cadbury, a small sixth-seventh century one c. 1 km to the east, and a less well documented find in 1878 of 'trenches full of human bones' 'thrown in without any order' on the west or north side of the hill,[52] but no burials later than the end of the Iron Age have been recorded from the hillfort itself. There are similarly ill-recorded cemeteries close to Cadcong in addition to that at Henley Wood.[53]

This evidence indicates that the religious significance of hill-top sites was considerable in the third and fourth centuries, and that attachment to some of the sites remained strong even after the Romanised buildings had been allowed to fall into ruin or been demolished, in two cases to be replaced by simpler rectangular structures. Evidence both from Somerset and elsewhere shows that this continuing sanctity maintained itself in some places throughout the study period, and this will affect our consideration of the Christian evidence which now follows.

c) Christian church (and associated settlement)

Christian activity in Somerset before the end of our period cannot be positively demonstrated. One inscribed memorial stone on Exmoor and a cross-marked stone at Culbone are presumably Christian,[54] but for the period before c. 400 AD we have only the ambiguous imagery of some villa mosaics to indicate the presence of Christians.[55] Dedications to Celtic saints, discussed in chapter 3, may in part originate in the AD 400-700 period. Their distribution, supported perhaps by that of 'sub-Roman' and other cemetery types, supports the model of a coastal evangelisation which made little headway in the south and east (Fig. 30).

Until the sixth century, the emphasis in Christian organisation was diocesan and not monastic, but after this time monasticism became dominant, especially in western Britain, whence any pre-English Christian influences on Somerset would most probably have come.[56] The nature of the pre-monastic church is uncertain, though it was apparently urban-based and found adherents among the upper classes in the fourth century.[57] Such an organisation could have survived through the later part of the study period, but its recognition archaeologically would be an even more formidable task than the identification of undocumented monastic sites.[58]

Whatever the details of the Christian organisation, the British and continental documentation makes it clear that support of the local secular powers was an important element in the successful establishment of Christian centre. Local 'grass roots' adherence to non-Christian beliefs often remained strong especially in rural areas where thw worship of classical deities continued.[59] The donation of defensive sites to Christian missionaries is a well-attested manifestation both of the links with local rulers cultivated by Christians, and of their need for secure resources to maintain their evangelisation. It must be considered probable that the donation of such sites was accompanied by a grant of estates in the area for the support of the religious community, and the likely antiquity of this type of arrangement links it with the functioning of non-Christian sites discussed above.

Can any of the Somerset sites therefore be interpreted as Christian centres? To a large extent such identifications must depend on overtly Chritian features: crosses, inscriptions, altars and ritual vessels, being located; and the example of Tintagel shows on how slender a basis the identification of even 'classic' sites rests.[60] The possible Christian significance of post-Roman imported wares has been exhaustively discussed elsewhere,[61] and it is not proposed to re-open the debate here. The case for so regarding these wares must, however, be regarded as unproven in a British context. 'A' ware vessels with impressed crosses on the bases were found at both South Cadbury and Cadcong, but this symbol need have had little significance for those who acquired them, perhaps at several removes from the 'primary' centres envisaged by Thomas, where on overtly Christian function might be more probable.[61] By themselves they cannot demonstrate a Christian religious element in the sites we are considering. In the period before the currency of this material there is little chance of demonstrating Christian usage from ceramics alone, although graffitti may provide evidence at all periods. No other overtly Christian evidence is known from any of the sites.

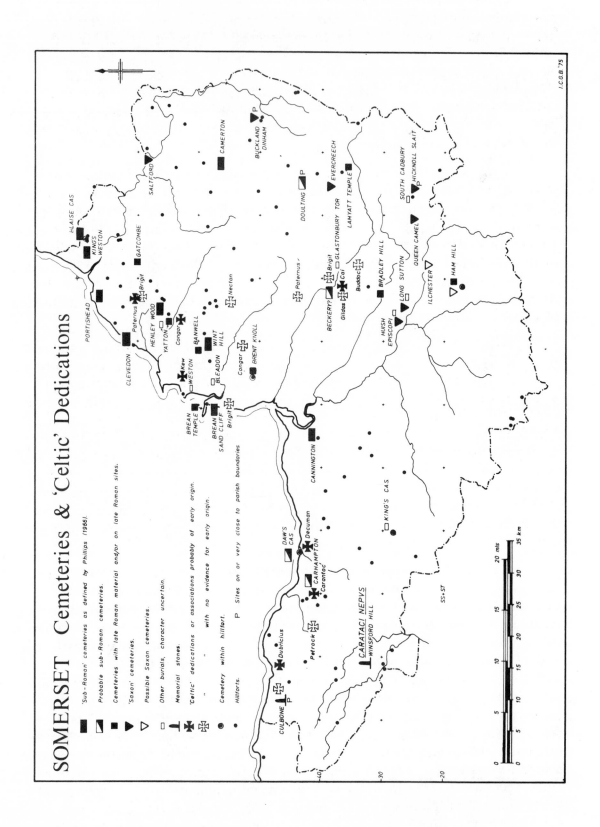

Fig. 30 Somerset; Cemeteries of the period AD 300-700 and Celtic
church dedications

164

The later sanctity of Glastonbury is not paralleled on the other sites (except possibly Blaise Castle). The eleventh century cruciform church at South Cadbury should be seen as part of the urban pretensions of the site at that time and cannot be seen as a reflection of earlier usage of the hilltop.[62] At Congresbury Alcock has argued that place-name evidence indicates a Christian use of the hillfort. He implies that the present parish name must have originally referred to the hillfort (there is in fact no evidence for this), suggesting that the burh element can only apply to a hillfort-type fortification. The discussion in chapter 3 showed this assumption to be false, and there is no difficulty in envisaging the name being applied to the area of the present village, as indeed the hagiographical material would imply.[63]

We are therefore left with the topographical data from the sites. In their general character and size, none of the sites occupied in the 400-700 period would be incapable of interpretation as monasteries. The use of pre-existing fortifications as monastic valla is well attested, though the new constructions of such early monasteries as Iona and Clonmacnois show that operations on the scale of the refurbishments of South Cadbury and Cadcong were undertaken in monastic contexts.[64] The much smaller site of Glastonbury Tor, naturally inaccessible because of its steep slopes and exposed position, would on this interpretation be more akin to the very small eremitic sites such as those in the Northern Isles,[65] or Western Ireland. Roman fort sites used in eastern England are nearer in size to the Somerset hillforts, but clearly a range of enclosure sizes was considered appropriate.

The concept of the monastic vallum, though perhaps ultimately derived from that of the temple temenos, was an intrusive element into non-Christianised areas. Its material expression would have been heavily influenced by local practices and materials, and thus its recognition archaeologically is unlikely to be straightforward. The vallum at Iona was a stone-faced bank fronted by a ditch, the whole scheme being about 3 m wide and 1.3 m high,[66] substantially smaller than the South Cadbury bank, and probably smaller than any turf superstructure on the stone banks at Cadcong.

This greater scale might, however, be related to a need for physical security, rather than for the more symbolic, legal and spiritual barrier represented by the vallum. Massive enclosing walls were constructed around monasteries in the East from an early date,[67] and the gate tower at South Cadbury and the elaborate entrance features at Cadcong (and Brent Knoll?) may be relevant here. Certainly the treatment of the entrances of later monastic establishments makes an impressive gateway a possibility on sites of our period. The reconstructions and discussion of the South Cadbury gateway have stressed its martial character and possible ancestry in Roman military architecture,[68] but its sophistication remains unparalleled on non-religious sites of this period in Britain, though our ignorance of monastic architecture at this time is such as to prevent us from knowing if such a structure is also out of place in a monastic context.[69]

Just as the vallum concept was expressed in a local idiom, the same may also be true of the functions of interior buildings. The specialised usage of buildings, especially churches and chapels, may be unrecognisable archaeologically without association with crosses, altars or Christian burials, none of which have so far been identified on the Somerset sites, except arguably at Cannington.

Radford and Thomas have argued that the rectangular conjoined buildings at Tintagel are an intrusive element in the local vernacular, but similar structures in pre-Norse contexts in the Northern Isles are regarded as Lamb as being in a local tradition there.[70] It can similarly be demonstratedthat the excavated buildings on the Somerset sites have local or insular antecedents, and no definitely exotic elements can be identified.[71]

At present the monastic model therefore lacks corroboration in Somerset, though a number of pieces of evidence—the post-Roman imported pottery, the general location of the known sites and their general character—would not positively preclude any of them. Determination of the political, social and/or religious function of such sites depends very much at present on documentary references wholly lacking in the Somerset area. Archaeological method is at present better equipped to study the general economic and subsistence bases of these settlements, and this aspect will next be considered.

III Economic models

In this section the function of the sites will be considered in relation to a series of models that can broadly be described as economic, though ranging from basic subsistence activities to long-distance exchange networks centring on hill-top settlements. The range of activities considered here is therefore wide, but all can be regarded as separate from the aspects we have been considering. A particular social, political or religious function for a site does not necessarily dictate the pattern of food production, technology or exchange patterns associated with the settlement though links between these may be discerned in particular cases.

a) Subsistence economy

In this case it is envisaged that the identified sites carried on their own subsistence activities. It is plain that throughout the period these would have essentially consisted of mixed farming, with local differences of emphasis on different resources such as cattle, sheep, grains etc., related both to the local resources and to the cultural importance attached to them by the local population.[72] We must therefore examine the subsistence base with the needs of mixed agricultural communities in mind. In this model it is assumed that the settlements could obtain all their basic subsistence needs by their own efforts.

Could the location of sites on hilltops be related in some way to basic subsistence activities? It was suggested in chapter 2 that some presumptively Iron Age enclosures may have had a specialised function related to food production, and the general location of the majority of hillforts close to a range of soils and topography has been stressed. The individual sitings, however, cannot be regarded as convenient bases for farming. The corralling of stock and the collection and storage of crops and hay would be simpler on lower ground, and other factors must have predominated in the selection of the sites. The only consideration of this sort which may have weighed with the users of some of the sites may have been the health of themselves and their stock. Although debate on the evidence continues, permanent inundation or at least seasonal flooding of parts of the Somerset Levels area was probably a feature of the latter part of the period.[73] This would restrict the area of available land and increase the prevalence of a range of diseases among humans and stock living in close proximity to the marshy inundated areas. A move to higher ground might have seemed desirable in some cases and could account for the occupations in sites around the periphery of the Levels. It can scarcely be relevant to all sites, however, since several are well away from areas thought to have been affected by flooding—South Cadbury being the primary example— and as it is argued here that the majority of settlements were not on hilltops the choice of these locations must be seen as exceptional.

The evidence from the sites themselves gives little indication of subsistence activities. In the earlier part of the study period only Kingsdown and Norton Fitzwarren have been excavated on a large enough scale for useful evidence to have been obtained. At Kingsdown sheep, cattle and deer bones were found, in addition to eight spindle-whorls and bone points made from sheep/goat tibiae. Norton Fitzwarren apparently produced little evidence of this kind, and iron working seems to have predominated in the excavated areas.

After AD 400 no evidence has yet been presented relating to subsistence activities at South Cadbury, but the stratigraphic problems of this site(above, chapter 5) probably render difficult the identification of faunal remains and other basic evidence of this date. Neither here nor at Glastonbury Tor can buildings be functionally related to this type of activity, though this may be the case at Cadcong (see below). At the Tor, the chief evidence again consisted of animal bones, here broadly indicating a community making use of its animals for a variety of purposes before slaughtering them.[74] Three small utilised stones from here are examples of a body of neglected evidence from sites of this period which are probably related to such activities as leatherworking.[75]

The areas surrounding the sites may ultimately be expected to yield evidence for food production in the form of field systems or other land divisions. The difficulties of relating these features directly to the contemporary hillfort /hill-top occupations will be considerable unless there is a direct stratigraphic relationship between them. The earthworks at Cannington, discussed in chapter 4 (Plan C) provide the only opportunity of this kind at present identified, and even the fields of possible Roman date in close proximity to the hillfort on the restricted site of Brean Down cannot be positively linked to the Roman activity on the settlement site.[76]

We may, however, attempt to define the land resources available to these communities by reference to geographical studies of the practices of arable economies, and possibly also by reference to the later evidence for land division provided by Anglo-Saxon land charters. By the use of these data theoretical territories related to the subsistence needs of hillfort populations might be constructed, and one example will be discussed in detail below. In chapter 2 the overall hillfort pattern was expressed in terms of Thiessen polygons (Fig. 5), and there it was seen that in general the larger the site the greater was its spacing from its nearest neighbours, and thus the greater the area enclosed within the polygons. This characteristic may be connected with economic or political influence, but it cannot readily be related to the subsistence needs of communities engaging in arable or mixed farming based on the hillforts, as the larger part of these activities would probably take place within a relatively small radius. This has been found by studies in various areas to be not normally greater than 4 km from the settlement site, and it is within this sort of area that evidence for main food production should be sought. Should links ever be positively demonstrated between field systems or other features and a hillfort significantly more than 4 km distant it could be suggested that the basic agricultural activity was being carried out at dependent settlements and only secondarily reaching the hillfort. This point will be returned to below.

The areas of land defined by the boundaries of Anglo-Saxon land charters vary considerably. While in some cases we may be dealing with small, self-sufficient estates worked from one centre, the early grants of large tracts of land, such as the 50 sq. km granted to Glastonbury Abbey around Brent Knoll (probably in the late seventh century), were clearly not intended to be regarded in this way.[78] Some smaller estate units within present parishes may have their origin in Roman or earlier land divisions, and some are coterminous with later parishes.[79] This variation suggests differing origins and development, and while it may be that in some cases later land units are direct survivals of small areas used by hillfort communities, the location of eleven Somerset sites on parish or charter boundaries[80] does not suggest that dates earlier than the later first millennium can be presumed for these units. Their value for determining territories relating to subsistence activities is therefore slight at present.

The evidence that these sites were engaged in basic subsistence activities therefore remains inadequate, and little progress can be made without much greater attention being paid to the recovery of reliable data in excavation. Some sites do, however, seem to have been involved in producing food for their own use, and the discussion on Cadcong will enlarge on this aspect.

b) Local trade or market centre

This model envisages the use of sites for the exchange of goods, and perhaps services, on a local basis, though a precise definition of 'local' cannot be made other than to suggest a journey-time of one day or less to the market centre as defining the hinterland—an area similar to that served by many medieval market towns and, in a different context, by West Saxon burhs.

Evidence to confirm this model could take the form of temporary enclosures or structures for the display and sale of goods and stock. In the period before c. AD 450 small denomination coinage in large quantities may provide the best clue to this type of activity. The possible use of Roman temple sites for this purpose has already been noted,[81] but on none of the Somerset sites has the distribution of coins and other relevant material been plotted in areas where exchanges of this type may have been carried on.[82] The numerous coin finds from Blaise Castle are unfortunately unprovenanced for the most part, but this interpretation might be confirmed here by further excavation.[83]

In periods without coinage, other criteria by which sites can be identified need to be defined. We might anticipate localised distributions of particular types of artifacts or goods on a site of this type, indicating the location of stalls or booths where these materials were offered for display, some items inevitably being broken, lost or discarded in the vicinity. Apart from perishable goods, the major items of local manufacture that might be anticipated on such sites would be utility goods such as pottery and metal utensils, and the local character of these could be established by the various methods of physical analysis now available. Once again, however, the available data is grossly inadequate to confirm or refute the model, which in this case would require the examination of a large continuous area in order to establish the character of the site and assess the significance of distribution patterns.

If the validity of this model could however be demonstrated, it would have implications for the general settlement pattern of the area. Hillforts or hill-top sites functioning in this way would be serving the needs of a number of surrounding communities depending on them for the disposal of their own surplus goods and the purchase of others. This economic dependence implies a simple settlement hierarchy in which the hillfort/hilltop is a higher order settlement surrounded by dependents. The hill-top sites themselves might in their turn be related to more important settlements, but it will be assumed in subsequent discussion that they are likely to be the most important sites in the region from an economic point of view. Central Place Theory would designate these market centres as the nodes of hypothetical lattices, the dependent settlements either making use of more than one higher order market centre (a K=3 lattice) or all owing allegiance to one centre only (a K=7 lattice),[84] the latter situation having implications for political and social models as well as economic ones, as will be discussed further below.

c) Long-distance exchange

The presence of pottery imported to the British Isles from the Mediterranean and Gaul on Somerset sites of the AD 400-700 period does not in itself demonstrate that these locations were acting as centres for trade in these goods at this time. Thomas has pointed out a possible distinction betwenn 'primary' sites where the pottery was first obtained from ships, and 'secondary' ones to which it could have been distributed by a variety of means.[85] It must also be questioned whether commercial transactions were involved at all if the material had a primarily liturgical use as Thomas suggests. The mechanisms by which the pottery and its contents reached the British Isles remain unknown, and its significance can therefore not be readily assessed. If its religious connotations were paramount, its importance as wine containers (a likely function of 'B' ware amphorae) and as liturgical vessels ('A' ware dishes and bowls) would be very great, both because of its origin within the heartland of Christianity and because of its rarity. Alternatively, if a purely commercial operation was involved the value of the traded goods must have been themselves considerable to warrant the long-distance transportation of such fragile material. The value of the pottery and its contents would presumably have increased if several groups of intermediaries were involved en route. We must not however discount the possibility that it arrived in Britain as gifts designed to obtain alliances or privileges from local rulers, in which case commercial considerations would not apply to the same extent.[86]

If a long-distance sea-borne trade is involved, sites close to the coast or to navigable rivers would be most favourably positioned, and Fox suggested that this explanation would best fit the evidence from the Devon estuary sites of Bantham and Mothecombe.[87] Requirements would include a safe anchorage in tidal water and a secure area in which exchange could be carried out. Neither South Cadbury nor Glastonbury Tor seem suitable for this purpose, the former because of its distance from a navigable waterway, and the latter because of its small size and difficulty of access. Cadcong and Cannington would, however, both be well-suited as exchange centres, although the small quantities of the material at the latter do not encourage any confidence in the hypothesis here.

The type of evidence required from the sites themselves is similar to that for the local market model discussed above. The crucial matter is, however, the identification of goods for which this exotic material might have been exchanged. Evidence for metal working at Glastonbury Tor and Cadcong indicates the manufacture of high quality jewellery or utensils, but such items have not been recorded on sites on the postulated trade routes to the Mediterranean.

The presence of small fragments of Germanic metalwork and glass does, however, present a more positive indication of long-distance exchange, probably overland from eastern England.[88] Small quantities of Teutonic glass were found at Cadcong, and two items of Anglo-Saxon jewellery at South Cadbury, one from the road surface associated with the postulated post-Roman gate, the second from the eastern side of the summit plateau. In these cases there is no evidence that these were scrap items intended for jewellery working as was suggested at Dinas Powys, though this is probably the case with the Cadcong glass.[89] The presence of a few exotic objects of this type cannot confirm that the site was a long-distance trading centre, though it must imply contact with populations with a 'Germanic' material culture though these were perhaps only a few miles to the east by the sixth and seventh centuries. Nor can the presence of an actual intrusive element in the population be ruled out.[90]

If any of the Somerset sites were involved in long-distance trade on a regular basis this activity has left little trade. Somehow they acquired exotic goods in the form of pottery and its unknown contents and perhaps a range of other perishable goods, but whether this is the result of an organised commercial trading pattern may be doubted. In particular it is difficult to envisage exchange goods, except perhaps slaves, valuable enough to justify the regular transport of these goods. The evidence for the re-use of metal scrap in the production of jewellery does not suggest either that metal ores were being exploited on a large scale, or therefore that the export of metalwork or precious metals could have been a major factor in the trade. A trading function for these sites, perhaps restricted to them in a manner similar to that of later Anglo-Saxon ports, must remain a possibility but cannot be demonstrated at present.

d) Specialised craft/industrial centre

Finally we may consider the possibility that the Somerset sites were used as enclosures within which essentially industrial activities were carried out. Analogies for this can be found in the third century coin-forging at Coygan Camp, in the small hill-top site of Kiondroghad (Isle of Man), a specialised metalworking centre of the AD 400-700 period, and at the Irish raths of Ballycateen and Garryduff.[91] The discussion of the Romano-British evidence in chapter 6 demonstrated that a specialist use related to industrial activity was likely in two forts in use before c. AD 400—Ham Hill and Norton Fitzwarren. The demand for the building stone produced at the former presumably declined after 400, but the demand for iron, apparently produced at the Norton Fitzwarren site, would have been maintained. The main issues, however, are firstly to distinguish between essentially domestic industrial production and a specialised centre whose occupants may not have been directly involved in food production, being dependent on the exchange value of their products. Secondly, if such a function can be distinguished, what is the significance of its location within the earthworks of hillfort or on a defensible hilltop?

Establishments such as the coin forgery of Coygan Camp and the Ham Hill quarries were clearly more than 'domestic' production centres, but the latter site provides the only firm example of this in Somerset, and here the critical locational factor was probably the unique outcropping of the stone and not the existence of the hillfort. The metalworking evidence from Cadcong and Glastonbury Tor is similar to that from sites of all kinds in western Britain in the AD 400-700 period although in the latter case the number of hearths probably associated with metal-working may indicate that this was the dominant activity. The loss of evidence from the area of the later church may, however, be giving too much weight to the material from excavated areas.

It has been suggested, chiefly on the basis of early Irish and Welsh documentary material, that the activities of smiths and, especially, of jewellers were closely associated with the ruling elements in society, both religious and lay, in the 400-700 period, and that individual craftsmen were peripatetic, undertaking work at centres where they obtained the best rewards.[92] If this model can be applied to Somerset at this time (and the relevance of other models based on documentary material has been questioned previously), it would not lead us to anticipate craft working on any very large or permanent basis, except perhaps on monastic sites.[93] Even here, however, production was essentially subsidiary to the needs of a community whose chief function was completely different. While we may therefore suggest specialised crafts were carried on on these sites, they were not the raison d'être of the settlements, nor were they likely to have been confined to them.

Having therefore reviewed the range of models which may be applicable to the Somerset sites, attention will now be concentrated on the site of Cadbury Congresbury, where alone the quality of the evidence and the scale of excavations to date enable a more detailed analysis to be undertaken. Even here, however, the discussion in chapter 5 demonstrated the present limitations of the stratigraphic data and this discussion should therefore be viewed as a basis for future analysis and research strategy, rather than a final statement on the status, role and functioning of the site.

Cadcong

In this discussion on overall treatment of Cadcong will be attempted, commencing with an examination of the local environmental and economic factors and only subsequently considering the political and religious elements which have in the past dominated discussion on sites of this type.

Before this is attempted it will be useful to state explicitly the basic relevant data on which the discussion will rely, since this does at least define the parameters within which a correct assessment of the site's purpose and function lies. The site is situated on a steep-sided Carboniferous Limestone hill in an area which falls into four main topographical zones: the alluvium and peat of the Levels, the outwash or 'Head' deposits at the bases of the limestone hills, the steep slopes of the hills themselves, and the undulating plateaux above. Modern settlements, including Congresbury, which is assumed here to be the location of the monastery in existence by the late ninth century,[94] are generally located on the Head deposits. The area is close to the sea, and Congresbury village was accessible to sea-going craft until this century. Despite the vulnerability of the Levels to flooding, the settlement and place-name evidence indicates that the area was well populated throughout the first millennium. A Romano-Celtic temple close to the hillfort demonstrates the wealth of the area in the later Roman period and its importance as a religious centre before the establishment of the Christian monastery.

The site itself is a defensible plateau of c. 3.5 ha. enclosed by earthworks partly of Iron Age type, and divided into two unequal parts by a N-S bank belonging to the AD 400-700 occupation phase. Excavation in the north part of the western half recovered evidence of at least eleven different structures including eight buildings of varying size, form and constructional technique, linear stone banks or platforms, and a laid stone platform delimiting an artificially constructed circular pit or timber emplacement, the fill of which contained a range of objects strikingly representative of the material culture of the site. Partly underlying this platform was a rubble deposit containing human skull fragments, some of them weathered. The superimposition of features indicates an occupation of some duration or at least two phases. Romano-British pottery was probably in use in the earliest stages of the occupation, supplemented by imported wares from the Mediterranean and possibly elsewhere, and by more local hand-made vessels. Other Roman material, especially roof and floor tiles, was present. Crucible fragments, fused glass, gold, and enamel, all suggest the production of fine metalwork. A large quantity of animal bones, most in a fragmentary state, provides the main evidence for agricultural practices and diet.

Although the evidence is defective, we may begin with an assessment of the relationship of the site to its immediate surroundings (Fig. 31). Here an attempt has been made to define areas of influence of the site related to its possible functions as a subsistence farming community, and as a local exchange or market centre. The Thiessen polygon expresses the geometrical relationship of the site to other hillforts. This might very crudely define the area of influence were the other sites in use contemporaneously, and within its limits any lower order settlements would be dependent in various ways on the hillfort. It will be noticed that there is a general correspondence between the polygon

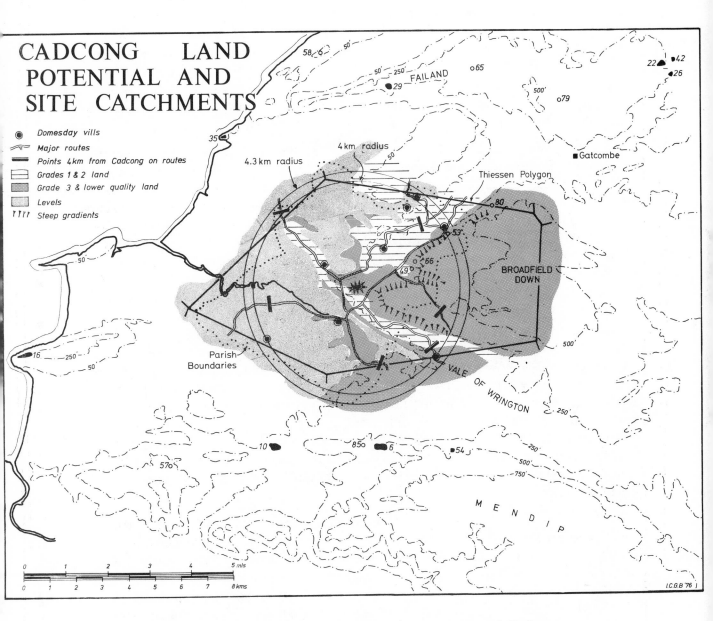

CADCONG LAND POTENTIAL AND SITE CATCHMENTS

- ◉ Domesday vills
- ⤳ Major routes
- ▬ Points 4km from Cadcong on routes
- Grades 1 & 2 land
- Grade 3 & lower quality land
- Levels
- ↑↑↑↑ Steep gradients

58 6   50
50 250   FAILAND   o65
50   o29
                          o79

35 o

4km. radius

4.3km. radius   Thiessen Polygon

                              80
                         53
                    o 66
               49 o
                          BROADFIELD
                          DOWN

50

250
50

16   250
      50

Parish
Boundaries

22 ▲ 42
        26

500

■ Gatcombe

500'

VALE OF WRINGTON   250

10   85 o   6   54   250

                                  500'
57 o   750'

M E N D I P

0   1   2   3   4   5 mls
0   1   2   3   4   5   6   7   8 kms

I.C.G.B.'76 J

Fig. 31 Site Catchments and land potential around Cadcong

and the boundaries of a land unit formed from the parishes of Puxton, Congresbury, Brockley, Cleeve and Yatton except on the east, where the area of the polygon bisects the upland plateau of Broadfield Down but the parish boundaries basically follow the summits of the side slopes. The antiquity of these boundaries cannot be firmly demonstrated in this instance, but some in other parts of the county were in existence in the eighth century.[95] No charter bounds survive for the Congresbury area, though it was assessed at twenty hides in a lost charter,[96] and it would be of the greatest interest to know the extent of the area granted with the Congresbury monastery to Asser in the late ninth century. The possibility can at least be raised here that a land unit based on the hillfort survived into the later first millennium AD as the monastic lands and was then gradually subdivided, several of the Domesday vills shown in Figure 31 being formed into later parishes.

This raises once again the question of the place of Cadcong in any local settlement hierarchy. An estimate of population size for the hill-top community suggests that other settlements are likely to have existed in the area, as indeed does the evidence of place names, church dedications and cemeteries already considered. Any wholly reliable estimate of population is impossible at this stage, but if a density similar to that suggested for Iron Age hillforts is assumed, a community of 150-200 would seem probable at Cadcong; approximately two persons per excavated building.[97] Assuming this to be of the correct order of magnitude, or at least that the population is unlikely to have been larger than that of an Iron Age hillfort (though it may have been smaller), the population density within the polygon 'territory' of c. 65 sq.km would be only about 2.5 per sq. km, or 3 per sq. km if the area defined by the parishes is adopted. This is approximately the same as the recorded 1086 population, but must be considerably less than the actual density at the latter period.[98] Unless we are to envisage a drastic population decline from a well-populated late Roman landscape and a subsequent increase, a figure four or more times lower than than at Domesday seems hard to accept in an agriculturally productive area such as this. There is therefore a high probability that other settlements existed in the area contemporary with the Cadcong occupation.

If the picture of Cadcong as a relatively populous and nucleated settlement is correct, it would appear to mark a departure from the preceding Roman rural pattern of villas and Romanised farmsteads. Gatcombe is the only known local site which may have supported a population on the same sort of scale in the preceding centuries, this site being interpreted as a large villa estate, and this model may be relevant to Cadcong.[99] Such a concentration of population on a dominant and well located position strongly suggests that Cadcong was a centre of social importance, and permits the inference to be made that the additional settlements in the area were of a lower order and dependent upon it both economically and perhaps socially and politically. Certainly the postulated predecessors of Congresbury, Yatton and Claverham would be well within the notional sphere of influence of the hillfort. The suggested pattern is one expressed by Christaller's administrative principal, in which the lower order settlements lie completely within the spheres of influence of the higher, instead of at their margin as in a more simple 'marketing' environment.[100] This line of argument would suggest that the hillfort was the central place in a local settlement hierarchy over which it exercised both economic and political control. This is certainly consistent with the evidence for wealth or power implied by the finds from the excavation itself.

It remains true, however, that much of the primary subsistence activities could have been carried on from the hillfort itself, despite the possible inconvenience inherent in the location. On Figure 35 circles of radii 4 km and 4.3 km have been drawn centring on the hillfort, together with actual 4 km distances along the major present-day roads, all of which follow obvious routes which are likely to be ancient. The basis for the 4 km figure has been discussed above, and the 4.3 km figure is derived from Hogg's formula for relating hillfort size to the population density of the surrounding area.[101] The correspondence of all these criteria can be seen on the map (Fig. 31).

The land resources within this area would have been ample for the postulated community, and their quality and accessibility must argue against any suggestion that Cadcong was a marginal settlement at the edge of an already ordered landscape.[102] Approximately 25% of the area within the defined territory is of grades 1 and 2 agricultural land as presently defined, most of it immediately north-east of the hillfort.[103] Here, any intensive arable cultivation would have been carried out. The Levels comprise some 60% of the area defined by the parish boundary unit, or 35% of that within the polygon. These, if not permanently flooded, would best be used for fuel and for grazing and fishing, as they were at Domesday, and would have been of considerable potential importance. The remaining zones, the plateau of Broadfield Down and the scarp slopes could also have been exploited; the latter for pannage, fuel and building materials if it was then wooded as at present. The former may have been regarded chiefly as an area for permanent grazing, and we may note that much of this area lies more than 4 km from the settlement.

The surrounding area therefore suggests that Cadcong was an important settlement controlling a large and varied area within which dependent settlements existed, and most of which could additionally have been managed from the hillfort. We may perhaps envisage a situation in which some functions were carried out at the site itself, and others were the responsibility of the postulated lower order settlements.[104] The evidence from the excavation can therefore be examined in the light of this hypothesis.

The preliminary analysis of the faunal remains from the site suggested that cattle predominated over sheep/goat and pig as at Gatcombe, but the sample was too small for useful data on age at death and other relevant information.[105] The quantities of bone from the site are large and include skull and horn cores, and this suggests that animals were slaughtered on the site. Bones were found over the whole site, and this distribution gives no indication of the location of the slaughter area or of cooking of refuse dumps. The only building which could at present be even tentatively linked to subsistence activities is the 'long house' (Structure I) so called from its plan similarity to a later medieval long house. If, however, its northern lower, end was used for stalling cattle there would only be room for three or four beasts, not in any way reflecting the scale of agricultural activity here envisaged. Nor within the excavated area is there sufficient open space for the penning of stock, although this may be present elsewhere on the hilltop. Nor can any of the buildings be at present interpreted as being for storage or processing of crops. Even the fragmentary rotary querns from the site cannot confirm that food processing was undertaken here, as they may have been brought to the site broken in common with some of the other Romano-British material.

If, however, the central place function of the site can be accepted we can proceed to a consideration of the political, social and possibly religious functions of a settlement with the suggested economic and population base. The discussion above indicated that the concept of some of the sites as communal refuges analogous to burhs deserves serious consideration. Cadcong is a defensible site in an area vulnerable to attack perhaps chiefly from the sea, and the discussion of the possible regional political situation above, together with more general historical analogies indicate that this is a possible interpretation here.

It was suggested above that adequate defence of the site (by tenth-century criteria) would require a force of about 650 men. The territory we have been considering would not have been able to provide such a force, even in the late eleventh century. If we accept the population estimates at Domesday as of the correct order of size for the 400-700 period, and assume that only one in four of the refugee population would be capable of bearing arms to defend the site, the catchment area of Cadcong would need to be some 260 sq. km, or an area within a radius of c. 9 km from the site.[106] Such estimates can only be tentative, but it is worth noting that such an area fits extremely closely the topographical region defined on the north by the Failand Ridge, on the south by Mendip and on the east by Broadfield Down, in the centre of which lies Cadcong.

There need be no conflict between this model and the concept of Cadcong as the economic and administrative centre of a smaller estate unit, but it does imply a wider political sphere of influence for the site. The crucial matter, however, is the archaeological evidence from the site itself. The area so far examined is densely covered in buildings which are apparently permanent, and the quantity of occupation debris does not suggest an infrequent usage in times of strife. It may be that the central areas of the site were open space, with buildings concentrated behind the banks, but features at the southern limits of excavation do not lend support to this suggestion. The excavation of a continuous strip north-south across the site would answer questions about the interior organisation of the site of relevance to this problem.

There is, however, little evidence to suggest a strongly military function for the site. The absence of weapons is not of direct relevance as these are rare on all western British sites, but the defensible capability of the stone banks is a more significant matter. The original form of these has been discussed in chapter 5. The post-bank apsidal structure (VII on Figure 11) resembles an open-gorge bastion in plan, and could be interpreted as a strengthening of the defences at the vulnerable junction of the western and eastern enclosures. This feature might therefore be a reflection of earlier Roman practices in the same way as the gate structure at South Cadbury, and would indicate a strong sub-Roman cultural element among the population of the site, also indicated by other evidence. If it is assumed that the stone banks as excavated were merely the base for a superstructure of organic materials, their present slight character may be wholly misleading and their defensive capability may have been adequate for the needs of the time.

The division of the site into two unequal parts by the N-S bank with its apparently non-defensive entrance gap is at present unparalleled on sites of this period, unless a link is seen with the Scottish nuclear forts or with the concentric monastic enclosures at Nendrum in Ulster. The excavated area does indicate that there were buildings in both parts, although they may not be strictly contemporary, but clearly both areas need investigation on a larger scale before any similarities or differences between them can be discerned. This division of the site must be seen as one of its most significant features and one which may finally resolve the questions relating to its political/religious functions. On the burh and market models it might be suggested that the eastern, outer enclosure, was intended for the periodic and infrequent influx of people and livestock, while the western portion was the permanently occupied administrative and economic centre, but this is hypothetical.

The diversity of the interior buildings is one of the most striking features of the site, especially when compared to those from contemporary lowland settlements such as Chalton and Catholme, or from Iron Age hillforts. There seems to be little element of planning although the area so far examined is too small to be certain and it may be that Structures I, II and VIII are flanking an E-W route from the entrance, though this is virtually blocked by Structure IV which is perhaps not contemporary. This diversity suggests either functional or social differences which do not indicate a simple agricultural community, and they must raise the possibility that the site possessed some urban characteristics. There is slight evidence (a concentration of glass and enamel fragments) that Structure IV was associated with jewellry production, Structure I contained a concentration of A and B ware and other finds associated with the use of the building, and Structure II contained few finds. It is impossible to define precise functions for the buildings on this basis alone, but the structural and artifactual variation does imply a complex community.

What is the ancestry of these buildings? They may either be a development of a local vernacular tradition or intrusive, and could be derived either from an urban or rural milieu. The only structures which appear to be in any way related to what would be anticipated in a late Romano-British urban centre are the 'bastion' structure (VIII)—just as possibly adapted from late Roman military models—and the 'long house', Structure I, resembling the series of latest structures on site 68 at Wroxeter, though only in a general way.[107]

The circular buildings can be readily related to the local rural tradition, good parallels being from an Iron Age context at Butcombe[108] and the summit structure at Cannington. Domestic circular buildings are not, however, known from the period c. AD 100-400 and parallels should perhaps be sought elsewhere, perhaps in the less Romanised areas to the west. If such a link could be demonstrated it would imply not only an intrusive element in the population (not at present supported by other evidence), but would also run counter to any suggestion that the site had roots in an urban-based society.[109]

However, late Romano-British religious parallels can be found for two of the buildings, Structures I and II, and a religious element on the site also seems indicated by the pit and its surround and the preceding rubble tumble containing human skull fragments. Given that the site was a permanently occupied one, and not a sporadically visited sacred area, we must consider whether any religious element in the settlement was the primary factor in its creation and function, and whether this religion was Christian or pagan, since resolution of the latter point will be of wide historical significance.

Figure 32 shows the formal similarities between Structure II and a number of late Roman shrines of circular plan. The main contrast is in the use of stone footings for the other buildings and the rock-cut trench, probably acting as a basis for upright timbers, at Cadcong. Some of the fourteen temple sites with which Structure II is comparable were perhaps more massive structures with footings at least of mortared stone,[110] but in general these buildings have a 'rustic' character which is in contrast to the more sophisticated Romano-Celtic temples. The majority have entrances facing east, the closest in alignment to Structure II (c. 110º) being Maiden Castle I (c. 100º). The elaboration of the Cadcong entrance seems unusual, but is reflected at the local Romano-Celtic temple sites.

The interior of Structure II was kept clean, and it was suggested in chapter 6 that this was in part due to its primary character in the site sequence and its continuous maintenance. Many of the earlier shrines do, however, contain large numbers of finds, although as these are chiefly of coins and mass-produced metalwork largely unavailable in the AD 400-700 period the contrast may not be significant. The most interesting finds from Structure II are the two bone plaques or pendants paralleled in bronze at Brigstock and Brean Down,[111] and the deposition in an adjacent post-hole of the entrance, of B ware amphora handle fragments. It seems probable that some significance was attached to both these items at the time of the construction of the building.

Specific similarities can, therefore, be demonstrated between Structure II and these slightly earlier ritual structures. A ritual context can also be argued for Structure I. The Romano-Celtic sites at Brean Down and Creech Hill were both succeeded by small rectangular buildings, the former perhaps a 2-cell structure, and at Maiden Castle a similar building was interpreted as a priest's house contemporary with the Romano-Celtic temple there.[112] The proximity of Structures I and II is reminiscent of the relationship at Maiden Castle and raises the possibility that at Cadcong a late Romano-British religious tradition continued into the AD 400-700 period. If the whole complex were to be viewed in this light the enclosure banks would form the temenos of a religious establishment on the scale of Lydney or Harlow.[113] However, the planned layout seen at the former and at Pagan's Hill is not apparently present at Cadcong. Nor is the shrine (if that is what Structure II is) in the dominant summit position normally chosen for the main religious building at these sites. It would have been immediately visible to anyone entering the inner enclosure, but is closely surrounded by other buildings which are almost certainly contemporary. It is of course possible that there were a number of small shrines, as at Collyweston, but this cannot yet be demonstrated.

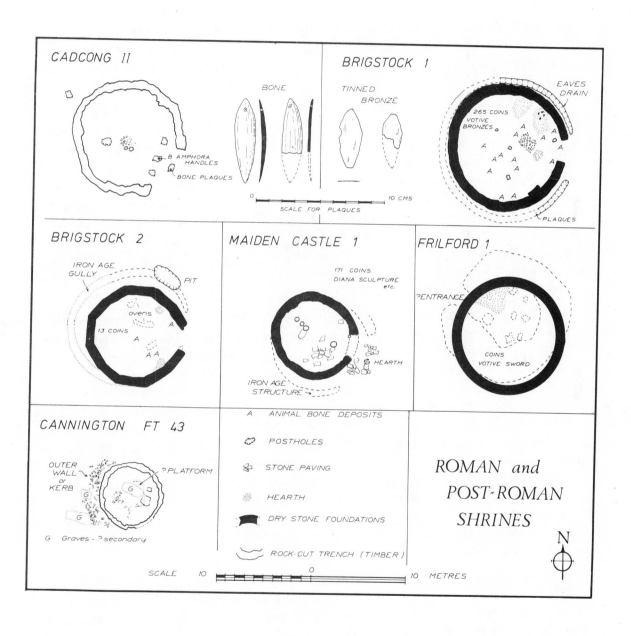

Fig. 32   Cadcong Structure II and comparable late or post-Roman
circular shrines

The size and complexity of the Cadcong settlement appears to make its interpretation as a large ritual centre unconvincing, even though such an establishment might conceivably have been able to exist into the sixth century even in the face of Christian expansion. However, the maintenance of a small shrine, perhaps with a priest, as part of a larger settlement complex with its cultural roots in the local area is not impossible. Certainly the slight evidence for the exposure of human skulls nearby may suggest at least an earlier pagan phase, [114] and the close proximity of the Henley Wood temple, although it was demolished in or ofter the fourth century, may be a further pointer to a strong local support for pagan worship. The evidence we have been considering would also suggest that it had support among the ruling group on the site.

The major alternative to this possibility is that this site is an early monastery, an interpretation ostensibly favoured by the proximity of a known later monastery at Congresbury and by the possibly religious associations of 'A' and 'B' wares. We have, however, questioned the significance of both these factors, and must therefore examine the other evidence for independent confirmation that a Christian monastic establishment existed here. A single significant find, such as an inscribed stone too large to have been brought in to the site from elsewhere, could resolve this question in a future excavation programme, but at present there is no unambiguous Christian evidence from the site apart from the stamped crosses on A ware bowls, of limited relevance to the status of the site itself.

The economic model put forward above for the site would be quite appropriate to a monastic status for it, any surrounding land perhaps being donated with the site itself by a local ruler, following documented practice elsewhere. Continuity between the hill-top site and a later establishment around the present church, the area 'shut in by water and reed beds', would in this case be complete, the only change being in the location of the main centre of activity. All the other economic activities we have examined would be appropriate to a large monastery at this time and this model of the site fits the data well in general terms. None of the features characteristic of early Christian sites —a cemetery, a building conclusively demonstrable as a church or the other criteria discussed by Rahtz[116] are however, present. We may regard the enclosure banks as the <u>vallum monasterii</u>, but nothing compels this interpretation and the unparalleled addition of the apsidal 'bastion'-like structure may in fact argue against it.

The inability to identify such a distinctive cultural institution as a monastery by archaeological means demonstrates the embryonic state of settlement archaeology of the AD 400-700 period in the British Isles. The preceding discussion has attempted to emphasize that the definition of these sites in such basic historical terms as <u>monastery</u>, <u>burh</u>, <u>llys</u> etc. should not be the only aim of archaeological research, and that the economic and social relationship of the sites to their surroundings forms an essential base to whatever political or religious system operated in the area.

The picture here presented of Cadcong in the AD 400-700 period therefore sees it as a permanently occupied and socially complex settlement of perhaps 200 people, probably acting as the central place to a number of, as yet unidentified, lower order settlements within an economic unit about 65 sq. km in area. This area, central to the North Somerset region, contains a high concentration of high quality arable land as well as upland grazing and areas on the North Somerset Levels. It is possible that the site exerted some political influenced over a wider area between Mendip and Failand, perhaps even acting as a refuge centre in times of war or unrest (monasteries could undoubtedly act in this way in the same manner as a secular power centre). The settlement was probably a wealthy one, as the imported pottery must indicate, although the basis for this wealth cannot be defined in the absence of evidence for large scale production of any kind; an agricultural surplus may, however, have been available for exchange purposes. This evidence suggests that the settlement was a major regional centre, although it does not at present appear to possess any urban characteristics. The population appears to have a cultural background derived from that of the local area in the preceding centuries, and this may be reflected in a continuing adherence to Romano-Celtic religious practices and beliefs. There is no direct evidence either that the population was intrusive into the area, or that the site was a Christian monastery at any stage in the occupation.

Future work

This thesis has attempted to explore in detail the relevance of arrange of data to the topic and to present the possible interpretations for the sites systematically. The inadequacy of the data available at present is manifest, and the aim of this final section is to suggest the lines of research which may be worth pursuing in future so that more positive answers may be obtained. The potential of Cadcong is such that the weight of future effort should clearly be put into this site, and this will be considered first.

a) Cadcong: future strategy

The ideal for this site would be total excavation, though as parts of the western enclosure have been destroyed by quarrying the picture of the site will never be a complete one. However, as this ideal is unlikely to be achieved given present resources, the need is to establish a sampling strategy which will answer as many questions as possible with minimum use of resources. The major questions may be summarised as follows; some are relevant to all models of the site, andothers to one or more. Strategies to recover the relevant data are then suggested.

1) Subsistence economy: Crops and animals eaten on site? Age and species structure of livestock? Implications for role of site as primary food producer or market centre? Exploitation of surrounding area? Food processing on site?

Adopting the territory suggested above, a programme of fieldwork supplemented by air survey and research on soils, drainage etc. could define more closely the resources available to the settlement and might identify the postulated contemporary lower order settlements. On-site recording of faunal evidence by a bone specialist will be essential, especially for identifying differences in distributions of bone indicating slaughtering debris, cooking rubbish etc. As animal bone seems to be prevalent over the whole site the choice of excavation area for this material does not seem crucial and can be subordinated to the needs of other questions.

2) <u>Interior layout</u>: Zoning? Planning? Open spaces? Different nuclei? Different arrangements in east and west enclosures?

A crucial point here is the difference or similarity between the areas each side of the N-S bank, and future work must attempt to examine these on a strictly comparable basis. The areas examined should therefore be similar in size, though if each were to be separately regarded as an individual sampling unit on a random basis the area examined in the eastern half would be slightly smaller.[117] Since past experience would suggest that the areas behind the defences are not representative of the whole interior space a solution would be to examine continuous north-south strips across the interior. That in the western enclosure could be immediately adjacent to the 1968-73 excavated area in order to see as large a continuous area of the site as possible. The strips would need to be sufficiently wide for buildings of the size and type so far encountered to be identified, and 20 m would be a possible minimum.

3) <u>Building types</u>: Range of plan types, constructional technique, size, function, distribution?

In the 5% of the site so far examined every building shows unique features and it will be important to know whether there are in fact a number of consistent techniques and plan forms and whether these occur in combination or in different areas of the site suggesting functional or social differences. One way of approaching this problem would be to examine an area the same size as that already excavated and to compare the structural evidence, but this would give less information on other aspects than a randomly selected transect across the hillfort such as has already been suggested.

3) <u>Artifact/ecofact distributions</u>: Uniform, random or agglomerated? Functional implications, activity areas etc?

Some idea of the overall distribution of certain key items—the A and B wares, Roman and post-Roman hand-made pottery, and animal bone—could be obtained by a sampling strategy which divided the area into a large number of sampling units which could then be excavated on a random basis. This might give an indication of the location of different types of activity, but only at the loss of information of other kinds. This procedure could be adopted if resources were very limited and understanding of overall intensity of occupation in the enclosed area was felt to be of overriding importance. On balance, however, the examination of a continuous area seems the best solution in this case also, since the scatter patterns of artifacts discussed in chapter 6 can clearly contribute to the understanding of the settlement's history and can only be recorded in this way.

4) <u>Form and function of the enclosure banks</u>

These may hold the clue to the social/political/religious aspects of the site and past experience here and elsewhere demonstrates that a considerable length of complex features such as these needs to be exposed simultaneously for their nature to be understood.[118] In addition there are two specific araas of interest: the junction of the western and eastern enclosure banks on the south side where a stratigraphical relationship can be established between the two, and the eastern entrance whose character has been discussed in chapter 4. Were a N-S strip immediately west of the 1968-73 area to be examined,

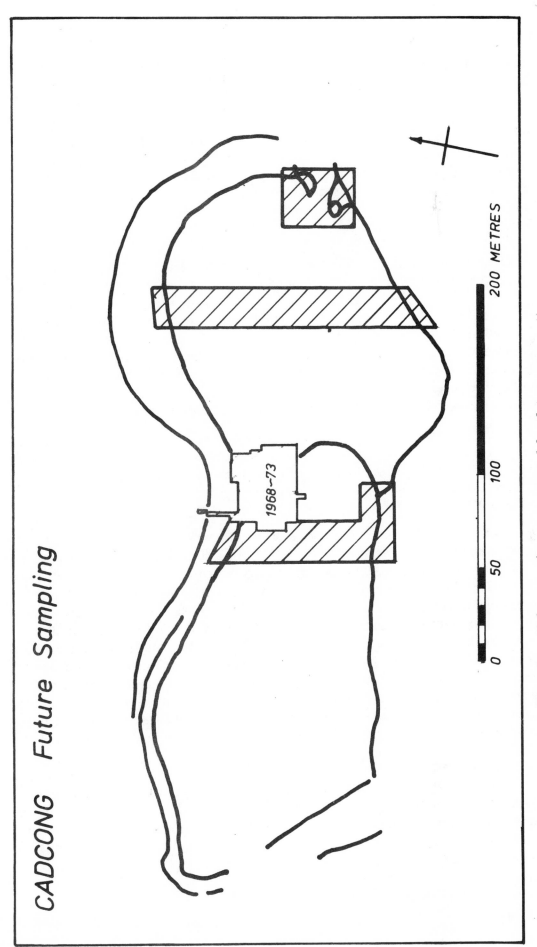

Fig. 33 Cadcong; Areas proposed for future excavation

its south end could be extended eastwards along and immediately behind the rampart as far as the junction of the two enclosures. The east entrance could be stripped completely.

The best solution for the future research on the site would therefore be to undertake more intensive fieldwork in the surrounding area, and to concentrate the excavation on at least two transects running N–S across the site, one connecting with the area already examined. Two specific areas of the defences could be examined at the same time. These proposals are shown on Figure 33 and would involve about 4500 square metres, bringing the total area excavated to over 12% of the enclosed area. At past rates of progress this would take about 15 years to complete.

b) Other Somerset sites

Despite the danger of perpetuating an existing bias, the discussions in chapters 4 and 6 drew attention to a number of sites where the evidence either from casual finds, excavation or fieldwork, indicated that examination by excavation would be worthwhile. Foremost among these must be Cannington, where the relationship of the earthworks to the outer bank of the hillfort and the Roman evidence behind it could be established by a small-scale programme. The common features this site shares with Cadcong in terms of topography and possible function, combined with the cemetery evidence suggest that limited research could be carried out at both sites simultaneously.

Both Maes Knoll and Stantonbury could be excavated on a small scale in order to confirm or refute the hypotheses put forward in relation to the Wansdyke in chapter 4. Similar small-scale work at Brent Knoll and Daw's Castle could establish basic stratigraphic sequences on the unusual earthworks at these two sites.

It is clear, however, that systematic fieldwork, both in the environs of sites and in the identification of unrecorded hillforts, still has a great potential, and the discussion in chapter 4 demonstrated the potential of this work at least in 'Western Lowland Britain' as here defined. The integration of all types of data has, however, been the aim of this study, even though the limitations of many of them have been such as to make this difficult. A basic conclusion that can be drawn is that at present hillfort and hill-top use from the first to the eighth centuries appears a complex phenomenon which cannot be covered by any single hypothesis. It may perhaps be argued that, in part at least, this apparent lack of patterning in the data is an inevitable consequence of concentration on a single element in the settlement pattern, rather than attempting a broader analysis. The need to identify other elements has been acknowledged above, and there is no doubt that the approach adopted here cannot lead directly to the reconstruction of the whole social organisation of Somerset in these centuries. The hill-top sites will not be fully understood until they can be related to the rest of the settlement pattern, but by studying them in relative isolation it has been possible perhaps to provide a sounder basis from which to attempt the much more complex task of defining and understanding the overall cultural pattern in this period in Somerset and elsewhere.

NOTES

1. For general discussion of source material, Alcock, 1971a, chaps. 1 and 6; Morris, 1973 passim. cf. Binford, 1972, esp. 94-96; Clarke, 1968.

2. See above, chap. 6.

3. Laing, 1973.

4. Branigan, 1972, 120-21.

5. Morris, 1973, 280. Guest, 1861.

6. Stenton, 1947, 66. Finberg, 1964c, no. 358 in which he is described as a king. The area name first occurs as Summurtunensis Pagae in Asser (Turner, 1952a, xix). The name is considered to mean 'dwellers dependent on Somerton' perhaps again stressing the importance of the Oolite and Lias areas in the south of the county.

7. Davies and Vierk, 1974, 245, 279-85 etc.

8. The example of Offa's Dyke comes to mind most readily, but Clawdd Mawr, Dyfed (Bull. Board Celtic Studs. 8 (1937), 383-85) and the Danewirke, Denmark, were also probably built under royal direction.

9. Fox and Fox, 1960; Myres, 1964, esp. 22.

10. cf. Hoskins, 1960. Rahtz and Fowler, 1972, 188-90.

11. Conveniently in Rahtz, 1971, 22.

12. Phillmore, 1888, 180; Morris, 1973, 308.

13. See above, chap. 1.

14. Rahtz, 1977, 58.

15. Above, chap. 4 and Plan C; Rahtz, 1969.

16. Rahtz, 1974a, 126. Despite the possible Christian associations of the 'B' ware from the site. For the latest discussion of this problem see Thomas, 1976 with refs.

17. Rahtz, 1971, 56-60; Alcock, 1963a, 34-38, but cf. Alcock, 1975 and Evans et al., 1975, 123.

18. Finberg, 1964b, 1967; Radford, 1962; Rahtz, 1971, 5-8.

19. Alcock, 1972a, 193.

20. Hill, 1969; Petrikovitz, 1971; Schlesinger, 1976.

21. Birch, 1885-93, ii, 222 (in relation to the burh at Worcester).

22. Alcock, 1971a, 219.

23. *Corpus Inscriptionum Latinarum* 12 (1888), no. 1524.

24. South Cadbury: T.P.Q. provided by coin of Honorius AD 393-402 (see chap. 5); Cadcong: Radio-Carbon Birm. 596, 320 ± 110 ad.

25. Freestone Hill, Co. Kilkenny (Faftery, 1969); Traprain Law (Feachem, 1956); Laing, 1975c.

26. Alcock, 1971a, 227.

27. *Sub annis* 552 and 556.

28. Calculated in relation to Fendoch (Perths) where the garrison defended a perimeter of 620 yards—4 men to 2.5 yards of rampart.

29. Morris, 1973, 99.

30. Clarke, 1972b; Haggett, 1965, chap. 5.

31. Sawyer, 1974; Jones, 1972; Alcock, 1963a, 197-199.

32. Wacher, 1975, 411-22.

33. P. J. Leach, *CRAAGS Interim Report 3, Ilchester, 1974* (Bristol, 1974), and pers. comm. Finds in Dobson, 1931, 182-3; Rahtz and Fowler, 1972, 203; Rahtz, 1974b, 112.

34. Alcock, 1972a, 197-201; above, note 20.

35. Lewis, 1966.

36. Rahtz *et al.*, 1958.

37. Clifford, 1938; Burrow and Bennett, forthcoming. See Appendix B, 29.

38. ApSimon, 1965, and *ex inf* R. H. Leech.

39. *Oxoniensia* 19 (1954), 15 ff. esp. fig. 12, and see below.

40. Bowes: *Yorks Archaeol. Journ.* 36 (1947), 383-6 and 37 (1948), 107-16. Cadbury Tickenham as n. 37.

41. Fox, 1952b, See Appendix B, 16.

42. e.g. Frilford (Berks), Bradford and Goodchild, 1939.

43. Branigan, 1972, 1974.

44. Although the refurbishment of mosaics at Lydney in the later fourth century was paid for by a non-local individual. Wheeler and Wheeler 1932, 102-4.

45. *Sussex Archaeol. Collections* 53 (1910), 131-7. Lewis, 1966, 85, 146.

46. Meaney, 1964, *passim*.

47. Thomas, 1971a, chap. 2, esp. 52.

48. Rahtz, 1977, 57. There was building material in the fill of some of the graves.

49. Creech Hill info. R. H. Leech; Brean Down: ApSimon, 1958, 206-11; Henley Wood: <u>JRS</u> 55 (1965), 216; Blaise Castle: Bartlett, 1919. Also Wint Hill villa, a non-hillfort example.

50. Page, 1890, 241; Godman, 1975, 45.

51. Rahtz, 1971, 12-14 & 61. Two young adults?

52. <u>PSANHS</u> 111 (1967), 67-9; 36(2) (1890), 9-10; <u>SDNQ</u> 5 (1887), 6.

53. 80 skeletons, $\frac{1}{4}$ mile from the hill in Yatton before 1911; <u>SDNQ</u> 12 (1911), 20-1. 13 burials at Yatton 1782; Collinson, 1791 vol. III. Unknown number 'at the foot of the encampment' in 1849; <u>PSANHS</u> 23(2) (1877), 8.

54. <u>CARATACI NEPUS</u> on a ridgeway at SS 890 336 (<u>Arch. Camb.</u> 8 (1891), 29-32). Culbone stone, an equal-armed cross in a ring cf. P OTITUS on Lundy (after <u>c</u>. AD 600), and VORTIPOR, Dyfed of <u>c</u>. AD 540. (Grinsell, 1970, 105; <u>Current Archaeology</u> 16 (1969), 139).

55. Barley and Hanson, 1968, 177-92 (J. M. C. Toynbee). The supposed Chi-Rho sherd from Gatcombe (Branigan, 1977, 179, 109 and Fig. 23) is not convincing. Leech 1977, 144-151 argues that Christianity was gaining ground in south Somerset by the end of the fourth century.

56. Hughes, 1966. Rahtz, 1977.

57. <u>Op. cit</u>. n. 55, 9-18, 37-49, 93-121, refs.

58. <u>Scottish Archaeological Forum</u> 5 (1973), 125-35.

59. Barley and Hanson, 1968, 15. Higgitt, 1973. cf. Gregory of Tours VIII, 15.

60. Burrow, 1973.

61. Thomas, 1959; 1969, 29, n. 14, 1976.

62. Alcock, 1968b, 12-13.

63. Alcock, 1971a, 219.

64. The <u>vallum</u> at Iona encloses <u>c</u>. 15 ha., that at Clonmacnois <u>c</u>. 20 ha.

65. <u>Scot. Arch. Forum</u> 5 (1973), 76-98.

66. Thomas, 1971b, 31.

67. Chitty, 1966 for Egyptian sites. Similar enclosures surround the early Syrian monasteries of Mar Gabriel and Der Zafaran S. Turkey (pers. obs.).

68. Alcock, 1971a, 224; Alcock, 1971b, 3: 1972a, 178.

69. The entrance at Mote of Mark is reported to have been strengthened by the addition of an interior 'barbican' of dry stone construction (Laing, 1973, 123). The status of the site is unclear and it could be a small monastery. cf. Chun Castle, Cornwall.

70. Thomas, 1971b, 25-26. Burrow, 1973, 101.

71. See below.

72. Alcock, 1964, Applebaum, 1972. The extinction of the Greenland
     Norse is an extreme example of cultural attitudes dictating inefficient
     use of available resources, and is a warning against the adoption of
     simplistic models based purely on modern assessments of available
     resources (Brock, 1975).

73. Hawkins, 1972, contra Cunliffe, 1966.

74. Above, n. 16.

75. Rahtz, 1971, 45, nos. 11, 13, 14.

76. Burrow, 1976a.

77. Chisholm, 1968, 66.

78. Sawyer, no. 372.

79. Fowler, 1970; Grundy, 1935; Bonney, 1972; Taylor, 1970, 49-83.

80. Cadcong, Ham Hill, Tedbury, Maesbury, Stantonbury, Ruborough,
     Burledge, Brent Knoll, Castle Wood and Creech Hill.

81. Above, n. 39.

82. Coin distribution was plotted at Brean Down, but the material here
     cannot readily be interpreted in this way. ApSimon, 1965, 222-24.

83. Boon, 1963.

84. Everson and Fitzgerald, 1969, chap. 9. Haggett, 1965, chap. 5.
     For the application of these concepts to archaeological material see
     Hodder, 1975, and Hodder and Orton, 1976.

85. Thomas, 1971b, 24-5.

86. Grierson, 1959; Hilgarth, 1961.

87. Fox, 1955.

88. Alcock, 1963a, 56 suggests that a Gaulish origin is possible for some
     of the material.

89. Alcock, 1968b, 12; 1970b, 3.

90. Rahtz and Fowler, 1972, 212.

91. Gelling, 1969, O'Kelly, 1962; O'Riordain, 1942. Proudfoot, 1961.

92. Alcock, 1963a, 54-5; Thomas, 1972a, 126-7.

93. Lawlor, 1925; Rahtz, 1974a, 130; cf. Bede Historia Ecclesiastica
     Gentis Anglorum V, 14.

94. Stevenson, 1904, chap. 81.

95. The Croscombe/Dinder Boundary bisecting Maesbury. Sawyer no.
     247 (AD 705).

96. Finberg, 164c, no. 372 (AD 688X726).

97. Cunliffe, 1974, 259.

98. Darby and Finn, 1967, 164; Morgan, 1938, plate XVI; Hogg, 1971, Fig. 27.

99. Branigan, 1977, esp. 174-212 where the discussion independently reaches similar conclusions in relation to the Gatcombe villa and its estate.

100. Above n. 84.

101. Hogg, 1971, 115-17.

102. Fowler, 1975b, 129. cf. Taylor, 1974b, 7.

103. Ministry of Agriculture, Fisheries and Food, Agricultural Land Classi-fication Map of England and Wales Explanatory note (1968), and map sheet no. 165 (1971).

104. Branigan, 1977, loc. cit. note 99.

105. Fowler et al., 1970, 38-9.

106. Assuming a pouulation density of c. 10 per sq. km, and therefore 2.5 defenders per sq. km.

107. Barker, 1973, fig. 3.

108. Fowler, 1970, 182.

109. Rahtz, 1976, Burrow, 1976a for Irish settlement. Documentary evidence in Meyer, 1912, 75 no. 883.

110. Comparable sites are Thistleton 1, Collyweston 2, 3, 4, Brigstock 1 & 2, Frilford 1, Maryport, Chanctonbury, Kelvedon, Maiden Castle 1, Bowes 2 and Housesteads 2. Lewis, 1966 with refs.

111. Ant. J. 43 (1963), 243 and 245. ApSimon, 1965, 251. cf. Cunliffe, 1974, 266 for possible Iron Age domestic use of bone plaques.

112. Wheeler, 1943, 132. The building here was 8.1 x 5.7 m with a length/breadth ratio of 1.4:1. Cadcong 7.8 x 3.4 m - length/breadth ratio 2.3:1. Brean Down 4.5 x 3.65 m - length/breadth ratio 1.2:1.

113. Victoria County History of Essex III (1963), 140.

114. Unless of course these are saints' relics.

115. The hagiographic material relating to Congar is discussed above, chap. 3.

116. Rahtz, 1974a, 127.

117. Binford, 1972, 135-62.

118. Guilbert, 1975a.

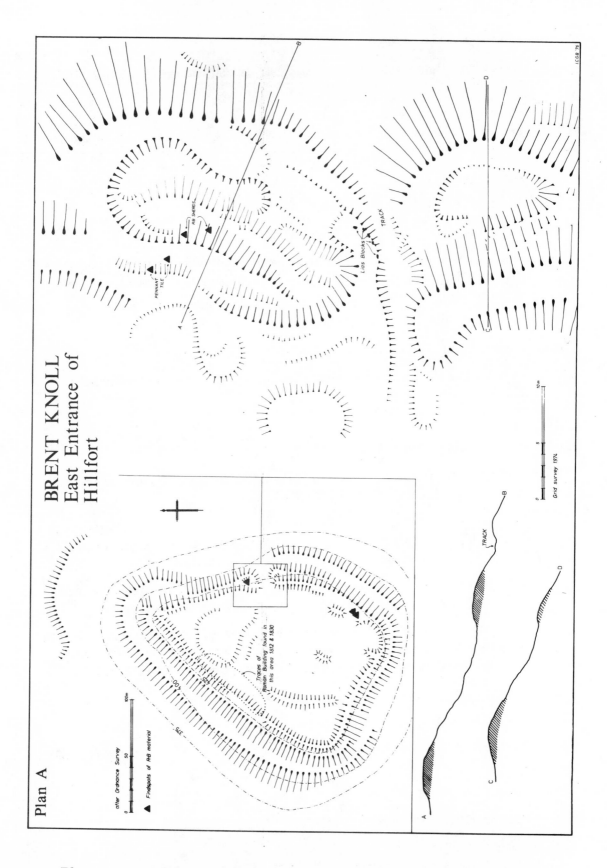

Plan A — text within the figure:

BRENT KNOLL
East Entrance of
Hillfort

Plan A

RB SHERDS.

PENNANT
TILE

Lias Blocks

TRACK

Traces of
Roman Building found in
this area 1812 & 1830

after Ordnance Survey

▲ Findspots of RB material

Grid survey 1974

TRACK

A   B   C   D

Plan A   Brent Knoll Hillfort: Plan of the hillfort and the earthworks
at the eastern entrance. (Based on Ordnance Survey, Crown
Copyright reserved.)

190

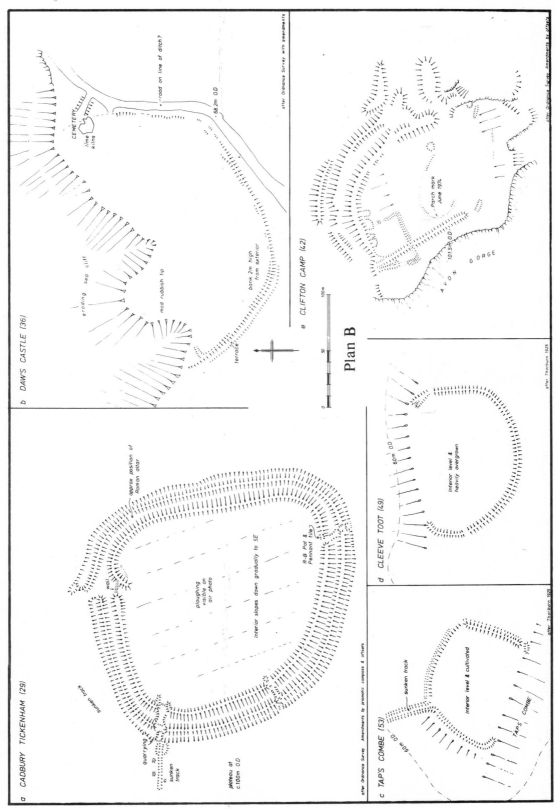

Plan B

Plan B   a) Cadbury Camp, Tickenham: revised plan
        b) Daw's Castle: revised plan
        c) Tap's Combe Camp (after Thorburn 1925)
        d) Cleeve Toot Camp (after Thorburn 1925)
        e) Clifton Camp: revised plan.

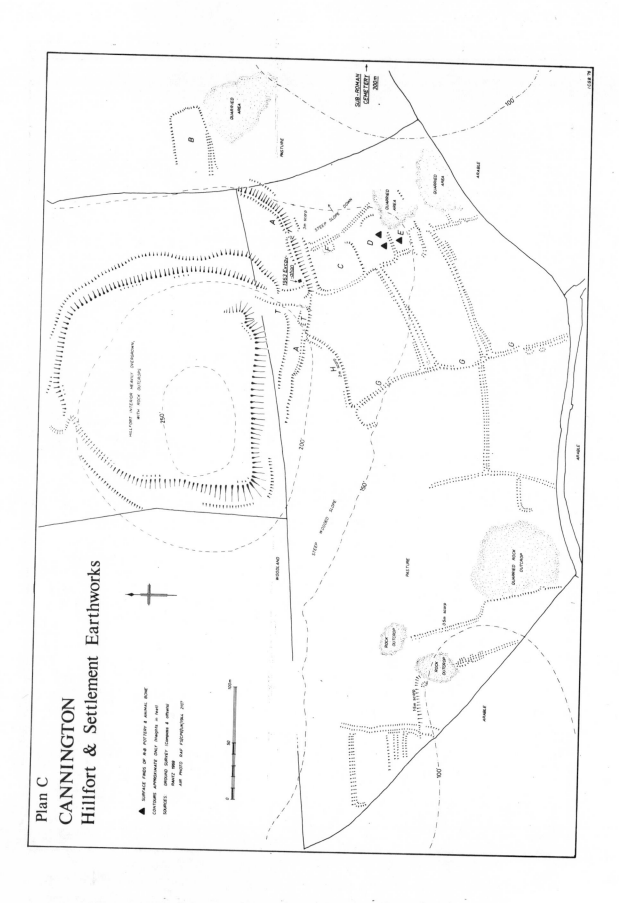

Plan C   Cannington Hillfort and the earthworks to the south.

192

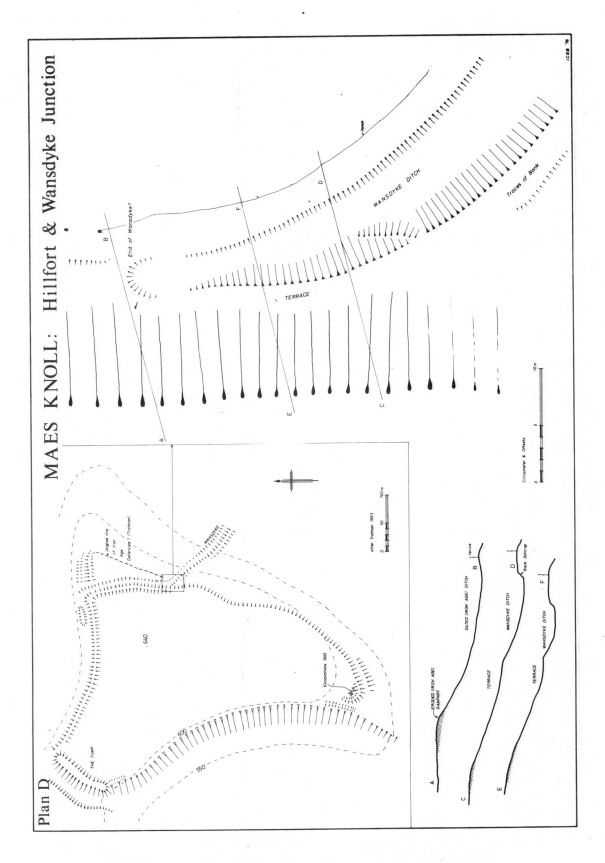

Plan D   Maes Knoll Hillfort: the junction of the Wansdyke and the east
         side of the fort.   (Based on Ordnance Survey, Crown Copyright
         reserved.)

Plan E   STANTONBURY (Merces Burh) & Wansdyke

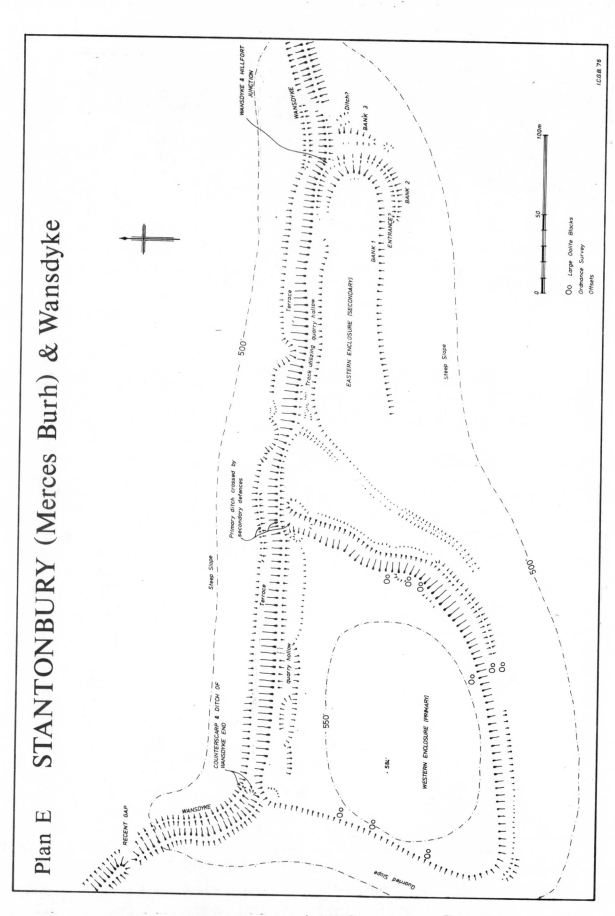

Plan E   Stantonbury Hillfort and the Wansdyke.   (Based on Ordnance Survey, Crown Copyright reserved.)

APPENDIX A

GAZETTEER OF HILLFORTS AND ENCLOSURES
IN THE STUDY AREA

This gazetteer is believed to be complete, within the frames of reference outlined in chapter 3, up to April 1975. The material is set out in a standard order as follows:

1. The number of the site in rank-size order, based on the enclosed area, the largest site being number 1.

2. The site name commonly found in published accounts. The Ordnance Survey usage is normally adopted, but some unpublished sites do not yet have standardized names.

3. The civil parish in which the site lies, or if in more than one parish, that normally used by the Ordnance Survey or other sources.

4. Grid Reference to six figures.

5. Type of site under the scheme of classification proposed in chapter 2.

6. Size of the enclosed area in hectares.

7. Whether scheduled.

8. The solid geology and topography of the site and its immediate surroundings, and the average height O.D. in metres.

9. Selected references to air photographs of high quality.

10. Brief description of site, including an assessment of the condition of the archaeological deposits, and present or future threats to them.

11. Surface finds, if any, summarized.

12. Brief summary of excavations, if any.

13. Derivation of name.

14. References. While not claiming to be absolutely exhaustive, this list includes all publications which contribute to the study of individual sites. The method of citation adopted is based on that in Cunliffe, 1974, 357-62, references in the text to a particular site being identified by their date of publication only. Some brief notes thought worth including here are not quoted in the full bibliography.

Alphabetic Index of Sites

Numbers on left refer to number in Appendix A

1 HAM HILL, Stoke-sub-Hamdon. ST 478 170

Group I

85.2 ha.

Scheduled

Siting
On Upper Lias limestone outcrop above low-lying Middle and Lower Lias deposits and alluvium. Plateau at about 120 m.

Air Photographs
UCCAP: ANN 24, FK 49 (Plates 9 and 10).

Description
The site is probably the largest 'classic' contour hillfort in Britain, the circuit of the defences being about 5 km around a roughly oblong plateau, from the north-west corner of which a fan-tail spur projects to the north, whence the majority of the finds from the site originate. The defences of this part of the fort are more massive and complex than those around the remainder of the circuit, consisting of two major banks and ditches fronted by a counterscarp bank, whereas elsewhere bank, ditch and counterscarp are normally present. The whole plateau is nevertheless very strongly defended, and there is no evidence that the northern spur was separately defended, as Collinson and others suggested. In the absence of excavation it is unclear which of the many gaps in the defences represent original entrances to the enclosure. The lower slopes on the north and south-east sides are covered by an extensive series of lynchets, the latter apparently associated with the earthworks of the deserted medieval settlement of Witcombe (ST 489 161).

The interior of the northern spur, with the exception of the north-east corner, as well as much of the western portion of the main plateau, have been quarried for Ham Stone. This activity, probably intermittent from Roman times, had destroyed or masked any stratified deposits in this part of the site. The rest of the plateau, having been used for rabbit warrens and rough grazing in the Middle Ages, is now mostly under plough, with resultant damage to the Roman building at ST 4878 1652, and to an extensive Roman site centring on ST 487 163. (Leech 1977, 119-121).

The area around the 'Prince of Wales' Inn, at the south-eastern corner of the northern spur, is probably the site of the hamlet of South Ameldon, the site of an annual fair documented from 1102-17th century, and of local courts. The location of a chapel, recorded in 1535, is perhaps indicated by the field name 'Ham Chapel', applied to the enclosure immediately to the east of the defences in this area on 1840 Tithe Award, and 'Hanging Chapple' 1666 (VCH III 1974, 245, 248) (visited 22.2.73).

Surface finds
Large quantities of material from Neolithic to Medieval data are recorded from the hill, predominantly from quarrying operations in the late 19th century. Taunton Museum holds much of this material. The Roman and post-Roman finds are summarized in Appendix B.

Excavations
1. Walter excavated a Roman building at the eastern end of the hill, and published an account and plan in 1907 (see Appendix B).
2. From about 1907 to 1920 Walter also undertook small-scale excavations at various places in the northern spur, the locations of which can be roughly identified from the information given. No details of the size of these cuttings, or of stratification or structures, appear to have been recorded, The finds are in Taunton Museum.
3. Gray initiated a programme of excavation on the hill in 1923, which continued until 1930, but which he uncharacteristically failed to publish fully. His cuttings I-VII were on the slopes immediately outside the defended area at the north-west corner of the northern spur, and cuttings IX-XIX were all within the north spur, concentrating on the defences. Reports were only published for cuttings I-IX and XIV, and on the evidence of Gray's notebook in Taunton Museum there appears to have been a decline in the standard of recording as the excavation proceeded, although the finds are in labelled bags in the museum which implies that some records were being kept. No details could be discovered about these contexts, many of which appear to have been no more than spits at successive depths.

It is clear from the notebook, however, that structural phases were encountered, and both pre-rampart occupation and successive phases of rampart construction are implied in places. Clearly an Iron Age sequence comparable to that at South Cadbury (9) may be anticipated here. An overall review of the Iron Age material from the site is needed in order for the undoubted importance of the site to be fully evaluated.

Roman material was found in all the cuttings on the spur, except XV, XVI, and XVIII, and is discussed in chapter 6 and Appendix B.

Name
Ekwall considers the full name, Hamdon, to be derived from O.E. Hamma-dun, 'the hill with or among the Hamms (meadows or enclosures)', having no connexion with ham (Ekwall, 1960).

References
1791 Collinson III (1791), 310. Suggested that the northern spur was separated from the rest of the plateau by 'a very strong and lofty rampire of stone and earth', but it is not clear whether he was referring merely to the wide natural valley, deepened by quarrying at the south-east corner of the spur.
1827 Colt-Hoare, 1827. First published plan of the fort.
1836 Phelps I, 1836, 78. Notes the interior 'intersected by divisions marked on the surface of the ground' on the northern spur. These are not now visible.
1853 Walter, 1853. General description of the site.
1884 Norris, 1884. Speculations on the name and history of the site.
(1886 PSANHS 32 (1) (1886), 43-51 Society visit; 81-83 illustrations of finds)
      Notes on donations of finds to the museum, all in part 1 of PSANHS by H. St. G. Gray:
1904 Vol. 50, 73-4.
1905 Vol. 51, 86-90.

Plate 9   Ham Hill (no. 1).   The western part of the hillfort from the south
(UCCAP neg. no. ANN24)

Plate 10   Ham Hill.   The western part of the hillfort from the north
(UCCAP neg. no. FK49)

1906 Vol. 52, 82-3.
1907a Vol. 53, 72-7.
1908 Voo. 54, 120-22.
1909 Vol. 55, 100-102.
1910a Vol. 56, 104-10.
1911 Vol. 57, 112-18.
1912a Vol. 58, 120-23.
1913 Vol. 59, 76-8.
1914 Vol. 60, 93-5.
1915 Vol. 61, xlvi, lvi-lvii.
1916 Vol. 63, xlvii.
1917 Vol. 64, lvii.
1918 Vol. 65, lxi-lxii.
1919 Vol. 66, lxxv-lxxvi.
1920 Vol. 67, lxxiii-lxxv.
1921 Vol. 68, lxxxvii-lxxxviii.
1902 Gray, 1902. Description of the Walter collection of prehistoric,
      Roman and post-Roman finds, predominantly from the northern spur.
1905 Gray, 1905, 145-48. Description of the Norris collection from the
      northern spur.
(1907b Gray in Proc Soc Antiq Lond 21, 1905-7, 128-39. Display of selected
      finds at the Society of Antiquaries.)
1907c Walter, 1907. Villa excavation.
(1910b PSANHS 56 (1) (1910), 50-61. Society visit.)
1910c Gray, 1910. Publication of selected finds.
1911 VCH 1911, 496-499. Fullest topographical description yet published.
1912b Walter, 1912. Summary of small-scale excavations and the description
      of 'six different sites of Roman habitation', although there is no indi-
      cation that structures were located, and in view of the extensive dis-
      tribution of Roman material on the northern spur it seems probable
      that Walter merely encountered Roman material in the general mixed
      humic layer identified by Gray.
1924 Gray, 1924. Report of excavation of cuttings I-VIII, XI and XII.
      Very full bibliography.
1925 Gray, 1925. Report on excavation of cutting XIV.
1926 Gray, 1926. Report on excavation of cutting IX, and brief accounts
      of other cuttings.
(1939 PSANHS 85 (1939), 40-1. Society excursion.)
1950a Seaby, 1950a. Brief summary.
1950b Seaby, 1950b. Roman coins in Taunton Museum.

2 COUNTISBURY, Countisbury (Devon). SS 740 493

Group III

34 ha.

Scheduled

Siting

Promontory on Devonian sandstone defined on north by almost precipitous
slopes to the sea on the north and to the river West Lyn on the south. Approach
from east across narrow neck of land c. 100 m wide. Interior of enclosure at
c. 250 m O.D.

Description

An extremely impressive site, under rough pasture, the defences of which consist of a massive bank up to 15 m high from an exterior ditch with counterscarp. The entrance is a simple gap in the centre. A change of direction can be seen towards the south end of the bank, possibly indicating an addition to the earthworks, which terminate where the slopes on the north and south become steep. There is no trace of defences on the north and south sides and the interior shows no archaeological features.

The chief interest of this site lies in its probable identification as the Arx Cynuit (or Cynwit or Cynwith) where a Danish force was defeated by the English in 878, according to the testimony of Asser (Stevenson, 1904; ch. 54). Although, as Stevenson points out (ibid., 265), there is nothing in Asser's text to confirm that the site was close to the sea. Asser claims to have seen the site itself and his description: locus situ terrarum titissimus est ab amni parte, nisi ab orientali; must therefore be given credence and fits the site perfectly, much more so than the alternatives of Cannington (no. 41) or Kenwith near Bideford (Stevenson, 1904, 262-5). There are philological arguments too for accepting the identification of Cynuit, which may be a Celtic name, with Countisbury (Place Names of Devon I (1931), 62f.; Ekwall, 1960; Devon Notes & Queries 16 (1931), 310-13).

The matter of most immediate interest is Asser's description of the site, which is pictured as 'ill-prepared and wholly unfortified' (imparatum atque omnino immunitam) 'as it had only walls made after our custom' (quod moenia nostro more erecta solummodo haberet). What does Asser mean by nostro more? There is ample evidence to show that he was a Welshman, probably writing for a Welsh audience, and it may therefore be supposed that the earth banks and ditches of hillforts were somehow thought of as a typically Welsh method of defence, even if a rather unsatisfactory one. It seems unlikely that Asser is using the adjective noster with reference to pre-Roman Celts, and we are therefore left with the possibility either that Asser was aware that his contemporaries were building and using earthworks of hillfort type for defence, or that he believed that similar sites he had seen had been so used in the recent past.

The details of the battle are also of some interest (although Athelweard contradicts Asser and the Anglo Saxon Chronicle in describing it as a Danish victory). The English forces (multi ministri regis cum suis) took refuge within the earthworks, but the Danish army did not attempt to break in through the weak defences, hoping to besiege the English, who were without water (nulla aqua illi arci contigua est). The latter made a dawn attack on the Danes, killing 1200 of them and driving the rest to their ships. We may note the reluctance of the Danes to attack even decayed and ill-prepared defences, the lack of water supply within the earthwork, and the apparently unpremeditated use of the site by the English. While it may be unjustifiable to project ninth-century conditions back into the fifth to seventh, one may suspect that the battles at Old Sarum and Barbury, and Badon also (if it was at a hillfort—cf. Alcock, 1971a, 71) may have developed in this way, rather than as deliberate attacks on refurbished and re-occupied hillforts. (Visited 6.4.73).

Surface Finds None.

Excavations None.

Name
Called 'Oldborough' by Davidson (1861). Cynuit may be a Welsh name (cf.
Kennet) which has become the first element in Countisbury (Place Names of
Devon loc.cit.).

References
1861 Davidson, J. Notes on the Antiquities of Devonshire (Exeter 1861), 26.
   Brief description.
1931 Alexander, J. J. 'Arx Cynuit', Devon & Cornwall Notes & Queries
   16 (1931), 310-13.

3 BATHAMPTON CAMP, Bathampton. ST 774 650

Group I

32.2 ha.

Scheduled

Siting
Oolitic limestone plateau at about 210 m O.D., the site lying on a promontory
formed by a loop of the river Avon. The land falls away steeply immediately
to the east and a short distance from the defences on the west and north, while
the plateau slopes downwards gently to the south.

Air Photographs
Crawford and Keiller, 1928, 147.

Description
   The hillfort is a large univallate site of roughly rectangular shape, the
eastern ends of the north and south defences apparently ending against the
steep eastern slopes on the east side, but later quarrying has confused the
original arrangement, especially on the north. The defences are generally
in very poor condition, being almost obliterated on the north and most of the
west sides, surviving as a scarp about 1.5 m high towards the south end of
the latter. The southern defences, set on a slight break of slope, are better
preserved, consisting of a scarp up to 2.5 m high. Landscaping of the interior
has in places created the appearance of a bank along the rear of the scarp, but
this is probably a recent feature. There are gaps at the south-west corner
(possibly original, but very much confused by later earthmoving) and in the
centre of the south side, proved on excavation to be secondary to the defences.

   The interior is generally level, and now used as a golf course. Extensive traces of a 'Celtic' field system are present both inside and outside the
enclosure, and although this appears to pre-date the hillfort on Crawford's
air photograph, Wainwright was able to show that it overlay the ditch fill on
the south side.

   Other earthworks, including 'two circular tumuli' near the southern defences, and 'two lines of long barrows' (? pillow mounds) on the north side
were noted by Seyer.

The site was for long considered to be joined to the Wansdyke, which was held to form its western and northern defences, but is is now clear that the Dyke ended at Horsecombe, some 3 km to the south-west. (Visited 10.2.73).

Surface finds None.

Excavations
1. A small trench was dug in 1905 near the south end of the western defences. 'Red and brown pottery' was found.
2. Three small cuttings were made across the south defences in the 1960s. Pre-Rampart occupation features associated with early Iron Age pottery underlay a bank 2.85 m wide, revetted at front and rear with a drystone wall. A berm separated this from the exterior ditch. A little Roman material was found (Appendix B).

Name
The hillfort probably takes its name from the settlement at Bathampton, recorded as Hamtun in 956 (BCS 973).

References
The Skinner Manuscripts (B.M. Add. MSS 33671 and 33673) include detail on the site and its environs, much of little value.
1888 Skrine, 1888.
1895 Skrine, 1895.   Excavation of ?Roman building outside the fort.
1897 Skrine, 1897.
1908 Winwood, 1908.   Excavation on the west side.
1911 VCH II, 472-3. Description.
1923 Major and Burrow, 1923. Discussion of the relation of the site to
      Wansdyke.
1924 Burrow, 1924, 50-1. Brief description.
1928 Crawford and Keiller, 1928, 144-7.
1958 Grinsell, 1958, 142-4, 146, 164.
1967 Wainwright, 1967. Excavation. Interpretation of the site as one of a
      number of large univallate early Iron Age 'stock enclosures'.

4 TEDBURY CAMP, Elm. ST 744 488

Group III

24.2 ha.

Scheduled.

Siting
Oolitic limestone promontory, above deeply incised streams converging to the NE, at about 105 m O.D.

Air Photographs None. Site under woodland.

Description
      A large promontory fort with a level wooded interior. The ramparts are also tree covered, and the use of the site for commercial forestry has probably resulted in severe damage to superficial deposits.

      The defences terminate at the head of near vertical slopes on north and south, the latter at the head of a small re-entrant. At present the earthworks consist of an inner bank about 3.5 m high rising from a slight ditch, with a second bank surviving on the north and south ends, where the defences are cut by a forestry road. The outer earthwork extant in 1836 is now destroyed. The inner rampart is surmounted by a drystone wall, normally constructed on rear slope of the bank.

The entrance was probably in the centre of the defences, where the ends of the inner rampart form an inturn flanking a narrow passageway. A second gap to the north is probably the result of quarrying, and close to the north end a track and associated embanked field boundary cut through the abraded inner and outer banks. (Visited 19.2.73).

Surface finds (See Appendix B

Excavations None

Name
Todanbrigge, Todanberghe AD 942 (Sawyer, no. 481)—personal name and burh?

References
1836 Phelps, 1836, 104-6 and illustrated. Notes that 'one part is more elevated than the rest', though his meaning is unclear. Account of finds of 'British implements and instruments of war' and Roman coins.
1903 Gray, 1903. Site compared to Ruborough (19).
1911 VCH, 1911, 476-7.
1924 Burrow, 1924, 56-7.

5 MAES KNOLL, Norton Malreward. ST 600 660

Group I

12.1 ha.

Scheduled

Siting
Lias limestone plateau at c. 185 m O.D. the hillfort occupying a southwards-projecting promontory joined to the main plateau of Dundry Hill by a narrow neck c. 75 m wide. Steep slopes on all other sides except the south.

Air Photographs
UCCAP HQ 59; Photo by J. Hancock published in Fowler, 1972, pl. XVI.

Description
Little need be added to the discussion above in chapter 3 and to Tratman 1963a. The geological instability of the western side of the enclosed area, which is being undermined by springs and animal activity, has exposed areas of burnt clay and slag stratified below a yellow clay soil containing lumps of stone. No dating evidence was found in these strata, but it is possible that the upper layer is the degraded remains of a bank on this side of the enclosure, of which slight traces can be seen in places between the south end and the major earthwork of the tump. Reasons have been put forward in chapter 3 for accepting the former existence of Iron Age defences on the west side also. (Visited 10.2.73).

Surface finds See Appendix B.

Excavations
Two small trial holes at the south end behind the rear of the rampart produced Iron Age 'A' pottery from an occupation layer and an overlying dump of clay soil.

Name
The name of the site probably includes the element <u>Mearc</u> 'boundary', referring to its position on Wansdyke (see chapter 5).

References
1821 Seyer, 1821, 87-8. Mentions drystone wall two feet high on the north side, entrances at both ends of the tump (which he regards as a barrow), and a spring outside the ramparts on the east. Illustrated.
1836 Phelps, 1836, 95-6. Suggests (cf. Tratman) that Wansdyke originally ran along the north side of the enclosure.
1911 <u>VCH</u>, 1911, 477-9.
1924 Burrow, 1924, 62-3.
1963 Rahtz and Barton, 1963. Excavations.
1963 Tratman, 1963a. Description and suggestion that the major ditches on east and west form part of the Wansdyke scheme and not Iron Age defences.

6 DOLEBURY CAMP, Churchill. ST 450 589

Group I

9.15 ha.

Scheduled

Siting
At western end of Carboniferous Limestone plateau at about 150 m O.D. with very steep descent on the south and steep slopes to north and west. Easy approach from the east.

Air Photographs
NMR nos. ST 4558/1-3 (UCCAP) ST 4558/4 (West Air Photography) Plate 5.

Description
A bivallate hillfort in a promontory location. The area of the fort is at present rough pasture, with some tree growth on the northern and western defences. The interior is crossed by at least four linear mounds running N-S, with two similar mounds running E-W shown in 1883 and 1911 but not now visible. In addition there is a rectangular depression in the SW corner (discussed in chapter 3) and a ruined building on the highest point on the east surrounded by a circular stone wall. Plate 5 indicates that much of the interior has been ploughed at some time, and the building and mounds are probably associated with warrening activities.

The defences are suffering damage from foot traffic and indiscriminate excavation on the north-East. The defences are bivallate on all sides except the south, where the inner rampart is little more than a scarp fronted by a terrace. Earlier accounts mention exposed drystone walling on the inner rampart, but this is no longer visible. Two outworks lie to the east of the camp, the nearer one, a bank rising 1.5 m from a ditch on its eastern side and running N-S across the ridge. This has been regarded by the Ordnance

Survey as a miner's rake and described as possessing a ditch on its western side also, but this was not confirmed by field investigation. A second earthwork, reportedly located on 'dead ground' to the north-east is now in a plantation of young trees.

No satisfactory explanation for the name has been put forward. (Visited 13.2.73).

Surface finds

'Roman and Saxon coins, iron spearheads and other weapons' and flints are reported (1911), and excavations in 1878 'at various points within the ramparts' producted a number of sherds of Glastonbury-type pottery, and some of this material is in Weston and Taunton Museum (Weston nos. A243-5, A3006 and un-numbered). See also Appendix B.

Excavations   None, other than the above.

References
1791 Collinson, 1791, III, 579. Description and notes of Roman and Saxon finds.
1821 Seyer, 1821, 85-6.
1829 Rutter, 1829, 114. Repeats Collinson.
1883 Dymond, 1883. A careful description and engraved plan reproduced from an instrument survey of 1872 (also published in JBAA 1882).
1885 PSANHS 31 (1885), 17. Society excursion.
1911 VCH, 1911, 487-8. Adds little to above.
1915a Knight, 1915, 199-208. Description based on Dymond. Quotes Leland on folklore associated with the site ' if Dolbyri dyggyd ware of Gold shud be the share' the first element dole in the sense 'to share out' being perhaps punned in the second line.
1915b PSANHS 61 (1915), xlv. Two hand-made sherds deposited at Taunton Museum.
1924 Burrow, 1924, 82-3.
1931 Dobson, 1931, 87, 196-7, 238. Summary.
1950 PSANHS 94 (1950), 51. Iron Age 'B' sherds found.
1958 Grinsell, 1958, 165.

7   SOLSBURY CAMP, Batheaston. ST 768 679

Group I

8.0 ha.

Scheduled.   National Trust ownership.

Siting
Oolitic limestone flat-topped triangular knoll separated from plateau to north by steep-sided combe. Fairly steep slopes on all sides. Avon valley to south. Summit at about 185 m O.D.

Description
The interior of the site, under pasture, is marked by a series of furlong boundaries running parallel to the SW and SE sides of the hilltop. Plough damage to underlying deposits may be anticipated. The defences are very poorly preserved, being in part affected by undermining from natural springs

below the summit and partly by quarrying, especially on the NW. The gap on the NW is probably an original entrance, though the quarrying has damaged the area. There are slight traces of a counterscarp bank on the SW side (Visited 10.2.73).

Surface finds See Appendix B. Iron Age bone pin (1968).

Excavations
1. Work in the early 1930s on occupation levels exposed by landslips produced large amounts of Iron Age material.
2. 1955 three trial cuttings 10 ft. (3 m) square towards the west end of the north side to the entrance.
3. 1956 a small rampart cutting on the north side showed that the rampart overlay an Iron Age occupation and its collapse was itself succeeded by further Iron Age activity. The pottery, mostly of Iron Age 'A' types, was identical from the two contexts.

Name
The first element is possibly derived from Sul, from Sulis Minerva of Bath (Hill, 1914, 26).

References
1791 Collinson, 1791 III, 23. Roman finds.
1836 Phelps, 1836, 102-4. Notes cultivation of the interior in progress. 'Flat stones placed sideways' on the northern rampart.
1908 The Antiquary, 1908, 284-5.
1911 VCH II, 472-3.
1924 Burrow, 1924.
1935 Falconer and Adams, 1935. Salvage excavation work.
1957 Dowden, 1957. Report on excavations 1955-6.
1962 Dowden, 1962. General account.
1968 PUBSS 11 (3) (1967-8) 251-2. Bone pin.

8 MILBOURNE WICK, Milbourne Port. ST 671 207

Group III

8.0 ha.

Scheduled

Siting
Oolitic limestone promontory with gentle gradients on N, W and S. Interior at about 110 m O.D.

Air Photographs NMR nos. ST6720/2-4.

Description
        The level interior is under grass but has been ploughed in the past (air photographs), and is flat and featureless except for a probable hedge-bank feature close to the north side where the ground falls away to the valley. The defences consist of a very large bank with a wide shallow ditch to the east, cutting off the promontory. The inadequacy of natural defences on the other sides, however, must suggest that the work is unfinished or that artificial works on these sites have been totally obliterated. The main bank is

about 6 m high from the exterior. There is a berm between it and the ditch, which is about 15 m wide and partly waterlogged. There are slight linear banks crossing the ditch at right angles to the defences to the north side of the entrance causeway, and the ditch narrows a short distance from the break of slope on the south side of the promontory, at which point it peters out. The causeway itself splays outwards, being some 3-4 m wider at the outer lip of the ditch than towards the bank. The entrance gap is not elaborated, but the top of the bank is flat to each side, with a marked depression of the north. The general appearance of the bank is rather uneven and hummocky, with a notably flat top near the north and south ends. (Visited 26.2.73).

Surface finds None

Excavations None

References
1857 Warre, 1857. A brief description. Notes a circular depression 25 yards south of the entrance and north of the entrance 'a small barrow, apparently formed from the soil of the mound itself', this probably referring to a mound of soil isolated by the removal of bank material to the north of it on top of the bank.
1911 VCH II, 527.
1924 Burrow, 1924, 136-7.

9 SOUTH CADBURY or CADBURY/CAMELOT, South Cadbury. ST 628 252

Group I

7.3 ha.

Scheduled

Air Photographs In Alcock 1972a, Plates I and 1.

Description
     The site has been fully described and interim reports on the recent excavations published in Alcock, 1967-72 (see below). Other excavations took place c. 1890 and 1913, when four small cuttings were made around the SW entrance area and one on the summit plateau. The recent work produced evidence for late Roman religious activity and major post-Roman refurbishing of the defences and at least two contemporary interior structures on the summit plateau.

Name See above, chapter 5.

References (major items only)
1542 Leland (Itinerary, ed. L. T. Smith, 1964, Vol. I, 151) description, finds, and identification with Camelot.
1776 W. Stukeley Itinerarium Curiosum (1776), 150. Quoted in Alcock, 1972a, 19.
1836 Phelps, 1836, 118-9. Small plan and description.
1883 Dymond, 1883, 110-16. Description and plan.
1890 Bennett, 1890. Folklore and brief accounts of excavations.
1911 VCH II, 484-5. Description. Notes the presence of bank across the east and north-east sides of the summit plateau.

1913 Gray, 1913. Excavations. Bibliography.
1924 Burrow, 1924, 74-5.
1967- Alcock, 1967a, b; 1968b, c; 1969a, b; 1970b, c; 1971b; 1972a;
1972 1972c.

10 BANWELL CAMP, Banwell. ST 409 590

Group I

7.3 ha.

Scheduled

Siting
Highest point of east-west Carboniferous Limestone knoll on north side of
Mendip at about 90 m O.D.

Air Photographs
West Air Photography, Weston-Super-Mare.

Description
        A badly damaged site. The defences are wooded and damaged by quarry-
ing, especially on the north side. The interior, within which a second line
of defences can be seen on air photographs, has been ploughed in the past.

The main defences consist of a bank about 3 m high from the exterior, but
less than 1 m from the interior, fronted by a ditch and counterscarp on the
north side. A hollow way leads into the camp through a gap in the bank at
the east end, but the only ancient entrance seems to be on the NE side where
the bank is slightly inturned on each side of an entrance passage. An entrance
described by Phelps on the west side cannot now be traced. (Visited 13.2.73).

Surface finds A number of Neolithic and Bronze Age flints from the interior.

Excavations
1958- Excavations on the central mound and through the inner defences.
The former produced Iron Age pottery and flints below post-medieval material,
the only older structural features being a row of posts in a trench.

References
1821 Seyer, 1821, 84.
1836 Phelps, 1836, 108-9. Notes entrance on west side, and discovery of
      'a regular foundation of bricks and freestone laid in mortar' below the
      mound on the summit.
1899 Clifton Antiquarian Soc IV (1899), 199-208—Finds.
1905 PSANHS 51 (2) (1905) 35-40.
1906 PSANHS 52 (2) (1906) 159.
1911 VCH II, 471.
1924 Burrow, 1924, 48-9.
1955 Journal Axbridge Caving Group & Arch Soc 2 (3) 1955, 28-34.
      Description and analysis of defences.
1961a Somerset & Dorset N & Q 27 (1961). Excavations (J. Hunt).
1961b Search 1 (1961), 15-23. Excavations.
1962 Search 2 (1962), 11-19.

11 <u>BLACKER'S HILL</u>, Chilcompton. ST 636 500.

Group II

6.0 ha.

Sche uled

<u>Siting</u>
Dolomitic Conglomerate area close to outcropping of Carboniferous Limestone.
Plateau edge at <u>c</u>. 215 m O.D., with steep drops on W and S to stream.

<u>Air Photographs</u>
UCCAP LX14 (plate 2)

<u>Description</u>
      The site lies in pasture land formerly ploughed. The defences are used
as field boundaries and are partly wooded. This hillfort has attracted little
attention, but shows some unique features of interest. The defences originally
consisted of two banks and ditches forming two sides of a roughly rectangular
area whose other sides are defined by steep natural slopes, apparently without
defences. The inner bank and ditch have been destroyed on the NE. Gaps
exist near the entre of the NW side, at the N angle and towards the southern
end of the NE side. The first two are clearly for modern agricultural access,
but the last, though confused by surface quarrying and recent field boundaries
appears to be original, with a slight inturn on the terminals of the outer bank.

      The most striking feature of the defences is the small scale of the inner
rampart, which is in places about 1 m lower than the outer. The ground
slopes gradually down to the SW across the enclosure and so there is a large
area of 'dead ground' in front of the outer bank concealed from an observer
standing on the inner rampart as it now exists. (Visited 15.2.73).

<u>Surface finds</u> None

<u>Excavations</u> None

<u>References</u>
1911 <u>VCH</u> II, 487.
1924 Burrow, 1924, 70-1.

12 <u>CLATWORTHY CAMP</u>, Clatworthy, ST 046 315

Group III

5.8 ha.

Scheduled

<u>Siting</u>
Devonian shale E-W promontory spur on Brendon Hills above valley of river
Tone (now flooded). Site at <u>c</u>. 275 m O.D.

<u>Description</u>
      A partly wooded site, the interior sloping down to SW and under pasture,
and steep drops on all sides except the E, where the land continues to rise
gently to a maximum of 306 m O.D. The earthworks have been much damaged
by badgers on the east and by agricultural activities on most of the south side,

but elsewhere consist of a bank and ditch with intermittent counterscarp bank. The ditch is steep sided and cut into the solid rock and there is a marked quarry scoop to the rear of the bank on the west and north sides. Examination of the body of the rampart in a badger scrape revealed a stratum of iron panning about 1.5 m below the crest. Above this the bank material was compact shale, below it looser with more earth.

There are entrances at the western apex and in the centre of the east side and towards its south end. The former is a simple gap; the second is also simple and may be relatively recent as it is not mentioned in published accounts, though it appears to pre-date a hedge bank on the outer lip of the ditch. The entrance towards the south end of the east side is mutilated and obscured by a hedge bank, but is clearly inturned. (Visited 3.4.73).

Surface finds None

Excavations None

References
1908 Allcroft, 1908, 75.
1911 VCH II, 489-90.
1924 Burrow, 1924, 78-9.

13 NORTON CAMP, Norton Fitzwarren. ST 195 262

Group I

5.2 ha.

Scheduled

Siting
Isolated Triassic sandstone knoll rising to about 50 m O.D., about 30 m above surrounding land.

Description
A badly damaged site, the gently domed interior and surroundings being under plough and the defences overgrown and eroded. The defences are univallate and now consist of little more than a scarp up to 3 m high. On the west side is a slight bank which appears to be a counterscarp to the main earthwork, but which has been shown by excavation to be of Bronze Age date. The most notable feature of the site is the three deep hollow ways which run towards the interior from the SW, SE and N. These are about 450 m long and up to 6 m deep where they approach the defences. At their inner ends the gradient is so steep at the point where they project into the interior that it is impossible to believe that they could have functioned as entrances in their present form. (Visited 2.4.73).

Surface finds
Flints and RB pottery before 1908 (1908b, 134).

Excavations took place in 1908, when Gray sectioned the ditch on the west side, and found Roman material stratified above Bronze Age material, including the rim of a cinerary urn. Excavations in 1968-71 were directed towards assessing the character of the Bronze Age occupation but also located evidence of considerable early Roman activity.

References

1850 PSANHS 1 (ii) (1850), 38-47. Description and sketch plan of site
      (F. Warre).
1872 PSANHS 18 (i) (1872), 43-6. Discussion, including mention of legendary
      dragon which inhabited the site. (H. M. Scarth) (cf. no. 59).
1898 Bidgood, 1898. Iron Age origin for the site accepted, but speculates
      on possible Saxon use and mentions dragon legend.
1908a Allcroft, 1908, 195, 631 n.
1908b Gray, 1908. Description and excavation report.
1911 VCH II, 51.
1968 Langmaid, 1968. Excavation interim.
1970 Langmaid, 1970. Excavation interim.
1971 Langmaid, 1971. Summary and discussion.

14 DUNDON HILL, Compton Dundon. ST 485 321

Group I

4.8 ha.

Scheduled

Siting
Isolated steep-sided hill of Lower Lias with flat summit at about 85 m O.D.
A lower hill to the west is separated from the hillfort site by a low col.
Higher ground to the east and north. Kings Sedgemoor to the west and
slightly higher ground to the east and south of the hill. Three Roman sites
lie close together about 1 km SSE of the hillfort.

Air Photographs None. Site under woodland.

Description
The site was visited under optimum vegetation conditions, but much of
the defences and interior are covered with impenetrable hawthorn and hazel
thickets. The interior rises gradually towards the south. The defences consist of a rather slight bank running along the edge of the plateau with a pronounced terrace about 6 m down the slope, perhaps a silted-up ditch with
counterscarp bank. At the south apex of the defences is a circular mound
about 4 m high the construction of which appears to have involved the destruction of the hillfort defences at this point. This feature has been thought
to be a bowl barrow, but seems more likely to be a motte or a beacon.
Entrance gaps are present at two places on the east side, the northern one
near the centre being largely altered by surface quarrying and possibly not
original. The approach from this side is very steep and it seems more probable that the main entrance was on the west side, but quarrying has taken
place here also and damaged the interior and defences. (Visited 20.2.73).

Surface finds
Iron Age pottery and flints found in the interior by Bulleid (1916).

Excavations None

References
1911 VCH II, 490-1.
1916 PSANHS 62 (1916), lx. Flint finds.
1924 Burrow, 1924, 84.

15 <u>KINGS CASTLE</u>, Wiveliscombe. ST 097 282

Group I

4.1 ha.

Scheduled

<u>Siting</u>
Isolated N-S flat-topped hill of Permian sandstone and conglomerate at about 160 m O.D. Fairly steep slopes on all sides and a stream on the north. The site is set within a valley surrounded by higher land on all sides except on the SE. The Roman fort of Minnington or Nunnington lies 1 km to the SSW.

<u>Description</u>
        The site is very badly damaged by quarrying and agriculture, though at the time it was visited the gently undulating interior which slopes down towards the north was under grass. The defences, where they survive, are overgrown with hard and softwood trees and are in poor condition. Isolated lengths of bank along the east side appear to be quarry waste and the north end of the fort has been destroyed by quarrying. On the northern part of the west side the defences comprise an inner bank about 1.75 m high from the interior with a possible outer ditch and counterscarp. On the southern side the defences, though overgrown, are better preserved. There are two banks and ditches and an entrance at this point. The entrance passage is quite steep and the banks on the east side are slightly inturned. On the west the outer bank bifurcates about 20 m W of the entrance so that there are three banks on this side. The outer bank mentioned by the <u>VCH</u> cannot now be seen. (Visited 3.4.73).

<u>Surface finds</u>
1. Human bones found in the north end of the site during quarrying before 1836 (1836).
2. Neolithic finds found at various times in the interior.
3. Coin finds see Appendix B.
4. Human bones on the slope of the bank and ditch (Taunton Museum A704-6).

<u>Excavations</u> None

<u>Name</u> The present name of Kings Castle does not appear to be ancient. In the C14 it was known as <u>Castrum de Hethenberi</u> (Grinsell, 1970, 93).

<u>References</u>
1791 Collinson II, 1791, 488. Coin finds.
1836 Phelps I, 1836, 115. Human bone finds.
1911 <u>VCH</u> II, 505. Description and plan.

16 <u>WORLEBURY</u>, Weston-Super-Mare. ST 314 626

Group I

4.0 ha.

Scheduled

<u>Siting</u>
Carboniferous Limestone ridge 4 km long, the western end projecting into

the Bristol Channel. The hillfort is located at the seaward end at about 90 m O.D. Steep slopes on the north and south and a level approach from the east. Low-lying levels to north, east and south.

Air Photographs None. Site under woodland.

Description

Tree-covered site but with little undergrowth and thin soil. The stone ramparts are for the most part free of vegetation. The interior is generally level but slopes down gradually to the south. A number of large pits, many of them excavated in the last century and now gradually filling up again, are present in the interior. Because of its proximity to Weston the site is suffering damage from visitors.

The hillfort is apparently of two phases, a N-S ditch dividing the enclosed area into unequal halves about 100 m west of the present eastern defences. At this point there is a marked re-entrant in the line of the southern defences partly caused by a deeply inturned NW-SE entrance at this point, but also indicating that the eastern parts of the defences were added to the enclosure from this point, continuing along the top of the slope for about 90 m and then turning north across the ridge, adding about 0.8 ha. to the enclosed area.

At the east end there are two main ramparts and ditches, and beyond this a scheme of four shallow steep-sided cross-ridge ditches about 5 m apart and with only slight traces of banks between.

The N side of the hillfort is defined by a vertical cliff at the base of which is a mass of scree material which may derive from a collapsed rampart but which is more probably natural. On the south side the defences have collapsed down the slope and merely consist of a spread of limestone rubble. To the east of the hillfort are two cross dykes, about 30 m and 200 m from the eastern defences respectively. They consist of banks averaging about 1 m high from the bottom of irregularly cut ditches on their eastern sides. They become slighter down the slope to the north and are best defined on the top of the ridge. (Visited 16.2.73)

Surface finds See Appendix B.

Excavations
1. 1851-3 Pits in interior and some other interior excavation (Warre, 1853).
2. c.1880 Dymond and Tomkins undertook small selective excavations to elucidate structural problems (Dymond and Tomkins, 1886; Dymond, 1902).

Name Wor leah - grouse wood burh (Ekwall, 1960).

References
1791 Collinson I, 1791, xii.
1821 Seyer, 1821, 83-4.
1836 Phelps, 1836.
1951 Warre, 1851. Description.
1953 Warre, 1853. Excavations.
1886 Dymond and Tomkins, 1886. A major work and possibly the first mono-graph on a British hillfort. Very full bibliography, description, plans and elevations and finds drawings. Re-issued with minor changes as Dymond, 1902.

1905 Gray, 1905b. Summary account.
1908 Allcroft, 1908, 88, 168, 173, 176, 179-81, 194, 213, 240, 247.
1911 VCH II, 501-3.
1924 Burrow, 1924.
1930 Arch. J. 87, 1930, 473-4, quotes Dymond and Tomkins and summary.
1946 Numismatic Chronicle 6th srs. 6, 1946, 153-6.
1951 Hill, 1951.

17 PITCHERS ENCLOSURE, Priddy. ST 549 546

Group IV

3.6 ha.

Not scheduled.

Siting
East facing slope on Carboniferous Limestone at c. 250 m O.D. above small stream.

Description
A rectilinear ditchless enclosure with a single bank 3-4 m wide with a possible original entrance near the SW corner. Possible surrounding field system. Largely destroyed. Seven interior hut circles. (Not visited).

Surface finds   None

Excavations
'A small trial trench near the entrance of one of the seven hut circles produced c. 1 lb of Iron Age pottery' 1968.

References
1967 Archaeological Review 2 (1967), 17 (N.V. Quinnell).
1968 Ibid. 3 (1968) 12 (N.V. Quinnell), excavation note.

18 CADBURY CONGRESBURY, or CADCONG, Congresbury. ST 440 650

Group I

3.5 ha.

Scheduled

Siting
Flat-topped steep-sided Carboniferous Limestone hill projecting into North Somerset Levels and separated from the main mass of Broadfield Down to the E and SE by a saddle about 50 m O.D., the summit of the hill being at about 150 m O.D.

Air Photographs published in Fowler, Gardner and Rahtz, 1970, plates I and II.

Description
The site is described in Fowler, Gardner and Rahtz, 1970, 7-8 and the probable post-Roman earthworks discussed above, chapter 3. Limestone quarrying has affected a large area in the SW corner of the enclosed area and other hollows are probably also attributable to this activity. The interior is

at present rough pasture, with the defences overgrown with trees and scrub in most places. Quarrying activities which destroyed the temple at Henley Wood may ultimately threaten the site.

The defences are univallate for most of the circuit where they can be traced, with an elaborate inturned entrance on the E. To the N of this the defences are bivallate with a counterscarp bank and beyond these on the E side is a very slight irregular length of ditch with a bank on its E side. A bank and ditch run from the perimeter bank on the S northwards across the middle of the site.

Surface finds
Possible Roman burial and Roman and medieval coins (Fowler, Gardner and Rahtz, 1970, 9).

Excavations
1. 1959 Small scale excavations at the E entrance, on three possible hut sites in the W part and in the area N of the summit area in the centre of the site, re-excavated in 1968. Iron Age, Romano-British and post-Roman material was found.
2. 1968, 1970-73 A continuous area of 1375 sq. m was excavated between the summit and the edge of the plateau on the north side. Interim reports 1968, 1970a and 1970b. Pre-Roman Iron Age features and finds were re-covered, but most of the structural evidence is related to a fifth-sixth century phase to which the main perimeter bank and perhaps the bank and ditch which divides the plateau are to be related. An entrance gap was excavated in this cross bank which lacked the structural complexity of that at South Cadbury. To the W of this bank the excavated area contained at least five buildings, one pre-dating the cross bank. To the E of this bank was a complex excava-tion in the bedrock with a complex sequence of deposits within it. The banks themselves consist of low spreads of limestone rubble in which little trace could be found of revetting or timber-lacing and their original form is obscure. The data will be published in a major report being prepared jointly by mem-bers of the excavation team.

Name See above, chapter 3.

References
1821 Seyer, 1821, 86.
1911 VCH II, 475-6.
1924 Burrow, 1924, 56-7.
1968 Current Archaeology 11 (1968) 291-5. Interim on 1968 season.
1970a Fowler, Gardner and Rahtz, 1970.
1970b Current Archaeology 23 (1970), 337-42.
1971 PSANHS 115, 1971, 51-2.

19 RUBOROUGH CAMP, Broomfield. ST 227 335

Group III

3.4 ha.

Scheduled

Siting

E-W spur of Devonian shale and slate between two steep-sided ravines on N and S. Dissected landscape on dip-slope of Quantock Hills. Hillfort at about 180 m O.D. with land rising to 289 m 1.5 km to the WSW.

Air Photographs None. Site under woodland.

Description

The hillfort is mostly under mature softwood commercial forest, with some ageing hardwood on the ramparts. Fairly free of undergrowth and otherwise in good condition. The site is unusual in having two lines of defences crossing the spur about 100 m apart, the area between them, or perhaps the whole area of the fort, being known as 'Money Field' in the late C19. This feature links it to Fox's class c or d south-western hillfort types (Fox, 1961). The western rampart ends against the steep slope at its northern end and does not appear to be connected with the main enclosure along this side, although a slight scarp runs westward for a short distance from the north end of the inner ditch. From the S end of the outer rampart, however, a slight bank with an interior quarry scoop runs eastwards along the top of the southern slope, surmounted for some distance by a hedge bank but continuing as the counterscarp along the S side of the inne enclosure. About 30 m E of the S corner of the main enclosure this counterscarp has been cut through and lowered by a terraced track running up from the SW.

The main entrance is at the E end where approach up the spine of the spur is easiest. The inner rampart is sharply inturned on the N side of the entrance passage, but apparently only thickened on the S, the termination of which is shown as a definite mound on the VCH plan of 1911. There is a second entrance in the middle of the western rampart which is a simple gap, and a possible one through the outer bank.

The interior is roughly level on the ENE, but slopes up more steeply to the WSW. No features are visible (Visited 31.3.73).

Name

Rugan beorh AD 854 (Sawyer, no. 311). Ruwan-beorge AD 904. 'Rough hill' (Ekwall, 1960).

References
1857 JBAA 13, 1857, 294 (J. Collins). A short speculative account.
      Mention of Roman material.
1878 PSANHS 24, 1878, 1 (H. M. Scarth)—Identified as Roman.
1890 Page, 1890, 280-81. Short account including statement that 'a sub-
      terranean passage, 100 yards long, now filled in, gave the occupants
      of the camp access to a spring of water on the side of the hill'.
1903 Gray, 1903. Description.
1911 VCH II, 483.
1924, Burrow, 1924, 66-7.

20 STANTONBURY CAMP, Marksbury. ST 672 636

Group I

3.1 ha.

Scheduled

Siting
Isolated Oolite hill at about 170 m O.D., surrounding land at c. 110 m

Air Photograph published in Fox and Fox, 1960 plate VIIIB (NMR no. ST 6763/1).

Description
The chief feature of the hillfort is the inclusion of its northern defences in the line of Wansdyke (see above, chapter 3). Early accounts of the site regarded it as a simple western enclosure of 2.5 ha. defined on the N, W and S by steep slopes and on the E by a broad but shallow ditch which divides it from an eastern, apparently unfinished enclosure which is defined by a bank running along the N side of the hill and which then turns S where it is flanked by additional banks to E and W forming a trivallate defence against the easy ridge. On the S this scheme has not been completed to join up with the western enclosure. Wansdyke runs up to the NW and NE corners of the hill-fort and it is possible that the N defence was refurbished at the time of construction of the dyke. Running SSW-NNE across the E enclosure is a slight hollow way which then turns E to run in the quarry hollow behind the N rampart and crosses the obscures the E defences adjacent to Wansdyke. The site is under scrub and woodland, but has been partly cleared and the W enclosure brought under cultivation, Plan F. (Visited 20.3.73 and resurveyed 1974).

Surface finds
'Hand-made pottery' before 1896 in interior. Iron Age 'A' pottery found on the SE side of the western enclosure rampart in 1974 in material thrown out by rabbits.

Excavations None

Name
Merces burh or Maerec's burh AD 941 (Sawyer, 476) 'boundary fort'. The site still lies in Marksbury parish but has some time been named after the settlement of Stanton Prior 1 km E of Marksbury itself.

References
1791 Collinson II, 438-9. Notes the N-S ditch 7 ft. (2 m) deep dividing the hill.
1836 Phelps, 1836, 95 notes earthworks forming the east defences of the eastern enclosure.
1896 CAC 3 (1893-6), 'hand-made' pottery from interior.
1911 VCH II, 500.
1924 Burrow, 1924, 92-3.
1960 Fox and Fox, 1960, 30-32, inaccurately describes the relation ofthe dyke to the hillfort.

21 HIGHBURY HILL, Clutton. ST 635 580

Group III

3.1 ha.

Not scheduled

Siting

Carboniferous sandstone NW–SE ridge with top at c. 125 m O.D. with steep sides on SW and NE sides. Site at SE end. Near precipitous slopes on the SW sides.

Air Photographs None. Site in woodland.

Description

A site covered with hardwood trees with little undergrowth. Univallate except on the easy approach on the NW where a slight outer bank and ditch are set in front of the main rampart which is itself only 0.5 m high. The rampart continues round the hillside on the NE, but is difficult to trace on the SW side where quarrying has taken place. A possible entrance on the SE has also been damaged by quarrying. (Visited 22.2.73.)

Surface finds None

Excavation None

References
1972 Archaeological Review 7, 1972, 24 (P. J. and R. L. Fowler).
Rediscovery of hillfort from reference in MS by Rev. J. Skinner, 1817.
Summary description of site.

22 STOKELEIGH CAMP, Stokeleigh. ST 559 733

Group III

3.0 ha.

Scheduled, National Trust ownership.

Siting

Carboniferous Limestone promontory on W side of Avon Gorge at c. 90 m O.D. South side formed by the Nightingale valley falling to the gorge on the E. Clifton Camp (42) and Burwalls (26) lie E across the gorge and S across the Nightingale valley.

Air Photographs None. Site under woodland.

Description

The hillfort is tree-covered but with little undergrowth. The use of the area for recreation may result in damage to the earthworks and interior. The promontory is defended by two banks and ditches on the W and NW both ending on the N against the steep drops of the gorge. On the S the outer rampart, fronted by a slight counterscarp, bifurcates a short distance from the edge of the slope to the Nightingale Valley, while the massive inner bank runs E along the slope top and is surmounted in places by massive blocks of a drystone wall. At its E termination the bank is turning N at the lip of the gorge but has been truncated by quarrying. The interior is generally level.

The position of the original entrance(s) is unclear. At present there are gaps on the NW and SW corners. The former is damaged and there is no inturn on either of the entrances. Ruins of a modern building lie just within it. The latter would appear to be a recent gap, since the contours of the banks are still present beneath the track, but there is a slight inturn on the north side of the gap on the inner rampart and the bifurcation of the outer bank occurs at this point.

A third bank and ditch is present on the NW about 30 m beyond the second. This runs SW for about 230 m, diverging gradually from the inner defences, and then turns W and runs for about 50 m before fading out. On the E side of the bank immediately before this change in direction two parallel banks about 20 m apart and 1.5 m high project ESE for about 30 m. These have ditches on the N in the case of the S bank and on the S on the other. (Visited 9.2.73).

Surface finds
Millstone and sword hilt (1789).

Excavations
1966-7 Six small cuttings behind inner rampart on NW side. Iron Age and R-B features (see Appendix B).

References
1789 Barrett, 1789, 20. Finds.
1802 G. Manby, Fugitive Sketches of Clifton, Bristol 1802, 12.
1821 Seyer, 1821, 64-6. Description including notes on long rectangular building on the NW and a 'square base with a circular foundation in the middle by the NW entrance'.
1873 Scarth, 1873. Discussion of the three camps in the area.
1900 Lloyd Morgan, 1900, 19-24.
1901 Lloyd Morgan, 1901.
1908 Allcroft, 1908, 62-4.
1911 VCH II, 470-1.
1924 Burrow, 1924, 46.
1946 Tratman, 1946, 177. Notes ford across Avon as possible motive for construction of forts.
1966 Haldane, 1966. Detailed account.
1968 Archaeological Review 3 1968, 11. Note on excavations.
1970 Haldane, 1970. Interim note on excavations.
1975 Haldane, 1975. Excavation report.

23 ELWORTHY BARROWS, Brompton Ralph. ST 070 337

Group I

2.9 ha.

Scheduled.

Siting
Sandstone plateau at c. 385 m O.D. with steep slope c. 0.5 km to E and S.

Description

An unfinished hillfort in pasture land formerly ploughed (? in the C19), the interior sloping down to the north. The defences are at present only intermittent and may have been levelled in recent times although it is clear that the enclosure was never completed. The inturned entrance on the E side is well preserved but the ditch is rather irregular and intermittent. (Visited 3.4.73).

Surface finds None

Excavations None

Name
Transferred from the village 2 km to NE Elwrde 1086—Ella/Elli's worthy (Ekwall 1960).

References
1883 PSANHS 29 (1883) 45-47. Society excursion.
1908 Allcroft, 1908, 77, 186, 525 n.
1911 VCH II, 508.
1924 Burrow, 1924, 106-107.
1971 Feachem, 1971, 25-7.

24 MAESBURY CASTLE, Dinder. ST 610 471

Group I

2.8 ha.

Scheduled

Siting
W end of Carboniferous Limestone ridge on S side of Mendip at c. 290 m O.D.

Air Photographs Plate 1 (West Air Photography, Weston-Super-Mare AJ 935/9).

Description
A multivallate contour fort. The ramparts are somewhat overgrown with hawthorn and small trees. The interior has been ploughed in the recent past. The defences consist on the S of a main inner bank fronted by a ditch beyond which is a berm about 10 m wide with a second bank, ditch and counterscarp bank beyond. On the N the inner bank is much wider and there is a counterscarp bank on the outer edge of the ditch. This is succeeded by a second scheme of bank, ditch and counterscarp for most of the N half of the defences.

The earthworks are broken on the W by an apparently original entrance with the inner rampart on the N side turning outwards to flank the entrance passage with later surface quarrying to the W and N. The gap on the SE (in foreground on air photo) is apparently a recent breach. It is at present c. 40 m wide, but slight traces of the bank on the S side are traceable for a further 20 m narrowing the gap to 20 m, and it is probable that the bank material has here been used to fill up the ditch.

Very slight traces of a bank and ditch branch off NE from the outer ditch opposite the N side of this gap. This earthwork is the remains of a triangular 'advance work' or 'outpost' mentioned by earlier sources, but is at present extremely degraded.

William Worcestre described the site:

'Maesbury Castle was built on a high hill by giant called Merk. It was thrown down, but more than a hundred thousand cartloads of stone are heaped there'
(William Worcestre: Itineraries ed. J. Harvey, Oxford, 1969, 293)

(Visited 15.2.73)

Surface finds   None

Excavations   None

Name
Merkesburi AD '705' (Sawyer, 247).
Fort on the boundary (Ekwall, 1960).

References
1908a PSANHS 53 (ii) (1908) 72-81 (Gray).   Description.
1908b Allcroft, 1908, 60, 188, 210.
1911 VCH II, 491-2.
1924 Burrow, 1924, 80-81.
1959 Tratman, 19 9. Detailed description.

25 WADBURY, Mells. ST 736 489

Group III

2.8 ha.

Scheduled

Siting
P romontory site on Ool tic Limestone at c. 115 m O.D., with very steep
descents to stream on W and S, steep slope on N and level approach from E
½ km W of no. 4 on opposite bank of stream.

Description
        A very badly damaged site, the defences of which have been terraced
and altered for gardens on the E side, although the single bank still stands
c. 3 m high on this side except on the NE where a modern house has destroyed
it. The north and NW sides have a bank, ditch and counterscarp bank, the
inner bank rising only about 30 cm from the interior, which is fairly level
and under pasture. At the W apex the artificial defences stop c. 20 m E of
the natural cliff falling to the stream. The area has been disturbed by surface quarrying but there was probably an entrance there. (Visited 19.2.73).

Surface finds   None

Excavations   None

Name
wad (woad), gewaed (ford) or Wada (personal name)   burh (Ekwall, 1960).

References
1908 Allcroft, 1908, 61.
1911 VCH II, 476, 477.
1924 Burrow, 1924, 58-9.

26 BURWALLS, Bristol. ST 563 730

Group III

2.6 ha. (estimated)

Not scheduled

Siting
Promontory site overlooking Avon Gorge and on its W side, with steep slopes down to Nightingale Valley on N. Ground falls away on SW and S. Level approach from W. c. 90 m O.D.

Description
The site was almost completely destroyed c. 1868, and small lengths of defences survive at ST 5609 7303 and ST 5625 7282, the latter showing a segment c. 20 m long of two banks c. 3 m high each fronted by a ditch in the garden of 'Burwalls'. Seyer, 1821, 62-4 and 57 describes the site as trivallate, the defences running for c. 415 m from the Avon Gorge in an arc, stopping just short of the lip of the Nightingale Valley on the N. Two entrance gaps are also described, the W being c. 15 m wide and 'within and in front of it the ground rises as if the foundation of a gatehouse or some such building were beneath'. The eastern gap was only c. 3.5 m wide; a track running through it then turned sharply left behind the main inner rampart, flanked on the N by a short additional length of bank.

The banks themselves are described by Seyer, Phelps and Scarth as showing evidence of mortar and stone walling. Mortar 'in great abundance' is described by Seyer on the inner rampart, and Scarth mentions a solid bed of 'concrete' within the rampart caused by the piling of limestone onto fires 2.75 - 4.5 m apart. These accounts have led to the site being regarded as a vitrified fort (Arch J 111, (1954), 85-6), but Lloyd Morgan, on the basis of sections cut through the banks of the SE, considered that the apparent mortaring was due to burnt limestone and charcoal washing down into the body of the bank from fires lit on its summit, and this seems to be confirmed by the section published in 1869.

The interior, now almost wholly built on or used for gardens was 'crossed in various places by stony ridges which have the appearance of being the foundations of long walls or ranks of houses' (Seyer). It is possible that this is an extension of the R-B field system in Ashton Park, 1 km to the W. (Visited 9.2.73).

Surface finds   None

Excavations
None to modern standards, though a section was drawn during demolition c. 1868.

Name   probably from burh, but possibly bur - cottage etc.

References
1789 Barrett, 1789. 17.
1802 Manby, Fugitive Sketches of Clifton (1802), 9. 12-13.
1821 Seyer, 1821, 62-64.
1836 Phelps I, 96-97.
1869 PSANHS 15 (pt. 2) (1868-9), 27-31. Section drawing p. 29.
1873 Scarth, 1873. Discussion of vitrification.
1900 Lloyd Morgan, 1900.
1901 Lloyd Morgan, 1901.

27 **BURLEDGE CAMP**, West Harptree. ST 582 585

Group III

2.6 ha.

Scheduled.

Siting
West-facing steep-sided spur of Burledge Hill at c. 155 m O.D. Lias
Limestone and Keuper Marl.

Description
    The hillfort was briefly described by Stukeley who called it 'Bow Ditches',
and rediscovered in 1948. The main defences are bank, ditch and counterscarp, well preserved only on the E and SE. On the north side the bank and
counterscarp are visible though overgrown and damaged, and on the W side
the counterscarp only survives on the N of the present track running up the
steep slope from the W. About 60 m E of the E defences is a second bank
and ditch running N-S across the ridge.

    The defences are light tree-covered; the interior, which slopes steeply
down to the E and is level in the W part of the enclosure is at present under
pasture but has been ploughed in the past. (Visited 15.2.73).

Surface finds None

Excavations
Twenty-six cuttings 1.21 m (4 ft) square were made in 1955. Interior features included evidence for iron working and an early Iron Age ditch overlain
by an occupation layer containing later Iron Age material. One sherd of
R.B. pottery was found.

References
1776 Stukeley, W. Intinerarium Curiosum Centura II (1776), 77-79.
1949 PUBSS 6 (1949), 42-54. Preliminary notice of rediscovery.
1954 Crook and Tratman, 1954. Description.
1957 PUBSS 8 (1957), 40 (ApSimon, A. M.) - excavation summary.
1977 Rahtz and Greenfield, 1977, 168-70 (A. M. ApSimon).

28 **DOWSBOROUGH**, Doddington. ST 160 391

Group I

2.5 ha.

Scheduled

Siting
Hill on dip slope of Quantocks, with deeply incised stream valley on W and
combe on S. Devonian Sandstone hilltop at c. 320 m O.D.

Description
    A contour hillfort with main rampart about 4 m high above an outer ditch
with counterscarp bank. The main entrance is on the east side, where
approach is easiest from lower ground, but has been mutilated and widened.
A second gap on the N side, where a ridgeway runs northwards down the spine

of the hill, may also be an original entrance. The defences are partly overgrown with oak trees, but most of the N side is clear.

The interior is almost wholly overgrown with neglected oak coppice and is impenetrable. (Visited 31.3.73).

Surface finds   None

Excavations   None

Name
Also called Danesborough (VCH II, 492) and Dawesbury (Hill, 1914, 312-13). Perhaps a corruption of Howsborough = hillfort (Page 18 0, 291) or containing the personal name Dagobert (Hill, 1914, 213-13). Perhaps the same personal name as at Daw's Castle (36) q.v.

References
1890 Page, 1890, 290-91.
1908 Alcroft, 1908, 631 n - Dragon legend associated with site.
1911 VCH II, 492.

29 CADBURY CAMP, Tickenham.   ST 454 725

Group I

2.5 ha.

Scheduled

Siting
Slight south-facing spur of Carboniferous Limestone Failand Ridge, running E-W at c. 100 m O.D. at this point.

Air Photographs   Plate 7 (West Air Photography, AN 1038/10).

Description
A bivallate site without a counterscarp bank outside the outer ditch. The defences are overgrown and suffering severe damage in places from cattle. The interior, which slopes down to the S has been ploughed in the past (certainly between 1939-45), but is now pasture. There are a number of modern breaches in the ramparts on the S and SW, but reasons have been put forward for suggesting that the gap on the NW side, though subsequent to the construction of the defences, is an ancient entrance (above, chap. 3). The banks themselves are up to 3.5 m high from the bottom of the ditches, but vary considerably. The entrance on the N side is elaborated by the outer and inner banks on the E side being turned outwards and inwards respetively to lengthen the entrance passage. Behind the inner bank a low bank 3 m long and 20 cm high runs from the inturn across to the rear of the main part of the bank. Quarry hollows can be seen at various points behind the bank. (Visited 11.2.73).

Surface finds   Roman altar and coins (Appendix B). Quern (Arch Review 2 1967, 27).

Excavations
Gray, 1922. Cuttings near gate and one trench in interior.
Iron Age and Roman material. No structures.

<u>Name</u> as nos. 9 and 18.   See chapter 5.

<u>References</u>
1821 Seyer, 1821, 80-81.   Mentions main entrance and other gaps in defences.
1875 Grover, 1875. Estimates defences to have required 72,000 man-hours
    for construction. Roman or later date. Plan.
1899 <u>CAC</u> 4 (1897-9), 160.
1911 <u>VCH</u> II, 500-501.
1922 Gray, 1922. Excavation report.
1924 Burrow, 1924, 76-77.

30 <u>TUNLEY CAMP</u>, Camerton. ST 684 592

Group I

2.5 ha.

Not scheduled

<u>Siting</u>
At W end of ENE-WSW trending ridge of lower Lias clay and Oolite at <u>c</u>.
160 m O.D.   Moderate slopes on N and S.

<u>Air Photographs</u>   UCCAP QA 48.

<u>Description</u>
        The remains of this hillfort are now so meagre that it is difficult to
assess its original form.   The N defences have been ploughed flat, although
a very slight scarp could be traced running across the middle of the field
(from left to right in photograph).   On the S and W sides the present hedge
sits on a scarp <u>c</u>. 2 m high and on the W a low wide bank is present immediately W of the hedge.   The whole area has been ploughed.   (Visited 22.2.73).

<u>Surface finds</u> None

<u>Excavations</u> None

<u>Name</u> Tunley is a hamlet $\frac{3}{4}$ km ENE of the site.

<u>References</u>
1958 Wedlake, 1958.

31 <u>SMALLDOWN CAMP</u>, Evercreech.   ST 667 406

Group I

2.4 ha.

Scheduled

<u>Siting</u>
On western side of Oolite plateau at <u>c</u>. 220 m O.D. with land falling fairly
steeply on W and N.   Easiest approach from the SE, where a farm pond
indicates water close to surface.

<u>Description</u>
        The site is pasture, possibly ploughed in the past, although the presence
of 11 small barrows along the E-W spine of the interior does not suggest that

this has been intensive and preservation of interior deposits may be quite good. The defences are bivallate except on the E side where a counterscarp bank c. 1 m high is also present. On the N, W and S the outer bank has been reduced to a scarp and the outer ditch is filled up. The inner bank on the south side has a sharp rear vertical profile, possibly caused by ploughing, and a flat top. Towards the E end of this side the bank shows as a flat-topped platform with a higher length of earthwork along its outer edge, creating an impression of a wall-walk behind a breastwork. The two entrances on the E and SE were shown by Gray (1904) to be original. (Visited 23.2.73).

Surface finds None

Excavations
Gray, 1904a. Eight small cuttings, four in the ditch terminals at the entrances, two on the interior barrows and one in the interior. Iron Age 'A' type pottery (Taunton Acc No. A 925-8) was found in the ditches and in the barrows, in addition to '2 fragments of rather later pottery' (perhaps RB) in the upper part of the ditch fill (Gray, loc. cit., 43).

Name
The hill is recorded as Smaledone 1262 - little hill (Gray, loc. cit., 33).

References
1903 PSANHS 49 (2) (1903), 32-39.
1904 Gray, 1904a.
1908 Allcroft, 1908, 107, 187, 533.
1911 VCH II, 495.
1924 Burrow, 1924, 90-91.
1958 Grinsell, 1958, 165, 322.

32 WESTBURY CAMP, Rodney Stoke. ST 492 511

Group IV

2.4 ha.

Scheduled

Siting
On W side of Mendip Carboniferous Limestone plateau at c. 260 m. On lip of steep slopes on SW down to Levels in hillslope position.

Description
    A hillslope enclosure damaged by surface quarrying. The main enclosure is surrounded by a small narrow-topped bank about 1 m high, possibly (O/S) a dry stone wall. The interior slopes to the SW. Apparently associated with enclosure are two linear banks, one running towards it from the N and the second from ENE. Both have been ploughed at their farther ends and are damaged. The first appears to continue into the interior of the main enclosure, while the second approaches it at an acute angle and terminates just before the main enclosure is reached. Earthworks to the W of the site may be remains of an early field system. The site is under pasture. (Visited 20.2.73).

Surface finds None

Excavations None

Name – from Westbury village.

References
1926 Tratman, 1926. Discovery and description.

33 WAMBROOK CAMP, Wambrook. ST 311 075

Group IV

2.4 ha.

Scheduled

Siting
Hilltop on Greensand Pebble Beds at c. 200 m O.D. Land rises gently to
NW, falling away on NE, SE and SW.

Description
        A site almost entirely obliterated by ploughing, the defences forming
an oval c. 200 x 150 m. These seem to have consisted of a bank and exterior
ditch. On the S this has been ploughed down and now appears as a much
spread bank c. 30 cm high. On the W and NW the bank is better preserved,
standing c. 50-75 cm high with a possible entrance gap on this side. On the
E a field boundary follows the line of the defences, and a scarp 2 m high is
present here. (Visited 25.3.74).

Surface finds
A crumb of Iron Age pottery was found behind the bank on the S side during
field investigation.

Excavations None

Name From village.

References
O/S Record Card ST30NW 4.

34 BURY HILL Winterbourne (Gloucs.) ST 652 791

Group I

2.2 ha.

Scheduled

Siting
Pennant Sandstone plateau falling away steeply to river on the W, gradually
dropping to N and S, level approach on E. About 75 m O.D.

Description
        A bivallate hillfort, partly quarried away on the W side. Interior
under pasture, defences partly tree covered. The interior has been used
for activities related to the quarrying and a number of the earthwork features
still visible and described in 1926 and 1927 may be related. The chief of
these is a low bank running E-W for 50 m from the rear face of the inner
rampart on the E side. A second bank runs N from this towards the rear

of the rampart on the N but fades out after about 10 m The excavated Roman
building (see chap. 6 and Fig. 33) is on the same alignment as the E-W bank.
At the E end of this is a rectangular earthwork, apparently also of a building,
set against its S side. Most other features appear to be the result of surface
quarrying. The inner rampart is about 4.5 m high from the bottom of the
inner ditch, and the outer about 3 m. There are apparently original entrances
on NE and SE.

Surface finds
Rotary quern from quarrying (Willmore and Tratman, 1927, 297).

Excavations
1926 (Davies and Phillips, 1927). Five areas excavated. Roman material
(Appendix B).

Name Bury Hill from OE burh (?).

References
1926 Willmore and Tratman, 1926. Detailed description and plan which is
     at variance with the 1927 plan. References.
1927 Davies and Phillips, 1927. Excavation report.

35 WAINS HILL, Clevedon. ST 391 706

Group III

2.2 ha.

Scheduled

Siting
Coastal promontory of Carboniferous Limestone at c. 30 m O.D. Site of
fort separated from land to E, on which the church stands, by a low saddle.

Description
Damaged by wartime installations and paths. Area now used for public
recreation and is grass covered for the most part. The interior is fairly
level. The single rampart runs N-S across the E side of the promontory at
the top of the slope down to the saddle, with a terrace below, possibly the
remains of a filled-up ditch. On the S the earthworks become very confused,
the main rampart turning E to flank an apparent entrance on its southern side.
There are traces of drystone walling on the bank at its N end. (Visited 11.2.73).

Surface finds
'Thin scatter of buff-coloured sherds of thumbnail size' below turf in interior
early 1930s. (Pers. comm. C. M. Sykes, 17.11.72) Roman material
Appendix B.

Excavations None

References
1924 Burrow, 1924, 142-3.

36 DAW'S CASTLE, Watchet. ST 062 433

Group II

2.0 ha.

Scheduled

Siting
Coastal cliff top at c. 75 m O.D. with unstable coastal slopes on N side.
Lias.

Air Photographs West Air Photography.

Description
        A univallate site, an uncertain proportion of which has been lost by
erosion of the cliff which is at present (1974) fairly stable. The site is
used as a council rubbish tip. The defences consist of a bank c. 2 m in
maximum height with a slight terrace in front on the SW side. On the E
the defences are barely traceable, but it seems clear that the modern road
follows the line of the ditch on this side. At the cliff top on the W side the
rampart appears to branch into two, one part turning E close to the top of
the cliff and this may be a 20 yd length of rampart described by the VCH,
but the main line of the bank is continued as a scarp right to the cliff top.
At the E end of the site late C19 lime kilns, which disturbed a cemetery,
have destroyed the earthworks. (Visited 10.4.73, 16.8.74).

Surface finds
Cemetery in area of lime kilns and in the cliff edge (Page, 1890, 241).

Excavations
A small excavation is believed to have taken place in the mid-1960s, directed
by Dr. D. Hill, but no information has been obtained.

Name
Also recorded as Dart's Castle and Danes' Castle, but a 16th century docu-
ment mentions Thomas Daw as occupier of the land (ex inf R. W. Dunning,
Victoria County History of Somerset).

References
1890 Page, 1890, 241-42.
1911 VCH II, 528-29.

37 COMBE HILL, Henbury. ST 561 782

Group II

2.0 ha.

Not scheduled

Siting
Cliff top site with river on NW side, ground falls away to S. Level approach
from E and W. Carboniferous Limestone.

Description
        The site is partly in woodland and partly incorporated in a golf course.
The earthworks are very badly eroded and now consist of little more than

low scarps. These run from the cliff top on the N, SE across the ridge and probably ran E-W along its S side to form a roughly parallelogram-shaped enclosure, but the S side has been destroyed. There are possible entrances in both E and W sides of the enclosure. (Visited 9.2.73).

Surface finds None.

Excavations None.

References
1946 Tratman, 1946, 178.
1968 Haldane, 1968.

38 CASTLES CAMP, Bathealton. ST 057 245

Group I

2.0 ha.

Scheduled

Siting
Hilltop of Devonian Sandstone at c. 220 m O.D. Easiest access from E, moderate slopes on N and S and steep drop to River Tone on W. Rolling countryside.

Description
    A univallate site under pasture with trees on the defences. These consist of a major bank and ditch on the E with a slightly inturned entrance in the centre. The bank is c. 4 m high on this side but decreases in scale markedly at the N and S ends where the defences run E along the edge of the hill, though a ditch and counterscarp is still present.

Surface finds See Appendix B.

Excavations None.

References
1791 Collinson III, 23, I, 134.
1908 Allcroft, 1908, 43.
1911 VCH II, 481.
1924 Burrow, 1924, 50-51.

39 HORSE POOL CAMP, Whitestaunton. ST 265 090

Group II

1.9 ha.

Scheduled

Siting
Hillslope location on W side of N-S Greensand ridge at c. 190 m O.D. Land falls steeply to River Yarty on W.

Description
    Hillfort with interior (pasture) sloping fairly steeply down to theW. The defences are mostly tree covered and enclose an oval area c. 250 m

N–S by 120 m transversely. They consist of a single bank with a wide flat-bottomed ditch in front. The bank is up to 3 m high from the bottom of the ditch on the E side and has a sharp steep profile which suggests the presence of narrow drystone walling on its summit. There is a simple entrance on the NE, but at the S Apex of the fort a second entrance is formed by the rampart turning outwards and running S for <u>c</u>. 30 m on each side of an entrance passage. Towards the S end of the entrance there is a break in the banks on either side, probably of recent origin. On the W side of the enclosure the bank is just discernible from the interior though masked by hillwash. (Visited 2.4.73).

<u>Surface finds</u> None.

<u>Excavations</u> None.

<u>References</u>
1911 <u>VCH</u> II, 503.
1924 Burrow, 1924, 96–97.
1930 <u>Transactions Devon Association</u> 62, 1930, 353 (Gray).
1931 Dobson, 1931, 205.

40 <u>LITTLEDOWN CAMP</u>, North Stoke. ST 709 689

Group III

1.8 ha.

Scheduled.

<u>Siting</u>
Oolite W-facing promontory at <u>c</u>. 220 m O.D. on W side of plateau of Lansdown Hill, N of Bath. Steep slopes on all sides except E.

<u>Air Photographs</u> UCAAP CD 71 (Plate 3)

<u>Description</u>
The interior of the site is cultivated, the rampart is degraded and surmounted by a stone wall. Artificial defences are only present on the E side, the ditch here being up to 3 m deep and the top of the bank <u>c</u>. 4 m from the bottom of the ditch. There are traces of a counterscarp S of the simple entrance which is in the centre of the E side, and the <u>VCH</u> shows other earthworks, now destroyed by ploughing, N of this. Two interior pillow mounds have been destroyed by ploughing, and two building foundations, at the rear of the N and S ends of the E defences, were under plough when the site was visited. No dating evidence was found but they are probably post-medieval agricultural buildings. (Visited 25.2.73).

<u>Surface finds</u> None.

<u>Excavations</u>
A trench 40 ft (**12.2** m) long was cut through the ditch S of the entrance in 1911. Animal bone was recovered.

<u>References</u>
1791 Collinson, I, 1791, 134.
1821 Seyer, 88.
1911a <u>PSANHS</u> Bath Branch, 1911, 125 (T. Bush). Excavation.
1911b <u>VCH</u> II, 480–81.

41 CANNINGTON CAMP, Cannington. ST 247 405

Group I

1.8 ha.

Scheduled

Siting
Isolated Carboniferous Limestone knoll at c. 70 m O.D., rising above
undulating country on Trias formations. A second, lower knoll to the E,
now largely quarried away, is the site of a major cemetery of Roman and
later date.

Air Photographs Series published in Rahtz, 1969.

Description
        The site and its surrounding earthworks are discussed in detail in
chapter 3 (Plan D), where it is argued that the settlement and field system
to the south post-dates the outer earthwork of the hillfort. The hillfort itself
is densely overgrown with hazel and bramble and little more can be said than
that it is a bivallate site with apparently original entrances at N and S.
(Visited 29.3.73; Earthwork Survey 1974).

Surface finds
Iron Age and RB pot in earthworks to south by wirter. (See also Appendix
B). Glastonbury pottery in interior (Rahtz, 1968, 60).

Excavations
1905 In interior.
1911 Behind rampart on N side.
1963 Behind outer bank on S. See Appendix B.

References
1907 Whistler, 1907. Excavation. Summary of earlier speculations that
      this was the site of Arx Cynuit (see Site No. 2).
1911 VCH II, 474-5.
1924 Burrow, 1924, 52.
1968 Rahtz, 1968. Description and excavation.

42 CLIFTON CAMP, Bristol. ST 566 733

Group II

1.7 ha.

Scheduled

Siting
Slight knoll at the E edge of the Avon Gorge slightly higher than Carboniferous
Limestone Clifton Downs on the N. Land falls away to E and SE. Sites 22
and 26 on S side of gorge.

Air Photographs West Air Photography Al1000/10 (Plate 6).

Description
        The site has suffered from its proximity to Bristol; the defences have
been landscaped and quarried, and the interior, at present under grass, was

used for a small reservoir and windmill (later converted into a <u>camera obscura</u>) in the last century. The interior earthworks are discussed in chapter 3 (Plan B). The defences originally appear to have been bivallate with an entrance on the E. A third bank is present on the N.

William Worcestre described the fort <u>c</u>. 1480:

> 'And which probable kind of hillfort (<u>castellum</u>) was founded in ancient times; it remains to this day as a large circle of great stones piled up and small ones scattered here and there, most remarkable to see; the said stones lying there, in a orderly ring and great enclosure, so that a very strong castle (<u>castrum</u>) is seen to have existed there, which hundreds of years ago was destroyed and thrown to the ground'.
> (translation by courtesy of Mrs. F. Neale from Corpus Christi College MS 210, p. 97).

<u>Surface finds</u> Roman coins, see Appendix B.

Excavations
1900 Cut through interior earthwork - no dating evidence.

References
1821 Seyer, 1821, 59-62. Plan p. 57.
1893 Fryer, 1893.
1896 Pritchard, 1896.
1900 Lloyd Morgan, 1900. Excavation.
1946 Tratman, 1946, 177-78.

43 <u>BRENT KNOLL</u>, East Brent. ST 341 510

Group I

1.6 ha.

Scheduled.

Siting
Highest point of a prominent 'island' of Lias sandstone and clay rising above the Somerset Levels. The larger part of the island consists of a steep-sided plateau at about 40 m O.D., and at the south end the knoll on which the hill-fort is located rises to 138 m, the easiest approach being from the N.

Air Photographs
UCCAP AFH 30 (Plate 5) and BMC 71. West Air Photography E224/11 (Plate 11).

Description
The interior of the site has been extensively quarried for the Lias limestone which caps the hill, but considerable areas, especially on the N and SW, are apparently intact. The whole site is under pasture, suffering damage from cows in places. The outer defences on the N have been used for military trenches. The main enclosure is defined by an inner bank, discontinuous on the W where it has been quarried away, and with an entrance on the E side with some unusual features (see chapter 3 and Plan A). About 5 m below the inner bank is a flat terrace about 3 m wide from which the

Plate 11   Brent Knoll Hillfort (no. 43) from the south-east
(West Air Photography neg. no. E224/11)

ground falls to a second major bank which surrounds the hilltop, except on the E side where a modern terraced trackway may reflect the original access route. There are several scarps across the spine of the hill on the N, but some of these may be medieval (?) strip lynchets which are also present on the S slopes of the hill. (Visited 14.2.73, re-survey May 1974).

Surface finds
Iron Age material. Roman material. See Appendix B.

Excavations
Skinner, early 19th century. See Appendix B

Name
Brente "AD 663'. Sawyer no. 238. Celtic root meaning 'high place'. (Ekwall).

References
1789 Barrett, 1789, 10. Roman coins.
1791 Collinson, 1791 I, 186. Repeat of Barrett?
    Skinner MSS Brit. Mus. Add MSS 33646 fol 10 (July 20, 1812);
    33719 fol 95 (September 30, 1830); 33726 fols 106 and 110 (June 1,
    1832) - notes on excavations.
1821 Seyer, 1821 I, 86.
1829 Rutter, 1829, 88.
1905 Gray, 1905c. Brief description. Quotes Skinner.
1911 VCH II, 482.
1924 Burrow, 1924, 66-7. Notes tradition of castle on the Knoll.
    (Enclosure Act Award of 1801 (Somerset Co. Record Office Q RE 40)
    shows a castellated tower on the knoll).
1948 Dobson, 1948. The hillfort claimed as the site of Mons Badonicus.
    Cites interpolation into De Antiquitate Glastoniae in which Arthur and
    Ider fight giants on Mons Ranarum, located to Brent. cf. Robinson,
    1926, 18 and 19 where John of Glastonbury states that the pagan Saxons
    took the lands of Brent, but later returned them to the abbey.
1967 Archaeological Review 2 (1967), 26 - Roman coin.
1972 Archaeological Review 7 (1972), 49-50. Fieldwork and surface finds.

44 CASTLE WOOD or KENWALCH'S CASTLE, Penselwood. ST 747 336
Group I

1.6 ha.

Scheduled

Siting
Greensand ridge at c. 230 m. The hillfort lies at the north end of the NNE-SSW ridge, with a level approach from the S and moderate slopes on the W, E and N.

Description
    The hillfort is covered by trees and much overgrown and the level interior shows no earthwork features. The defences are univallate with a counterscarp bank on the NE side, and are most massive on the SSE and NNW where there appear to have been entrances. That on the S has been altered

by the present road, but on the N the modern road runs slight E of an earlier gap, and a small segment of bank survives between the two. A third gap, apparently recent, is present at the SW corner.

Surface finds None.

Excavations None.

Name
The ascription to Cenwalh is probably recent, due to the location of the battle aet Peonnum in this area. The VCH quotes a corruption of this to 'Kenny Wilkins Castle'.

References
1904 Gray 1904b. Excursion notes.
1911 VCH II, 511-12.

45 CREECH HILL, Milton Clevedon. ST 666 367

Group III

1.6 ha.

Scheduled

Siting
Oolitic limestone ridge at about 180 m. The site located on a W-facing promontory.

Air Photographs
RAF CPE U.K. 1924 Jan. 16; 1947 3273/4 (site first identified from aerial photography).

Description
    A univallate promontory fort, much damaged by ploughing. On the E side the approach is level and there may be an entrance in the centre of this side, though the defences are almost obliterated here. On the remainder of the circuit the defences run along or slightly below the edge of the steep sided plateau, consisting chiefly of a simple scarp, but with a ditch and counter-scarp bank on the NW. (Visited 23.2.73).

Surface finds None.

Excavations None.

References
1957 PUBSS 8(1) 1957, 42 (Plan).

46 BLAISE CASTLE, Henbury. ST 558 783

Group I

1.6 ha.

Sheduled.

Siting
Steep-sided Carboniferous Limestone hill at about 85 m O.D.

Description

The interior of the site is fairly level and undisturbed apart from the folly of 1768 in the centre. The defences have been extensively altered by landscaping in the C18 and C19 and it is now difficult to assess their original form though there appear to have been at least three concentric banks and ditches on the W and N sides. On the S there are now no signs of artificial defences, the steep slopes being perhaps regarded as adequate protection, though on the E a low much spread bank runs N-S across the summit about 20 m W of the break of slope, and there is a possible entrance in the centre. A second entrance gap, comprising a deeply cut quarried track is present at the SW corner. (Visited 8.2.73)

Surface finds Roman material: see Appendix B.

Excavations
1918 and 1957 Roman? building and Iron Age 'B' material.

Name
Perhaps originally called Henbury. Chapel of St. Blaise documented in Henbury Parish (Bartlett, 1919).

References
1768 Sir R. Atkyns The Ancient & Present State of Gloucestershire, 2nd ed. 1768. Describes discovery of 'vault' in 1707 with Roman material and burials.
1779 Rudder, J. A New History of Gloucestershire, 1779, 491. Roman coins found during construction of folly.
1821 Seyer, 1821, chap. 1, 66-68, chap. 2, 59-62, 156-7. Description, plan and coin list.
1919 Bartlett, 1919. Excavation.
1958 Rahtz and Brown, 1958. Excavation.
1963 Boon, 1963. Coin list.

47 MOUNSEY CASTLE, Dulverton. SS 852 295

Group I

1.5 ha.

Scheduled

Siting
Semi-promontory position with steep drop to river on W. Devonian Sandstone at c. 215 m O.D. Plateau to N rising to 300 m.

Air Photographs None known. Site under woodland.

Description
A roughly triangular-shaped fort with apex to the N. The interior slopes down gradually N-S, but any interior features are obscured by trees and forestry disturbance. The defences are univallate on the SE and E sides, with a ditch and counterscarp on the S. On the W the rampart runs along the top of a very steep slope down to the Barle, and behind it is a pronounced quarry hollow, the E side of which is formed by a steep craggy natural cliff, interpreted by the VCH as part of the rampart. On the S the inner rampart can be seen to consist of a drystone wall about 3 m thick still surviving several

courses high. Inturn—out-turn entrances are present at the SW and N corners. Behind the W rampart about 40 m N of the SW entrance is a large recumbent slab, possibly a fallen standing stone. (Visited 1.4.73).

Surface finds None.

Excavations None.

Name
Possibly from the Monceaux family (Page, 1890, 85-6).

References
1890 Page, 1890. Brief description.
1911 VCH II, 492-3.
1924 Burrow, 1924, 88.

48 OLDBERRY CASTLE, Dulverton. SS 909 282

Group I

1.4 ha.

Scheduled

Siting
Devonian Sandstone flat-topped ridge at c. 230 m O.D., above river Barle, which runs in steep-sided valley to N and E. E-W ridgeway to the south.

Description
    A site badly damaged by ploughing. Defences only survive on the NE in woodland immediately above precipitous drops to the river. Here there is a single bank rising about 2 m from the exterior ditch with a possible simple entrance giving access to the spine of a ridge running down to the NE. The remainder of the circuit is incorporated in massive hedge banks, though the ditch can just be seen at the W corner. The interior is gently domed and under continuous cultivation. (Visited 1.4.73).

Surface finds None.

Excavations None.

Name Presumably 'the old fort'.

References
1911 VCH II, 493-4.
1924 Burrow, 1924, 90.

49 CLEEVE TOOT, Cleeve. ST 462 657.

Group II

1.2 ha.

Not scheduled

Siting
Gentle N-facing slope on S side of small steep-sided ravine, with higher Carboniferous Limestone ridge immediately to the S. Site at c. 70 m O.D.

<u>Air Photographs</u> None. Site in woodland.

<u>Description</u>
       Undergrowth was so dense at the time of the field visit that the site could only be partially examined. The earlier account describes it as an enclosure of about three acres defined by a low bank without a ditch and about 1 m high and 10 m wide, terminating against the edge of the cliff on the N. The interior is level. Plan B(d) (Visited 16.2.73).

<u>Surface finds</u> None.

<u>Excavations</u> None.

<u>References</u>
1829 Rutter, 1829, 68. Brief mention.
1925 Thorburn, 1925, 281-2.

50 <u>BAT'S CASTLE</u>, (or Caesar's Camp), Carhampton. SS 988 421.

Group I

1.0 ha.

Scheduled.

<u>Siting</u>
NW-SE Devonian Sandstone ridge with steep drops on N, W and S side, moderate slopes on the NE and E. Hillfort on highest point of ridge at <u>c</u>. 205 m O.D.

<u>Air Photographs</u>
NMR No. SS 9842/1 (UCCAP) site from the west (16.6.49).
          SS 9842/2 (West Air Photography) shows past ploughing in the
                    interior of the fort (29.4.74).
          SS 9842/4 (West Air Photography) view from SE (29.5.74).
          UCCAP reproduced in Grinsell, 1970, 72.

<u>Description</u>
       A strongly defended univallate hillfort on a hill crest. The area is open moorland and the interior is featureless, the traces of early C19(?) ploughing being visible only from the air. There are two entrances, facing E and W and askew to the trend of the ridge, perhaps a defensive device. The W entrance is inturned and the ditch is very steep and deep at this point. The E entrance is extremely unusual and from the air photographs does not appear to be original. The inner banks are slightly inturned, but the terminals of the ditch turn eastward for about 45 m flanking a causeway 8 m wide at its inner end and 6 m at the outer (eastern) end. The ramparts have been damaged in several places and partly pushed forward into the ditch. 125 m to the SE is a linear earthwork which follows a sinuous course across the ridge. (Visited 4.4.73).

<u>Surface finds</u> None.

<u>Excavations</u> None.

References
1830 Savage, 1830, 289. Describes the back of the rampart 'terraced like
    steps'.
1890 Page, 1890, 200-201.
1911 VCH 1911, 484-5.
1924 Burrow, 1924, 84-5.
1964 Forde-Johnston, 1964, 86. Links site to Black Ball (69).

51 COW CASTLE, Exmoor. SS 794 373

Group I

0.9 ha.

Scheduled

Siting
Sandstone knoll with summit at c. 235 m O.D. lying at confluence of River
Barle and Whitewater; a saddle separating the knoll from higher moorland
rising to 378 m on the N. High moorland all round, mostly unenclosed.

Air Photographs UCCAP (reproduced in Grinsell, 1970, 89).

Description
        A remote site set in a steep-sided valley with high ground to the N.
The defences consist of a mostly flat-topped bank which is apparently stone-
revetted on both outside and inside. There is a silted ditch around the circuit. The entrance gap on the SW is about 3 m wide and the passage formed
by the inturned ramparts is 9 m deep, with vertical revetment stones visible
on the S side. The interior has very steep slopes on the W and N, but slopes
down more gently on the other two sides and there are possible hut platforms
on the E side. (Visited 30.3.73).

Surface finds None.

Excavations None.

References
1890 Page, 1890, 95-6.
1908 Allcroft, 1908, 174.
1911 VCH 1911, 495.

52 PLAINSFIELD CAMP, Over Stowey. ST 184 362

Group IV

0.9 ha.

Scheduled

Siting
Sandstone SW-NE ridge on dip slope of the Quantocks with steep-sided valleys
on the NW and SE. Site lies on slope at 230 m O.D. with land rising gently
to the SW, and falling more steeply on the NE.

Description
 A hillslope enclosure set at the point at which the gentle gradient of the dip slope increases as the land falls away to the stream to the N. The interior is without archaeological features and is tree covered, but there are a number of field banks about 30 cm high in the surrounding area. The defences are univallate, with a ditch surviving on all sides except the N, where its position is occupied by a modern track. There is an out-turned entrance on the E side. (Visited 31.3.73).

Surface finds None.

Excavations None.

References
1911 VCH 1911, 511.

53 TAP'S COMBE, Brockley. ST 477 670

Group II

0.8 ha.

Not scheduled

Siting
On Carboniferous Limestone terrace at c. 70 m O.D. with steep slope on S and gentle drop to W and NW.

Description
 One of the three small Group II sites on the NW edge of Broadfield Down. The level interior of the site is now used as a garden and the embanked hollow-way approach from the NW is partly blocked and mutilated. The defences end against a steep slope on the S and consist for the most part of a scarp or bank up to 2 m high with a shallow exterior ditch. Traces of stone wall in places on top of the bank. The whole site is subject to piecemeal damage from gardening and domestic activities. (Visited 16 & 24.2.73).

Surface finds None.

Excavations None.

References
1925 Thorburn, 1925, 279-80.

54 BURRINGTON CAMP, Burrington. ST 478 588

Group II

0.8 ha.

Scheduled.

Siting
On gentle N-sloping side of Carboniferous Limestone plateau, with higher ridge to S and precipitous drop to the W. Land falls away steeply c. 50 m N of the site, which lies at c. 170 m O.D.

Plate 12   Burrington Camp (no. 54) from the west
(UCCAP neg. no. HQ81)

Air Photographs

HQ 81 (UCCAP) the site from the W (Plate 12).

NMR ST4758/1 (West Air Photography) the site from the NW. Good highlights (5.11.73).

Photograph by J. Hancock in Rahtz and Fowler, 1972, pl. xv.

Description

Site lies in bracken-covered rough pasture, and the interior shows no features, sloping gradually down to the N. The defences are not strong and the site is overlooked from the S. The hillfort consists of a roughly rectangular enclosure defined by a bank with an outer ditch and an inner quarry dicth which is almost continuous and regularly cut. On the SW this quarry ditch diverges from the bank and outer ditch to run N forming the W side of the main enclosure, while the bank runs W for a further 50 m to end at the edge of the combe. A similar arrangement may have been present at the NW corner but has been disturbed. On the NE the outer ditch continues N beyond the NE angle where the N defences run up to it, in a similar manner to the arrangements at the NW and SW. This area has been damaged by quarrying and it is possible that there was an entrance here. There is a spring by this gap just outside the defences. (Visited 13.2.73).

Surface finds   None.

Excavations

1948   Rampart section on E side. No finds apart from Old Red Sandstone pot lid.

1960   Cleaning down of 1948 section; 15 trial pits 4 ft (1.2 m) square dug in interior. No finds or structures.

Name

A back-formation, the village of Burrington being byrig-tun; the byrig element probably referring to the hillfort (Ekwall 1960).

References

1908   Allcroft, 1908, 207; 582-4. Because of the inner ditch considers site to be a religious one.

1911   VCH II, 483-4.

1924   Burrow, 1924, 68.

1958   Grinsell, 1958, 165.

1963   Tratman, 1963b. Description, plan and excavation report on work done in 1948 and 1960.

55 ROOK'S CASTLE, Goathurst.   ST 253 323

Group I

0.8 ha?

Not scheduled

Siting

SW-facing spur on S side of E-W ridge at c. 170 m O.D., steep slopes on W and S, with level access from the N.

Description
The N and W sides of a probable univallate rectangular enclosure. The other sides have been confused by medieval stone tile quarrying and it is possible that the bank and external ditch remaining is in some way associated with the latter activity. On balance, however, it appears likely that there was an enclosure here.

Surface finds None.

Excavations None.

Name
Probably a corruption of Roc (personal name recorded in 14th century) or rock.

References
1964 Ordnance Survey Archaeological Record Card ST23SE4.
1970 Grinsell, 1970, 91.

56 RODDENBURY, Selwood. ST 798 439

Group I

0.7 ha.

Scheduled

Siting
Near summit of E-W Greensand ridge at c. 170 m O.D. Moderate slopes on all sides. Site no. 63 lies 300 m to the N.

Air Photographs. None. Site in woodland.

Description
A univallate enclosure set just to the W of the highest point of a wooded ridge. The interior is much overgrown and has been damaged by surface quarrying, though some hut platforms may be present. The defences on the W side, where approach to the site is easiest, have been almost obliterated. On the E and N the defences are in good condition, the bank rising c. 5 m from the bottom of the ditch on the E. (Visited 19.2.73).

Surface finds None.

Excavations None.

Name
First element Reddene 1086, either ra denu or raeg-denu 'roe deer valley' plus Burh (Ekwall, 1960).

References
1911 VCH II, 510-11.
1924 Burrow, 1924, 110.
1958 Grinsell, 1958, 165.

57 <u>ELBOROUGH</u>, Hutton. ST 369 583

Group III

0.7 ha.

Not scheduled

<u>Siting</u>
Carboniferous limestone knoll at the E end of E-W ridge. Site at <u>c</u>. 100 m O.D. Ground falls away on N giving extensive views over the North Somerset Levels. Higher ground to S.

<u>Description</u>
        The earthworks of this site are now extremely slight and seem to have been damaged and ploughed since first recorded by Tratman in 1935. On the N and S sides of the ridge the domed interior, at present under pasture, is defended by steep rocky slopes. On the E side the defences now comprise a slight scarp which could be mistaken for an ancient field boundary, though Tratman describes it as a bank 2 ft (0.6 m) high and 25 ft (7.6 m) wide with an internal ditch. On the W side the bivallate defences described by Tratman can now only be traced with difficulty. (Visited 10.6.74).

<u>Surface Finds</u> None.

<u>Excavations</u> None.

<u>Name</u>
Present settlement 1 km to the N. Probably a personal name plus <u>bearu</u> wood (Ekwall, 1960).

<u>References</u>
1935 Tratman, 1935.

58 <u>WALTON 'BANJO' ENCLOSURE</u>, Walton. ST 428 738

Group IV

0.6 ha.

Scheduled

<u>Siting</u>
On flat-topped Carboniferous Limestone ridge at <u>c</u>. 80 m O.D. Ridge runs SW-NE with steep drops to SE and NW.

<u>Air Photographs</u> See Phillips, 1931a.

<u>Description</u>
        A typical 'Banjo' enclosure, some examples of which have been dated to the late Iron Age (Perry, 1966). It consists of a univallate circular enclo-sure with a flat featureless interior, now much overgrown with thorn scrub. An entrance gap on the NE side leads into an embanked straight passage about 110 m long, at the end of which further banks run off at right angles to NW and SE. A second gap, on the SW of the main enclosure, appears to be a later breach. There are traces of field systems in the surrounding area. (Visited 11.2.73).

Surface finds None.

Excavations None.

References
1931 Phillips, 1931a. Description and plan.

59 TRENDLE RING, Bicknoller. ST 118 393

Group IV

0.6 ha.

Scheduled

Siting
On W-facing scarp slope of the Quantocks (Devonian Sandstone) on slight spur at c. 170 m O.D., about 60 m above the valley floor to the W and 140 m below the summit plateau.

Air Photographs
ARJ 4 (UCCAP). The site from the SW (Plate 4).

Description
      The best preserved and most classically   located of the hillslope enclosures of Somerset. It lies in rough pasture and the interior slopes steeply down to the W; there being no visible features. The defences are univallate, and most massive on the E, uphill, side where there is a simple entrance gap. Here the bank rises about 2 m from a wide U-shaped ditch On the W side of the enclosure the bank is much slighter, and even when the effects of hillwash piling up against the rear of the bank are taken into account it is clear that the greatest attention was paid to defending the E side. (Visited 4.4.73).

Surface finds None.

Excavations None.

Name Trendle = circle (Ekwall, 1960).

References
1908 Allcroft, 1908, 205, 631 n. Notes a dragon legend associated with
      the site (cf. 13).
1911 VCH II, 506.
1924 Burrow, 1924, 102.
1968 Haldane, 1968a.

60 BREAN DOWN, Brean. ST 298 588

Group III

0.5 ha.

Scheduled

Siting
E end of isolated Carboniferous Limestone promontory at about 50 m O.D. Level approach from W with steep, in places precipitous, drops on the S and fairly steep slopes on the N. To the E the ridge narrows into a series of crags ending in a sea cliff.

Plate 13   Brean Down Hillfort (no. 60) from the south-east
(West Air Photography neg. no. BB1343 2)

Air Photographs
BB 1343 2 (West Air Photography).   View from the SE (Plate 13).

Description
      The interior of the site has been much disturbed and terraced by military activity in the last 100 years, and is now under grass. The defences form an L-shape with the foot of the L running along the top of the steep slopes on the S, and the stem, fronted on the W by a ditch, runs N-S across the ridge. There are no clear indications of defences on the N side, though these may have been destroyed. The simple gap in the centre of the W side may be an original entrance, but is now occupied by a military road and is not mentioned in earlier accounts. (Excavated and Surveyed April, 1974).

Surface finds Roman coins, see Appendix B.

Excavations
April, 1974 by writer.
A section through the defences at the SW corner showed the defences to consist of rubble banks faced at front and rear with massive stone walls. The southern bank was structurally later than the western. Radio-carbon dates from beneath the W bank and in the lower part of the ditch indicated a date in the Iron Age. Roman material also found.

References
1836 Phelps I, 1836, 109, 136.
1864 PSANHS 12(1) (1864), 65-6 (F. Warre).
1902 Knight, 1902, 298.
1911 VCH II, 1911, 473-4.
1958 ApSimon, 1958, 109. Coin finds.
1976 Burrow, 1976a. Excavation report and description.

61 CONYGAR HILL, Portbury. ST 499 751

Group I

0.4 ha.

Scheduled.

Siting
Small flat-topped knoll of Dolomitic Conglomerate rising to about 35 m O.D. Levels to the N.   Higher ground to S.   Streams at base of hill on W and E.

Air Photographs None known. Site partly tree-covered.

Description
      The interior, under grass and trees, contains a low circular mound, considered by the VCH to be a barrow, but in view of the hillfort's name (see below) may be a pillow mound. The defences consist of a low stony bank visible around the whole circuit but best preserved on the SW, where it stands up to 75 cm high from the interior. The entrance, at the W angle, is approached from the NW by a terrace-way and there are probable strip lynchets on the SW and NW. On the S side of the entrance gap the earthwork is clubbed and inturned, though the arrangements have been confused by the construction of a small reservoir here, and the inclusion into the rampart of mortared rubble. (Visited 11.2.73).

Surface finds None.

Excavations None.

Name
Conygar = enclosure for rabbits. Perhaps the hillfort was originally called Portbury (see chapter 5).

References
1829 Rutter, 1829, 255-56.
1881 PSANHS 27 (1) (1881), 71 (H. M. Scarth).
1911 VCH II, 479-80.
1923 Major and Burrow, 1923, 14-20. Attempt to show that Wansdyke ran up to this hillfort, which formed its western end.
1924 Burrow, 1924, 64.

62 KINGS WESTON, King's Weston. ST 555 780

Group III

0.4 ha.

Scheduled

Siting
E end of SW-NE Carboniferous Limestone ridge at c. 90 m O.D. Steep drops on NW, E and SE, level approach from the SW.

Description
A rectangular enclosure, under grass with wooded slopes on N and S. The defences consist of a bank and exterior ditch on the W and S, with no apparent defences on N and E where the slopes are steepest. There are gaps at the NW and SW corners. To the W are two earthworks, a circular bank and exterior ditch about 55 m in diameter and beyond it, about 240 m from the main enclosure, a bank and western ditch running N-S across the ridge and possibly running back eastwards along the contours along the top of the steeper slopes for a short distance. There is a large gap in the centre of this bank. (Visited 8.2.73).

Surface finds None.

Excavations
1956 Ditch section on the W side and seven small test holes in the interior. Two of the cuttings behind the south rampart produced Iron Age occupation material. The ditch section produced Roman material in the rubble collapse from the rampart, lying above Iron Age deposits, cf. Brean Down (60).

References
1821 Seyer, 1821, 72-3.
1924 Tratman, 1924.
1946 Tratman, 1946.
1957 Rahtz, 1957.
1972 Goodman, 1972. Salvage of possible sub-Roman cemetery outside the enclosure, and observations.

63 <u>HALES CASTLE</u>, Frome. ST 797 442

Group IV

0.4 ha.

Scheduled

<u>Siting</u>
N-facing slope on side of E-W combe on Greensand, with Oxford Clay nearby
—very water retentive soil. About 135 m O.D.

<u>Description</u>
      A circular univallate enclosure under pasture. The bank rises about
2.5 m above the present bottom of the exterior ditch. A slight counterscarp
is present in places. There is no obvious entrance, though a disturbed area
on the N side, where the approach is steepest, may be such. A causeway
across the ditch on the SE side does not have a corresponding gap in the bank.
The interior slopes down to the NW. A hollow, possibly a well, is present
on the W side of the interior. Former field boundaries are present in the
surrounding fields. (Visited 19.2.73).

<u>Surface find s</u> None.

<u>Excavations</u> None.

<u>Name</u>
Perhaps from <u>Halh</u>, corner or valley in a hillside (Ekwall, 1960).

<u>References</u>
1911 <u>VCH</u> II, 508.
1966 King & Alcock, 1966, 121. Suggest that the site is a ringwork castle
      of C11-C13 and mention traces of a bailey which were not confirmed in
      field investigation.

64 <u>KING'S CASTLE</u>, St. Cuthbert Out. ST 569 456

Group IV

0.4 ha.

Scheduled

<u>Siting</u>
West end of E-W Carboniferous Limestone ridge with steep slopes on N
and moderate slopes on S and W. Fairly level approach from the E dropping
to slight saddle. Site at <u>c</u>. 105 m O.D.

<u>Description</u>
      An unusual site consisting of a line of at least three conjoined stone-
walled enclosures along the ridge. The interior is overgrown, heavily wooded
and quarried. The western enclosure is defined by a stone bank without a
ditch and about 1 m high on the N and W. On the S the bank continues E to
form the S side of the middle and E enclosures, but a decrease in scale and
slight change of direction suggests that these enclosures are secondary.
This bank returns N and W towards the NE side of the W enclosure leaving
a gap about 3 m wide up to which an exterior terraced way runs from the W.

The defences on the E side of the middle enclosure consist of double banks and ditches, with the ditches on the E. The E enclosure is similar and the largest of the three, its E side—a bank with ditch on the W (i.e. internal) side running along the top of the slope down to the saddle on the E. There are traces of another bank running E from the centre of this bank. The whole complex is regarded by the Ordnance Survey (ST54NE 7) as part of a field system but the scale of the enclosing features and their disposition suggest a settlement site, perhaps of two phases. (Visited 15.2.73).

Surface finds   None.

Excavations   None.

References
1911 VCH II, 146.
1924 Burrow, 1924, 146.

65 MOAT HOUSE FARM, Wraxall. ST 487 732

Group IV

0.3 ha.

Not scheduled

Siting
Level Carboniferous Limestone plateau of the Failand Ridge.   Site at c. 140 m O.D.

Description
        A circular embanked enclosure, the S part of which has been destroyed by agriculture and the N part is now badly eroded. The interior is level and the bank, with a probable entrance gap on the NW, is about 40 cm high. The enclosure forms part of a complex of slight earthworks, probably a field system. (Visited 11.2.73).

Surface finds   None.

Excavations
1929 Trench across N interior and earthwork showed that the bank was a rubble spread about 40 cm deep with an exterior ditch 1 m deep and a shallow (? earlier) ditch at the rear of the bank. The exterior ditch produced Roman pottery in the upper 30 cm of the fill and Iron Age material below. The interior space produced finds but no structural evidence.

References
1929 Antiquity 3 (1929) 352. Note on excavations.
1931 Phillips, 1931b. Excavation summary.

66 CLEEVE HILL CAMP, Cleeve. ST 463 658

Group IV

0.3 ha.

Not scheduled

Siting
Gentle S-facing slope above combe. Carboniferous Limestone at $\underline{c}$. 70 m O.D.

Description
A univallate hillslope enclosure. The bank, with slight indication of ditch and entrance on the W is about 0.75 m high and much spread. In the surrounding area are a number of linear banks and slight ditches, possibly a field system. The site is under woodland, but is not heavily overgrown. (Visited 24.2.73).

Surface finds None.

Excavations None.

References
1829 Rutter, 1829, 68. 'A Danish Camp'.
1925 Thorburn, 1925, 280-81.

67 BLACKDOWN CAMP, Rowberrow. ST 465 568

Group IV

0.3 ha.

Scheduled.

Siting
SW facing slope of Dolomitic Conglomerate forming NE side of steep-sided combe. Site at $\underline{c}$. 235 m O.D. in woodland.

Description
A hill-slope enclosure with a featureless interior crossed by a more recent track. The defences have been mutilated by forestry operations, but consist of a bank rising up to 1.5 m from the bottom of the ditch and 30 cm from the interior. It is possible that the present track utilizes an original entrance on the W. (Visited 13.2.73).

Surface finds None.

Excavations None.

References
1911 VCH II, 512.
1927 Tratman, 1927a.
1949 Donovan, 1949, 87.

68 BREWER'S CASTLE, Dulverton. SS 883 297

Group I

0.3 ha.

Scheduled

Siting
Sandstone promontory above loop of river Barle and its tributary, the Danes' Brook, with approach difficult from the W along the ridge at $\underline{c}$. 180 m O.D., and steep drops on the N, E and S. Mounsey Castle (47) across river to SE.

<u>Air Photographs</u> None. Site under woodland.

<u>Description</u>
      A site which is very strongly fortified both by artificial defences and by natural features, despite its small size. The main defence is on the W side where there is a bank rising 2 m from an external ditch. The entrance gap in this side is slightly angled to the S. Around the other sides the defences are slighter, a low rubble bank and scarp being traceable around the circuit except on the NE where there is a gap 4 m wide to the south of which is a large recumbent stone, possibly a gate-post. The interior is marked by a series of natural crags and terraces sloping down from N to S. (Visited 1.4.73).

<u>Surface finds</u> None.

<u>Excavations</u> None.

<u>Name</u> Of unknown significance.

<u>References</u>
1911 <u>VCH</u> II, 477.
1924 Burrow, 1924, 58.

69 <u>BLACK BALL</u> or <u>BRITISH CAMP</u>, Dunster. SS 984 426

Group IV

0.3 ha.

Scheduled

<u>Siting</u>
Gentle W-facing slope at <u>c</u>. 160 m O.D. on sandstone moorland with steeper drop to W plateau on which Bat's Castle (50) lies 600 m SE, just to E of site.

<u>Air Photographs</u>
NMR no. SS 9842/2 (West Air Photography) showing ancient ploughing in the interior of the site, 29.5.74.

<u>Description</u>
      A univallate hill-slope enclosure just visible from the ramparts of Bat's Castle. The ditch is generally about 2 m deep and the bank 3m high. There is a counterscarp bank on the NW side. The entrance is on the SW side, opening towards the steepest approach. The area around the entrance gap is disturbed. (Visited 4.4.73).

<u>Surface finds</u> None.

<u>Excavations</u> None.

<u>References</u>
1890 Page, 1890, 202.
1911 <u>VCH</u> II, 508. Notes a 'circular breastwork or tower about 15 ft in diameter' behind the bank on the N side of the entrance. This is not now discernible.
1924 Burrow, 1924, 106.
1964 Forde-Johnston, 1964, 86. Regards the site as an outpost of Bat's Castle.

70 SWEETWORTHY, Luccombe, SS 890 425

Group IV

0.25 ha.

Scheduled

Siting
N-facing slope at c. 310 m O.D. Steep combe on the E and fairly steep fall
to the East Water valley on N. Immediately below a hedge bank marking
the upper limit of C19 enclosure in this area. Moorland to S, site in pasture.

Description
        A hill-slope enclosure with ditch and internal bank. The ditch is
widest and deepest on the E side, probably due to its present use as a N-S
track at this point. On the N it is very slight and on the S has been re-cut
for drainage purposes. The bank is well-preserved on the SW and E sides
and there is a marked quarry-scoop in the interior. A gap on the SE may
be original, but seems to be partly recent. (Visited 30.3.73).

Surface finds None.

Excavations None.

References
1911 VCH II, 521. Interpreted as a medieval moated site.

71 WORTHEAL I, Wambrook. ST 274 085

Group IV

0.25 ha.

Scheduled

Siting
Greensand with water retentive soil. Site on gentle W-facing slope at c.
200 m O.D. falling to stream 0.5 km to W, and land rising to plateau at c.
250 m to E.

Description
        An oval univallate enclosure under pasture close to a farm and incor-
porated into modern field boundaries. The defences consist of a rubble bank
3 m wide and 1 m high with an external ditch 6 m wide and 0.5 m deep on the
E side. The W half has been levelled by cultivation but still shows as a scarp
in the field. There are traces of a field system to the W. (Visited 5.4.75).

Surface finds None.

Excavations None.

References
1977 Carter, R. Parish Surveys in Somerset: 1. Wambrook (Taunton 1977),
        13 & Plate 2a.

72 ROAD CASTLE, Winsford. SS 862 375

Group IV

72 <u>ROAD CASTLE</u>, Winsford. SS 862 375

Group IV

0.2 ha.

Scheduled

<u>Siting</u>
Slight knoll at <u>c</u>. 235 m O.D. set in loop of River Exe which runs around
NW, N E and SE sides with steep drops on these sides. A saddle separates
the knoll from higher ground to the south. Slate.

<u>Description</u>
        A strongly fortified site set at lip of N-facing slope and under improved
pasture. The bank and dtich defences dnclose a roughly rectangular featureless and flat area. The bank is 4.5 m high on the S, where it is best preserved. On the N side ploughing has masked the ram art, the ditch is slight
and two breaches have been made in the defences. On the E most of the defences have been destroyed by a hedge bank which runs NS across the N part
of the site but then turns SE, leaving a gap between the field and the surviving
defences on the S and it is probable that this is the original entrance.
(Visited 30.3.73).

<u>Surface finds</u> None.

<u>Excavations</u> None.

<u>Name</u> Rode 1086, O E <u>rod</u> 'clearing' (Ekwall, 1960).

<u>References</u>
1908 Allcroft, 1908, 383 n.
1911 <u>VCH</u> II, 504.
1924 Burrow, 1924, 96.

73 <u>SHIPHAM</u>, Shipham. ST 457 568

Group IV

0.2 ha.

Scheduled

<u>Siting</u>
At <u>c</u>. 200 m O.D. On S-facing slope on N side of Longbottom Valley, which
runs E-W. Carboniferous Limestone.

<u>Description</u>
        Site on improved pasture and much degraded by cultivation. The ground
slopes down to the S across the interior, which shows no features. It forms
a roughly rhomboidal enclosure now delineated by a slight scarp on the S and
traces of a ditch on the other sides. There is no sign of an entrance.
(Visited 13.2.73).

<u>Surface finds</u> None.

<u>Excavations</u> None.

References
1911 VCH II, 412-13.
1927 Tratman, 1927a.
1949 Donovan, 1949, 78.

74   EAST MYNE or FURZEBURY BRAKE, Minehead Without.   SS 936 483

Group IV

0.2 ha.

Scheduled

Siting
E end of spur of Devonian Sandstone at c. 230 m O.D. with very steep
descent on S and E to stream and coastal slope on the N.   Level approach
from W.

Description
      A badly eroded site on improved pasture.   The interor is level and
featureless.   The defences form an oval with its long axis N-S.   They consist of a degraded bank, no more than a scarp in many places, and an outer
ditch.   No indication of entrance.   (Visited 5.4.73).

Surface finds   None.

Excavations   None.

References
1911 VCH II, 496.
1924 Burrow, 1924, 86.

75   BURY CASTLE, Selworthy.   SS 917 471

Group IV

0.2 ha.

Scheduled

Siting
E end of NW-SE spur of Devonian Sandstone at c. 230 m O.D. with steep
drops on N, E and S.   Level approach from the NW.

Air Photographs
NMR no. SS9147/1 (West Air Photography). 29.5.74.

Description
      A wide-spaced rampart enclosure, with an inner univallate enclosure
set on slightly sloping ground falling to the E.   30 m W of this enclosure is
a cross bank running across the spur.   A second bank crosses the ridge
150 m further NW.   This appears to be a later field boundary, although
Allcroft regarded it as part of the defensive scheme.   The main crossbank,
which is an open V-shape in plan with a gap at the apex, stands up to 4 m
high, with a ditch on the W side.   The outer side of the ditch is revetted in
dry-stone masonry.   Between this and the main enclosure the ground falls
slightly and the cross bank is clearly sited for a better view to the NW than

can be obtained from the inner enclosure. The earthworks of the latter are smaller in scale with an entrance on the SW. It is possible that the northern end of the cross bank runs ESE along the top of the N slope to join up with the inner enclosure making the whole complex a 'dependent enclosure' hillfort (Fox, 1961). (Visited 5.4.73).

Surface finds None.

Excavations None.

Name Presumably from OE burh.

References
1836 Phelps I, 1836, 117.
1908 Allcroft, 1908, 112-13.
1911 VCH II, 499-500.
1924 Burrow, 1924, 72.
1967 Whybrow, 1967.

76 KINGSDOWN, Mells. ST 718 517

Group IV

0.15 ha.

Scheduled

Siting
SW side of Oolite plateau with steep slopes to W and SW and level approach from E and N. Site at c. 185 m O.D.

Description
        A small univallate enclosure with further earthworks around. The whole area under pasture. The main enclosure is a rough quadrilateral with an entrance on the NE. The bank is up to 0.75 m high with an external ditch surviving on the W and N about 0.25 m deep. From the NE entrance a low causeway runs NE as far as a sinuous bank which runs from N-S across the ridge E of the enclosure. This bank is about 0.3 m high and 3 m wide. From the NW side of the enclosure a low bank 0.2 m high runs NW to the road and thenturns 90° to run SW. Other slight earthworks are present in the area. (Visited 19.2.73).

Surface finds None.

Excavations
1927-9 excavation of the larger part of the interior and defences and three through the outer banks. The main enclosure was shown to be of two phases, with the earlier ditch overlain by the stone wall of the later. The first phase was Iron Age and early Roman and the second 2nd century and later. Finds included a hoard of currency bars (see Appendix B).

References
1791 Collinson II, 1791, 462.
1911 VCH II, 524-27.
1929 Antiquity 3 (1929), 352.
1930 Gray, 1930. Excavation report.
1958 Grinsell, 1958, 164, 171, 322.

77 BERRY CAMP, Porlock & Stoke Pero.   SS 859 449

Group IV

0.15 ha.

Scheduled

Siting
Steep spur between two combes.   Site on sandstone and at c. 349 m O.D.
Spur running SW-NE, rising to plateau at c. 425 m O.D. to the SW.

Description
        NW, SW and part of the SE sides of a rectangular enclosure, perhaps
unifinished, with an outer crossbank 115 m up the ridge to the SW.   The
earthworks are quite massive and the Ordnance Survey's interpretation of
the site as a medieval hunting lodge enclosure seems improbable.   On the
SW side the rampart is c. 2.5 m high and fronted by a ditch 7.5 m wide.
No sign of an entrance, although its position may have been obscured by the
massive field wall, forming the parish boundary, which bisects the site from
SW and NE.   The lack of defences on the E may be explained by the steep
slope on that side.   (Visited 5.4.73).

Surface finds
Savage (1830) notes 'swords and other instruments of war' from the vicinity
of the site.

Excavations   None.

References
1830 Savage, 1830, 92.
1908 Allcroft, 1908, 207.
1911 VCH II, 478-9.
1924 Burrow, 1924, 62.
1928 PSANHS 74 (1928), 73.
1967 Whybrow, 1967, 9-11.

78 STADDON HILL, Winsford.   SS 887 376

Group IV

0.1 ha.

Scheduled

Siting
Devonian Slate.   N-facing slope at N end of spur between Larcombe Brook
on NE and tributary on NW.   Site at c. 320 m O.D. with steep drops on NW
and NE and land rising to S.

Air Photographs
UCCAP reproduced in Grinsell, 1970, 72.

Description
        A hillslope enclosure with one or possibly two outer cross banks at
distances of 20 m and 130 m south of it.   The main enclosure and first bank
are under bracken, but the surrounding area is under commercial forestry

and the outer bank could not be located. The Ordnance Survey (SS83NE 4) believe it to be a field boundary unrelated to the site. The main cross bank is about 2 m high from the ditch on the S side without any sign of an entrance gap, and ends where the slope becomes steeper on NW, but ending on level ground on the E. A low bank running SW-NE connects the inner enclosure ditch with this cross-bank and seems to pre-date the latter, as it continues beyond it to the SW for about 30 m. The inner enclosure, with a sloping interior, has an entrance on the SW with a slight inturn on the NW side and a low bank connecting the angle of the inturn with the rear of the inner bank. The site is a Fox (1961) type 'd' crossbank enclosure. (Visited 30.3.73).

Surface finds None.

Excavations None.

References
1908 Allcroft, 1908, 206 n.
1911 VCH II, 504.
1924 Burrow, 1924, 98.
1961 Fox, 1961, 58.
1967 Whybrow, 1967.

79 WRAXALL CAMP, Wraxall. ST 494 680

Group IV

0.1 ha.

Scheduled

Siting
Plateau at c. 140 m, with land falling away gradually to N. Failand Ridge. Carboniferous Limestone.

Description
        A small circular earthwork set on a gentle N-facing slope in a copse. Improved pasture around with traces of early field systems in vicinity. The enclosed area is about 45 m in diameter and is raised c. 1 m above the surrounding land. The bank around the site is about 1.2 m high, though lower on the N where there may have been an entrance. There is no visible ditch. (Visited 11.2.73).

Surface finds None.

Excavations
1933 6 ft. (1.8 m) square excavation across the defences, which were shown to consist of a utilized natural outcrop with additional material piled above. Finds included Kimmeridge shale and sherds of Glastonbury-type Iron Age pottery.

References
1911 VCH II, 513.
1933 Phillips, 1933. Excavation report.

80 <u>BACKWELL CAMP</u>, Backwell. ST 484 680

Group II

0.1 ha.

Not Scheduled. Destroyed.

<u>Siting</u>
NE side of NW-SE combe on Carboniferous Limestone. Site lay on summit
of very steep drop to valley bottom at <u>c</u>. 110 m O.D.

<u>Description</u>
This site has been destroyed by quarrying. It was described in 1935
as a triangular area, its south side formed by the cliff and artificial defences
running E and NE from the cliff edge. The east-running bank was 7 ft.
(2.1 m) high and ran 60 yd (55 m) to the apex from which the second bank
ran to the cliff top. The banks were 30 ft. (9 m) wide and showed evidence
of drystone wall construction. (Area investigated 24.2.73 and 13.4.75).

<u>Surface finds</u> None.

<u>Excavations</u> None.

<u>References</u>
1935 Tratman, 1935, 252.

81 <u>DINIES CAMP</u>, Downhead. ST 676 458

Group IV

0.1 ha.

Scheduled

<u>Siting</u>
NE-facing slope on Carboniferous Limestone at head of shallow SW-NE
valley. At <u>c</u>. 240 m O.D.

<u>Description</u>
A hillslope enclosure in pasture with woodland to S. The site is a
univallate oval with a ditch 2 m deep and a slight inner bank. The position
of the entrance is unclear, but probably on the E. (Visited 19.2.73).

<u>Surface finds</u> None.

<u>Excavations</u>
1961 A section across the NE bank and ditch showed that the extant features
had succeeded a small circular enclosure, the ditch of which was overlain
by the later bank. No dating evidence was obtained, but charcoal from both
ditches should be susceptible to radio-carbon determinations.

<u>Name</u> Origin unknown.

<u>References</u>
1967 <u>Archaeological Review</u> 2 (1967), 12.

82   BROOMFIELD CAMP, Broomfield.   ST 216 320

Group IV

0.6 ha.

Not scheduled

Siting
South-facing sandstone slope near head of SW combe.   Ridgeway running
NW-SE immediately to the NE.   240 m O.D.

Description
        A sub-rectangular univallate enclosure with a possible outwork 100 m
up slope to the NE.   Ploughed, but still in fair condition especially on the W.
(Visited 15.3.79).

Surface finds   None.

Excavations
1968   Trench 50 ft (15.2 m) long cut through the bank and ditch produced
Iron Age pottery.

References
1968 SDN&Q 28 (1968), 187-9.
1970 Grinsell, 1970, 91.

83   WORTHEAL II, Wambrook.   ST 274 086

Group IV

0.1 ha. ?

Not scheduled

Siting
Gentle W-facing Greensand slope at c. 200 m O.D. falling to stream 0.5 km
to W.   Land rising to plateau at c. 250 m to E.

Description
        Possible hillslope enclosure identified in 1974.   It is very badly dis-
turbed and not certainly an artificial feature.   (Visited 5.4.75).

Surface finds   None.

Excavations   None.

References
1977 Carter, R. 1977 Parish Surveys in Somerset: 1 Wambrook (Taunton
        1977) 13 and Plate 2a.

84   BERWICK CAMP, Bath.   c. ST 740 627

Group I?

Unknown size

Not scheduled.   Destroyed.

Oolite plateau at <u>c</u>. 160 m with ground falling to Avon valley to N.

Description
        A possible multivallate(?) contour fort set on the plateau of Odd Down south of Bath. The area is now occupied by a factory and playing fields and there are no certain traces of earthworks of hillfort type. (Visited 16.4.73).

Surface finds None.

Excavations None.

References
1836 Phelps I, 1836, 102 (plan), 103-104. Brief description.

85 DINGHURST CAMP, Churchill. ST 442 591

Group III

Unknown size

Not scheduled

Siting
N-facing promontory flanked by cliffs of Churchill Gap on the E and combe on the W. Level approach from S. Carboniferous Limestone at <u>c</u>. 110 m O.D.

Description
        A promontory fort almost totally destroyed by quarrying and the area now much overgrown with gorse and difficult to distinguish. A short length of E-W bank on the E side of the promontory is possibly the only remaining part of the defences. (Visited 13.2.73).

Surface finds None.

Excavations None.

References
1836 Phelps I, 1836, 100.
1927 Tratman, 1927b, 25.
1964 Fordge-Johnston, 1964, 89 suggests that the site is a 'satellite' of Dolebury (6).

86 ROWBERROW CAMP, Rowberrow. ST 456 584

Group III

Uncertain size

Scheduled

Siting
Gentle N-facing spur on N slope of Blackdown (Dolomitic Conglomerate). Site at <u>c</u>. 130 m O.D.

Description
        This site was not located on field investigation and appears to have been destroyed by forestry operations. It is described by Tratman (1927b) as a

bivallage promontory fort, the inner bank 24 ft (7.3 m) wide and a maximum of 9 ft (2.7 m) high fronted by a ditch 3 ft deep and 10 ft (3 m) wide. 100 m S a damaged second bank standing 7 ft (2.1 m) from the bottom of its ditch and 18 ft (5.5 m) wide. (Visited 13.2.73).

Surface finds None.

Excavations None.

References
1927 Tratman, 1927b, 30.
1949 Donovan, 1949, 79.

87 CROYDON HILL, Dunster. SS 981 403

Group IV

0.1 ha.

Not scheduled

Siting
SE-facing slope on side of valley running NNE. Sandstone at c. 300 m O.D.

Description
    Univallate hillslope enclosure with entrance on the S side. The interior slopes down to the SE and the earthworks have been damaged by forestry (Visited 4.4.73).

Surface finds None.

Excavations None.

References
1830 Savage, 1830. Map opp. p. 1.
1890 Page, 1890, 203.
1970 Grinsell, 1970, 87.

88 CURDON CAMP, Stogumber. SS 981 403

Group IV

0.1 ha.

Scheduled but largely destroyed.

Siting
E-facing slope at c.75 m O.D. above Doniford Stream. Low lying and on Trias Marl.

Description
    The site has been largely destroyed. Described by the VCH as a rectangular univallate enclosure, the defences surviving only on the W and W sides, and consisting of a bank about 2.5 m high with an outer ditch. (Visited 6.4.73).

Surface finds None.

Excavations None.

Name
Page, 1890, 260 suggests W. Caer Dun.

References
1890 Page, 1890, 260.
1911 VCH II, 479-80.
1924 Burrow, 1924, 64.

89 RODHUISH COMMON, Withycombe.   SS 995 392

Group IV

Unknown size

Not scheduled

Siting
NE-facing slope on sandstone at c. 340 m O.D.

Air Photographs;
Identified from RAF CPE/UK/1980 3289 by Grinsell (1970).

Description
    A small univallate hillslope site on a featureless bracken-covered hillside.   A search of the area failed to locate it.   (VIsited 20.4.74).

Surface finds None.

Excavations None.

References
1970 Grinsell, 1970, 88.

APPENDIX B

ROMAN AND POST-ROMAN MATERIAL FROM
SOMERSET HILLFORTS AND ENCLOSURES

The detail with which this material is presented is related to the
extent to which it has been published elsewhere, and to its value in the context of this study. It is thus not a definitive account of Roman and post-
Roman finds. The latter in particular does not include the major groups
of post Roman material from Cadcong and South Cadbury, neither of which
is yet fully evaluated. A distinction has been made between casual finds
and material recovered under broadly controlled archaeological conditions.

1 HAM HILL

a) Excavation

   1. Building - Villa at ST 4878 1652 c. 1906 (Fig. 33)

      A 12-room building measuring 49 x 13 m (160 x 40 ft) associated with
a coin series running from Carausius (287-293) to Valentinian II (375-392).
Two decapitated interments with the skulls missing were also found. The
villa is clearly of at least two phases. The southern block is apparently a
corridor villa with the corridor on the east side, an axial group of rooms
(? or yards) and a line of smaller chambers on the west. To the north,
possibly separated by a passage or alley from this range are two large rooms
or structures. This building is, from surface finds, part of a larger complex extending to the south and west (see below). Building material and
pottery can be found over a wide area in this part of the hillfort. See Leech
1977, 119-121 for discussion of this site and its status.

   2. Excavation by H. St. George Gray 1923-1930

      These cuttings were all confined to the Northern Spur. Details of
the excavations are contained in St. George Gray's notebook at Taunton
Museum, but the 'plans' and 'sections' which he refers to on occasion can
no longer be located. The position of most of his cuttings can be pinpointed
with the exception of nos. XVII-XIX which can only be placed behind the rampart towards the eastern end on the north side. No structures of Roman
date were apparently encountered, although the records are extremely scanty
in most cases. The quantities of pre-Roman material, especially pottery in
Taunton Museum, are very great, only a relatively small amount of Roman
material being present. This is in contrast to the 'several hundredweights'
of coarse RB pottery found in quarrying (1920b, 53). Details of the cuttings
and finds follow.

Cutting I, 1923: 'on the lower sloping ground on the north-west of the
northern spur of Ham hill'. In the heavily lynchetted area. No stratigraphic
details of this cutting have been located. Dimensions 16 x 3 m (50 ft x 10 ft)
(Gray, 1924).

Cutting II, 1923

Close to, and same dimensions as, Cutting I. No stratigraphic details (Gray, 1924).

From this cutting come two possible sherds of Thomas' class Bii (Fig. 38). The sherds, which may be from the same vessel, are in a hard grey fabric with white and dark grey/black grits. The exterior surface is buff, speckled with the same grits, and shows the marked regularly-spaced ribbed bands characteristic of Bii. The sherds were thin-sectioned at Southampton but the fabric could not be matched with available sections (Dr. D. P. S. Peacock, pers. comm. 24.4.75). Thomas has recently stressed the great range of fabric of this material (Thomas, 1976, 247) and in the apparent absence of earlier Roman parallels a consensus opinion would see these sherds as probably of post-Roman date (cf. Cadcong, 1970, 34-6 nos. 25-28).

Cutting III, 1923

In the same area as nos. 1 and 20. 30.4 m (100 ft) long. No details or finds (Gray, 1924).

Cutting IV, 1923

Connecting I and II. No details or finds (Gray, 1924).

Cutting V, 1923

On the lip of a lynchet east of I and II. No details or finds (Gray, 1924).

Cutting VI, 1923

South of I and II. 30.4 m x 1 m (100 x 3 ft). No details or finds (Gray, 1924).

Cuttings VII and VIII, 1923

Trenches forming a group with VI. No details or finds (Gray, 1924).

The absence of any stratigraphic details from these cuttings in the published accounts implies that the 1923 layer numbers refer to the excavations in cuttings IX and X.

Cutting IX, 1923 'Ham Turn'

This is described as 'on the south-west side of the northern spur' and is probably at ST 4775 1690. Finds from this cutting are not ascribable to well-defined stratigraphy. A photograph (Gray, 1926, plate XIII) shows a hearth probably sealed by the rampart and 'well below the level at which remains of the Roman period were found'.

The only Roman finds from this cutting are two body sherds in a fine soft orange fabric from 'Extension, layer 4'. This may be inferred to be the old turf line in the rampart referred to in the notes on cutting X.

Cutting X, 1923 'Ham Turn'

Described as 'North of cutting IX' and 'on top of the vallum'. Six layers are recorded, though the impression gained from the notebooks is that these are spits rather than defined stratigraphic units. Dimensions 6.6 x 5.2 m (20 ft x 16 ft).

Layer 1 'Vallum layer 1': 3 sherds of samian. 1 rim orange mortarium. 1 cream-white ring base with smooth pale orange surface. (Iron Age material also.)

Layer 2 'Vallum between 2 and 3 feet from the crest': Pedestal base in pale brown sandy micaceous fabric (Iron Age material including Glastonbury types).

Layer 3 '3¾ to 4' deep': Lattice marked black-burnished cooking pot. Lattice-marked brown vessel.

Layer 4 'Old turf line in Vallum'. This may imply that the material above this layer is the result of recent quarry upcast, though Gray nowhere offers an interpretation of this evidence.
1 sherd of fine cream-white fabric (much Iron Age material).

Layer 5 (No.RB. Huge quantities of I.A. coarse wares. Also Glastonbury and Haematite wares.)

Layer 6 (No RB. Huge quantities of I.A. coarse wares.)

Cutting XI, 1923

400 ft. (131 m) north of the 'Prince of Wales', between the tip from a quarry and the inner vallum, on the E side of the northern spur. Few details of stratification. Most of the finds were from a 'black layer' (Gray 1924, 109-10).

A 'large amount' of RB material, including one piece of first-century samian is recorded in Gray, 1924, but the following only are present at Taunton: 5 sherds fine cream sandy fabric
2 sherds soft fine orange fabric.

Cutting XII, 1923

750 ft (229 m) north of the 'Prince of Wales' and 167 ft (50.9 m) south of the middle of the ancient entrance through the vallum and 120 ft (36.5 m) from the top of the incurved vallum on the S side of the entrance. The dimensions are given as 42 ft (12.8 m) east-west and 16 ft (4.8 m) north-south in the notebook, but 42 ft (12.8 m) and 31 ft (9.5 m) in Gray, 1924, 112-3. The cutting straddled the inner rampart. No details of stratification.

1 sherd samian (burnt)
1 sherd mortarium in fine micaceous ware with a grey core (?
  Oxford ware)
1 sherd black sandy micaceous 'black burnished' ware
1 sherd greenish-grey hard gritty fabric
2 sherds orange sandy wares
(Late I.A. bead-rim bowls also).

Cutting XIII, 1923-6, 1929

'5½ ft (1.7 m) north of cutting X'. 18 ft (5.5 m) north-south and 28 ft (8.5 m) east-west. No RB below 4.3 ft (1.3 m). Clay pipe at below 3 ft (1 m). The stratification here may be the same as that in cutting X:

'From surface to 3 feet' (1926): sandy red fabric with white slip (Glastonbury types).

Layers 1 and 2 (1925):

4 sherds from same vessel as above
1 flanged 'Black Burnished' ware bowl
(Coarse I.A. pottery)

Layer 3 (1925):

17 sherds sandy red fabric with white slip
1 sherd smooth soft orange fabric
5 sherds buff fine fabric
(I.A. material)

(The large number of sherds from one vessel may suggest that these layers are not redeposited.)

Layers 4-8 (1925) (no RB)

'Extension' 1925

Layer 4:

39 sherds sandy red fabric with white slip
14 sherds buff fine fabric
1 grey smooth mortarium sherd
(I.A. material)

'Hearth VIII' 1 sherd buff fine fabric.
The other contexts: 'Extension, top of layer 5 but mostly from bottom of layer 4', 'Deep, but not from actual bottom', 'Bottom of extension' and 'Hearth IV below oven' contain only I.A. material.

Cutting XIV, 1925-6

Across the supposed entrance on the east side of the north spur. Dimensions 20 ft (7 m) north-south by 25 ft (7.6 m) east-west, with a later L-shaped extension across the causeway, which proved to be secondary (Gray, 1925, plan and section of cutting p. 59).

'3' to 4'': 1 mortarium sherd (I.A.)

'5' to with 1' of bottom': (I.A. only)

Bottom 3' of silting 1 Roman rim sherd amongst Durotrigian counter-sunk handled jars.

Cutting XV, 1929 North side of spur

The only context 'Not Vallum' has I.A. material only 65 ft long (19.8 m) and 6 ft (1.8 m) wide.

Cutting XVI, 1929

In the NE corner of the fort, $84\frac{1}{4}$ ft (25.6 m) east of XV. Dimensions 70 ft (21 m) north-south, 4 ft (1.2 m) east-west. Across quarry hollow and a section across the north bank of the 'Equestrian Camp'. No finds.

Cutting XVII, 1929-30

On the N spur, 8 ft (2.4 m) by 4 ft (1.2 m) but unlocated.

Surface finds (I.A.)

'Black earth above the pits'

1 sherd orange fine soft fabric
(large quantities of I.A. material)

Cutting XVIII, 1930 'Trenching'

Unlocated.
'From below stones of fallen wall'
(medieval sherds and clay pipe)
'Front side of wall'
(I.A. only)
'Top of Black Earth'
1 frag of scale armour (lorica squamata)
Several sherds sandy red fabric with white slip
3 sherds in white chalky fabric.

Eight pits (out of an implied total of 24) all have I.A. material.

'Infilling 1925' (probably cutting XIII)

2 sherds sandy red fabric with white slip
2 sherds buff fine fabric

The following general comments may be made:

1. Roman pottery was found in half of the cuttings, and in each part of the northern spur sampled.

2. In relation to the Iron Age material, the quantity of Roman material is small.

3. Where it is possible to assess the stratification it appears that intact sequences do exist as Roman material consistently occurs in the upper parts of the cuttings and the earlier Iron Age material lower down. Opportunities for controlled excavation to assess the Roman and earlier occupations therefore exist even in the apparently heavily disturbed area of the Northern Spur.

3.   Excavations by R. H. Walter, 1907-2

Walter opened at least eleven cuttings on the eastern part of the northern spur, the earlier ones noted in Walter, 1922, the accessions from the work being noted by Gray in 1910-13 and 1918-21 (see Appendix I). The sites can be roughly located from these sources. The finds are in no way stratified and the lists in Gray's accession notes will not be duplicated here. Walter describes finding '6 sites of Roman habitations, probably huts of timber or turf'.

D 10 1912-17 Taunton Accession no. A1860 (Fig. 34)

Body sherd and handle from an amphora in sandy fabric with small white inclusions and surface pitting where the grits have weathered out.

There is also a little mica and some quartz grits of 1-2 mm diameter. Orange-brown surface with redder core. The handle is offset in relation to the ribbing, which averages 5 mm wide. Dr. D. P. S. Peacock (pers. comm. 13.3.77) notes the similarity of this vessel to early Roman 'carrot' amphorae, although it is somewhat larger than these normally are. Similar wares have, however, been located in late levels at Exeter and Lincoln and a fourth or fifth century date might therefore be possible.

b)   Casual finds

A. Northern Spur

Quarrying of this area has produced a very large amount of Roman material of all dates, but predominantly first century. The majority of these are summarized in Gray's papers from 1904 to 1921, including most of the recorded nineteenth century finds. Remains other than small finds are:

(i) Cemetery? ST 4765 1730 found during the cutting of access to the quarry outside the NW corner of the camp in 1866 at least 29 individuals were found. (Ordnance Survey ST41NE 14)

(ii) Cemetery? ST 4781 1728 a female skull found with weapons and a coin hoard (Ordnance Survey ST41NE 15) (Taunton Acc No. A1758)

(iii) Enclosure ST 478 172 A rectangular enclosure (not now traceable) thought by Colt Hoare to be Roman and termed an 'Equestrian Camp'. (Colt Hoare, 1827, 40)

(iv) 'Amphitheatre' ST 4795 1728 also called the 'Frying Pan' this is a sub-circular depression about 30 m (98 ft) in diameter. There is however no direct evidence for its date or function (Ordnance Survey ST41NE 16)

(v) Cemetery ? 'Near cutting D'10' (Walter, 1912). The arm of a young adult female with four late Roman Bronze rings. (Taunton Acc No. A1770)

(vi) The Saxon Shield Boss (Fig. 34)

Apart from a brief mention in Gray, 1910c, this object has never been published or described. Its precise position of discovery is unknown, but is almost certainly from the Northern Spur of the hillfort.

The boss is of Evison's type B (Evison, 1963, 40), not securely dated but probably fifth or sixth rather than seventh century (ibid., 50). It is of iron, 16.6 cm (6.6 in.) in diameter and 6.6 cm (2.8 in.) high, with five rivets spaced around the rim. Macroscopic examination suggests that the concave portion and stud may have been welded onto the wall and flange.

(vii) Ham Stone object, function unknown (Roof finial?)

From O'15 on Northern Spur
A small rectangular piece of Ham stone, roughly square in plan and broken at one end. The other end widens into a plinth-like base. Diverging grooves run up one side of both 'plinth' and 'shaft'. The similarlity to a Roman altar is notable , but its actual date and function are not clear. In view of the amount of Roman material from this area it seems likely to be Roman.

HAM HILL, SOMERSET
Possible Post-Roman Pottery

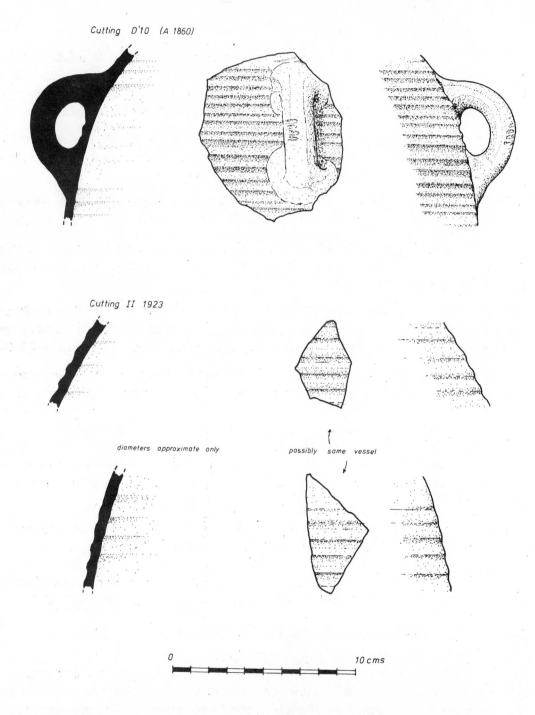

Cutting D'10 (A 1860)

Cutting II 1923

diameters approximate only

possibly same vessel

0   10 cms

Fig. 34 Ham Hill; Possible post-Roman imported wares and Saxon
Shield Boss, all from the Northern Spur

HAM HILL, SOMERSET
Saxon Shield Boss

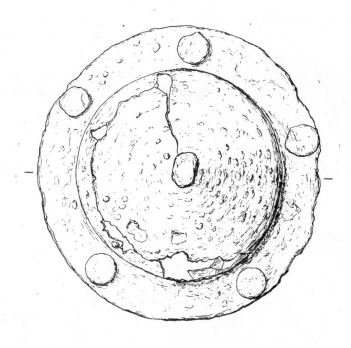

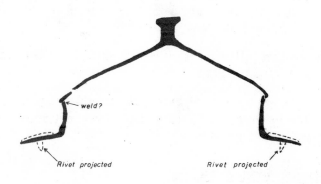

weld?

Rivet projected

Rivet projected

Taunton Museum
A 879

0

10 cms

(viii) A very large amount of Ironwork, especially early Roman spears and other weapons and tinned bronze scale armour.

Coins from the Northern Spur (Seaby, 1950b)

(i) Hoard coins from Domitian (81) to Constantine (306) found with the female skull at ST 4781 1728.

(ii) Coin of Valens (364-378) ST 480 171 on the east rampart of the Northern Spur (Taunton Museum Catalogue).

(iii) Valentinian-type coin ST 477 173 (Taunton Museum Catalogue). The majority of the other coins in Taunton Museum probably come from the Northern Spur, especially those from the Walter collection. The range is from Augustus to Arcadius, with a chronological emphasis on the late third and fourth centuries, as the rough breakdown of the Taunton Catalogue indicates:

AD	
0-50	14
50-100	2
100-150	33
150-200	2
200-250	16
250-300	66
300-350	118
350-400	61

Coins probably from the Northern Spur

(i) Hoard of 30 Roman coins (unspecified types) and the pottery vessel in which they were found (PSANHS 32(1) (1886), 79).

(ii) Three Roman 1st brass coins and fragment of vessel in which they were found (PSANHS 40(2) (1894), 48).

(iii) 300 large brasses Domitian (81-96) to Philip I (244-249). (Numismatic Chronicle 1886, 96).

(iv) An urn full of copper coins 'chiefly of the later Roman emperors'. (PSANHS 4(1) (1853), 11).

(v) A large number of base silver and copper coins in a large earthen vase. Of the period from Philip (244-249) to Constantine (306-337). (PSANHS 4(2), (1853), 87).

B.   Bedmore Barn Area

Coins from Bedmore Barn, in the vicinity of the villa

(i) Hoard of 491 antoniniani found in or before 1814 in a biconical pot, dug out of the 'eastern extremity of the camp'. Date range from Gallienus (253-68) to Tetrici (271-73). (Numismatic Chronicle 1936, 30-42).

(ii) Hoard of at least 1089 coins in three pots, of which 796 are in the Taunton Museum Collection found close to the probable eastern entrance to the hillfort. Date range up to c. 260, most coins being of the second century. ST 4888 1642.

Museum Acc Nos. A 1862-7, 1841-2, 1999, 2000, 333-9. (PSANHS 95 (1950), 150-1, 158).

(iii) Unlocated hoard of third-century coins, possibly the same as above. (JRS 21 (1931), 241).

(iv) Surface finds from Bedmore Barn (Taunton Museum Collection). 9 coins from Antoninus Pius (138-61) to Valentinian (364-375).

Other Surface Finds

(i) 'Spears' were recorded in an area of irregular ground (c. ST 4886 1634) (Walter, 1853, 83). The whole area of Butchers Hill is ploughed regularly and produces large quantities of pottery and building material. It appears to be an extensive settlement area continuous and apparently roughly contemporary with the villa.

Pottery from this area in Taunton Museum (Acc nos. 50 A1110, 61 A10 49A17 and 67AC) includes Iron Age, Samian, and New Forest and Oxford ware types.

3   BATHAMPTON CAMP

Excavation 1967

Pottery: Roman pottery was found in the ploughsoil above the rampart in excavations on the S side. Two dozen sherds of 'indeterminate' Roman types. (Wainwright, 1967, 49).

4   TEDBURY

Casual find c. 1691

Coin hoard—A hoard of coins, mostly of Constantine II (317-40) found within the camp. (VCH I, 362)

5   MAES KNOLL

Surface finds, before 1977

'Occasional scraps of R.B. pottery come to light in animal disturbances.' (Branigan, 1977, 162)

6   DOLBURY CAMP

Casual finds
(Collinson III 1791, 579) Roman and Saxon coins frequently found within the hillfort. The only well-attested find is a third brass found in 1904. (Knight, 1915, 201)

There appear to be no grounds for the suggestion by the Ordnance Survey (ST45NE 3) that most of the Roman finds were made in the small depressed area in the SW corner.

7   SOLSBURY CAMP

Casual find before 1791

Coin hoard?

Roman coins of the Lower Empire found 'inside an earthwork ½ mile west of the church'. This can only refer to the hillfort. (Collinson III, 1791, 23)

9   SOUTH CADBURY

a)   Casual finds

Roman Temple?

Evidence for a temple within the hillfort is based on accounts of the finding of stonework, some of it apparently blue lias (Gray, 1913, 7), in the 16th-18th centuries, and of pieces of sawn and hammer-dressed stones incorporated into the post-Roman bank at the south-west entrance and site I during the excavations 1966-70 (Alcock, 1970b, 17). Additionally, the gilt bronze letter 'A' from site B (Alcock, 1972a, 51) and the large amounts of Roman coins reportedly found in the past support the suggestion.

b)   Excavation 1913

Gray's small trial excavations have been discussed by Alcock (1972a, 20-21, 1967, 71). Five cuttings were made, one on the summit plateau, two at the SW gate, one across the inner ditch and one outside the SW entrance. Some quantity of Roman pottery was found, including a piece of Samian from the summit plateau, but no structural remains. (Gray, 1913)

c)   Excavations 1966-70

Since this material is not fully published, and the interim accounts readily accessible, no attempt is made here to present the Roman evidence in overall detail. The detailed accounts of the rampart sections Site J, kindly made available by Professor Alcock, are here made use of in the context of the Roman finds from them.

The other Roman evidence may be summarized as follows:

1.   Early Roman Military

a) At least three buildings, represented by a series of wall trenches in Site B. Overall these form a row of regularly-spaced parallelogram-shaped structures. Late Iron Age pottery and a Roman hob-nail in the wall trenches provide termini post quem. An oven was also located in the same area. Samian pottery indicates that this occupation was in the Flavian period or after the Boudiccan revolt (Alcock 1969a, 35, 38; 1970b, 19; 1972a, 170-72).

b) Evidence for assault and massacre at the south-west gate, followed by burning and demolition of the gate structure and rampart (Alcock, 1971b, 4).

c) A number of finds of Roman military equipment and coins from the interior (Alcock passim).

2. Agricultural use of hilltop?

Humus collected over the rear of the final Iron Age rampart to a depth of 1 metre or more (Alcock, 1968b, 38) and a cobbled 'farm track' was laid over the collapse of the latest Iron Age walling at the south-west gate (Alcock, 1968b, 1971b, 3).

3. Roman Temple?

See above, Coins from 222-35 to 393-402 also found (Alcock, 1973b, 5).

Roman Material from Site J

This excavation consisted of two sections across the inner rampart on the west side immediately below the summit plateau. J67, 3 x 7 metres (9.8 x 22.9 ft) in size produced over 220 Roman sherds (at least 13 vessels) from nine contexts. J69, 5.5 x 10 m (18 x 32.8 ft) produced over 300 Roman sherds from at least 22 vessels from eleven contexts (numbers based on catalogue and examination of material by writer, August, 1974). Reduced to its simplest terms, this gives a density of about five sherds per square metre (cf. Cadcong 0.3 sherds per square metre). The material from these contexts is summarized, the contexts being in stratigraphic order based on the manuscript account, catalogue, and drawings.

J67

J115 Humus accumulation on top of latest pre-Roman bank

26 Roman sherds, chiefly from two vessels, a cooking pot in red-grey-red fabric with dark wiped surfaces, and a black-burnished type dish. (Iron Age material much more prolific than Roman in this context).

J114 Main body of Rampart E—late/post-Roman bank
Coin of Honorius (393-402). Over 50 Roman sherds including a sherd from a castor-ware beaker, the remainder from late Roman lattice—ornamented grey cooking pots (relatively small quantity of Iron Age material).

J111 Dark soil forming rear part of the late/post-Roman bank
59 sherds of late Roman sand tempered fabric, 37 from lattice-marked cooking pots. Small size of sherds. (c. 10 possible Iron Age sherds).

J112 Front Revetment of late/post-Roman bank
'Black burnished' ware flanged dish and a jar with typologically late lattice.

J110 Humus accumulation on late/post-Roman bank
About 80 mostly small late Roman sherds including black/grey flanged dishes and one base castor ware sherd. Also one early Roman sherd. (20 Iron Age sherds).

J107 Build up (or earlier phase?) of Aethelraedan burh defences
Six rims of early Roman vessels. 62 sherds from burnished lattice decorated late Roman vessels. Neck and rim of a coarse grey sandy fabric with eroded surface, this vessel does not appear to have been made on a fast wheel.

J109 Gravel layer contemporary with J107
Seven sherds from vessels as in J107.

J103   Aethelraedan bank

'Few small derived sherds' from late Roman lattice cooking pots.

J104   Robbing of Aethelraedan bank

Four sherds from late Roman lattice cooking pots.   Coin of Constans.

J69

J175   Quarried area, probably underlying tail of post-Roman bank

Bronze bangle, probably late Roman.   Two sandy grey ware vessel sherds
(earlier material present).

J125   Pit sealed by Aethelraedan bank

(Migration period Iron knife).   Late Roman lattice-marked cooking pots.
(Iron Age material).

J012   Late/post-Roman bank

Seven sherds probably from an amphora and 33 sand tempered sherds, some
of which may be Roman.   Six sherds from an early Roman grey/black dish.

J010b   Humic soil on tail of late/post-Roman bank

Large part of same early Roman vessel in J012.   About 30 sherds from at
least four grey/black sandy lattice decorated jars.   One small sherd late
Roman (Oxford) mortarium, burnt.

J010a   Gravel in lowest layer of Aethelraedan bank

27 probable late Roman sherds.   One rim sherd from early Roman vessel
in J012, J010b (Iron Age material).

J010   Lowest layer of Aethelraedan bank

Two late Roman lattice-decorated sherds as J010b.   One early Roman sherd.

J005-009   Aethelraedan bank

A number of sherds of grey/black sandy lattice decorated cooking pots,
some grey wares and one colour coat (Castor ware).

13   NORTON FITZWARREN

a)   Excavations 1908

Gray dug a trench 7.9 m (26 ft) by 3.6 m (12 ft) across the ditch and
outer bank on the west side.   No structural remains were encountered as
he only sectioned the ditch stratification.   Over 200 Romano-British sherds,
probably from a local kiln (Gray, 1908, 135) were recovered, mostly from
depths of less than 1 m (3 ft) and in 'fine light-coloured silting' (the upper
60 cm (3 ft) of stratification) or from the under-lying 'tenacious red marl'.
There was a preponderance of rims and bases.   No other Roman material
was found.   (Gray, 1908).

b)   Excavations 1968, 1970-71

Eleven cuttings were made, seven of them (D-G, Langmaid, 1971, 117)
designed to trace the Middle Bronze Age ditch feature, two on the summit
and one behind the rampart on the SE.   This work has only been published
in short interims (Langmaid 1968, 1970 and 1971).   The sequence in trench
'D' confirmed that of Gray's work, with R-B pottery in the upper part of the

ditch. Cobbling of Roman date was found in trenches C and E, in the former lapping against the rear of the earlier rampart. Ditches and gullies containing Roman material were located in features in cuttings B, G, and the pottery was found in association with quantities of iron slag.

The pottery from both excavations was examined in August, 1974 at Taunton Museum. The bulk of the material consists of greyish-pink gritty fabrics (very similar to some of the Congresbury fabrics), probably from the local source discussed by Gray, as there are wasters among the sherds. The amount of material is considerable (c. 2000 sherds).

Most of the pottery is early Roman, but there are late sherds, including an Oxford ware ring base (surface find). Leech 1977 145-166 suggests that the site was occupied throughout the Roman Period.

There is no other datable Roman material. The records of the excavations were not examined.

15   KINGS CASTLE, WIVELISCOMBE

a)   Casual find in plouging

Coin hoard. A large hoard dating from 270/4-388, three-quarters of the coins being of Valentinian. Contained in an everted rim jar in red fabric with a darker wash. Possibly a Valentinian hoard to which earlier material has been added. (Gray, 1946; Num. Chron. 1946, 163 5).

b)   Casual find 1711

Coins of the late C2 found on the slopes of the hillfort. (Collinson II, 1791, 488)

16   WORLEBURY

a)   Casual finds

Coins 1833 on the SW side of the hillfort, probably outside the ramparts. 11 coins from Tiberius (14-37) to Constantius II? (324-61). (Dymond, 1902, 81)

b)   Excavation

F. Warre's excavations 1851-3 were directed at the many large pits visible in the interior. Skeletons, some with sword cuts, were found above burnt grain and charcoal in the pits. The burials were regarded as of much later date than the use of the pits as hut sites.

'Within an area' (not located) 'the breadth of which was not more than five or six yards we found similar pottery' (to other finds) 'enough to fill several baskets; upwards of 200 coins of the later Empire; a great many glass beads, and fragments of bronze ornaments.'
(Warre, 1853, 126)

Some of this material is in Woodspring Museum, (Weston) and Taunton Museum. The Taunton material is as follows

A646   Flanged dish rim in sandy black-burnished fabric
A647   Flagon handle

A648   Flanged dish rim in sandy brown fabric, possibly same vessel
        as A646
A665   Glass beads as shown in Dymond and Tomkins, 1886, pl. X
        no. 16.
A678   194 coins from 241 reported in Numismatic Chronicle 1946,
        153-6. The coin range of the hoard is Constantine I (306-337)
        to Honorius and Arcadius, with three late third-century radiates.
        The deposition date has been put as late as AD 500 (Hill, 1951,
        25).
A685   Five 3 Æ 'probably from the camp'
A3019 Small quantity of black-burnished ware sherds.

at Weston:

    Black-burnished and grey ware sherds and some Oxford ware colour-
    coated sherds
    Coins from the above hoard from Constantine to Gratian
    Bronzes including two fragments of decorated bracelet, a strap end,
    rings and a bow brooch
    Further glass beads as above.

'Saxon' finds

1.   A 'Saxon dagger and spearbutt' were found 'in one of the hut circles'
      by Warre. (PSANHS VII (2), 51, 1856-7)

2.   Saxon spearhead? (same as above?)
      In Weston museum. Included by M. J. Swanton in his Corpus of Anglo-
      Saxon Spear Types (BAR 7, 1974) as of his Type L and provenanced
      to the hillfort.

18   CADCONG

      Roman pottery from the 1968-73 excavations

      General comments

      The wider significance of the Roman pottery is discussed elsewhere
(chapter 6), the material being there exhaustively analysed in order to assess
its function on the site, and to discover whether it is to be associated with
the post-Roman occupation. The total of 466 sherds, from an estimated 150
individual vessels, was classified macroscopically into fabric types, indicated
by Arabic numerals, and then further sub-divided into individual vessels,
shown by Roman numerals. The fabric types are grouped together for con-
venience according to shared characteristics of colour, and to a lesser extent
of fabric. The groups thus defined are

Group 1 - 9	Grey Wares	213 sherds
Groups 40 - 44	Black (mostly 'Black burnished') Wares	115
Groups 61 - 67	Buff-red-orange wares	43
Groups 81 - 84	Colour-coated fine wares	9
Groups 91 - 95	Mortaria and miscellaneous	30
Samian		56
		466

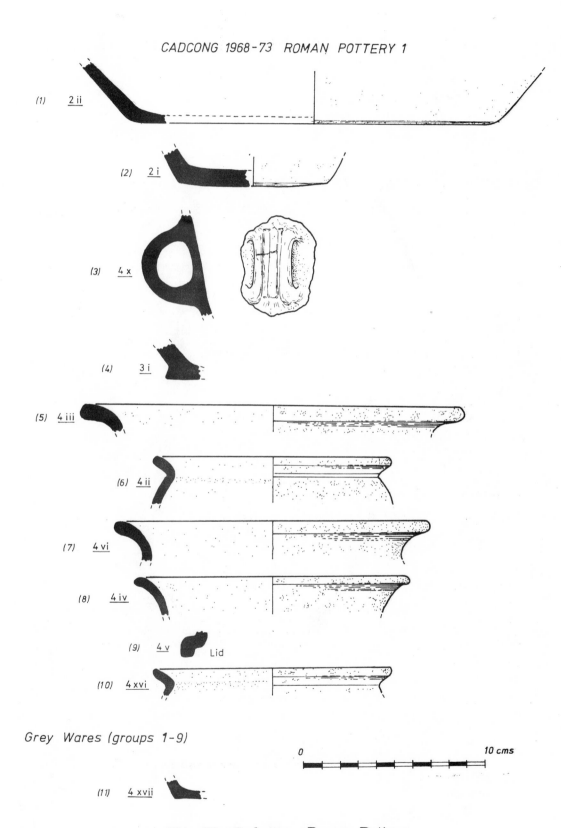

CADCONG 1968-73 ROMAN POTTERY 1

(1)   2 ii

(2)   2 i

(3)   4 x

(4)   3 i

(5)   4 iii

(6)   4 ii

(7)   4 vi

(8)   4 iv

(9)   4 v   Lid

(10)   4 xvi

Grey Wares (groups 1-9)

0   10 cms

(11)   4 xvii

Fig. 35 Cadcong; Roman Pottery

Grey Wares (groups 1-9)

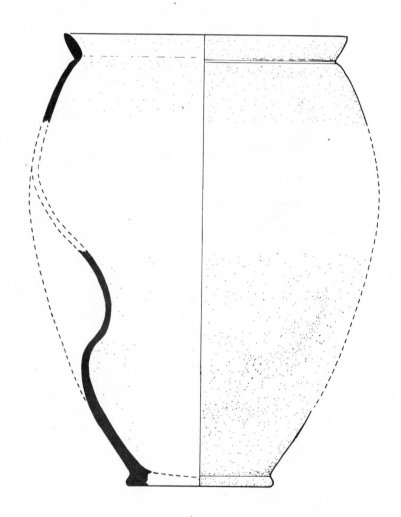

(12)   *suggested reconstruction of Vessel 4i*

0   10 cms

Fig. 36 Cadcong; Roman Pottery

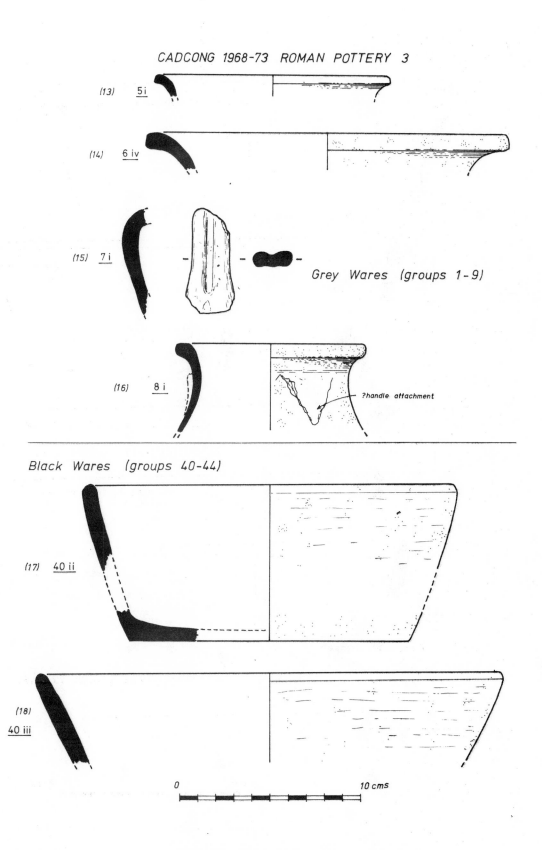

CADCONG 1968-73 ROMAN POTTERY 3

(13) 5 i

(14) 6 iv

(15) 7 i

Grey Wares (groups 1-9)

(16) 8 i

?handle attachment

Black Wares (groups 40-44)

(17) 40 ii

(18) 40 iii

0   10 cms

Fig. 37 Cadcong; Roman Pottery

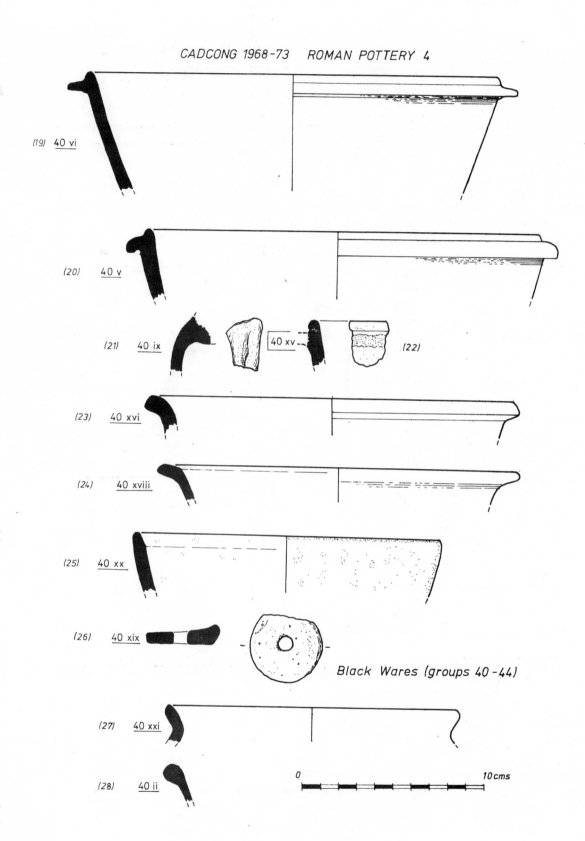

(19) 40 vi

(20) 40 v

(21) 40 ix   40 xv   (22)

(23) 40 xvi

(24) 40 xviii

(25) 40 xx

(26) 40 xix   Black Wares (groups 40-44)

(27) 40 xxi

(28) 40 ii   0   10 cms

Fig. 38 Cadcong; Roman Pottery

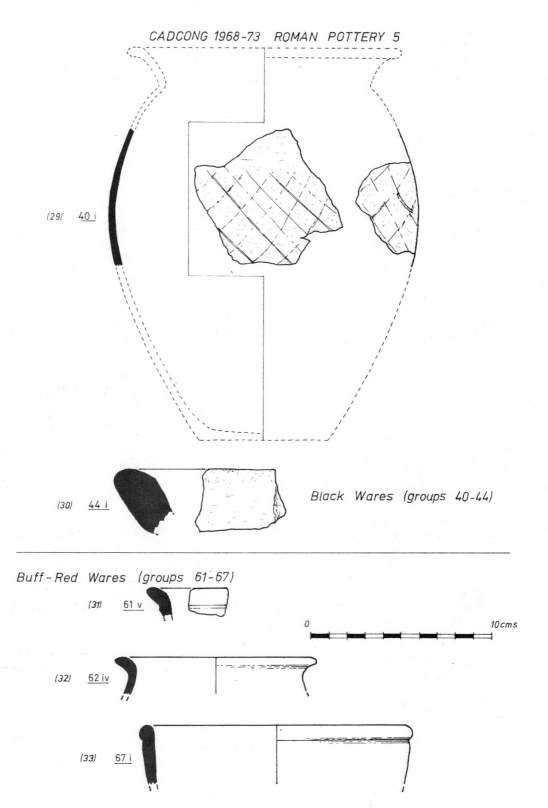

CADCONG 1968-73   ROMAN POTTERY 5

(29)   40 i

(30)   44 i   Black Wares (groups 40-44)

Buff-Red Wares (groups 61-67)

(31)   61 v

0   10cms

(32)   62 iv

(33)   67 i

Fig. 39 Cadcong; Roman Pottery

Colour Coats (groups 81-84)

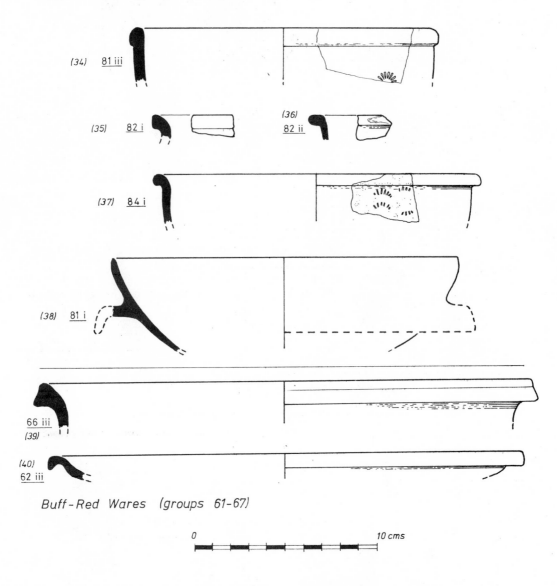

Buff-Red Wares (groups 61-67)

0   10 cms

Fig. 40 Cadcong; Roman Pottery

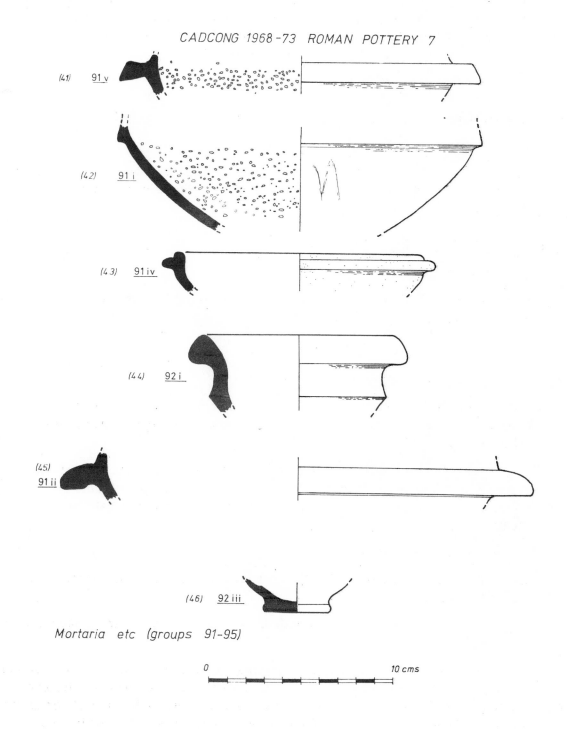

CADCONG 1968-73 ROMAN POTTERY 7

(41) 91 v

(42) 91 i

(43) 91 iv

(44) 92 i

(45)
91 ii

(46) 92 iii

Mortaria etc (groups 91-95)

0   10 cms

Fig. 41 Cadcong; Roman Pottery

Gaps in the numerical sequence are designed to accommodate additional groups into the scheme when excavation is resumed on the site. This classification replaces the Butcombe scheme adopted for the 1968 report (29-30). The material is re-published here but the three illustrated vessels are not reproduced. The main parallels cited are from Butcombe (3) and Chew Valley Lake (CVL). A complete catalogue is not given here as this will be published in the full report with the other Roman material. The drawn vessels are illustrated on Figures 39-45.

19   RUBOROUGH

Casual finds ?

Coins ?

The area of the hillfort, more particularly that between the inner and outer ramparts on the west side, was known as 'the Money Field'. (JBAA 13 (1857), 294)

22   STOKELEIGH CAMP

a)   Casual finds ?

before 1789: a quern and sword hilt found within the camp (Barrett, 1789, 20).
1890s Roman material on the Avon below the hillfort (CAC 2 (1893), 178).

b)   Excavation 1966-67

Six small cuttings to the rear of the inner rampart on the NW side, one (A) on the tail of the bank. The total area excavated is about 40 sq. m (430 sq ft).

Area A: No RB finds. Iron Age material in material interpreted as rampart collapse apparently prior to an undated phase of refurbishment comprising the construction of a rough revetment drystone wall on the rear of the tumble.

Area D : 5 m square.

(Layers 5 and 5a, associated with two hearths and four post-holes. Iron Age material only).

(Layer 4b, reddish-brown earth with an associated pit and three post-holes. Iron Age material only).

Layer 4a dark brown clayey soil overlying 4b with one hearth and a post-hole. Pottery from these contexts includes late Iron Age types and late Roman coarse wares including everted rim jars and flanged dishes mostly of grey/black quartz gritted fabrics. These made up about one-fifth of the total pottery group from Area D. AE Radiate.

Layer 3 reddish-brown clay and limestone fragments. Pit cut through Layer 4a (Iron Age material). Late Roman coarse ware dishes.

Layer 2 Reddish-brown clay with weathered limestone (rampart tumble)
    1 ? Roman sherd
    coin of Gallienus (253-268)

Area J

A possible rectangular structure consisting of very rough walling with some associated post and stake holes was found in this cutting but the stratification was disturbed and included a medieval glazed sherd as did the layer overlying it (2a). No Roman material was found.

Cutting I (1 m square) 1 RB sherd.

(Haldane, 1975)

27   BURLEDGE

Excavation 1955

Pottery: 1 sherd of 1st-century pottery found in excavations in the south-west corner of the hillfort, stratified above a two-phase Iron Age occupation deposit.
University of Bristol Spelaeological Society Museum
(ApSimon, 1957, Rahtz and Greenfield, 1977)

29   CADBURY TICKENHAM

a)   Casual finds: before 1922

1. Fragments of Roman pottery in molehills in the interior.
2. A coin of Claudius Gothicus (268-69) 'in the entrance' of the hillfort.
(Gray, 1922, 11 and C. M. Sykes
pers. comm. 3.11.75)

after 1945:

3. Coin of Valentinian II (375-392) 'well inside the ramparts'
(C. M. Sykes)

1974:

4. Roman Altar (Fig. 42)

Found in the inner ditch of the hillfort on the north-east side about 60 m (196 ft) east of the entrance. Moss on its surface showed that it had been partly exposed for some time, perhaps after eroding out of the inner bank. The stone is to be fully published elsewhere (Burrow and Bennett, 1979). The iconography suggests that a Mars figure is portrayed on the die. (Bristol Museum Accession No. 65/1975)

5. Roman pottery and tile. Investigation of an eroded area on the rear of the inner bank on the south side on the eastern flank of the recent gap through the defences (Plan Ba) showed Roman and Iron Age sherds in the topsoil with fragments of Pennant sandstone roofing tiles, some pieces showing typical bevelled edges.

b)   Excavation 1922

? Roman pottery from Cutting III, a 73 ft (22 m) long trench in the interior.

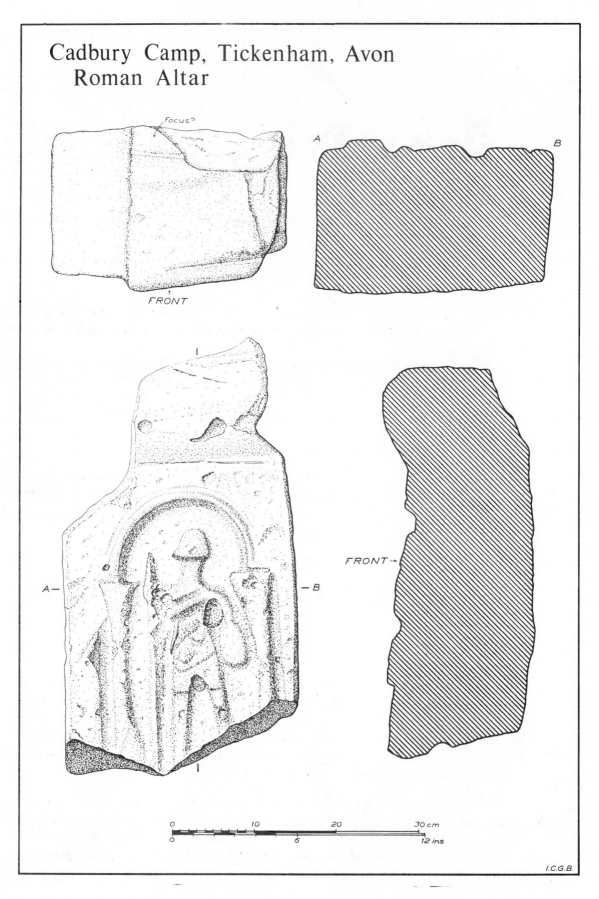

Cadbury Camp, Tickenham, Avon
Roman Altar

Fig. 42 Cadbury Tickenham; Roman altar

'A number of fragments of coarse black and brown pottery, including pieces of vessels exceeding $\frac{1}{2}$" (1 cm) in thickness. A rim piece of a very large vessel measured $\frac{3}{4}$" (2 cm) in thickness at the neck. Some of the sherds were weathered: none was ornamented. Half a circular disc of pottery diameter 11/16 in (2.7 cm) was also found'.

(Gray, 1922, 19)

This material cannot be located at Taunton Museum but the description suggests Iron Age material, though it must have been distinct from that found in the two cuttings in the entrance, which Gray describes as all Iron Age.

34   BURY HILL

Excavation 1926

1. Building: Early Roman barrack block?

The western part of this feature had been destroyed by quarrying. The excavated portion consisted of a ditch 1.2 m (4 ft) wide and 15-30 cm (6 in - 1 ft) deep enclosing a rectangular area 21 m (70 ft) by 5 m (17 ft). Along the inner lip of this ditch and 'flush with the bottom' was a fragmentary drystone Pennant wall 5-6 courses high and about 30 cm (1 ft) high. Inside the wall were north-south rows of Pennant slabs set vertically into the ground and dividing the interior into at least seven unequal compartments. Three small axial post sockets were also found on the lines of these subdivisions, perhaps forming post-holes for a ridge piece.

The pottery described from the area of this structure is predominantly early Roman, but as none of it is stratigraphically related to the building the date of the latter is conjectural. The plan suggested to the excavators that it was an early barrack block.

2. Structure: Late Roman?

A roughly square 'platform' of Pennant Sandstone 3.3 m (11 ft) N-S and E-W, with four possible post sockets at the corners of a square 1.8 m (6 ft) on a side within it, was located below mounds containing early 19th century material. Late Roman pottery was abundant in the centre of the area, including New Forest and Castor Ware types.

3. Other

Roman material was found in small quantities in trenches across a slight bank and ditch on the west side, below an oval mound at the south end, and 'a few sherds of coarse dark wheel-made ware ... probably Romano-British' from an ash and charcoal deposit in the top of the inner ditch silt on the north side.

The material from the excavation is believed to have been destroyed in the War, and the published account of the pottery is inadequate for present purposes. The assemblage clearly, however, includes jars with typologically late flaring rims, flanged bowls and straight-sided dishes in addition to castor ware and indented beakers.

Other Roman material:

'6 small copper coins' from the 'platform', apparently badly corroded; 1 piece of Roman bottle glass and quern fragments, also from the 'platform'.

There was also evidence for probable Roman iron-working.

(Davies and Phillips, 1926)

35   WAINS HILL

Casual finds

Pottery, early 1930s

Work on the footpath around the promontory. Late Roman sherds 'definitely of the types found in villas of the late 3rd or 4th centuries' found on the top of the inner rampart on the south side just below the turf. Lifting of the turf in places in the interior revealed 'a very thin scatter of buff-coloured sherds of thumbnail size' (? Iron Age). (Pers. comm. from Mr. C. M. Sykes, 6 Oldville Avenue, Clevedon, 17.11.72 and 3.4.75).

36   DAW'S CASTLE

Casual finds before 1890

Roman or later cemetery?

'When excavating for the (lime) kilns a quantity of human bones was discovered, and quite recently others were laid bare by the breaking away of a portion of the cliff.'

(Page, 1890, 241)

In view of adjacent field name evidence (Old Minster), it is possible that this is a late Saxon cemetery (ex inf. R. W. Dunning, Victoria County History of Somerset).

38   CASTLES, BATHEALTON

Casual finds before 1791

Coins. 'Some Roman coins of the Lower Empire have been found within its circuit'. (Collinson III (1791), 23).

41   CANNINGTON

1.   Excavation 1905

Roman sherds? Excavation behind the rampart on the north side produced wheel-turned pottery, contrasted by the excavator with the Glastonbury sherds found elsewhere. The sherds were with a small group of slingstones. (C. W. Whistler 'Further Notes on Kynwich Castle' Saga Book of the Viking Club 5 (i) (1907), 47-8).

2.   Excavation 1963

A 3 m (10 ft) square behind the outer bank to the east of the entrance (see Plan C). Immediately below the topsoil was an occupation level containing Roman and Iron Age material, with a stone packed post-hole containing an RB sherd and area of burnt daub. Within the latter was a darker area, possibly a second post-hole. Below these features was a layer of clean red clayey soil on the bedrock. The lack of any Iron Age levels behind the bank suggested that the bank itself might be of Roman or later date.

42 sherds of Roman pottery were found, the majority in the definition of the occupation level

27 'Black burnished' sandy ware	(Fabric H)	Cannington type series fabrics
13 grey micaceous	(Fabric I)	
2 red ware	(Fabric J)	

(Rahtz, 1969)

3.   Casual finds 1975

During the survey of the earthworks immediately to the south of the hillfort, and physically connected to the outer bank 26 sherds were found in the locations shown on Plan C, in superficial deposits disturbed by cows.

1 sherd samian (unidentifiable form)

4 sherds soft sandy micaceous wheel-made fabric with grey/buff or orange core

6 sherds hard grey micaceous wheel-made fabric (Cannington Cemetery Fabric I)

6 sherds very hard black sandy wheel-made fabric with small white grits and mica. 1 sherd buff (Cannington Cemetery Fabric H)

9 sherds as above, but with smoothed burnished surface.
(4 sherds of Iron Age pottery also found)

42   CLIFTON

Casual finds

Coins of Constantine (306-337) Crispus (317) and Constantius II (324-361) from unknown contexts in the camp.

(CAC iii (1896), 146)

43   BRENT KNOLL

a)   Excavation

Building: ?Temple (or villa)

Cemetery? Human remains associated with Roman material

On at least two occasions the Rev. J. Skinner undertook excavations on the Knoll, apparently on the north-west side behind the inner rampart. As his accounts show he located Pennant Sandstone roof tiles, 'foundation stones' and painted wall plaster, all indicative of a substantial building. In a location such as this a temple would be more appropriate than a villa establishment, the prominent topographical position being similar to that of the Brean Down temple, 8.5 kms to the NNW. Skinner's record of 'foundation stones' is especially important as it may imply that intact deposits undisturbed by quarrying are present on the site. His sketch section (B.M. Add MSS 33719 f97) shows a pre-quarrying horizon of 'dark mould'.

B.M. Add MSS 33646 f10   (1812)
33719 f95-8   (1830)
33726 f106, 110 (1832)

Two pieces of Pennant tile and some mortar fragments are in Weston Museum.

B.M. Add MSS 33646 f10

'We took a pickaxe and shovel, and climbed the knoll in order to dig within the entrenchment; the course of a few minutes Mr Phelps and his brother, my companion, collected a good many pieces of the coarse Roman pottery, namely some stoneware, black and brown, and also one of the flat-headed nails, of the same kind I found in the Winter at Camerton, which was used for keeping on the stone tiling of their dwellings. I understand, at different times, a variety of coins have been discovered here, and lately, a piece of iron or steel, which is now in the posession (sic) of Mr Antstis, at Bridgwater, which he denominates a stylus, or pen..... The ground at present is very unequal within the vallum, having been turned up by the quarrymen, who without doubt removed the foundation stones of the buildings and walls; yet towards the east there is a considerable space of ground which remains untouched, and perhaps yet contains many interesting reliques (sic) beneath the surface. On mentioning this to my companions, they promised to occupy some of their leisure, in having it explored, and inform me of the result.'

J. Skinner, July 20th 1812

B.M. Add MSS 33719 f95

'Having engaged two labourers we ascended from the church by a ridge which led to the camp or acropolis on the summit of the Knoll, which ridgeway was guarded by linchets and high banks as I have shown in my sketches. I put the men to work in the black mould where I found the fibula about six years ago. They soon turned up fragments of Roman ware, black grey and samian; also roofing stones of the pennant kind; bones of animals, charcoal, and the blades of two cutters or cutting instruments. Mr Williams, who was occupied in digging a little beyond, though within the agger of the camp, which contains eight acres, turned up some unbaked British ware, also the flint head of an arrow, a clear indication of the place having been a settlement of the ancient Britons before the arrival of the Belgae or Romans ..... The workmen engaged in digging informed me that coins of various kinds had been found within the lines of the camp, and that one, a gold one, had been purchased by Mr Fry at Axebridge .....'

J. Skinner, September 30th 1830

f96   sketch clearly showing interior quarrying

f97   section drawing showing 'dark mould' above yellow subsoil and below 'earth thrown up by the quarry men'

f98   birds'-eye view of site showing area excavated, apparently near the centre of the north-west side. Interior quarried.

B.M. Add MSS 33726 f100, f110

'I am now fully assured that this was the Uxela (sic) of Ptolemy which gave name to the Aestuary flowing up to Glastonbury; Eux signifying water stronghold, and el an elevation.... (here) the Romans themselves had a strongly fortified camp, and I am inclined to think a specular watchtower on the summit of the Knoll to keep a good look-out on the Severn, and to communicate by signals with the coast of Wales, the Country of the Silures since, when digging in the camp I found not only foundation stones, but painted stucco, which were indicative of a permanent building on the spot.'

J. Skinner, June 1st 1832

b)   Casual finds

1. Coins

An urn containing coins of Trajan and Severus was found 'on Brent Knoll' before 1790 (Barrett, 1789, 10). These or other finds may be referred to by Collinson who notes bronze and silver coins from the Knoll (Collinson I, 196).

Skinner found coins on his excavations, but does not record them.

A coin of Victorinus (268-70) from the Knoll was presented to Bristol Museum in 1967 (Arch Rev 2 (1967), 26).

2. Pottery

A total of 580 sherds are in the collections at Taunton (Accession numbers A3033 (on north side of entrance top layer of rampart material), A3344 and 30 A117) and Weston (unmarked) and 31 vessels, comprising a majority of the forms represented, are illustrated. The material is catalogued and identified on the same principle as the pottery from Cadcong, and only a few fabrics at Brent Knoll are absent from Congresbury, and these can mostly be paralleled in the Chew Valley Series.

On both form and fabric the bulk of the pottery appears to be of the third or fourth centuries AD, with the exception of the small quantity of samian and the grey jar of group 3 (no. 1). The sherds are large and unabraded.

The collections consists overwhelmingly of coarse wares, probably of local origin, and breaks down as follows

Grey wares	51%
Black wares	44%
Others	5%

Especially noteworthy is the total absence of mortaria or late colour-coated vessels from Oxford or New Forest sources, with the exception of one sherd.

Roman Pottery in Weston and Taunton Museums

(Much of this material is illustrated by Leech 1977, Fig. 146).

Grey Wares

As at Congresbury, Butcombe and Chew Valley Lake it is probable that most of these are from the Congresbury kilns or other as yet unidentified sources nearby.

294 sherds, of which only 8 cannot be paralleled among the above series. Where possible these are related directly to the Cadcong series, but otherwise to CVL and Butcombe.

The material at Taunton is marked A30333, A3344 or 30 A117 but is without exact provenances within the hillfort. The Weston material is unmarked.

Cadcong Group 1 (Fourth century?)

5 body sherds (A3033)

Cadcong Group 2 (Third and Fourth centuries?)

4 body sherds (A3344)

Cadcong Group 3 (Fourth century?)

39 sherds (A3033, 1, A3344 5, 30 A117 19, Weston 14)
(1) Rim of large jar, form paralleled in period Ib contexts at CVL (e.g. no. 51), but fabric later. (Weston)

Cadcong Group 4 (Third and Fourth centuries?)

9 sherds (A3033 2, A3344 1, 30 A117 2, Weston 4)
(2) Jar rim (A3033)
(3) Mug (CVL no. 161, late 2nd and 3rd centuries)] [Weston]
(4) Jar with grooved rim, similar to some Congresbury rims at CVL. (Weston)
(5) Small jar (50 A117).

Cadcong Group 6 (mostly Fourth century) Typical Congresbury ware

134 sherds (A3033 3; A3344 10; 30 A117 108; Weston 13)
(6) Jar rim (A3344)
(7) Mug (CVL nos. 157-61 later 2nd and 3rd centuries) A3344)
(8) Jar rim (A3344)

Cadcong Group 9 (wide dating range at CVL, possibly Caldicot kilns)

95 sherds (A3344 1, 30 A117 94)
(9) Jar rim (30 A117)
(10) Jar rim (30 A117)
(11) Double rim jar or jug. (Chew Park Well 293 AD - nos. 305-9)

In addition are eight sherds of a fabric not at Cadcong, CVL or Butcombe, with a very rough dark grey surface and core with occasional large calcareous grits (aal A3344).

Black Wares

These fall into groups 40 and 41 at Cadcong, but the Brent Knoll examples are mostly possibly of BB2 type (Farrar, 1974), being probably wheel-made and very highly burnished in most cases. The rim forms in general indicate a late Roman date.

Cadcong Group 40

243 sherds (A3033 3, A3344 28, 30 A117 124, Weston 108)

(12) Rim sherd in ? local sandy ware (A3344)

(13) Rim sherd in ? local sandy ware (A3344)

(14) Rim sherd in ? local sandy ware (A3344)

(15) Small jar with shallow tooled lines at base of rim (30 A117)

(16) Shoulder of lattice marked cooking pot in BB1 or local version.
    Angle of lattice suggests a date within third century (Weston)

(17) Jar (Weston)

(18) Jar (Weston)

(19) Jar (Weston)

(20) Jar (Weston)

(21) Jar (Weston)

(22) Bowl or dish (30 A117)

(23) Flat-based bowl in sandy fabric (Weston)

(24) Flat-based bowl in sandy fabric (Weston)

(25) Flat-based bowl in sandy fabric (Weston)

(26) Flanged dog dish bowl – normally a late Roman type (Farrar,
    1974, 70) (30 A117)

Cadcong Group 41 (? early Roman – CVL group N)

10 sherds (A3344 4; Weston 6)

(27) Footring (Weston)

(28) Jar (Weston)

Other Fabrics

1.   Five sherds in a buff smooth fabric with small white grits and a
burnished surface. Possibly CVL fabric L (early) but Butcombe XXIV is
post AD 350).

(29) Mug with grey core and burnished surface (30 A117)

(30) Jar rim (Weston)

(31) Body sherd with two irregular rouletted bands of hollows above
    a girth groove (Weston)

2.   Hard, sandy red-orange wares, one with a white slip. Similar to
material in Claudio-Neronian contexts from Ham Hill (Taunton Museum,
St. G. Gray excavations)

17 sherds (30 A117)

3.   Samian. 10 plain body sherds (A3033 1, 30 A117 9)

Totals	579 sherds examined	Cadcong
Grey wares 51%		46.4%
Black wares 44%		25.2%
Rest	5%	28.2%

4.   1 sherd New Forest (30 A117)

Comparison with Cadcong

(1)   This material is purely surface finds.

(2)   Sherds are much larger in general than those at Cadcong.

(3)   Higher proportion of exotica etc. at Cadcong - note no mortaria or colour coats at Brent Knoll.

Dating

On form and fabric the majority of the groups appear to be of 3rd or 4th centuries AD exceptions to this may be the hard sandy red wares and the samian and some vessels such as group 3 jar.

46   BLAISE CASTLE

a)   Casual finds

1. Coins: Coin finds made at various dates show a chronological distribution throughout the Roman period. Of 114 published, 76 are of fourth-century date. (Boon, 1963, Rahtz and Brown, 1958, 153)

2. Pottery (Bristol musems) c̲. 200 sherds including Flavian, Samian and New Forest indented beakers. (Rahtz and Brown, 1958, 152)

b)   Excavation

Roman Temple and Cemetery?

1707   A vault 6 yd (5.9 m) broad and 10 yd (9.9 m) long, with many interments and Roman coins 'and other Roman antiquities' found.

1918   This was possibly re-excavated by Bartlett, who located a building 28 ft (8.5 m) by 14 ft (4.25 m) internally with angle buttresses at the corners and pilasters centrally on the long sides. Two wall stubs running westward from the west wall were interpreted as a porch. Bartlett's plan shows the east wall projected north and south and a 'bed of brown mortar' on the SW side. The structural remains were very slight, the foundations consisting of limestone set in brown lime mortar, in places on a bed of mortar on the levelled bedrock.

In the interior were fragments of 'Lias' tile, (probably of Pennant Sandstone). At the east end was a platform, possibly paved with red tile. On the west side of the platform was a 'fissure or trench' 6 ft (1.8 m) deep and filled with 'black greasy soot' containing Roman pottery. Under the platform was a piece of sandstone, possibly from a Roman altar.

A number of graves were found in the vicinity. One an extended inhumation with head to the east was excavated below the platform at the eastern end. Some of the others (east-west, heads to west) were in graves cut in the bedrock and covered by slabs of stone occasionally mortared in place. Bones were also found on the line of the walls, and near the east end of the north wall the latest of three superimposed burials was cut through the foundations.

1957   Seventeen small trial holes were dug in the interior of the hillfort, ten of which produced Roman material. In cutting 10, traces of walling with Roman sherds were located, and a possible Roman post-hole in cutting 6. A child inhumation (E-W, head to west) with a coin of FEL TEMP REP type under the skull was located in cutting 9. Roman building material included

tegulae and imbrices, Pennant Sandstone roof tiles, seven kinds of mortar and six of painted plaster. A fragment of Bath Stone roof coping was noted built into the wall of Blaise Castle (1768).
(There is also a strap end, probably of 9th century date found in 1819).
(Rahtz and Brown, 1958)

60 BREAN DOWN

a) Casual finds

1. Coins, before 1902. Quarrying on the north side of the enclosure c. 1870 produced Roman coins including gold pieces of Augustus (23 B.C. - 14 A.D.), Nero (54-68) and Drusus (early 1st century). (Knight, 1902, 298)

2. Coins. Fourth-century Roman coins from the enclosure.
(ApSimon, 1958, 109)

b) Excavation 1974

Second century brooch and mortarium found in upper levels of ditch. Eleven sherds on occupation deposit on rear of bank. Thirteen sherds, possibly late Iron Age, below rampart collapse in ditch.
(Fully published in Burrow, 1976)

62 KINGS WESTON

Excavations 1956

Seven small cuttings were made in the interior of the inner enclosure, and a section across the inner ditch. Pottery of second-century date, probably in the first half of the century, was found both in the interior cuttings and in the ditch silt, including one sherd in soft orange fabric in layer 7, the destruction rubble from the bank.
(Rahtz, 1957)

Casual finds 1966

A pipe trench across the outer bank and ditch revealed an inhumation in the lowest observed layer of the stratification. This had its head to the north, in contrast to the orientated burials found 400 m (1300 ft) to the east. The date is uncertain, but could be late or post-Roman.
(Goodman, 1972, 45)

65 MOAT HOUSE

Excavation 1931

Pottery: 'A few poor pieces of Romano-British pottery from the upper part of the ditch'. Nine pieces of thin greyish-blue pot, and six thicker brownish-red. (Present location unknown).
(Phillips, 1931b, 46, 49)

76 KINGSDOWN CAMP

Excavations 1927-9

Gray's excavations on this site examined the entire length of the inner ditch of the central enclosure, selective sectioning of the outer ditch and stone enclosing wall, the entrance on the north-east and the trenching of about half the interior. Cuttings were also made on the surrounding earthworks.

The stratigraphic record of this excavation is such that it is impossible to reconstruct the structural history of the site in other than broad terms. The sequence of the enclosing earthworks is as follows:

1.   The inner ditch, an irregular feature averaging just over 1 m deep with an entrance on the south. The lower parts of this were filled with a yellow clay and silt containing only prehistoric material of Iron Age date. Above this level were a series of ashy deposits and five hearths. Roman material, including Flavian and other mid-1st century Samian was found at this general level, but as finds and 'layers' were only recorded in terms of absolute depths below the turf, despite the acknowledged variability in depth of the ditch, there are no valid associations. The top 45 cm ($1\frac{1}{2}$ ft) of ditch silt contained an AS of Domitian (86 AD) and two dupondii of Hadrian, one dating to 133-5 AD.

2.   The stone wall, with an entrance on the NE and associated in plan with the outer ditch, The drystone wall was faced and well constructed in places, and about 2.5 m (8 ft) wide. On the south it ran over the silted-up inner ditch. This wall was nowhere sectioned. The outer ditch was a regularly cut V-shaped feature averaging 1.6 m (5 ft 3 in.) deep.

Roman pottery was found throughout the silting of the ditch in most cuttings, including what Gray describes as 'imitation Samian', and is apparently Oxford ware (sherds handled at Taunton Museum). These sherds were found at the bottom of the ditch in cuttings I and V (for discussion of this see chapter 6). Flavian Samian was also found in this ditch.

3.   The interior produced eight structural features, all excavations in the bedrock. The remaining untouched area of the site clearly has considerable potential for the recovery of coherent area plans. Hole 4, a large oval feature 2.7 m (8.9 ft) deep, contained Roman pottery sherds down to the bottom. Holes 2 and 5 produced Roman pottery in their upper parts. None of the remainder of the material is in any way stratified.

The inner ditch was used for infant burial of eleven individuals, apparently contemporary with or later than the outer ditch and wall, as an interment in cutting XII (south-east corner) was covered with a slab probably from the wall.

The material is in Taunton Museum. The pottery was examined in August 1974, chiefly to search for late/post-Roman wares. Of the c. 3000 Roman sherds (292 published) five were of Samian and 23 of a soft orange ware with a red colour coat—apparently Oxford ware. The remaining material is fine smooth wheel-made grey pottery, the majority from cooking pots or jars. Most of the sherds are from the body, but the rims present are comparable with those from Period I at Chew Valley Lake (late 1st-2nd century).

APPENDIX C

PLACE NAMES IN SOMERSET
CONTAINING CELTIC ELEMENTS
(Fig. 9)

a)   <u>River names</u>

Source: Ekwall, 1928 and Turner, 1950-4.

The majority of the rivers shown on Figure 9 are those named on the Ordnance Survey One-Inch maps. Smaller streams and rivers appear to possess names generally of more recent origin, but these have not been systematically treated and are not shown.

Rivers of Celtic derivation:

Alham, Avill, Avon, Axe, Brue, Cam Brook, Cary, Chew, Exe, Frome, Isle, Kenn, Parrett, Tone, Yeo (South Somerset), Wellow Brook, Winford Stream, Wring (former name of Congresbury Yeo).

Rivers of English derivation:

Banwell, Barle, Fivehead, Land Yeo (Clevedon), Lox Yeo, Mells Stream, Pulham, Mells.

b)   <u>Other place names</u>

For the reasons outlined in chapter 3 no definitive list of Celtic place names can yet be produced. The following list was compiled from places named in the Domesday Survey and in earlier material, predominantly charters (Finberg 1964c and Sawyer 1968; numbers quoted, prefixed by F or S). The chief authorities are Ekwall 1960 (E) and Turner 1950-4 (T).

	Name	Grid Ref	Authority	First Reference
r	Avill	SS 978 431	E	Domesday Book (DB)
	Bath	ST 750 645		Alcock, 1972a, 70-1 suggests that the Œ Baðum could derive from a British *Baðon, and that the battle of Badon was fought on the vicinity. Other authorities regard it as a wholly English name.
	Brean	ST 561 296	E, T	DB
	Brent	ST 519 344	E, T	AD 693 (S 238)
r	Brewham	ST 720 361	E	DB
r	Bruton	ST 685 348	E	DB

	Name	Grid Ref	Authority	First Reference
	Camel	ST 590 255	T	AD 939–46 (Finberg, 1964c, no. 455)
r	Camerton	ST 686 575	E	AD 946–55 (F 462–3)
	Cannington	ST 258 395	E	AD 873–88 (will of Alfred)
r	Cary	ST 561 288	T	DB
	Cedern	ST 537 594	E	AD 760 (Turner 1952a)
	Cheddar	ST 460 535	T	AD 880 (Birch no. 553) (Ekwall treats as an English name)
r	Chew	ST 557 620	E, T	DB
	Chinnock	ST 462 128	T	AD 950 (Whitelock, 1930, will of Winflaed)

Turner, 1952c, derives this from Cynnog –
a milk pail, or from OE cinu – a fissure.
Ekwall regards it as English.

	Name	Grid Ref	Authority	First Reference
	E. Coker	ST 538 123	E	DB
	W. Coker	ST 516 136	E	DB
	Churchill	ST 449 598	T	DB
	Churchill	ST 580 440	T	DB
	Congresbury	ST 436 638	E, T	AD 688–726 (F 372)
	Corston	ST 695 653	E, T	AD 941 (S 476)
	Creech	ST 275 253	E	DB
	Creechbarrow	ST 247 255	E, T,	AD 682 (S 236)
	Crewkerne	ST 440 098	E	873–88 (Whitelock, 1930, will of Alfred)
	Cricket St. T	ST 374 086	E, T	DB
r	Curry	ST 391 255	E, T	AD 934–9 (F 437)
	Dommett	ST 276 145	T	AD 762 (F 392)
r	Doulting	ST 646 432	E, T	AD 702–6 (S 248)
r	Doverhay	SS 890 466	E	DB
r	Dowlish	ST 375 130	E	DB
	Dunkerton	ST 711 594	E, T	DB
	Evercreech	ST 649 387	T	DB
r	Frome	ST 774 489	E, T	AD 955 (ASC)
	Glastonbury	ST 500 390	E, T	AD 688 (ASC)

	Name	Grid Ref	Authority	First Reference
r	Ilchester	ST 353 210	E	DB
r	Isle	ST 353 210	E	AD 762 (F 392)
r	Ilton	ST 351 175	E	DB
r	Kenn	ST 416 690	T	DB
	Kewstoke	ST 335 635	T	DB
	Lantocai	ST 490 360	T	AD 677-81 (S 1249)
r	Limington	ST 542 224	E	DB
	Lydeard	ST 168 299	E, T	AD 854 (S 363)
	Minehead	SS 967 466	T	DB
	Myne	SS 940 480	E	DB
	Oare	SS 802 473	E	DB
	Pamborough	ST 471 456	E	DB
	Pennard	ST 570 382	E, T	681 (S 236) (Charter possibly a forgery)
r	Petherton	ST 290 330	E	DB
r	Petherton	ST 433 169	E	DB
	Priddy	ST 528 518	T	AD 688-726 (F 372)
	Priston	ST 678 616	T	AD 934-9 (F 435)
	Quantockhead	ST 136 437	E, T	DB
	Ridgehill	ST 539 626	T	DB
r	Tarnock	ST 380 526	T	AD 946-55 (F 464)
r	Taunton	ST 225 247	E	AD 722 (ASC)
r	Tolland	ST 101 321	E	DB
r	Tone	ST 126 219	E	AD 705-6 (F 371)
r	Trent	ST 590 186	E	DB
	Watchet	ST 065 428	E	AD 918 (ASC)
r	Wearne	ST 425 281	E	DB
r	Williton	ST 076 411	E	AD 904 (Brich 612)
r	Winford	ST 540 649	T	DB
r	Wincanton	ST 711 284	E	AD 956 (Birch 923)
r	Yeovil	ST 555 160	E	AD 873-88 (will of Alfred)
r	Yeovilton	ST 546 230	E	AD 955-9 (F 489)
	(Quantock	Unlocated	E, T	DB)

Name	Grid Ref	Authority	First Reference
(Stretmersh	Unlocated	T	AD 693 (F 365)). Turner, 1952c 'horses brook'. M. Gelling does not accept this as a Celtic name (pers. comm.)

r indicates place name formed from a river name.

Where there are a number of adjacent places with the same name (e.g. West, East and Queen Camel) only one has been shown on the distribution map.

c)   Additional Celtic place names cited by Turner, from post-Domesday sources

Alham, Cale, Christon, Conkwell, Croscombe, Dinder, Dundry, Edingworth, Foss, Keyford, Locks Brook, Peart, Pen Hill, Pinksmoor, Ponteside, Rodney, Tolchet, Ros (Welcroft), Wellow, Wilmington, Winterhead, Wrington.

BIBLIOGRAPHY AND ABBREVIATIONS

Addyman, P. V. et al., 1973a. 'Anglo Saxon Houses at Chalton, Hampshire', Med Arch 16 (1972), 13-31.

Addyman, P. A. et al., 1973b. 'The Anglo Saxon Village at Chalton, Hampshire: second interim report', Med Arch 17 (1973), 1-25.

Alcock, L., 1962. 'Settlement Patterns in Celtic Britain', Antiquity 36 (1962), 51-5.

Alcock, L., 1963a Dinas Powys, Cardiff 1963.

Alcock, L., 1963b. 'Pottery & Settlements in Wales & and Marches; A.D. 400-700' in I. LL. Foster and L. Alcock (eds.) Culture and Environment, London 1963, 281-302.

Alcock, L., 1964. 'Some Reflections on Welsh Society & Economy', Welsh History Review 2 (1964), 1-7.

Alcock, L., 1965a. 'Hillforts in Wales and the Marches', Antiquity 39 (1965), 184-95.

Alcock, L., 1965b. 'Wales in the Fifth to Seventh Centuries A.D.: Archaeological Evidence' in I. Ll. Foster and G. E. Daniel Prehistoric & Early Wales, London 1965, 177-211.

Alcock, L., 1967a. 'A Reconnaissance Excavation at South Cadbury Castle, Somerset, 1966', Antiq Jour 47 (1967), 70-76.

Alcock, L., 1967b. 'By South Cadbury is that Camelot', Antiquity 41 (1967), 50-53.

Alcock, L., 1968a. 'Wales in the Arthurian Age' in G. Ashe (ed.) The Quest for Arthur's Britain, London 1968, 101-118.

Alcock, L., 1968b. 'Excavations at South Cadbury Castle 1967: A Summary Report', Antiq Jour 48 (1968), 6-17.

Alcock, L., 1968c. 'Cadbury Castle 1967', Antiquity 42 (1968), 47-51.

Alcock, L., 1969a. 'Excavations at South Cadbury Castle 1968, A Summary Report', Antiq Jour 49 (1969), 30-40.

Alcock, L., 1969b. 'South Cadbury Excavations 1968', Antiquity 43 (1969), 52-56.

Alcock, L., 1970a. 'Was There an Irish Sea Culture Province in the Dark Ages?' in Moore, D. (ed.) The Irish Sea Province in Archaeology & History (Cardiff 1970), 55-65.

Alcock, L., 1970b. 'Excavations at South Cadbury Castle 1969: A Summary Report', Antiq Jour 50 (1970), 14-25.

Alcock, L., 1970c. 'South Cadbury Excavations 1969', Antiquity 44 (1970), 46-49.

Alcock, L., 1971a. Arthur's Britain, London 1971.

Alcock, L., 1971b. 'Excavations at South Cadbury Castle 1970', Antiq Jour 51 (1971), 1-7.

Alcock, L., 1972a. By South Cadbury is that Camelot, London 1972.

Alcock, L., 1972b. 'The Irish Sea Zone in the Pre-Roman Iron Age' in Thomas (ed.) 1972a, 99-112.

Alcock, L., 1972c. 'Excavations at Cadbury/Camelot 1966/70', Antiquity 46 (1972), 29-38.

Alcock, L., 1973a. (Review of Brodribb et al. 1972), Med Arch 17 (1973), 189-90.

Alcock, L., 1973b. 'Towards a Culture Sequence for Cadbury Camelot' MS. May 1973.

Alcock, L., 1974. 'Fenestrae Obliquae: a Contribution of Literate Archaeology', Antiquity 48 (1974), 141-3.

Alcock, L., 1975. 'Dry Bones & Living Documents' in Evans et al. 1975, 117-122.

Alcock, L., 1980a. 'Populi Bestiales Pictorum Feroci Animi: A survey of Pictish Settlement Archaeology' in Hanson, W. S. and Keppie, L. J. F. (eds.) Roman Frontier Studies 1979, British Archaeol. Reports International Series 71 (1980), 61-95.

Alcock, L., 1980b. 'The Cadbury Castle sequence in the First Millennium B.C.', Bulletin Board of Celtic Studies 28 pt IV (1980), 656-718.

Alföldy, G., 1974. Noricum, London 1974.

Allcroft, A. H., 1908. Earthwork of England, London 1908.

Angles & Britons 1963, Cardiff, University of Wales Press, 1963.

Anon., 1968 (Broomfield Enclosure) SDN&Q 28 (1968), 187-9.

Antiq Jour Antiquaries Journal, London.

Applebaum, S., 1972. 'Roman Britain' in Finberg, H. P. R. (ed.), 1972 The Agrarian History of England and Wales Vol I, pt. 2, Cambridge 1972, 3-277.

ApSimon, A. M., 1957. 'Excavations at Burledge Camp, Somerset', PUBSS 8 (1957), 40.

ApSimon, A. M., 1958. 'The Roman Temple on Brean Down, Somerset', PUBSS 8 (2) (1958), 106-9.

ApSimon, A. M., 1965. 'The Roman Temple on Brean Down, Somerset', PUBSS 10 (3), 195-258.

ApSimon, A. M., Donovan, D. T., Taylor, H., 1961. 'The Stratigraphy and Archaeology of the Late Glacial and Post-Glacial Deposits at Brean Down, Somerset', PUBSS 9 (2) (1961), 67-136.

Arch Rev Archaeological Review, Bristol 1965-73.

Arch Camb Archaeologia Cambrensis, Cardiff.

Arch J Archaeological Journal, London.

Armitage-Robinson, J., 1921. 'On the Antiquity of Glastonbury' in
    Somerset Historical Essays, London 1921, 1-25.

Armitage-Robinson, J., 1926. Two Glastonbury Legends, Cambridge 1926.

Atkinson, G. M., 1869. 'Clifton Camps', PSANHS 15 (2) (1868-9), 27-31.

Avery, B. W., 1955. Soils of the Glastonbury District of Somerset, Soil
    Survey, London 1955.

Avery, M., 1976. 'Hillforts of the British Isles: A Student's Introduction',
    in Harding 1976, 1-58.

Baddely, H. St. C., 1930. 'The Battle of Dryham' TBGAS 51 (1930), 95-101.

Barley, M. W. and Hanson, R. P. C., 1968. Christianity in Britain 300-700,
    Leicester 1968.

Barker, E. E., 1961. Somersetshire Charters to A.D. 900 (M.A. Thesis
    London University 1961).

Barker, P. A., 1970. 'Some Aspects of the Excavation of Timber Buildings',
    World Archaeology 1 (1969-70), 220-235.

Barker, P. A., 1973. Excavations on the Site of the Baths Basilica at
    Wroxeter 1966-73, Birmingham 1973.

Barrett, W., 1789. History and Antiquities of Bristol, Bristol 1789.

Bartlett, J. A., 1919. 'Report on a Search for the Site of the Chapel of St.
    Blasius, Henbury', TBGAS 41 (2) (1919), 163-9.

Barton, K. J., 1964. 'Star Roman Villa, Shipham, Somerset', PSANHS 108
    (1964), 45-93.

Bates, E. H., 1905. 'The Dedications of the Churches of Somerset',
    PSANHS 51 (1905), 105-135.

Bennett, J. A., 1890. 'Camelot', PSANHS 36 (2), 1890, 1-19.

Benson, D. and Miles, D., 1974. The Upper Thames Valley: an Archae-
    ological Survey of the River Gravels, Oxford 1974.

Bidgood, W., 1898. 'Norton Camp', PSANHS 44 (2) (1898), 198-202.

Biddle, B. and Biddle, M., 1969. 'Metres, Areas and Robbing', World
    Archaeology 1 (1969), 208-219.

Binford, L. R., 1972. An Archaeological Perspective, New York and London
    1972.

Birch, W. G., 1885-93. Cartularium Saxonicum, London 1885-93.

Bonney, D. J., 1972. 'Early Boundaries in Wessex' in Fowler, 1972,
    168-86.

Boon, G. C., 1963. 'Roman Coins from Blase Castle', PUBSS 10 (1)
    (1962-3), 7-8.

Boon, G. C., 1963. 'Roman Coins from Blaise Castle', PUBSS (10 (1) (1962-3), 7-8.

Bowes, H. C. and Fowler, P. J., 1966. 'Romano-British Rural Settlements in Dorset and Wiltshire' in Thomas, 1966a, 43-67.

Bradford, J. S. P. and Goodchild, R. G., 1939. 'Excavations at Frilford, Berks', Oxoniensia 4 (1939), 1-70.

Branigan, K., 1968. 'The North-East Defences of Roman Gatcombe', PSANHS 112 (1968), 40-53.

Branigan, K., 1972. 'The End of Roman West', TBGAS 91, (1972), 117-28.

Branigan, K., 1974. 'Gauls in Gloucestershire?', TBGAS 92, 1973 (1974), 82-95.

Branigan, K., 1975. 'Gatcombe' in Rodwell and Rowley, 1975, 175-82.

Branigan, K., 1976. 'Villa Settlement in the West Country' in Branigan and Fowler, 1976, 120-41.

Branigan, K., 1977. 'Gatcombe Roman Villa', British Archaeological Reports British Series 44, 1977.

Branigan, K., and Fowler, P. J., 1976. The Roman West Country, Newton Abbot and London 1976.

Brock, C., 1975, The Extinction of the Norse Greenland Colony: A Carrying Capacity Model, B.A. Honours Thesis, University of Alberta, Edmonton, Canada, 1975.

Brodribb, A. et al., 1972. Excavations at Shakenoak Farm (Roman-early Anglo Saxon site) near Wilcote, Oxfordshire: III, Site F, Privately Published 1972.

Brown, P., 1971. The World of Late Antiquity, London 1971.

Burrow, E. J., 1924. Earthworks and Camps of Somerset, Cheltenham 1924.

Burrow, I. C. G., 1974. 'Tintagel - some problems', Scottish Arch Forum 5 (1973 (1974) 99-103.

Burrow, I. C. G., 1976a. 'Brean Down Hillfort 1974', PUBSS 14 (2) 1976, 141-54.

Burrow, I. C. G., 1976b. 'Possible Irish Earthworks in Somerset', Proc Royal Irish Acad 76 (c), 1974 (1976), 228-9.

Burrow, I. C. G., 1979. 'Roman Material from Hillforts', in Casey, P. J. (ed.) The End of Roman Britain, British Archaeological Reports British Series 71 (1979), 212-229.

Burrow, I. C. G., Forthcoming. 'Hillforts after the Iron Age - The Contribution of Surface Fieldwork' in Guilbert G. C. (ed.) Hill-Fort Studies —Essays Presented to A. H. A. Hogg, Leicester.

Burrow, I. C. G. and Bennett, J., 1979. 'A Romano-British Relief from Cadbury Camp, Tickenham (Avon) in Rescue Archaeology in the British Area I (Bristol City Museum) (1979), 1-5.

Bush, T. S., 1911. 'Tumulus in British Camp', PSANHS (Bath) (1911).

Bush, T. S., 1913. 'Summary of the Lansdown Explorations 1905-1912', SANHS (Bath) (1913), 251.

CAC   Clifton Antiquarian Club, Bristol.

Campbell, J. A., Baxter, M. S. and Alcock. L., 1979. 'Radiocarbon dates for the Cadbury massacre', Antiquity 53, 31-38.

Cameron, K., 1969. English Place Names, London 1969.

Chadwick, N., 1954. Studies in Early British History, Cambridge 1954.

Chadwick, N., 1961. The Age of Saints in the Early Celtic Church, Oxford 1961.

Chisholm, M., 1968. Rural Settlement and Land Use, London 1968.

Chitty, D., 1966. The Desert a City, Oxford 1966.

Clarke, D. L., 1968. Analytical Archaeology, London 1968.

Clarke, D. L., 1971a. Models in Archaeology, London 1972.

Clarke, D. L., 1972b. 'A Provisional Model of an Iron Age Society and its Settlement System' in Clarke, 1972a, 801-70.

Clifford, E. M., 1938. 'Roman Altars in Gloucestershire' Trans Bristol Gloucestershire Archaeol Soc 60 (1938), 297-307.

Coles, J., 1973. Archaeology by Experiment, London 1973.

Coles, J., 1975. 'The Somerset Levels' in Fowler, 1975a, 12-26.

Collingwood, R. G. and Myres, J. N. L., 1937. Roman Britain and the English Settlements (2nd Ed.), Oxford 1937.

Collinson, J., 1791. History and Antiquities of the County of Somerset 3 Vols, Bath, 1791.

Colt-Hoare, R., 1827. 'Account of Antiquities found at Hamden Hill' Archaeologia 21 (1827), 39-42.

Colvin, H. M., 1963. The History of the King's Works   Vol I, London 1963.

Cook, K. M. and Tratman, E. K., 1954. 'Burledge Camp', PUBSS 7 (1) (1953-4), 39-41.

Cornwall, I. W., 1969. 'Soil, Stratification and Environment' in D. Brothwell and E. Higgs Science in Archaeology, 2nd ed. London 1969, 120-34.

Cottam, M. B. and Small, A., 1974. 'The Distribution of Settlement in Southern Pictland', Med Arch 18 (1974), 43-65.

Cramp, R. J., 1958. 'Beowulf and Archaeology', Med Arch 1 (1957), 57-77.

Craw, J. H., 1930. 'Excavations at Dunadd ...' Proc Soc Ant Scot 64 (1930), 111-27.

Crawford, O. G. S. and Keiller, A., 1928. Wessex from the Air, Cambridge 1928.

Cunliffe, B., 1966. 'The Somerset Levels in the Roman Period', in Thomas, 1966a, 68-73.

Cunliffe, B., 1969. Roman Bath, Soc. Antiq. London Res. Rpt. 24, London 1969.

Cunliffe, B., 1971a. 'Some Aspects of Hillforts and their cultural environments' in Jesson, M. and Hill, D., 1971 The Iron Age and its Hillforts Southampton 1971, 53-70.

Cunliffe, B., 1971b. 'Danebury, Hampshire: First Interim Report ...' Antiq Jour 51 (pt. 11), 1971, 240-52.

Cunliffe, B., 1973a. 'Saxon and Medieval Settlement Pattern in the region of Chalton, Hampshire', Med Arch 16 (1972), 1-12.

Cunliffe, B., 1973b. 'Chalton, Hants: The evolution of a landscape', Antiq Jour 53 (1973), 173-90.

Cunliffe, B., 1974. Iron Age Communities in Britain, London 1974.

Curle, A. O., 1914. 'Report on the Excavation of a vitrified fort at Rockcliffe', Proc Soc Ant Scot 94, (1913-14), 125-68.

Curwen, E. C. and Williamson, R. P. R., 1931. 'The date of Cissbury Camp', Antiq Jour 11 (1931), 14-36.

Darby, H. C. and Finn, R. W., 1967. The Domesday Geography of South West England, Cambridge 1967.

Davidson, J., 1861. Notes on the Antiquities of Devonshire, Exeter, 1861.

Davidson, J. B., 1884. 'On the Charters of King Ine', PSANHS 30 (2) (1884), 1-31.

Davies, J. A. and Phillips, C. W., 1927. 'The Percy Sladen Memorial Fund Excavations at Bury Hill Camp, Winterbourne Down, Gloucestershire, 1926', PUBSS 3 (1) (1927), 8-24.

Davies, W., and Vierk, H., 1974. 'The Contexts of the Trbal Hidage: Social Aggregates and Settlement Patterns', Frümittelalterliche Studien 8 (1974), 223-93.

Davison, B. K., 1973. 'Castle Neroche: an abandoned Norman Fortress in South Somerset', PSANHS 116 1972 (1973), 16-58.

Detsicas, A., 1973. Current Research in Roman-British Coarse Pottery CBA Res Rept 10, London 1974.

Dewar, H. S. L., 1949. 'Pottery Mounds of the Brue Valley', SDN&Q 25 (1949), 161-64.

Dickinson, F. H., 1877. 'The Banwell Charters', PSANHS 23 (2) (1877), 49-64.

Doble, G. H., 1945. 'St. Congar' Antiquity 19 (1945) 32-43; 85-95.

Doble, G. H., 1970. The Saints of Cornwall Part 5, Truro 1970.

Dobson, D. P., 1931. The Archaeology of Somerset, London 1931.

Dobson, D. P., 1948. 'Mount Badon Again', Antiquity 22 (1948), 43-5.

Donovan, D. T., 1949. 'A Revised Account of the Earthworks between Shipham and Charterhouse-on-Mendip', PUBSS 6 (1) 1946-8 (1949), 76-84.

Dowden, W. A., 1957. 'Little Solsbury Hill Camp, Report on Excavations of 1955 and 1956', PUBSS 8 (1) (1957), 18-29.

Dowden, W. A., 1962. 'Little Solsbury Hill Camp', PUBSS 9 (3) (1961-2), 177-182.

Dumville, D. M., 1977. 'Sub-Roman Britain: History and Legend', History 62 (no. 205) (June 1977), 173-92.

Dunning, R. W., 1975. 'Ilchester: A Study in Continuity', PSANHS 119 (1975), 44-50.

Dymond, C. W., 1883. 'Dolbury and Cadbury', PSANHS 29 (1883), 104-116.

Dymond, C., 1902. Worlebury, Bristol 1902.

Dymond, C. and Tomkins, H. G., 1886. Worlebury: An Ancient Stronghold in the County of Somerset, Bristol 1886.

Dymond, D. P., 1974. Archaeology and History: A Plea for Reconciliation, London 1974.

Earle, J., 1890. 'Camps and Hundreds', SDN&Q 1 (1890), 12.

Ekwall, E., 1928. English River Names, Oxford, 1928.

Ekwall, E., 1960. The Concise Oxford Dictionary of English Place Names 4th ed., Oxford 1960.

Elkington, H. D. H., 1976. 'The Mendip Lead Industry' In Branigan and Fowler 1976, 183-97.

Ellison, A., and Harriss, J., 1972. 'Settlement and Land Use in the Prehistory and Early History of Southern England: a Study based on Locational Models' in Clarke, 1972a, 911-62.

Evans, E. E., 1975. 'Highland Landscapes: Habitat and Heritage' in Evans et al., 1975, 1-5.

Evans, J. G., et al., 1975. Effect of Man on the Landscape: the Highland Zone, CBA Res Rept 11 (1975), London.

Everson, J. A. and Fitzgerald, B. P., 1969. Settlement Patterns, London 1969.

Evison, V., 1963. 'Sugar-Loaf Shield Bosses', Antiq Jour 43 (1963), 38-96.

Falconer, J. P. E. and Adams, S. B., 1935. 'Recent Finds at Solsbury Hill Camp, near Bath', PUBSS 4 (3) (1935), 183-222.

Farrar, R. A. H., 1973. 'The Techniques & Sources of Romano-British Black-Burnished Ware' in Detsicas, 1973, 67-103.

Feachem, R. W., 1955. 'Fortifications' in F. T. Wainwright (ed.) Problem of the Picts, London 1055, 66-86.

Feachem, R. W., 1956. 'The Fortifications of Traprain Law', Proc Soc Ant Scot 89 (1955-6), 284-9.

Feachem, R. W., 1966. 'Hillforts of North Britain', in A. L. F. Rivet (ed.) The Iron Age in North Britain, Edinburgh 1966, 59-88.

Feachem, R. W., 1971. 'Unfinished Hillforts' in Jesson and Hill, 1971, 19-40.

Finberg, H. P. R., 1964a. Lucerna, London 1964.

Finberg, H. P. R., 1964b. 'Sherbourne, Glastonbury, and the Expansion of Wessex' in Finberg, 1964a, 95-115.

Finberg. H. P. R., 1964c. The Early Charters of Wessex, Leicster, 1964.

Finberg, H. P. R., 1967. 'St. Patrick at Glastonbury', Irish Ecc Record (June 1967), 345-61.

Findlay, D.C., 1965. The Soils of the Mendip District of Somerset, Soil Survey, London 1965.

Fleure, H. J. and Whitehouse, W. E., 1916. 'The early distribution and valleyward movement of population in South Britain', Arch Camb 16 (1916), 100-140.

Forde-Johnston, J., 1964. 'Earls Hill, Pontesbury and Related Hillforts in England and Wales', Arch J 119 (1964), 66-99.

Forde-Johnston, J., 1976. Hillforts of the Iron Age in England and Wales, Liverpool U.P., 1976.

Fowler, P. J., 1970. 'Fieldwork and Excavation in the Butcombe Area, North Somerset', PUBSS 12 (2) 1970, 195-202.

Fowler, P. J., 1971. 'Hillforts, A. D. 400-700' in Jesson, M. and Hill, D. The Iron Age and its Hillforts, London 1971, 203-13.

Fowler, P. J. (ed.), 1972. Archaeology and the Landscape, London 1972.

Fowler, P. J., 1973. (Note on Highbury) Arch Rev 7 (1972) (1973), 24.

Fowler, P. J., 1974. 'Motorways and Archaeology' in Rahtz, P. A. (ed.) Rescue Archaeology, London 1974, 113-29.

Fowler, P. J. (ed.), 1975a. Recent Work in Rural Archaeology, Bradford-on-Avon, 1975.

Fowler, P. J., 1975b. 'Continuity in the Landscape?' in Fowler, 1975a, 121-36.

Fowler, P. J., 1976. 'Farms anf Fields in the Roman West Country' in Branigan and Fowler, 1976, 162 82.

Fowler,, P. J., 1978. 'Pre Medieval Fields in the Bristol Region' in Bowen, H. C. and Fowler, P. J., 'Early Land Allotment': British Archaeological Reports 48 (1978) 29-48.

Fowler, P. J., Gardner, K. S., Rahtz, P. A., 1970. Cadbury Congresbury, Somerset, 1968 (Bristol, 1970).

Fox, A., 1952a. 'Hillslope Forts', <u>Arch J</u> 119 (1952), 1-22.

Fox, A., 1952b. 'Roman Objects from Cadbury Castle', <u>Trans Devon Association</u> 84 (1952), 105-114.

Fox, A., 1955. 'A Dark Age Trading Site at Bantham, S. Devon', <u>Antiq Jour</u> 35 (1955), 55 ff.

Fox, A., 1961. 'South-Western Hillforts' in Frere, S. S., (ed.) <u>Problems of the Iron Age in Southern Britain</u>, London 1961, 35-60.

Fox, C., 1943. <u>The Personality of Britain</u> 4th ed., Cardiff 1943.

Fox, C., 1955. <u>Offa's Dyke</u>, Oxford 1955.

Fox, A., and Fox, C., 1960. 'Wansdyke Reconsidered', <u>Arch J</u> 115 (1960), 1-48.

Frere, S. S., 1966. 'The End of Towns in Roman Britain' in Wacher, J. S. (ed.) <u>The Civitas Capitals of Roman Britain</u>, Leicster 1966, 87-100.

Frere, S. S., 1967. <u>Britannia</u>, London 1967.

Fryer, A. C., 1893. 'Subsidence of Land on Clifton Hill Camp Bristol' <u>JBAA</u> 49 (1893), 159-61.

Gardner, W. and Savory, H. N., 1964. <u>Dinorben</u>, Cardiff 1964.

Gelling, P. S., 1969. 'A Metal-working site at Kiondroghad, Kirk Andreas', <u>Medieval Archaeology</u> 13 (1969), 67-83.

Goodman, C., 1972. 'Kings Weston Hill, Bristol: Its Prehistoric Camps and Inhumation Cemetery', <u>PUBSS</u> 13 (1) (1972), 41-48.

Gray, H. St. G., 1902. 'The Walter Collection in Taunton Castle Museum', <u>PSANHS</u> 48 (2) 1902, 25-49.

Gray, H. St. G., 1903. 'Ruborough Camp', <u>PSANHS</u> 49 (2) (1903), 173-82.

Gray, H. St. G., 1904a. 'Excavations at Smalldown Camp, Evercreech', <u>PSANHS</u> 50 (1904), 32-49.

Gray, H. St. G., 1904b. (Excursion Notes), <u>PSANHS</u> 50 (1940) 43-4.

Gray, H. St. G., 1905a. 'The Norris Collection in Taunton Castle Museum' <u>PSANHS</u> 51 (2) (1905), 136-59.

Gray, H. St. G., 1905b. 'Worlebury Camp', <u>PSANHS</u> 51 (1) (1905), 17-28.

Gray, H. St. G., 1905c. 'The Camp of Brent Knoll', <u>PSANHS</u> 51 (1905), 43-5.

Gray, H. St. G., 1908. 'Excavations at Norton Camp, near Taunton', <u>PSANHS</u> 54 (2) (1908), 131-43.

Gray, H. St. G., 1910. 'Notes on Archaeological Remains found on Ham Hill', <u>PSANHS</u> 56 (2) (1910), 50-61.

Gray, H. St. G., 1913. 'Trial excavations at Cadbury Castle, S. Somerset, 1913', <u>PSANHS</u> 59 (2) (1913), 1-24.

Gray, H. St. G., 1922. 'Trial excavations at Cadbury Camp, Tickenham', <u>PSANHS</u> 68 (2) (1922), 8-20.

Gray, H. St. G., 1924. 'Excavations at Ham Hill', <u>PSANHS</u> 70 (1924), 104-116.

Gray, H. St. G., 1925. 'Excavations at Ham Hill', <u>PSANHS</u> 71 (1925), 57-76.

Gray, H. St. G., 1926. 'Excavations at Ham Hill', <u>PSANHS</u> 72 (1926), 55-68.

Gray, H. St. G., 1930. 'Excavations at Kingsdown Camp, near Mells, Somerset', <u>Archaeologia</u> 80 (1930), 59-96.

Gray, H. St. G., 1940. 'Excavations at Burrow Mump', <u>PSANHS</u> 85 (2) (1940), 95-132.

Gray, H. St. G., 1946. 'A Hoard of Late Roman coins found on Castle Hill, Wiveliscombe, 1946', <u>PSANHS</u> 92 (1946), 65-75.

Greene, J. P., 1975. 'Bath and Other Small Western Towns' in Rodwell and Rowley 1975, 131-8.

Greenfield, E., 1963. 'The Roman-British Shrines at Brigstock, Northants.' <u>Antiq Jour</u> 43 (2) (1963), 228-63.

Gregory of Tours <u>Historia Francorum</u> (ed. L. Thorpe, London 1974).

Greswell, W., 1901. 'King Ina's Grant of Brent to Glastonbury', <u>SDN&Q</u> 7 (1901), 255.

Greswell, W., 1905. <u>The Forests and Deer Parks of Somerset,</u> Taunton 1905.

Grierson, P., 1959. 'Commerce in the Dark Ages', <u>Trans Royal Hist Soc</u> 5 (1959), 123-140.

Grinsell, L. V., 1958. <u>The Archaeology of Wessex,</u> London 1958.

Grinsell, L. V., 1970. <u>The Archaeology of Exmoor,</u> Newton Abbot, 1970.

Grover, J. W., 1875. 'Cadbury Camp and similar works near Bristol', <u>JBAA</u> 31 (1875), 68-75.

Grundy, G. B., 1935. <u>The Saxon Charters and Field Names of Somerset,</u> Taunton 1935.

Guest, E., 1861. 'On the boundaries which separated the Welsh and English Races during the 75 years which followed the capture of Bath AD 577; with speculations as to the Welsh Princes who ... were reigning over Somersetshire', <u>Arch Camb</u> 3rd Srs. 7 (1861), 269-92.

Guilbert, G., 1975a. 'Moel-y-Gaer 1973: an Area Excavation on the Defences', <u>Antiquity</u> 49 (1975), 109-117.

Guilbert, G., 1975b. (Ratlinghope/Stitt Hill Shropshire: Earthwork Enclosures and Cross-Dykes', <u>Bull. Board Celtic Studies</u> 26 pt. 3 (1975), 363-73.

Haggett, P., 1965. <u>Locational Analysis in Human Geography,</u> London 1965.

Haldane, J. W., 1966. 'Stokeleigh Camp, Somerset ', <u>PUBSS</u> 11 (1) (1965-6), 31-8.

Haldane, J. W., 1968a.   Note on Trendle Ring, Arch Rev 2 1967 (1968), 12.

Haldane, J. W., 1968b.   'Combe Hill Enclosure, Bristol', PUBSS 11 (3) (1967-8), 249-51.

Haldane, J. W., 1970.   (Interim note on Excavations at Stokeleigh), PUBSS 12 (2), 133.

Haldane, J. W., 1975.   'Excavations at Stokeleigh Camp, Avon', PUBSS 14 (1) (1975), 29-63.

Harding, D, W., (ed.), 1976.   Hillforts - Later Prehistoric Earthworks in Britain & Ireland, London 1976.

Hawkes, C. F. C., 1931.   'Hill Forts', Antiquity 5 (1931), 60-111.

Hawkes, C. F. C., 1948.   'Britons, Romans and Saxons round Salisbury and in Cranbourne Chase', Arch J 104 1947 (1948), 27-81.

Hawkes, S. C. and Dunning, G. C., 1961.   'Soldiers and Settlers in Britain, Fourth to Fifth Century'   Med Arch 5 (1961), 1-70.

Hawkins, A. B., 1973.   'Sea Level Changes around South-West England', in Marine Archaeology Colston Papers 23, London 1973, 66-87.

Hayes, J. W., 1977.   'North African Flanged Bowls: A Problem in Fifth-Century Chronology', in Dore, J. and Greene, K., (eds.) 'Roman Pottery Studies in Britain and Beyond', British Archaeological Reports International Series 30 (1977), 279-83.

Henken, H. O'N., 1942.   'Ballinderry Crannog No. 2', PRIA 47 C 1941 1942, 1-67.

Henken, H. O'N., 1951.   'Lagore Crannog, an Irish Royal Residence of the Seventh to Tenth Centuries AD', PRIA 53 C (1950-51), 1-248.

Higgitt, J. C., 1973.   'The Roman Background to Medieval England' JBAA 3rd Srs. 36 (1973), 1-15.

Hill, D., 1969.   'The Burghal Hidage, the Establishment of a Text' Med Arch 13 (1969), 84-92.

Hill, J. S., 1914.   The Place Names of Somerset, Bristol 1914.

Hill, P. V., 1951.   'The Coinage of Britain in the Dark Ages', British Numismatic Journal 26 (1949-51), 1-27.

Hillgarth, J., 1961.   'The East, Visigothic Spain and the Irish', International Conference of Patristic Studies 4 (1961), 442-456.

Hodder, I., 1975.   'The Spatial Distribution of Romano-British Walled Towns' in Rodwell and Rowley, 1975, 67-74.

Hodder, I. and Orton, C., 1976.   Spatial Analysis in Archaeology, Cambridge 1976.

Hogg, A. H. A., 1957.   'A fortified round hut at Carreg-y-Llam near Nevin', Arch Camb 106 (1957), 46-55.

Hogg, A. H. A., 1960. 'Carn Boduan & Tre'r Ceiri, Excavations at two Caernarvonshire Hill-sorts', Arch J 117 1960, 1-39.

Hogg, A. H. A., 1966. Native Settlement in Wales' in Thomas 1966a, 23-38.

Hogg, A. H. A., 1971. 'Some Applications of Surface Fieldwork' in Jesson and Hill, 1971, 105-122.

Hogg, A. H. A., 1972a. 'Hillforts in the Coastal Area of Wales' in Thomas, 1972a, 11-24.

Hogg, A. H. A., 1972b. 'Size Distribution of Hillforts in Wales and the Marches' in Lynch, F. and Burgess, C., (eds.) Prehistoric Man in Wales and the West, Bath 1972, 293-305.

Hogg, A. H. A., 1973. 'Gaer Fawr & Carn Ingli: Two Major Pembrokeshire Hillforts', Arch Camb 122 (1973), 69-84.

Hogg, A. H. A., 1974. 'Carn Goch, Carmarthenshire', Arch Camb 123 (1974), 43-53.

Hope-Taylor, B., 1961. The Site of Ad Gefrin, Cambridge Ph.D. 1961, (no. 4048) (St. Johns Coll.).

Hope-Taylor, B., 1979. Yeavering: An Anglo-British Centre of Early Northumbria, HMSO London 1979.

Hoskins, W. G., 1960. The Westward Expansion of Wessex, Dept. Eng. local History Occ. Paper 13, University of Leicester 1960.

Hughes, K., 1966. The Church in Early Irish Society, London 1966.

Hughes, K., 1972. Early Christian Ireland: Introduction to the Sources, London 1974.

Institute of Geological Sciences, 1948. Bristol and Gloucester District, 2nd Ed., London 1948.

Institute of Geological Sciences, 1969. South West England, 3rd Ed., London 1969.

Isaac, P., 1976. 'Coin Hoards & History in the West' in Branigan & Fowler, 1966, 52-62.

Jackson, K., 1953. Language and History in Early Britain, Edinburgh 1953.

JBAA Journal of the British Archaeological Association, London.

Jesson, M. and Hill, D., 1971. The Iron Age And Its Hillforts, Southampton, 1971.

Jobey, G., 1966. 'Homesteads & Settlements in the Frontier Area' in Thomas (ed.) 1966a, 1-14.

Jones, G. R., 1959. 'Rural Settlement: Wales', British Assoc Adavancement of Science 15 (1959), 338-42.

Jones, G. R., 1960. 'Pattern of Settlement on the Welsh Border' Agricultural History Review (1960), 66-81.

Jones, G. R., 1961a.   The Tribal System in Wales: A Reassessment in the Light of Settlement Studies', Welsh History Review (1960-1), 114-132.

Jones, G. R., 1961b.   'Settlement Patterns in Anglo-Saxon England', Antiquity 35 (1961), 221-32.

Jones, G. R., 1961c.   'Early Territorial Organization in England & Wales', Geografiska Annaler 43 (1961), 174-81.

Jones, G. R., 1963.   'Early Settlement in Arfon: The Setting of Tre'r Ceiri', Transactions Caernarvon Historical Society (1963), 11-17.

Jones, G. R., 1964.   'The Distribution of Bond Settlements in North-West Wales', Welsh History Review 2 (1964), 19-36.

Jones, G. R. J., 1972.   'Post Roman Wales' in H. P. R. Finberg (ed.) Agrarian History of England and Wales Vol 1, pt. 2, Cambridge 1972, 283-382.

JRS   Journal of Roman Studies, London.

Joseph, J. K. S. St., 1973.   'Air Reconnaissance in Roman Britain 1969-72', JRS 63 (1973), 214-46.

Kemble, J. M., 1839-48.   Codex Diplomaticus Aevi Saxonici, London 1839-48.

King, D. J. C. and Alcock, L., 1966.   'Ringworks of England and Wales' Chateau Gaillard Conference for Castle Studies III, London 1966, 90-127.

Knight, F. A., 1902.   The Seaboard of Mendip, Bristol 1902.

Knight, F. A., 1915.   Heart of Mendip (Reprinted Bristol 1971).

Knowles, D. and Hadcock, R. N., 1971.   Medieval Religious Houses in England & Wales, London 1971.

Laing, L., 1973.   'The Mote of Mark', Current Archaeology 39 (1973), 121-25.

Laing, L., 1975a.   The Archaeology of Late Celtic Britain & Ireland c. 400-1200 AD, London 1975.

Laing, L., 1975b.   'The Mote of Mark and the Origin of Celtic Interlace' Antiquity 49 (1975), 98-108.

Laing, L., 1975c.   'Settlement Types in Post-Roman Scotland', British Archaeological Reports 13, 1975.

Lane-Fox, A., 1878.   Untitled—Sigwells Camp, PSANHS 24 (2) (1878), 84-88. 84-88.

Langmaid, P. A., 1968.   'Norton Camp Excavations 1968' PSANHS 112 (1968), 107-108.

Langmaid, N., 1970.   'Excavations at Norton Fitzwarren 1970', PSANHS 114 (1970), 105-106.

Laingmaid, N., 1971. 'Norton Fitzwarren', Current Archaeology 28 (1971), 116-20.

Lawlor, H. C., 1925. The Monastery of St. Mochaoi of Nendrum, Belfast 1925.

Leech, R. H., 1976. 'Larger Agricultural Settlements in the West Country', in Branigan and Fowler, 1976, 142-61.

Leech, R. H., 1977. Romano-British Rural Settlement in South Somerset and North Dorset (Ph. D. Thesis, University of Bristol 1977).

Leeds, E. T., 1947. 'A Saxon Village at Sutton Courtenay Berkshire. Third Report', Archaeologia 92 (1947), 79-94.

Leggatt, L. Fullbrook, 1935. 'Saxon Gloucestershire', T B G A S 57 (1935), 110-135.

Lewis, M. J. T., 1966. Temples in Roman Britain, Cambridge 1966.

Lilly, D., and Usher, G., 1972. 'Romano British Sites on the North Somerset Levels', PUBSS 13 (1) (1972), 37-40.

Limbrey, S., 1975. Soil Science & Archaeology, London 1975.

Lloyd Morgan, C., 1900. 'Notes on Clifton, Burwalls and Stokeleigh Camps', CAC 5 (1900), 8-24.

Lloyd Morgan, C., 1901. 'Burwalls and Stokeleigh Camps', PSANHS 47 (2) (1901), 217-229.

Maitland, F. W., 1897. Domesday Book and Beyond, Cambridge 1897.

Major, A. F., 1913. The Early Wars of Wessex, Cambridge 1913.

Major, A. F. and Burrow, E. J., 1923. The Mystery of Wansdyke, Cheltenham 1923.

Maxwell, G., 1969. 'Duns & Forts - a note on some Iron Age Monuments of the Atlantic Province', Scottish Archaeological Forum 1 (1969), 41-52.

McDonnell, R., 1980. Report on the Survey of Aerial Photography in the CRAAGS Region, (typescript).

Meaney, A., 1964. A Gazetteer of Anglo-Saxon Burial Sites, London 1964.

Med Arch Medieval Archaeology, London.

Meyer, K., 1912. Anecdota from Irish Manuscripts IV, Halle 1912.

Miles, H. and Miles, T. J., 1969. 'Settlement Sites of the Late Pre-Roman Iron Age in the Somerset Levels', PSANHS 113 (1969), 17-55.

Miles, H. and Miles, T. J., 1974. 'Trethurgy', Current Archaeology 40 (1974), 142-46.

Morgan, F. W., 1938. 'The Domesday Geography of Somerset', PSANHS 84 (1938), 139-55.

Morris, J., 1973. The Age of Arthur, London 1973.

Musson, C. R., 1970. 'The Breiddin 1969', Current Archaeology 19 (1970), 215-18.

Musson, C. R., 1972. 'Two winters at the Breiddin', Current Archaeology 33 (1972), 263-67.

Musson, C. R., 1976. 'Excavations at the Breiddin 1969-73' in Harding 1976, 293-302.

Myres, J. N. L., 1964. 'Wansdyke and the Origin of Wessex' in Trevor Roper, H. R. (ed.) Studies in British History, London 1964, 1-27.

Myres, J. N. L., 1969. Anglo-Saxon Pottery and the Settlement of England, Oxford, 1969.

NMR National Monuments Record, Fortress House, London.

Norris, H., 1884. 'The Camp on Hamdon Hill', PSANHS 30 (1) (1884), 138-48.

O'Kelly, M. J., 1956. 'An Island Settlement at Beginish, Co. Kerry', PRIA 57 (c) (1956), 159-94.

O'Kelly, M. J., 1958. 'Church Island, Co. Kerry', PRIA 59 C2 (1958), 57-136.

O'Kelly, M. J., 1962. 'Garryduff', PRIA 63c (1962), 17-120.

O'Neil, B. St. J., 1952. 'The Roman Conquest of the Cotswolds', Arch J 109 (1952), 23-38.

Ordnance Survey, 1962. Map of Southern Britain in the Iron Age, Southampton 1962.

O'Rian, P., 1972. 'Boundary Association in Early Irish Society', Studia Celtica 7 (1972), 12-29.

O'Riordain, S. P., 1942. 'The excavation of a large earthen ring-fort at Garranes, Co. Cork', PRIA 47 (C) 1941-1942, 77-150.

O'Riordain, S. P., 1943. 'The Excavation of Ballycateen Fort Co. Cork', PRIA 49C (1943), 1-43.

Overend, E. D., 1968. (note on Dinies Camp), Arch Rev. 2 1967 (1968), 12.

Page, J. L. W., 1890. An Exploration of Exmoor, London 1890.

Peacock, D. P. S., 1967. 'Romano-British Pottery Production in the Malvern District of Worcestershire', Trans. Worcs Arch Soc 3rd Srs. 1 (1967), 15-28.

Peacock, D. P. S., 1973. 'The Black-Burnished Pottery Industry in Dorset', in Detsicas 1973, 63-5.

Pearce, S. M., 1973. 'The dating of some Celtic Dedications and Hagiographical Traditions in SW Britain', Transactions Devon Association 105 (1973), 95-120.

Pearce, S., 1978. The Kingdom of Dumnonia, Padstow 1978.

Perry, B. T., 1966. 'Some Recent Discoveries in Hampshire', in Thomas 1966a, 39-41.

Petrikovits, H. V., 1971. 'Fortifications in the North-Western Roman Empire from the third to the fifth centuries AD' JRS 61 (1971), 178-218.

Phelps, W., 1836-9. History and Antiquities of Somersetshire 2 vols 1836 and 1839, Bristol.

Phillips, C. W., 1931a. 'Earthworks on Walton Common Down, near Clevedon', PUBSS 4 (1) (1931), 34-42.

Phillips, C. W., 1931b. 'Field Work, 1929' PUBSS 4 (1) (1931), 45-52.

Phillips, C. W., 1933. 'Note on Excavations at Wraxall' PUBSS 4 (2) (1933), 150.

Phillips, C. W., 1934. (The Excavation of a Hut Group at Pant-y-Saer ... Anglesey', Arch Camb 89 (1834), 1-36.

Phillips, C. W., 1974. 'The English Place Name Society', Antiquity 48 (1974), 7-15.

Phillmore, E., 1888. 'The Annales Cambriae and Old Welsh Genealogies from Harleian MS 3859', Y Cymmrodor 9 (1888), 141-83.

Pollard, S. H. M., 1966. 'Neolithic and Dark Age Settlements on High Peak, Sidmouth, Devon', Proc Devon Arch Exploration Society 23 1956, 35-59.

Porter, H. M., 1967. The Saxon Conquest of Somerset and Devon, Bath 1967.

PRIA Proceedings of the Royal Irish Academy, Dublin.

Pritchard, J. E., 1896. (Untitled) CAC 3 (1896), 146.

Proc. Soc. Ant. Scot. Proceedings of the Society of Antiquaries of Scotland, Edinburgh.

Proudfoot, V. B., 1961. 'The Economy of the Irish Rath', Med Arch 5 (1961), 94-122.

PSANHS Proceedings of the Somersetshire Archaeological and Natural History Society.

PUBSS Proceedings of the University of Bristol Spelaeological Society.

Quinnell, N. V., 1967. (Note on Pitchers Enclosure), Arch Rev 2 (1967), 17.

Quinnell, N. V., 1968 (Note on Pitchers Enclosure), Arch Rev 3 (1968), 12.

Radford, C. A. R., 1951. 'Report on the Excavations at Castle Dore', Journal Royal Institution of Cornwall N.S. 1 appendix 1951, 1-119.

Radford, C. A. R., 1957. 'Excavations at Glastonbury Abbey 1956', Antiquity 31 (1957), 171.

Radford, C. A. R., 1958. 'The Saxon House: a review and some parallels', Med Arch 1 (1957), 27-38.

Radford, C. A. R., 196?. 'The Church in Somerset to 1100', PSANHS 106 (1962) 28-45.

Radford, C. A. R. and Swanton, M. J., 1975. Arthurian Sites in the West, Exeter University, 1975.

Raftery, B., 1969. 'Freestone Hill, Co. Kilkenny: An Iron Age Hillfort and Bronze Age Cairn', PRIA 68 C (1969), 1-108.

Rahtz, P. A., 1951. 'The Roman Temple at Pagans Hill, Chew Stoke, N. Somerset' PSANHS 96, 112-42.

Rahtz, P. A., 1957. 'Kings Weston Down Camp, Bristol, 1956', PUBSS 8 (1), 1957, 30-38.

Rahtz, P. A., 1968. 'Sub Roman Cemeteries in Somerset' in Barley and Hanson 1968, 193-5.

Rahtz, P. A., 1969. 'Cannington Hillfort 1963', PSANHS 113 (1969), 56-68.

Rahtz, P. A., 1971. 'Excavations on Glastonbury Tor ...', Arch J 127 (1971), 1-81.

Rahtz, P. A., 1974a. 'Monasteries as Settlements', Scottish Archaeological Forum 5 (1973), (1974), 125-35.

Rahtz, P. A., 1974b. 'Pottery in Somerset AD 400-1066', in V. I. Evison et al. (eds.) Medieval Pottery from Excavations, London Baher, 1974, 95-126.

Rahtz, P. A., 1975. 'How likely is likely?', Antiquity 49 (1975), 59-61.

Rahtz, P. A., 1976. 'Irish Settlements in Somerset', PRIA 76 (C) 1974 (1976), 233-30.

Rahtz, P. A., 1977. 'Late Roman Cemeteries and Beyond', in Reece, R., Burial in the Roman World, CBA Research Report, London 1977.

Rahtz, P. A., et al., 1958. 'Three Post-Roman Finds from the Temple Well of Pagans Hill, Somerset', Med Arch 2, 1958, 104-111.

Rahtz, P. A. and Barton, K. J., 1963. 'Maes Knoll Camp, Dundry, Somerset', PUBSS 10 (1) (1962-3), 9-10.

Rahtz, P. A. and Brown, J. C., 1958. 'Blaise Castle Hill 1957', PUBSS 8 (2) (1958), 147-71.

Rahtz, P. A. and Fowler, P. J., 1972. 'Somerset A.D. 400-700' in Fowler (ed.) 1972, 187-221.

Rahtz, P. A. and Greenfield, E., 1977. Excavations at Chew Valley Lake, Somerset, London, 1977.

Rahtz, P. A. and Harris, L. G., 1957. 'The Temple Well and Other Buildings at Pagans Hill, Chew Stoke, N. Somerset', PSANHS 101/2, 1956-7 (1957), 151-51.

Rahtz, P. A. and Hirst, S., 1974. Beckery Chapel, Glastonbury 1967-8, Glastonbury 1974.

Ravenhill, W. L. D., 1970. 'The Form and Pattern of Post Roman Settlement in Devon', Proceedings Devon Arch Exploration Society 28 (1970), 83-94.

Rees, W., 1963. 'Survivals of Celtic Custom in Medieval England' in Angles and Britons 1963, 148-68.

Rivet, A. L. F., 1964. Town and Country in Roman Britain, London 1964.

Rodwell, W. and Rodwell, K., 1973. 'The Roman Villa at Rivenhall, Essex: an interim report', Britannia 4 (1973), 115-27.

Rodwell, W. and Rowley, T., 1975. 'The "Small Towns" of Roman Britain', British Archaeological Reports 15, 1975.

Rowley, T., 1974 (ed.). 'Anglo-Saxon Settlement and Landscape', British Archaeological Reports 6, 1974.

Rutter, J., 1829. Delineations of the North-West Division of the County of Somerset, London 1829.

Saunders, C., 1973. (Note on Grambla), Arch Rev 7 1972 (1973), 26.

Savage, J., 1830. History of the Hundred of Carhampton (Minehead, 1830).

Savory, H. N., 1960. 'Excavations at Dinas Emrys, Beddgelert, Caernarvonshire 1954-6', Arch Camb 109 (1960), 13-77.

Savory, H. N., 1971. Excavations at Dinorben 1965-9, Cardiff 1971.

Savory, H. N., 1976. 'Welsh Hillforts: A Reappraisal of Recent Research' in Harding 1976, 237-291, esp. 282-91.

Sawyer, P., 1974. 'Anglo Saxon Settlement: The Documentary Evidence' in Rowley, 1974, 108-119.

Sawyer, P. H., 1968. Anglo Saxon Charters: An Annotated List and Bibliography (ed. P. Sawyer) London, Royal Historical Society.

Scarth, H. M., 1873. 'The Camps on the River Avon at Clifton', Archaeologia 44 (1873), 428-34.

Schlesinger, W., 1976. 'Early Medieval Fortifications in Hesse: a General Historical Report', World Archaeology 7 (3) (1976), 243-60.

SDN&Q Somerset and Dorset Notes and Queries.

Seaby, W. A., 1950a. 'The Iron Age Hillfort on Ham Hill', Arch J 107 (1950), 90-91.

Seaby, W. A., 1950b. 'Coinage from Ham Hill in the County Museum, Taunton' PSANHS 95 (1950), 143-58.

Seyer, S., 1821. Memoirs Historical and Topographical of Bristol and its Neighbourhood, Bristol 1821.

Sheail, J., 1972. Rabbits and their History, Newton Abbot, 1972.

Simpson, Grace, 1964a. 'The Hillforts of Wales and their Relation to Roman Britain', in Gardner and Savory, 1964, 209-220.

Simpson, Grace, 1964b. Britons and the Roman Army, London 1964.

Skrine, H. D., 1888. The Belgic Camp on Bathampton Down ..., Bath 1888.

Skrine, H. D., 1895. 'President's Address', PSANHS (1895), 9-16.

Skrine, H. D., 1897. Some Account of the Belgic Camp on Hampton Down ... Bath, 1897.

Smith, C. A., 1974. 'A Morphological Analysis of Late Prehistoric & Romano-British Settlements in North-West Wales' Proceedings Prehistoric Society 40 (1974), 157-169.

Solley, T. W. J., 1967. 'Excavations at Gatcombe 1954', PSANHS 111 (1967), 24-37.

Stenton, F. M., 1947. Anglo Saxon England (2nd Edition), Oxford 1947.

Stevens, C. E., 1966. 'The Social & Economic Aspects of Rural Settlement' C.B.A. Res Rept. 7 (1966), 108-128.

Stevenson, W. H., 1904. Asser's Life of King Alfred, Oxford 1904.

Swan, Vivien, 1973. 'Aspects of the New Forest late-Roman Pottery Industry', in Detsicas, 1973, 117-34.

Taylor, C. C., 1970. The Dorset Landscape, London 1970.

Taylor, C. C., 1974a. Fieldwork in Medieval Archaeology, London 1974.

Taylor, C. C., 1974b. 'The Anglo Saxon Countryside' in Rowley, 1974, 5-15.

TBGAS Transactions of the Bristol and Gloucester Archaeological Society, Bristol.

Thomas, C., 1959. 'Imported Pottery in Dark-Age Western Britain', Med Arch 3 (1959), 89-111.

Thomas, C., 1966a. Rural Settlement in Roman Britain, C.B.A. Research Rpt. 7, London 1966.

Thomas, C., 1966b. 'The Character ond Origins of Roman Dumnonia', in Thomas, 1966a, 74-98.

Thomas, C., 1969. 'Are These the Walls of Camelot?', Antiquity 43 (1969), 27-30.

Thomas, C., 1971a. Britain and Ireland in Early Christian Times, London 1971.

Thomas, C., 1971b. The Early Christian Archaeology of North Britain, Oxford 1971.

Thomas, C., 1972a. The Iron Age in the Irish Sea Province CBA Res. Report 9, London, 1972.

Thomas, A. C., 1972b. 'The Irish Settlements in Post-Roman Western Britain: A Survey of the Evidence', Journal Roman Institution of Cornwall New Srs 6 (1972), 251-74.

Thomas, C., 1976a. 'Imported Late Roman Mediterranean Pottery in Ireland and Western Britain: Chronologies and Implications', PRIA 76 (C) (1976), 245-255.

Thomas, C., 1976b. 'The End of the Roman South-West', in Branigan and Fowler, 1976, 198-213.

Thomas, C. and Peacock, D. P. S., 1967. 'Class E Imported Post-Roman Pottery: A Suggested Origin', Cornish Archaeology 6 (1967), 35-46.

Thorburn, M., 1925. In 'Field Work', PUBSS 2 (3) (1925), 279-82.

Tinsley, H. M. and Smith, R. T., 1974. 'Ecological Investigations at a Romano-British Earthwork in the Yorkshire Pennines', Yorkshire Archaeol J 46 (1974), 23-33.

Todd, M., 1976. 'The Vici of Western England', in Branigan & Fowler, 1976, 99-119.

Tratman, E. K., 1924. 'First Report on Kings Weston Hill, Bristol', PUBSS 2 (1), 76-82.

Tratman, E. K., 1926. In 'Fieldwork' PUBSS 2 (3), (1926), 284-5.

Tratman, E. K., 1927a. 'Note on Blackdown', PUBSS 3 (1) (1927), 27-28.

Tratman, E. K., 1927b. 'Notes on Dinghurst and Rowberrow', PUBSS 3 (1) (1927), 25, 30.

Tratman, E. K., 1935. 'Field Work' (Elborough), PUBSS 4 (3) (1935), 256-68.

Tratman, E. K., 1946. 'Prehistoric Bristol', PUBSS 5 (3) (1944-6), 162-182.

Tratman, E. K., 1959. 'Maesbury Castle, Somerset', PUBSS 8 (3) (1958-9), 172-178.

Tratman, E. K., 1963a. 'The Iron Age Defences and Wansdyke', PUBSS 10 (1) (1962-3), 11-15.

Tratman, E. K., 1963b. 'Burrington Camp, Somerset', PUBSS 10 (1), 1963, 16-21.

Tratman, E. K., 1966. 'A Supposed Roman Camp in Cloford Parish', PUBSS 11 (1966), 256.

Turner, A. G. C., 1950. 'Notes on some Somerset Place-Names', PSANHS 95 (1950), 112-24.

Turner, A. G. C., 1951. 'A Selection of North Somerset Place Names', PSANHS 96 (1951), 152-9.

Turner, A. G. C., 1952a. The Place Names of North Somerset, (Ph. D. Thesis, University of Cambridge, 1952).

Turner, A. G. C., 1952b. 'Some Aspects of Celtic Survival in Somerset', PSANHS 97 (1952), 148-151.

Turner, A. G. C., 1952c. 'Some Somerset Place-Names containing Celtic Elements', Bulletin Board of Celtic Studies 14 1950-52, 113-118.

Turner, A. G. C., 1954. 'A further selection of Somerset Place-Names Containing Celtic Elements, Bulletin Board of Celtic Studies 15 (1952-4), 12-20.

UCCAP University of Cambridge Committee for Aerial Photography.

Usher, G. and Lilly, D., 1964. 'A Romano-British Kiln Site at Venus St. Congresbury', PSANHS 108 (1964), 172-4.

VCH The Victoria County History, London.

Vetters, H., 1956. 'A Propos des Oppida Celtiques', Ogam 8 (1956), 38-81.

Wacher, J. S., 1975. The Towns of Roman Britain, London 1975.

Wainwright, F. T., 1962. Archaeology and Place Names and History, London 1962.

Wainwright, G. J., 1967a. 'The Excavation of an Iron Age Hillfort on Bathampton Down, Somerset', TBGAS 86 (1967), 42-59.

Wainwright, G. J., 1967b. Coygan Camp, Cardiff, Cambrian Archaeological Association, 1967.

Walter, R. H., 1912. 'Hamdon or Ham Hill Somerset', PSANHS 58 (2) (1912), 45-52.

Warner, R. B., 1974. 'Clogher' in Excavations 1973, Belfast 1973.

Warre, F., 1851. 'Worle Camp', PSANHS 2 (2) (1851), 64-85.

Warre, F., 1853. 'Appendix to Worle Camp', PSANHS 4 (ii) (1853) 124-7.

Warre, F., 1857. 'Milbourne Wick', PSANHS 7 (1856-7), 60-62.

Watts, S., 1957. 'Creech Hill Camp, Milton Clevedon', PUBSS 8 (1) (1957), 42.

Webster, G., Hobley, B., 1965. 'Aerial Reconnaissance over the Warwickshire Avon', Arch J 121 (1965), 1-22.

Wedlake, W. J., 1958. Excavations at Camerton, Somerset, Camerton Excavation Club, 1958.

West, S., 1974. 'West Stow', Current Archaeology 40 (1974), 151-8.

Wheeler, R. E. M., 1922. 'Roman and Native in Wales: An Imperial Frontier Problem', Trans Soc Cymmrodorion 1920-21 (1922), 40-96.

Wheeler, R. E. M., 1925. Prehistoric and Roman Wales, Oxford 1925.

Wheeler, R. E. M. and T. V., 1932. Report on the Excavations at Lydney Park Gloucs., London 1932.

Wheeler, R. E. M., 1943. Maiden Castle, Dorset, London 1943.

Whistler, C. W., 1907. Further Notes on Kynwich Castle', Saga Book of the Viking Club 5 (1) (1907), 47-8.

Whitelock, D., 1961. The Anglo Saxon Chronicle, London 1961.

Whybrow, C., 1967.   'Some Multivallate Hillforts on Exmoor and in North Devon', <u>Proceedings Devon Archaeological Exploration Society</u> 25 (1967), 1-18.

William Worcestre <u>Itineraries</u> (ed. J. Harvey), Oxford 1969.

Willmore, K. M. and Tratman, E. K., 1926.   'Bury Hill Camp', <u>PUBSS</u> 2 (3) 1926, 294-7.

Wilson, D. M. (ed.), 1976.   <u>The Archaeology of Anglo-Saxon England,</u> London 1976.

Winwood, H. H., 1908.   'The Wansdyke, Hampton Down', <u>PSANHS</u> (Bath) 1904-8, 56-8.

Young, C., 1973.   'The Pottery Industry of the Oxford Region', in Detsicas 1973, 105-115.